Hip Hop and Political Voice for Young South Sudanese Australians

Hip Hop and Political Voice for Young South Sudanese Australians

Born to Stand Out

Sarah J. Williams

Foreword by Mandisi Majavu

LEXINGTON BOOKS
Lanham • Boulder • New York • London

Lexington Books
Bloomsbury Publishing Inc, 1385 Broadway, New York, NY 10018, USA
Bloomsbury Publishing Plc, 50 Bedford Square, London, WC1B 3DP, UK
Bloomsbury Publishing Ireland, 29 Earlsfort Terrace, Dublin 2, D02 AY28, Ireland
www.rowman.com

Copyright © 2025 by The Rowman & Littlefield Publishing Group, Inc.

All rights reserved. No part of this publication may be: i) reproduced or transmitted in any form, electronic or mechanical, including photocopying, recording or by means of any information storage or retrieval system without prior permission in writing from the publishers; or ii) used or reproduced in any way for the training, development or operation of artificial intelligence (AI) technologies, including generative AI technologies. The rights holders expressly reserve this publication from the text and data mining exception as per Article 4(3) of the Digital Single Market Directive (EU) 2019/790.

British Library Cataloguing in Publication Information Available

Library of Congress Cataloging-in-Publication Data Available

ISBN 9781666971903 (cloth: alk. paper) | ISBN 9781666971910 (ebook)

For product safety related questions contact productsafety@bloomsbury.com.

∞™ The paper used in this publication meets the minimum requirements of American National Standard for Information Sciences—Permanence of Paper for Printed Library Materials, ANSI/NISO Z39.48-1992.

Contents

List of Figures and Tables	vii
Foreword	xi
Acknowledgements	xiii
Acronyms and Key Terms	xvii
1 Introducing Born to Stand Out	1
2 Freedom to Enact Political Voice and Develop Forms of Resistance	27
3 The System	53
4 'Oh Yeah, I Am African': Identity Politics and Celebrating Blackness in the Consciousness-Raising Journey	93
5 'My Skin Ain't Apex': Presenting Counter-Narratives to Racialising Discourses	141
6 Born to Stand Out: 'We Want to be Free from Our Chains'	179
7 Discussion: Alternative Forms of Artivism for Young South Sudanese Australians through Hip Hop	225
8 Creating Sites for Social Change: Implications and Conclusion	251

A Note on Terminology	271
Glossary of Terms and Key Events	275
References	277
Index	311
About the Author	325

List of Figures and Tables

FIGURES

Figure 0.1	Artist Tèbir Performing at Footprints Pop-up Performance at the State Library, Naarm in 2017	xiv
Figure 0.2	Erjok Nai (Eeh) Memorial	xvi
Figure 1.1	Young SSAs' Experiences from 'We Don't Fit In' to 'I Have Absolutely No Desire to Fit In'	18
Figure 1.2	Artist Ayuen K Bol – to Represent the Research Theme – 'Born to Stand Out'	20
Figure 1.3	Map of Greater Naarm (Melbourne) and Bordering Regions, Featuring Common Resettlement Zones	21
Figure 2.1	Research Design for PhD Thesis	31
Figure 2.2	Researcher's Positionality Statement	34
Figure 2.3a to 2.3i	Born to Stand Out (BTSO) Artivists	41
Figure 2.4	Grounded Project Planning Meeting at Gua Performance and Leadership Camp, 2017, Featured in the *Grounded* Documentary, 2018	46
Figure 3.1	Categorising Political Rap Songs	77
Figure 3.2	Artist Élkato Standing at the Intersection of Federation Square and Flinders St Station, Naarm CBD	83
Figure 4.1	Gua Workshop Discussion Topics and Process, 2019	116
Figure 4.2	Workshops at Gua Performance and Leadership Camp	117
Figure 4.3	Gua Performance and Leadership Camp, 2019	117
Figure 5.1	Krown – 'Let Us Live' Music Video	142
Figure 5.2	Spoken-word Artist Abe Nouk Performing at the Grounded Festival, 2017	162

Figure 5.3	The Grounded Youth Stage Featured at the Harmony Festival, March 2019, at Harmony Square, Dandenong	164
Figure 5.4	Footprints Vice-President (Stage Manager) and Co-founder Thank the Audience for Attending the Grounded Youth Stage, 2019	167
Figure 5.5	Audience Members Enjoying the Grounded Youth Stage, Including a Police Officer Standing with the General Public	168
Figure 5.6	Up-and-coming Melbourne-based Artist Krown Invites to the Stage His Students from Mushroom Group's 'On Track' Program, to Showcase Their Collaborative Song at the Grounded Youth Stage at Harmony Square Hosted by Footprints	171
Figure 5.7	Jacki Tut Performing at the Grounded Youth Stage, 2019	172
Figure 5.8	Burn City Movement (BCM) Members Wearing Their Own Fashion Styles	173
Figure 6.1	Lerato Masiyane – Afrobeats and Dancehall Dancer from Burn City Queens and Jungle City Projects (Footprints Project Partner) Is Born to Be Seen	189
Figure 6.2	Artist Daniel Elia Is 'Born to be Heard'	190
Figure 6.3	Artist i.OG from BCM Is 'Born to Stand Out' at the Dandenong Market Pop-up Performance as Part of the Grounded Project	192
Figure 6.4	Jungle City Project Teaching the Pop-up Performance Dance at the Gua Performance and Leadership Camp in 2019, Followed by Practices at YSAS in March 2019	194
Figure 6.5	Krown, A1 Krashn, Wantu ThaOne and i.OG from Burn City Movement (BCM), and Karabo and Lerato from Culture Queenz Pictured with Footprints Co-founder Sarah Williams at Dandenong High School Harmony Day Event during Cultural Diversity Week, 2019	197
Figure 6.6	Burn City Movement (BCM) Performing at Dandenong High School's Harmony Event in CDW, 2019	198
Figure 6.7	Artist i.OG from BCM Performed at the Dandenong Market Wearing a 'Sudanese Are Dope Though' T-shirt, an Example of Involvement in a Standpoint Project	200
Figure 6.8	Burn City Queens Dance Crew as Part of Jungle City Projects Leads the Pop-up Performance of Their Choreographed Dance at the Brunswick Street Parade in March 2019 as Part of the Grounded Project	201
Figure 6.9	Grounded Youth Stage Flyer, 2019	204

List of Figures and Tables ix

Figure 6.10	Grounded Youth Stage MC Simba Mak Hosting the Event and Performing Spoken-word, 2019	207
Figure 6.11	Achai and Soli Tesema (above) Performing at the Grounded Youth Stage, 2019	210
Figure 6.12	FLEXX and Malesh P Performing with Their Live Band at the Grounded Youth Stage, 2019	212
Figure 6.13	Akimera Engaging the Audience in Dance Moves at the Grounded Youth Stage, 2019	213
Figure 6.14	Jungle City and Culture Queenz Interactive Dance with Crowd at the Grounded Youth Stage, 2019	214

TABLES

Table 1.1	Key Racialising Discourse Moments in Recent Naarm (Melbourne) History That Portray Young SSAs Negatively and Their Responses	6
Table 1.2	Common Descriptors for 'African Refugees' Adapted from Windle 2008	11
Table 2.1	Research Theoretical Frameworks	30
Table 2.2	Born to Stand Out (BTSO) Artivists	38
Table 3.1	Participants Development of Their Sense of 'Voice' and Political Voice	79
Table 4.1	Gua Performance and Leadership Camp Key Themes	133
Table 4.2	Gua Performance and Leadership Camp Key Themes Cntd.	134
Table 5.1	Alternative Narratives to Racialising Discourses	168
Table 6.1	What Makes You Born to Stand Out? – Themes 'Be Seen'; Perspectives on Being BTSO	190
Table 6.2	What Makes You Born to Stand Out? – Themes 'Be Heard'; Perspectives on Being BTSO	191
Table 6.3	What Makes You Born to Stand Out? – Themes 'Born to Stand Out'; Perspectives on Being BTSO	193
Table 6.4	Summary of the Grounded Project Communication Strategies and Pop-up Performances Key Themes	202
Table 6.5	Summary of the Grounded Youth Stage Key Themes	203
Table 6.6	Afrocentricity and Afropolitanism – An Expression of Political Voice through Blackness	216
Table 8.1	Participants Contribution Statements towards Australian Multiculturalism	255

Foreword

Hip Hop and Political Voice for Young South Sudanese Australians: Born to Stand Out is not only original but makes a substantive contribution to knowledge because it tells us something new about how South Sudanese Australians develop their political voice to resist racialising discourses. Through developing this voice, South Sudanese Australians develop a Black identity which they express via South Sudanese Australian spoken-word poetry or Hip Hop. This monograph breaks away from the narrative that perpetually portrays black people as victims by documenting the role of black agency in the way in which African Australians develop their political voice. This is the first study of its kind in Australia to document black self-emancipation.

Sarah J. Williams' scholarship reflects a deep commitment to an Antiracist ethic, something that gives her work authoritative judgement and liberatory politics. The data generated from the interviews with African Australian youth contribute new empirical data and new insight into the conversation about the lived experience of black Africans in Australia. Williams' critical discussion and analysis of her empirical data showed deep insight, outstanding expertise, and sensitivity to the lived experience of her research participants presented in this monograph. As a co-founder of the grassroots community non-profit Footprint Enterprises, Williams' work embodies what the African American scholar, Patricia Hill Collins, described as 'scholarship in service to social justice'.

The monograph is presented as an ethnography and draws on empirical data generated through interviews and art artefacts, data which was triangulated against evaluations of other similar projects run by Footprints over the 2008–2021 period, demonstrating a rare intellectual leadership initiative and the intellectual autonomy that in my view gives us a blueprint for how to conduct blue sky research with political praxis. This monograph will be a game changer!

Dr Mandisi Majavu
Senior Lecturer
Department of Political and International Studies
Faculty of Humanities
Rhodes University, South Africa

Acknowledgements

I acknowledge the traditional custodians of this unceded land, the Kulin Nations and pay my respects to the elders as intergenerational ancestors and present, for they hold the memories, the traditions, the culture and hopes of First Nations peoples in the lands we now call Australia (Prentis 2017). May we truly listen.

Through this, I would like to acknowledge the Creator Spirit who hovers over the land and waters, sustaining us and, through Trinity relationship, calling us to stand with those 'whose backs are against the wall' (Thurman cited in Hart 2020, 352). My faith and commitment to following a revolutionary path influenced by liberation and black liberation theology (Hart 2020) have sustained me throughout this journey that has had many ups and downs.

My PhD research featured in this monograph was based on the motto 'born to stand out' investigating the role of Hip Hop for young South Sudanese Australians in building their political voice to resist racialising discourses (see figure 0.1).

This book is dedicated to the memory of Erjok Nai (Eeh) and others Joseph Arima, Kuda Pwiti, Tendai Dzvairo, Franco Lokiru, Joseph Aklilu – black-African friends and Hip Hop artists/producers who either migrated or came to Australia as refugees for a better life. They represent countless others who have passed too soon (sometimes mysteriously, desperately) and due to preventable causes. They would still be here if only we did some inward gazing. It is not too late to begin. In the context of an emerging global uprising relating to racial justice and equity, I conduct this research with the notion that:

> Literature follows great social changes – . . . it always 'comes after'. To come after, however, does not mean to repeat ('reflect') what already exists, but the exact opposite: to [seek to] resolve the problems set by history. *Modern Epic* (Moretti cited in Salvídar 2006, 152)

Figure 0.1 Artist Tèbir Performing at Footprints Pop-up Performance at the State Library, Naarm in 2017. *Source*: Footprints.

I would not be the person I am today without Footprints' family and networks (2020), cultural leaders and scholars such as David Nyuol Vincent, Dr William Abur and Dr Santino Deng, youth-led organisations such as South Sudanese Australian Youth United, so many others from the South Sudanese communities in Australia and South/North Sudan, and the artists who trusted me with their precious stories and encouraged me to continue. May this research truly be a reflection of your cultural tales and ambitions.

To my supervisors of my PhD research of which this monograph is derived, Dr Vicki-Ann Ware, Professor Anita Harris, and Dr Leanne Kelly from Deakin University, I am truly indebted to your dedication to me and this research project, upholding similar values such as peacebuilding through arts-based practice and supporting Antiracism scholarship and towards decolonising conversations. I am excited for the future if we can continue trailblazing in these fields. Thank you to Dr Deb Wain who conscientiously edited my PhD thesis and demonstrated similar passions in the sectors mentioned.

Through activist ethnography and transformative leadership paradigms, the former Oases Graduate School and California Institute of Integral Studies (CIIS) have always embedded the notion that 'another or a new world is possible'. I was blessed to complete a seminar series in *Social Movements and Social Change* during my candidature at CIIS. I continue to be informed by your legacy as we creatively disrupt, dismantle, and imagine alternative futures. My Inverse community supported me to unpack what this means through praxis, unlearning old paradigms, imagining new possibilities, and with a global network of change-makers focused on Antiracism. Finally, I would like to acknowledge the contributions of industry partners such as Footprints, Jungle City Projects, and Youth Support and Advocacy Service (YSAS), who supported my fieldwork journey and these values.

It is important to acknowledge the extensive lived experience of global BIPOC and their pivotal contributions to scholarship and movement practice. I express my gratitude to all the authors and artists whose work I have cited in this literature. In my mind, and through praxis, we have been dancing together, learning and unlearning, and hopefully offering nuanced insights. Ngũgĩ (1986, ix) acknowledges that

> there are so many inputs in the actual formation of an image, an idea, a line of argument and even sometimes the formal arrangement. The very words we use are a product of a collective history.

I wish to express my unending appreciation of my immediate family and best friends. Only you truly know what this journey has been like and what it has meant to me. Thank you for continuously helping me to get through (especially during a pandemic), encouraging me to follow my often-crazy dreams, and supporting my big ideas.

I would like to dedicate the following poem, which demonstrates our collective hopes, resistance, and beloved community to Eeh (James 2013; Smith and Zepp 1986) despite the struggles faced (see figure 0.2):

BORN TO STAND OUT – RESISTANCE AND UPRISING

Spoken-word piece composed by the author Sarah Williams in 2019

Resistance
the power of persistence
It can challenge our existence
Persuade you to go the distance

So many lost to the challenge of the dark night of the soul
Challenged by racism and discrimination
Told you don't belong
Those lost
Here today, gone tomorrow
We light a candle for you
Our collective memories lift up your spirit
Each day you are gone, but not forgotten

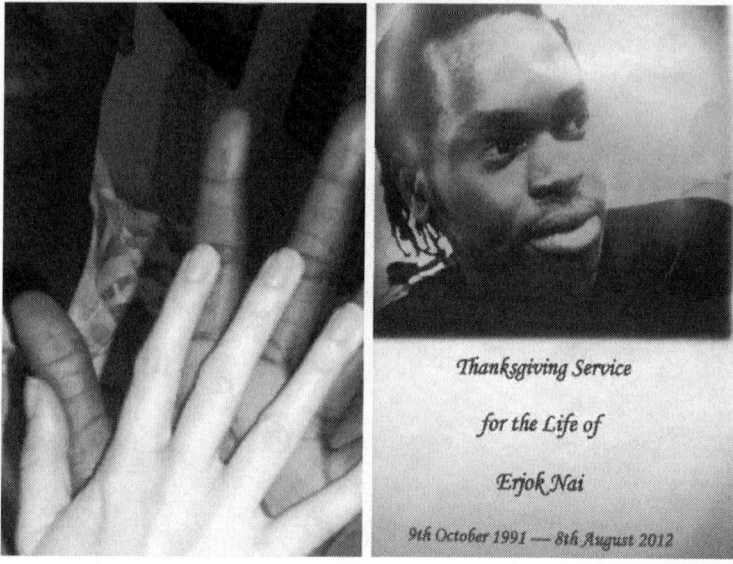

Figure 0.2 Erjok Nai (Eeh) Memorial. *Source*: Footprints.

Uprising
Rise up all you warriors of the youth
Each new day brings a different level of consciousness

Keep rising to the challenge to decolonise our minds
Like the great thinkers through history
Let's not take the easy road in the Matrix

Let's push forward to create new ways of thinking
New communities to be a part of
Irrespective of our backgrounds
A new subculture merging forward

We are the futurists
Born to stand out
Raise a fist in the air
And give a hug to your neighbour
This will be a constant labour
But worth the path less travelled

I'm looking forward to seeing how the story unravels
With my friends the misfits, the forgotten ones
Still so much more to be done!

(Williams 2021)

Acronyms and Key Terms

ABCD:	Asset-Based Community Development
AI:	Appreciative Inquiry
AOD:	Alcohol and Other Drugs
BIPOC:	Black, Indigenous, People of Colour
Bla(c)k:	Referencing Australian First Nations people's identification with Blackness
BLM:	Black Lives Matter (movement or organisation)
BTSO:	Born To Stand Out
CALD:	Culturally and Linguistically Diverse
CACD:	Community Arts and Cultural Development
CBD:	Central Business District (also known as 'downtown' in other countries)
CD:	Community development
CDW:	Cultural Diversity Week
CGD:	City of Greater Dandenong
CHHP:	Critical Hip Hop Pedagogy
CRT:	Critical Race Theory[ies]
Footprints (Fam):	Footprint Enterprises Inc.
LGA:	Local Government Area
Naarm:	First Nations term for the city Melbourne, Australia on Kulin lands
NGO:	Non-Government Organisation
NSMs:	New Social Movement/s
POC:	People of Colour
SPLA:	South Sudanese People's Liberation Army
SPLM:	South Sudanese Liberation Movement
SSA:	South Sudanese Australian
YPAR:	Youth Participatory Action Research

Chapter 1

Introducing Born to Stand Out

SOUTH SUDANESE POPULATIONS IN AUSTRALIA

A brief exploration of the political history of Sudan and South Sudan and the origins of predominantly South Sudanese in Australia is imperative to understanding participant narratives in this monograph. This chapter, therefore, provides the background context as to why Hip Hop was chosen by young South Sudanese Australians as a means of building their political voice and, therefore, as a methodology and form of social change studied to resist racialising discourses in Australia.

Sudan gained independence from Britain and Egypt in 1956 and was the largest country in the African continent. Two prolonged civil wars, 1955–1972 and 1983–2005, marked one of the longest periods of civil war on record. Following the peace agreement, the independence of South Sudan was achieved in 2011, six years after the war ended. The cause stemmed from inter-ethnic and religious tension between the North, whose people are largely of a Arabic-speaking and Muslim faith background, and South Sudan who consist of diverse African peoples following traditional religions or who have converted to Christianity (Cockett 2016). This intense fighting, combined with widespread starvation, led to the internal displacement of 5 million people in this region, and a death toll (noted as genocide) as high as 2 million. The following exodus of people made [then] Sudan the second largest originator of refugees in the 'modern world' (Milner and Khawaja 2010, 20).

When South Sudan gained independence from the North, a 'unity government' formed with President Salva Kiir, who is from the Dinka tribal group, and Vice President Dr Riek Machar from the Nuer tribal group. Extensive civil unrest between these two military rivals broke out in 2013, and armed conflict has continued to erupt until today, despite attempts at weapon removal amongst faction and renegade groups allegedly supporting their tribal counterparts. Kiir and Machar's forces signed a peace agreement in 2018 that ended a five-year civil war fought primarily along ethnic lines. However, implementation has been slow, and the opposing forces have clashed frequently over disagreements about how to share power. Current armed inter-communal youth conflict is also escalating; additionally, there is growing concern that the world's newest country will resume civil unrest if the 2018 peace agreement is not implemented (Jineffer 2022; Al-Jazeera 2022). The International Crisis Group publication *Toward a Viable Future for South Sudan* describes the discussion in the tribunal around South Sudan being a 'failed state' (International-Crisis-Group 2021).

This national and civil history is important when considering the intersectional identities of the participants in this study who identify as being of South Sudanese descent but, due to forced migration, have spent time living in North Sudan (in the capital Khartoum), in refugee camps in Kenya (Kakuma), and Egypt as displaced peoples. Whilst youth populations' identities may be political for many reasons (Gentry 2018), whether young SSAs articulate it or not, their identities are in fact political due to the very nature of this extensive conflict and identification with rivalling tribal groups such as being Dinka or Nuer (predominantly) (Moussa and Tony 2017; Bernstein 2005; Alcoff et al. 2006).

Relocating to Australia as former refugees fleeing civil unrest under the Humanitarian Resettlement Program cements this political identity into new territory. This is due to exposure to the type of minoritised border thinking (*pensamiento fronterizo*) that Chicano/a Studies theorist Gloria Anzaldúa argues is due to the very nature of them being former refugees who have faced major structures of dominance and subordination due to geopolitical events in their lives (Salvídar 2006, 2007). Upon arrival in Australia, young SSA identities revolve around the intersections of local histories and global designs, including the modern (colonial) world-system. Young SSA evolving identities are now additionally exposed to what Peruvian historical social scientist Aníbal Quijano calls the 'coloniality of power'. These forms of power are 'entangled relations of power between the global division of labour, racial and ethnic hierarchy, identity formation, and Eurocentric epistemologies' and can be traced through the 'continuous forms of hegemonic dominance produced by colonial cultures and structures' (Salvídar 2006, 152). This history in an Australian context is now detailed.

Since the early 1990s, the largest intake from African countries under the humanitarian resettlement scheme has come from Sudan. By 2001, Australia had accepted over 8,000 refugees from Sudan alone, with arrivals peaking between 2002 and 2007. As of 2008, the *Australian Bureau of Statistics Population Census* reported that there was an estimate of 24,796 Sudanese born in Australia (as a result of the influx of refugees since 1992 and especially since 2006) with a strong concentration living in metropolitan areas such as Sydney and Naarm (Melbourne) (see figure 1.3) (Williams 2022b). However, the South Sudan-born were previously included in the census count of the Sudan-born and were first counted separately in the 2011 census. The 2011 census recorded 3,487 South Sudan-born people in Australia, yet, it was likely that many still identified as being Sudan-born and as Sudanese, and this may still be the case in the 2016 census. The latest census in 2016 recorded 7,699 South Sudan-born people in Australia, an increase of 120.9 per cent from the 2011 census (Australian Government 2016). It is important to note that due to being born in transit countries, capturing data from South Sudanese populations in Australia has always been a challenge and is a cause for concern, particularly when recording alleged criminal activity (Zihabamwe 2022). The 2016 census data indicated more specific tribal ancestry identifications, whereby 4301 indicated they were from the Bari (Equatorian tribal group), 4,303 Dinka, and 4,304 Nuer tribal groups (A.B.o.S. 2016b, 1).

The recent wave of black-African immigration is dominated by former refugees who have left war-torn countries (Colic-Peisker and Tilbury 2008). The arrival of a large intake of Africans in the post-World War II period marks the unprecedented arrival of large communities from Africa, where 'increasing African immigration has been part of the post-war transformation of Australia from an overwhelmingly British-dominated population to a multicultural society' (Hugo 2009, 17). The establishment of the *White Australia policy* (introduced by the Australian government from 1901 to 1973)

> effectively prevented the settlement of Africans and others of non-European origin in Australia. Accordingly, in 1947 there were only 75,506 Africa-born people in Australia and 78.3% of these were South African.
>
> Hence, in the period before World War Two, there were only small numbers of Africa-born persons and they were overwhelmingly the children of colonial functionaries and Anglo Saxons from Southern Africa. (AHRC 2010, 16)

It is clear from this period that there exists a large-scale prejudice by white Australian counterparts towards those with noticeably darker skin, demonstrating a long neo-colonial history of racialisation. Following this period and from very early on since their arrival, battling negative stereotypes, prejudice, racism and discrimination were said to be the key factors undermining SSAs' potential for equal rights as equal citizens in Australia (AHRC 2010). These undermining factors are due to the Whitening regimes of multicultural policy in an Australian context (Henry-Waring 2008; Stratton 2020; Majavu 2018). Over a decade later, human rights breaches and forms of *necropolitics* (death-dealing regimes) continue because forms of Australian Whiteness have not been dismantled (Zihabamwe 2022; OHCHR 2022; Mbembe and Corcoran 2019). A recent visit in December 2022 by the UN Working Group of Experts of People of African Descent (UN WGEPAD) claimed that people of African descent living in Australia are 'living under the siege of racism' (OHCHR 2022, 1). The UN WGEPAD experts reported the experiences of people of African descent continue to be

> impacted by the country's settler-colonial past, its White Australia immigration policy, which was dropped in 1973, and its legacy, still endured by the First Nations peoples, including Aboriginal people, Torres Strait Islanders, and South Sea Islanders. 'People of African descent' experience a culture of denial of this racialised reality, and the legacies of this via pervasive 'Othering' in public spaces and entrenched disadvantage. (OHCHR 2022, 1)

This background of Sudanese and South Sudanese populations in Australia provides the context for the accounts of experiences faced by young SSAs in Australia.

SOUTH SUDANESE EXPERIENCES IN AUSTRALIA

> Home Affairs Minister Peter Dutton blasted the Victorian Labor government over African street crime, claiming residents of Australia's second-largest city were scared to go out to restaurants at night. (Hunter and Preiss 2018, 1)

This article filled the front page of the *Sydney Morning Herald* on the 3rd January 2018. In it, Minister Peter Dutton vilified young people from the South Sudanese community in Naarm (Melbourne, Australia) allegedly involved in crime by stating that 'they don't belong in Australian society' (Hunter and Preiss 2018, 1). It is not new for politicians to use fear-mongering tactics in election years. However, concerned citizens found ways of retaliating against this hyperbole by posting photographs of white Melburnians enjoying eating in restaurants safely with no disturbances and using a counter-narrative hashtag #Melbournebitesback (R. Morgan 2018, 1).

Naarm's African leaders called for 'bipartisanship and not sensationalism' (Ryan 2018, 1). In response, the Victorian Police Chief Commissioner Graham Ashton released a statement rebuking the misrepresentation of crime statistics, stating that crime had been reduced in the last 10 years. He clarified news reports from December 2017 depicting the alleged involvement of young SSA with the 'Apex gang' (further discussed in chapter 5) by stating:

It's not a structured or organised gang, it doesn't have a name or organised meetings. . . . It's [multicultural] young people coming together in an ad hoc way and engaging in public misbehaviour. (Faruqi 2018, 1)

Members of the local City of Greater Dandenong (CoGD) community additionally advised that 'Apex' was taken from a street sign in Dandenong. Despite ongoing clarifications, Dutton's statements led to a media frenzy and continued misleading political statements. The negative perceptions portrayed in the media were also countered by young SSAs who reclaimed the #*AfricanGangs* hashtag. They posted pictures of the positive contributions they make to Australian society, including photographs of them attending awards ceremonies, social events, and graduations (Bowden 2018). However, the achievements of SSAs are rarely acknowledged in the mainstream media. What is depicted instead are deficit stories that detail a community struggling to settle or integrate, and young people within their communities are portrayed as criminals (Windle 2008). These narratives are an example of how the system of *Australian Whiteness* works, producing *racialising discourses*, a term used in this research to describe these phenomena of racist propaganda exacerbating inter-ethnic tensions. Noting the insidious nature of perpetuated racialising discourses as a form of *necropolitics* (an analytical lens which details forms of social and political power to dictate life and death-dealing discourses) (Mbembe and Corcoran 2019), it is important to see Dutton's statements as part of a broader political discourse that benefits Australian Whiteness, rather than as isolated comments.

Table 1.1 was developed with participants taking part in my PhD research detailing a timeline of media and political discourses and important racialising discourses related to incidents affecting SSA communities in Naarm. Whilst this was the research locale of this monograph, a wealth of other research demonstrates that the trends and issues that these young, urban SSAs face do extrapolate to the broader population across Australia (Abur 2019; Baak 2019; Atem-Deng 2016; Macaulay 2020; Maher, Atem-Deng, and Kindersley 2018; Marlowe, Harris, and Lyons 2013; Nunn 2010; Williams 2022a; Pittaway and Dantas 2021).

Despite acculturative and social resettlement stressors, the vast majority of recently arrived young SSAs have made Australia their new home, expressing gratitude for being provided the opportunity for a fresh start in a new country. In addition, they demonstrate that they are 'proud of their contributions to Australian society and their desire to contribute to changing narratives of what it means to be African in a country like Australia' (Gatwiri and Anderson 2022, 139). This was after experiencing significant conflict in war-torn South Sudan at their time of departure (Abur 2019). They have been described by scholars Shepherd et al. (2018, 3) as 'integrat[ing] successfully

Table 1.1 Key Racialising Discourse Moments in Recent Naarm (Melbourne) History That Portray Young SSAs Negatively and Their Responses (as developed by the author in consultation with participants).

Year	Key racialising discourse moments in recent Naarm (Melbourne) history that portray young SSAs negatively and their responses
2007	• Murder of young SSA Liep Gony portrayed initially in mainstream media as South Sudanese gangs being responsible for cause of death. Described by SSAs as a racially motivated hate crime perpetrated by two Caucasian males. • Kevin Andrews states South Sudanese are not 'integrating' in Australian society, limits African diaspora immigration to Australia as a result. This was in an Australian federal election year. • South Sudanese Australian former refugee David Vincent protests Andrews by daubing his face with white zinc cream to represent the white-only migrants Andrews seems to want.
2008	• The mother of Liep Gony Martha Ojulu speaks to Australian news broadcaster SBS stating: 'Liep was killed due to his skin colour'.
2013	• The *Insight* current affairs program broadcast on ABC network conducts media report on the story around Liep Gony's murder uncovering how he was murdered and revealing misreporting amongst mainstream media.
2014–2015	• Crime statistics focused on African youth results in a racial profiling investigation of Victoria Police.
2015	• Associated multicultural network offenders roughly affiliated with the name Apex were involved in serious carjackings and robberies across Naarm. Originating in the South-east of Naarm, Apex is a street name in Dandenong.
2016	• The 'Moomba [festival] riots' was a significant episode of public disorder in Victoria involving multicultural young people but alleged to be South Sudanese young people who had formed the 'Apex gang'. This event, incorrectly labelled as a riot sparked a resurgence in the wave of heavily racialised media narratives about 'African gangs' resulting in major political consequences regarding the narratives of public safety.
2016–2017	• Media outlets mention the 'Apex gang' 145 times in one year.
2017	• The Black Lives Matter (BLM) founders visit Australia to meet with BIPOC groups. Racialised media and political narratives of bla(c)k and incarcerated youth is one agenda item. • The BLM protest was hosted in Naarm.

(Continued)

Table 1.1 (Continued)

Year	Key racialising discourse moments in recent Naarm (Melbourne) history that portray young SSAs negatively and their responses
2018	• Former Home Affairs Minister Peter Dutton makes statements about Naarm not being safe due to African gangs. This was a key narrative in a state election campaign. • Former Prime Minister Malcolm Turnbull backs his claims stating 'there is a real concern about Sudanese gangs in Australia'. • People across Australia respond with #AfricanGangs hashtag, highlighting positive achievements of the African diaspora and South Sudanese communities. • Raquel Willis (BLM Organiser) visits Australia and attends Liep Gony memorial. • *A Current Affair* program on Channel 7 network covered a story on African gangs. The Australian Communications and Media Authority (ACMA) ruled that Seven's current affair program breached guidelines presenting factual inaccuracy and resulted in misleading the public. • Channel Seven protests, organised primarily by two young SSAs invited Victorians to protest against the portrayal of African gangs and harmful racialised narratives.
2019	• African youth crime reporting continues in mainstream media alleging that young SSAs are filling youth justice precincts. • Police operations are conducted to arrest a series of network offenders. Those with South Sudanese cultural background were threatened with deportation.
2020	• BLM march Australia, involved further solidarity with First Nations and BIPOC peoples around the nation.

into the fabric of Australian society'. For the purpose of this research, integration is described in an 'open non-normative fashion as the process of becoming an accepted part of society' (Penninx and Garcés-Mascareñas 2016, 11). By juxtaposing Dutton's statement of 'failing to integrate' and the claim by many SSAs of 'successful integration', participants in this research actually question whether the notion of 'integration' is, in fact, their goal. They do this by questioning the heuristics of integration (on whose terms).

Bypassing media and political portrayal of effective 'integration' into normative Whiteness, this monograph, based on my PhD research looks at how young SSAs build their political voice to resist racialising discourses. This political voice is represented through the expressed conviction that they are 'born to stand out'. The aim of this monograph is to examine young SSAs' sense of agency through their development of arts projects involving Hip Hop as a form of activism/artivism (defined in chapter 3). They use Hip Hop as a vehicle through which to campaign to bring about political or social change, specifically through building counter-narratives to racialising discourses. I explore how their actions may counteract negative perceptions of their communities and, more importantly, involve public displays of resistance. Whilst establishing themselves as social agents in the world, young SSAs reframe and assert their multiple identities rooted in their Blackness, as well as their pride in culture.

WE DON'T FIT IN – PREVIOUS RESEARCH

Mainstream and tabloid media have targeted South Sudanese communities in Australia over a decade, which has had negative effects on their well-being (Milner and Khawaja 2010; Gatt 2011; Farquharson, Marjoribanks, and Nolan 2018; Abur and Mphande 2020). Young SSAs frequently express feeling misunderstood and thus struggle to 'fit into' Australian society (Henry-Waring 2008; Gatt 2011; Marlowe, Harris, and Lyons 2013; Colic-Peisker and Tilbury 2008). These narratives align with broader racialising discourses about black-African young people, which question whether black bodies are in or out of place (Windle 2008; Kwansah-Aidoo and Mapedzahama 2018). The racialised narratives are key to the rhetoric of 'mediated multiculturalism' (deciding who constitutes the Other) (Nolan et al. 2011). This approach of perpetuating media and moral panics targeting communities such as SSAs has resulted in a range of 'unfreedoms' (detailed in chapter 2) that prevent this minoritised group from realising the fulfilling lives that every human should have the right to attain, regardless of socio-cultural, political or religious background (Sen 2001[1999]; Freire et al. 2018[1968]).

This background drives aspects of an identity crisis faced by many migrant young people who may have had similar experiences struggling to forge a new hybrid identity in Australia. The decisions that a small number of struggling young people make, such as being involved in criminal behaviour, can influence the broader community's perceptions of all young people from that ethnic group (Shepherd, Newton, and Farquharson 2018). Due to misleading media reporting, broader forms of prejudice towards African diaspora communities have also developed (Farquharson, Marjoribanks, and Nolan 2018).

My previous 'Master of Sustainability and Social Change' research explored the concept of 'fitting in' within the lens of social inclusion. It depicted the voices and experiences of young SSAs growing up in Naarm, primarily from the period of 2004 onwards (Williams 2016). The research found that whilst some of these young SSAs do feel it is possible to fit in or feel a sense of belonging, depending on one's definition of 'fitting in', many more rejected this possibility. Rather, 'standing out' and being able to express yourself was seen as a more important goal for opening up a dialogue about identity and belonging. This idea of 'standing out' was adapted into the motto 'born to stand out' embraced by participants throughout subsequent discussions with SSA communities hosted by Footprints through youth participatory action-research (YPAR) processes (described in chapter 3). This monograph extends this body of research and longitudinal approach beyond belonging to explore the alternative notion of 'standing out' and how this enables young SSAs to carve out a space to be who they aspire to be in the Australian context.

When Henry-Waring (2008) and Ipsos Eureka Social Research Institute (2011) conducted research around the notion of belonging for South Sudanese and immigrant communities, many participants were clear that they wanted to belong to Australian society. Yet, 'there was a realisation amongst a number of migrants and [former] refugees that they could never fully belong' (Henry-Waring 2008, 6). This was due to a 'constant questioning of their presence and the largely negative and pervasive public and political discourse about migrants and refugees as a problem' (Henry-Waring 2008, 6). Nevertheless, there was a 'hope and expectation that it would be different for their children' (Henry-Waring 2008, 6).

Lentin and Titley (2011) demonstrate that 'fitting in' and belonging can be shaped by racism. Along with other social researchers such as Henry-Waring (2008); Colic-Peisker (2008); Khan and Pederson (2010), I suggest that because African diaspora communities in Australia, such as the South Sudanese, have noticeably darker skin than most Australians, this has fuelled racism based on visible differences. These indicators of social exclusion inhibit the ability of young people from African backgrounds to 'fit in' or belong (Williams 2016).

Colic-Peisker (2005) discusses the topic of identity and social inclusion of Bosnian former refugees in Australia (who display a white-skinned appearance). Whilst acknowledging that all humans often make adjustments to 'fit in' through their exploration of their social identities, a pertinent sentiment expressed towards Bosnians in this study was 'at least you're the right colour' (Colic-Peisker 2005, 615). Majavu (2018) argues that the African diaspora faces significant challenges due to the Whiteness regimes of multiculturalism (discussed in chapter 2) which denigrate Blackness and prioritise Whiteness. These claims demonstrate the interconnection between multicultural and migration policies and prejudice, whereby integration policies moderate the link between immigrant presence and anti-immigrant prejudice (Kende et al. 2022). This monograph details some of these experiences from the perspectives of SSA communities.

WHAT IS IT THAT YOUNG SOUTH SUDANESE AUSTRALIANS ARE RESISTING? RACIAL PROFILING AND MORAL PANICS DIRECTED TOWARDS SOUTH SUDANESE AUSTRALIAN URBAN YOUTH

Young SSAs reside at the intersection of multiple vulnerable populations: they are young, they tend to come from a former refugee background, and they navigate social complexities which often cause them to feel excluded in the Australian landscape. Young SSAs may also have experienced trauma and they, or their immediate families, arrived in Australia from difficult economic, political, and social conditions, resulting from civil war and tribal disputes spanning 50 years (Abur 2019). Negative stereotypes, prejudice, racism, and discrimination are key factors undermining SSAs and other African diasporas' potential for equal rights as equal citizens in Australia (Milner and Khawaja 2010; Shepherd, Newton, and Farquharson 2018; AHRC 2010). The young people taking part in this research portray how they can respond with agency and resilience in dangerous and distressing situations and, moreover, have ownership over the narration of their experiences and the meanings they give to them, preferring to prioritise articulation of their strengths and dignity and their cultural tales. The description of Immigration Minister Peter Dutton's statements and table 1.1 are examples of media and moral panics that young SSAs have faced for almost two decades in the Australian context. Media and moral panics utilising specific integration and criminality discourses are described as *racialising discourses* and are the specific cultural phenomena that young SSAs are resisting. Forms of resistance such as through protest, dissent or through arts-based development projects are further explored in each chapter.

Young people in public places have always been a contentious issue (Furlong 2013; R.E. White 2009), often regardless of whether they are presenting in a perceived antisocial way or not (Smith 2011). Whilst youth gangs and 'cliques' do exist in Australia (Grossman and Sharples 2010; R.E. White and Mason 2006), multiple sources identify that fear of groups of young people in public spaces is often fuelled by media reports that label young people as 'troublemakers' (R.E. White 2009; Furlong 2013; YACVIC 2017). These media frenzies have been termed 'moral panics' (Young 1971, 2009; Cohen 1987) which have been constructed by the 'opportunistic behaviour of politicians scapegoating youth in attempts to appear connected with what is happening in local electorates to win votes' (Furlong 2013, 362). The media focus on youth gangs in Victoria, Australia dates back to mid-late 1990s, when young Vietnamese migrants were stereotyped in the media as *ethnic youth gangs* (R.D. White 1999).

Mainstream media often presents young SSAs and other African-origin 'youths' as homogenous. For example, they are sometimes identified as being of 'African appearance' and vulnerable, or engaging in criminal or gang-related behaviour (see Windle 2008 and table 1.2).

After former immigration minister Kevin Andrews questioned their ability to integrate in 2007 (Cowan 2007; Collins 2007), SSAs identified difficulties recovering from what they felt was a harmful denigration of their communities as similar racial profiling continued in Australia (Topsfield 2008; Oakes and Cooke 2007; VEOHRC 2008). Following 2011, an increase in popular media articles included misleading and alleged crime statistics throughout leading newspapers (Oakes 2012). From 2011 to 2015, attention shifted to issues of racial profiling of East African communities in Australia by Victoria Police (Green 2015; Waters 2011). Despite attempts at internal reform, this was still of concern in 2017 (Hopkins 2017). Allegations of young SSAs' involvement with the 'Apex gang' (Wahlquist 2018) surfaced following a public brawl during the March 2016 Moomba Festival in Melbourne.

One mainstream news source reportedly published 173 racialised and sensationalising stories linking back to the Apex gang, frequently embellishing crime statistics. These articles were published despite Victoria Police maintaining the alleged gang was not primarily Sudanese and had been disbanded (Shepherd, Newton, and Farquharson 2018). Then-prime minister of Australia Malcolm Turnbull claimed that African gangs still

Table 1.2 Common Descriptors for 'African Refugees' Adapted from Windle 2008. Newspaper articles appearing in Naarm (Melbourne), 26 September–3 December 2007.

Common descriptors for 'African refugees' adapted from Windle 2008*				
Racial Attributes	Collective Attributes	Age Attributes	Migration Attributes	Moral Qualities
African	A mob	Youths	Refugees	Delinquent
North African	Packs	Kids	Immigrants	Lawless
Of African descent	A gang	Children	Migrants	Thugs
Black	Gangs	Under-age		Offenders
(South) Sudanese	A group	Teenagers		
Sudanese-born	Community	Teens		
		Juvenile		

existed despite Victorian (state) Premier Daniel Andrews establishing that 'he [Turnbull] doesn't know what he is speaking about' (Andrews cited in Ferguson 2018, 1).

Dan Harris' (2017) earlier exploration of the social exclusion of South Sudanese communities in Australia also reports young people's experiences of frequent and aggressive racism, noting how this directly relates to skin colour. Experiences of exclusion are attributed to their settlement history in Australia. With SSAs' recent arrival (predominantly from 2004 onwards, and relatively sudden influx into Australian society, this triggered 'ongoing and often ugly backlash from some sectors of the majoritarian white Australian community and media' – a common pattern with earlier waves of particular migrant groups (D. Harris 2017, 7).

Mainstream media, in particular, has a profound influence on the attitudes of the Australian public, manipulating the population to form biases against recent migrant groups (Dandy and Pe-Pua 2015; Schweitzer et al. 2005; Entman 2007; Elias, Mansouri, and Paradies 2021). Examples of other moral panics include rhetoric from the period of Hansonism in the late 1990s; young people of Islamic faith and their potential involvement in terrorism post-September 11; asylum seeking to enter borders depicted as criminal 'boat people' or the visual dehumanisation and changing images of refugees (Martin 2015; Kabir 2006; Bleiker et al. 2013).

A study of the refugee experience of social cohesion in Australia found that 'racism, intercultural contact, and the media had multiple and interrelated effects on aspects of social cohesion such as belonging, participation, and inclusion' (Dandy and Pe-Pua 2015, 339). Adverse media coverage and stereotyping of young SSA communities have been relentless and somewhat unprecedented in terms of focusing on a specific cultural community for over a decade (Nolan et al. 2011; Marjoribanks, Nolan, and Farquharson 2010; Gatt 2011; Windle 2008; Majavu 2020; Macaulay and Deppeler 2020; Run 2013). This has resulted in significant negative effects on young SSAs' health (Abur 2018; Abur and Mphande 2020; AHRC 2010; VIC-Health 2005, 2008).

Structural disadvantage faced by ethnic minority groups such as SSAs, including racism or concentration in particular locations, likewise significantly contributes to health disparities (Rambaree and Knez 2016; Nazroo et al. 2007; Mansouri 2009; VIC-Health 2008; Land and Stovall 2009). As a result, newly arrived black African Australians report discrimination and economic disparity, which contributes to feeling socially excluded (AHRC 2010). As a largely misunderstood population in Australian society, multiple studies report on the social exclusion of South Sudanese communities (Colic-Peisker and Tilbury 2008; Gatt 2011; Marlowe, Harris, and Lyons 2013) as they 'face a unique set of challenges as a result of their age, ethnicity, migration and direct/indirect trauma experience' (Windle cited in Griffiths, Sawikar, and Muir 2009, 32).

Globally, there is a growing concern that migrant young people may opt to estrange themselves from their host societies due to the perception that some migrant young people cannot simultaneously hold multiple allegiances (Mansouri, Beaman, and Hussain 2019). SSAs have also demonstrated awareness of issues surrounding their community in response to acculturation stressors and incidences of violent crime (Daughter's-of-Jerusalem 2017; Atem-Deng 2016). Despite this, Mansouri et al. (2019) suggest migrant youth identities are far more nuanced, highlighting how migrant identities are mediated through complex layers that can include personal, local and cross-border networks. These scholars engender new possibilities to create and express multiple attachments to cultural systems and socio-political communities. These findings suggest that scholars have begun to understand these multiple attachments as transcultural processes (*transculturalism*) which involve young people identifying with multiple or hybrid cultural identities. With this in mind, the focus of this monograph around the theme of 'born to stand out' (BTSO) notes the importance of freedom to choose how one might express one's hybrid identities in order to flourish. One way this occurs is through challenging misrepresentations of themselves.

WHAT DOES IT MEAN TO CHALLENGE REPRESENTATIONS?

Throughout history, one way that disaffected young people have enacted their political voice is through protests and social movements where groups of young people or various subcultures act together to disrupt the status quo and form sites of resistance (Subcultures-Network 2014; Wray-Lake and Abrams 2020; Rogers and Kelly 2024). This often occurs due to government failure to support or prioritise these groups (Wyn and Woodman 2006). For young SSAs, this is made more difficult now due to the lengthy period of over a decade of media and moral panics directed towards young SSAs since young SSA Liep Gony's 2007 murder, which turned out to be a racially motivated crime (New-Matilda 2010). Following this significant event, which essentially brought SSA communities to the attention of the nation, young SSAs continued to express dissatisfaction with racialising narratives that they are criminals involved in gangs and are not integrating into Australian society. For example, the alleged Moomba riots in 2016 (K. J. Benier et al. 2018) are another significant period when the *African gangs narrative* came to the forefront. This was followed by the Channel 7 protest organised in 2018 by young

SSA Hip Hop artists in response to the same narratives depicted in national TV news broadcasting (Eddie 2018) (see table 1.1).

This monograph posits that actions of young SSAs mirror similarities with BIPOC elsewhere across the globe where 'contemporary "moral panics" around gang culture have also been interpreted through these models of resistance and the criminalisation of young people in public' (Gildart et al. 2017, 4). For SSAs, this is an ideal time to continue to work out what forms of resistance they wish to enact in response to racialising discourses, not just through their migration experiences or through the lens of their visibility and experiences of racism, but also through asserting their positive contributions (Gatwiri and Anderson 2022). Here, it is not just about tolerance or feelings of social inclusion, but an opportunity to express their identity in Australia on their own terms, as expressed through the notion of being 'born to stand out' (described below, and why Hip Hop was chosen as a method of social change pedagogy). Nunn (2010) presents one form of this resistance by contrasting false media representations with the audio-visual output of a collaborative arts-based research project with SSA young women. Nunn discusses how the film constitutes both a reply to, and a complication of, the dominant representations of SSAs. Similarly, this monograph describes how an action-research process through arts-based community development and standpoint projects provided the possibility to explore how young SSAs are challenging representations through this methodology.

It is important to explore the micro-level everyday practices of the cohort under investigation by documenting the 'causal connections that can encompass dynamism, interdependence, and contingency' (Bevington and Dixon 2005, 187). This involves understanding the impact of the socio-political and structural forces that pervade research participants' lives, the effects on their identity and social relations, and other people's responses, which can be examined through a close engagement and reading of popular actions. It also involves an investigation into the

> processes of articulation that start out of submerged networks of meanings, proceed through cultural innovation in the domain of everyday life, and may result in visible and sizable forms of collective action for the control of historicity. (Escobar 1992, 420)

Some of the local and global causal forces can therefore be described through the concept of *identity politics,* where identities can be politicised, as experienced by many identity-based groups (discussed in chapter 3). Identity politics is defined in cultural terms as expressing 'the belief that identity itself, its elaboration, expression, or affirmations should be a fundamental focus of political work' (Kauffman cited in Bernstein 2005, 49). The Australian context of bla(c)k identity politics (incorporating blak First Nations peoples and other peoples who identify as black) is nuanced and requires further interrogation beyond the scope of this research (Colic-Peisker and Tilbury 2008; Gatwiri and Anderson 2020). One aim of this monograph, however, is to narrate the diversity and complexity of young SSAs' individual and community experiences as it pertains to their identity politics in Australia. As Idriss (2021) notes, this takes place in a settler colonial context, identifying the difficulties of incorporating race and ethnicity as central to an Australian youth studies agenda. The renewed driver of this interrogation is the global resurgence of the Black Lives Matter (BLM 2021) movement in 2020–1, which further revealed ongoing experiences of bla(c)k deaths in custody and daily experiences of systemic racism. Racialising discourses are therefore at the forefront of many agendas (Henriques-Gomes and Visontay 2020; Gatwiri and Anderson 2020). Understanding this context is imperative for the positioning of this research as it articulates a gap in knowledge for young SSAs' experiences with Australian racialising discourses. Additionally, acknowledging young SSAs' global links with social movements further highlights racism, discrimination, and inequality experienced by black peoples worldwide (O'Brien 2017) whilst positioning them as active agents in matters that affect them. It is therefore important to turn to a brief statement on my own positionality as a researcher, which is taken up further in chapter 2.

As a Caucasian Australian, I am not of South Sudanese origin and do not profess to speak for South Sudanese communities. I have, however, been closely relating with South Sudanese communities in Naarm and South Sudan for over a decade as a friend, community development practitioner, and academic. I have a strong affiliation with organisations such as Footprints, where I continue to walk alongside young emerging artists from culturally diverse backgrounds whilst following a *researching with* process (Exley, Whatman, and Singh 2018).

Practically, this process involves recognising that young people who were involved as participants in this research have strong voices in their chosen elements of forms of Hip Hop, emceeing (rap, spoken-word), or dance (M. Morgan and Bennett 2011) or other forms of Afrocentric and Caribbean dance styles or street dance, including Afrobeats and Dancehall. This monograph supports the amplification of their voices as they articulate self-representation in challenging circumstances of oppression and Othering. The monograph also addresses how young SSAs negotiate identity politics whilst acknowledging that terminology such as the use of 'BIPOC' can be highly contested because individuals prefer to self-select their identify terminology (Shoneye 2018). This research does not seek to generalise all African Australian or SSA experiences, noting that experiences are complex and vary considerably (Gatwiri and Anderson 2022).

QUESTIONS EXPLORED THROUGHOUT MONOGRAPH

Common conceptualisations in social science literature depict young SSAs as refugees displaying potential for criminality or gang behaviour (K. Benier, Wickes, and Moran 2020; Majavu 2020; Shepherd, Newton, and Farquharson 2018). This obscures the opportunity to comprehensively explore this population, not only as resilient social agents with a political voice but also as individuals making choices in unique circumstances. Despite an overwhelmingly negative media portrayal, and their position in a vulnerable stage of early resettlement in Australia, I have repeatedly observed young SSAs actively partaking in the complex activity of forming their identity, building their political voice, and contributing to Australian society (Gatwiri and Anderson 2022; Gatwiri and Moran 2022; C. Moran and Gatwiri 2022; C. Moran and Robards 2020; L. Moran 2016). Khan (2021) identifies this trajectory as a type of pragmatic analysis of belonging, foregrounding the practical and political contexts in which forced-migrant young people's statements of belonging are put to work making claims on the nation.

Community arts initiatives and arts-based research methods have the potential to bring diverse people together and build strong relationships through various forms of artistic expression (D. Harris 2017; Hickey-Moody 2013; Clammer 2015; Ware and Dunphy 2020). Coupled with critical arts-based *standpoint project* methodology stemming from a social position on racism and involving *transformative youth organising* (Ritzer 2005; Bautista 2018) (discussed in chapter 3), the PhD research explored in this monograph discusses the value of the arts in urban youth cultures, stimulating creativity and the social imagination, which in turn flow back into wider processes of social transformation (Clammer 2015). Through observation of the ways being BTSO manifests, this research investigates the effectiveness of arts-based standpoint project initiatives in the Footprints YPAR project – particularly those utilising Hip Hop – for sustaining agency, countering stereotypes, and building resistance and political voice through self-determination.

The overarching questions explored in this monograph asks: *What is the role of Hip Hop to support young South Sudanese Australians in building their political voice to resist racialising discourses?* To unpack this question, the sub-questions explored are:

- How do young SSAs build agency and develop their political voice?
- What role does Hip Hop specifically play in this building of political voice?

- What role does political voice play for young SSAs in resisting racialising discourses?
- How might this contribute to enhanced freedom and affirmations of identity?

The following section outlines the ethnographic site on which this monograph is based.

LOCALE – FOOTPRINTS YOUTH PARTICIPATORY ACTION RESEARCH AND SOCIO-POLITICAL CONTEXT

Footprints is a grassroots community development non-profit organisation, which I co-founded in outer southeast Naarm (Melbourne), Australia in 2008 to 'create spaces to bring about social change through the creative arts' (Footprints 2020). Projects involving camps, festivals, school tours, workshops, and pop-up performances feature SSA Hip Hop artists who use their art to describe the evolution of their identity formation. They express this through the tracks they perform and community initiatives. This monograph uses Footprints as a site to investigate the notion of being 'born to stand out' (BTSO), which supports young SSA participants in negotiating their Blackness (black identities) through Hip Hop.

The idea for the BTSO motto (motivational saying) came from seeing images such as the one with the giraffe of many colours, portraying its multiplicity and uniqueness, as displayed in figure 1.1. My PhD research, from which this monograph is drawn, utilises this metaphor to demonstrate that despite young people's 'sameness' as humans, they nonetheless value the differences in their unique identities, and thus have no desire to 'fit in'. Rather, they deliberately and strategically utilise tools such as Hip Hop to define themselves, thus 'standing out'. The phrase BTSO emerged through my observations of a Footprints' YPAR project that ran from 2011 to 2015, and which is documented in my master's thesis described earlier (Williams 2015). It aligns with popular culture literature and imagery, such as photo 3 that suggests that fitting in does not necessarily equate to belonging (Brown 2010).

This YPAR project, as part of my PhD research, was developed to support young SSA Hip Hop artists who were trying to discern their diaspora identities in a nation that deploys harmful political agendas relating to their presence (Majavu 2015, 2018, 2020). Through Footprints YPAR periods 2017–20, I identified that participants involved in this PhD research continued to adopt and relate to the BTSO phrase, which became a communal motto. When 'checking in' with participants during this research process,

Figure 1.1 Young SSAs' Experiences from 'We Don't Fit In' to 'I Have Absolutely No Desire to Fit In'. *Source*: Photo courtesy of public domain.

they repeatedly confirmed this metaphor was a useful way of expressing their intent regarding their multiple identities within Australian society.

This motto was adopted publicly by SSAs in a short documentary describing what 'born to stand out' means to them as artists (Summer and Footprints

2022a, 2022b). In addition, young people of African descent with noticeable darker skin referred to the difficulties of forming strong, healthy identities, which are often restricted by social identity categories imposed on them through frequent Othering by white Australians. *Otherness* refers to a racial inferiority or a non-white Other (E. Said 1994; 2003[1968]) (see note on terminology). Through the lens of urban youth culture, Dimitriadis (2007) attributes this term to misconceptions of young people and their cultural politics. He focuses on racialising discourses that mark people, primarily by their race (visibility of skin colour), in ways that Other or distance them and create power imbalances.

For young people who may identify as BIPOC in Australia, Othering has serious implications for how they perceive themselves and how others perceive them in society (Eitle and Eitle 2002). I have written previously on how identity politics plays tricks on young SSAs (Williams 2022a). The tricks play out through mainstream media and politicians using persuasive media devices to create moral panics associating Blackness with criminality (Majavu 2020). As a result, young SSAs must navigate complex cultural codes on a daily basis (Abur 2019).

The being BTSO motto suggests reclaiming identities involving being strong in culture, championing multiple identities, celebrating difference and diversity, displaying dignity, and fearlessly challenging societal norms (Mahana-Culture 2022). Having the capacity to stand out and focus on self-determination necessitates a level of assertiveness and confidence – not compromising on affirmations of, and self-articulation of, evolving identities. Figure 1.2 is used with permission from the artist Ayuen K. Bol to visually represent this notion of BTSO. It does so by depicting vivid portraiture and the use of colour over dark melanated skin. It is overtly political but visually accessible, inviting the viewer to look at the subject's face through a surreal and constructed lens.

Ayuen Bol accompanied this picture with a poem describing the opposite of following a BTSO motto, that is, having to fit in (look and act like 'us'), which limits one's ability to truly express identity. The abstract from her poem[1] displays some of the angst she felt as she longed for home and a sense of belonging in South Sudan as well as her feelings of being Othered as a forced migrant (former refugee) in Australia:

I was convinced to shed my skin
And wash my mind
The mirrors told me I was one of them
Shrinking even smaller, in this hate
(for full poem see Appendix [2]).

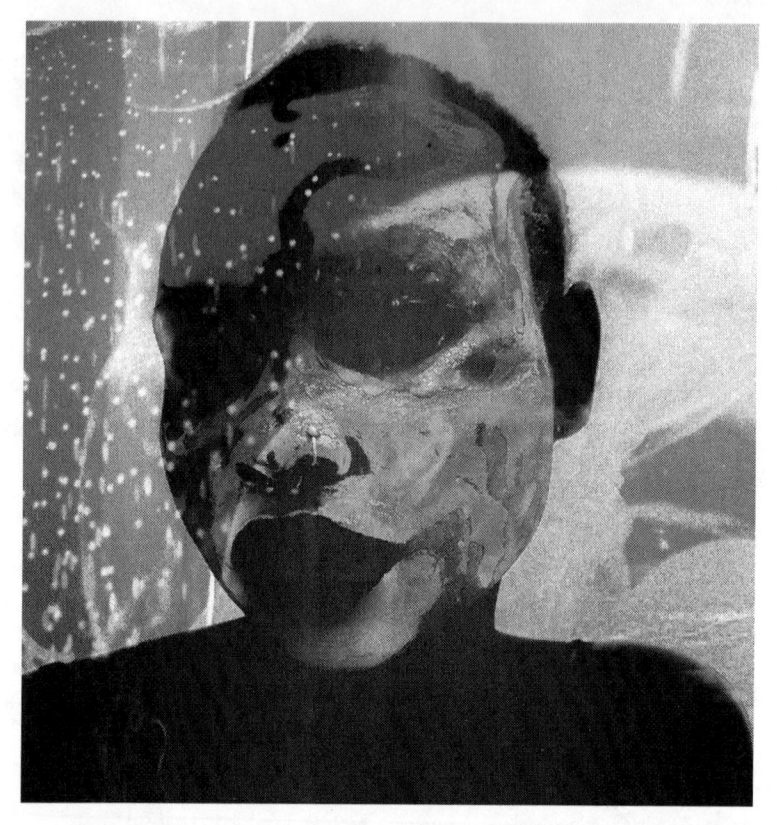

Figure 1.2 Artist Ayuen K Bol – to Represent the Research Theme – 'Born to Stand Out'.
Source: Ayuen K Bol.

Having chronicled the genesis of the BTSO concept and motto in relation to cultural codes and the need for critical creative agency as used in this monograph, the remainder of this section further details the PhD research setting and background of the Footprints organisation that provides a platform for young SSAs to build their political voice.

This study takes place in Naarm (Melbourne) on the lands we now call Australia (see figure 1.1). Whilst these lands were never ceded, the moniker 'Australia' will be used throughout the text. However, the name 'Naarm' will be used to acknowledge traditional custodians' terminology for the region colonially known as 'Melbourne'. The prime research locale for this monograph is the CoGD local government area (LGA), which is on Boon Wurrung and Bunurong lands in outer suburban Naarm where I have lived and worked for 17 years.

Footprints was started in CoGD, which is the most culturally diverse locality in Australia (CGD 2018, 1)(figure 1.3 below). This and neighbouring municipalities form a common resettlement zone for former refugee communities.

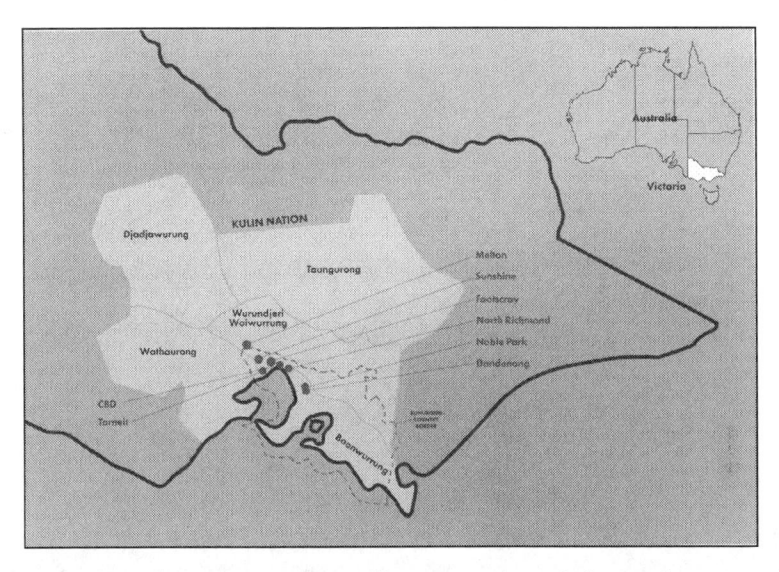

Figure 1.3 Map of Greater Naarm (Melbourne) and Bordering Regions, Featuring Common Resettlement Zones. *Source*: Kimberley Summer.

Research participants also come from other areas across Naarm including Footscray, Melton, Sunshine, North Richmond, Tarneit (Wurundjeri Woiwurrung), and Pakenham, Noble Park (Southern Boonwurrung/Bunurong). According to the most recent census data (A.-B.-o.-S. 2016a), the City of Casey (a neighbouring LGA located in Southern Boon Wurrung/Bunurong) has 9,693 residents born in Africa whilst CoGD has 4,398 out of a total population in both LGAs of 152,050. Casey is mentioned as CoGD is a nearby hub which Casey residents frequent for shopping, socialising and working purposes.

In CoGD in 2016, 234 residents were born in South Sudan, whilst 434 were born in Sudan. However, these numbers are not indicative of the total residents who identify with South Sudanese cultural heritage due to many people being born in transit countries such as Kenya, Uganda, and Egypt, or in the destination of Australia (CGD 2016). In 2018, there were 2,840 young people aged between 12 and 25 years and a further 3,694 young adults and adults aged between 25 and 44 years originating from Sudan and South Sudan residing across Naarm (Victorian Government 2018, 65).

SIGNIFICANCE OF RECLAIMING IDENTITIES

Using the example of young SSAs, this chapter has discussed the limited understanding in Australian society around the circumstances surrounding multicultural young people and those from former refugee backgrounds.

These include potential experiences of significant trauma, struggles with identity issues, and feeling excluded from the wider Australian community (Majavu 2015, 2018; Abur and Mphande 2020; Abur 2018, 2019; Windle 2008; Henry-Waring 2008; Williams 2016; Pittaway and Dantas 2021). Alternatively, this monograph explores how young SSAs develop and sustain critical creative agency despite their portrayed vulnerability. The purpose of this research was to understand what this process of self-actualisation might look like for young SSAs seeking to forge their own transcultural identities and paths in Australia (Mansouri and Modood 2021; Wyn, Cuervo, and Cook 2019). Reclaiming identities therefore involves moving beyond the racist tropes of Othering to understand young SSAs' assertions of their own emerging transcultural (hybrid) identities. The power of this process of reclaiming identities is pivotal for seeking to understand how they enact agency and resilience rather than focusing on deficit narratives.

This monograph highlights how young SSAs and the ethnographer (me) seek to understand how they enact agency and resilience rather than focusing on deficit narratives. This is expressed through the theme 'born to stand out'. The main themes highlighted throughout demonstrate new contributions to knowledge, as the topic of young SSAs' senses of freedom (Sen 2001[1999]) and aspirations (Appadurai 2004) (discussed in chapter 6) in Australia has not been covered extensively. As suggested, what is often documented are deficit narratives further restricting our understanding of populations such as SSAs, rather than demonstrating capabilities through a strengths-based imagining of their futures.

A growing body of research points towards the value of arts-based community development initiatives and standpoint projects involving transformative youth organising, which seek to support people in the exploration and self-expression of their identities, develop their sense of agency, and highlight resilience (VIC-Health 2009; Ware and Dunphy 2019; Sonn and Baker 2016; Cañas 2013; Bautista 2018). This specific mode of creative inquiry prioritises participants' voices and seeks to convey the complexities of their stories (A. Harris 2013; Baker, Sonn, and Meyer 2020; Akom 2009; Hickey-Moody 2013). Through my own experiences walking alongside young people from migrant and former refugee backgrounds, I observe that creating an open or 'third' space for dialogue through arts activities supports processes of identity transformation for young people. Scholars such as De Block and Buckingham (2007, 177) recognise the potential role of the arts in renegotiating identities, stating that it 'can provide a powerful means of representing identity, and of asserting cultural difference'. However, whilst participation in various art forms can demonstrate a sense of the artist's voice (not always overtly) which involves freedom of self-expression, a knowledge gap persists around how young SSAs create and use the art form of Hip Hop to develop and broadcast their political voice as a site of resistance, particularly to racialising discourses. Through a focus on racial social justice issues, this research bridges this gap by examining how Hip Hop provides a medium for young SSAs to enact and build their political voice and develop spaces and counter-narratives that may influence public perceptions and challenge representations amongst broader Australian society.

Using empirical research and an interdisciplinary approach drawing on anthropology, sociology, youth studies, community development, and migration studies, my findings regarding the assertion of cultural identity, agency, and political voice demonstrated by young SSAs contribute to discourses of diversity, difference, and the creation of sites for social change in the Australian context, offering meaningful exchanges and collaborations through arts-based initiatives and standpoint projects.

The implications of this monograph are primarily epistemological, providing impetus to impact social and cultural policy and community development programmes by informing service providers, local government, the public sector, and creative industries working across sectors about the ways South Sudanese Australians make sense of their lives and how this understanding drives their decision-making and actions.

MONOGRAPH STRUCTURE

The metanarrative of this monograph explores how political voice manifests in various forms of artivism (further defined in chapter 4) for young SSAs through Hip Hop expression. This section details the aims of each chapter.

In chapter 2, I briefly survey the overarching theoretical frameworks of *Critical Race Theories* (CRT) and *New Social Movements* (NSMs) that form the basis of this monograph. Explanation of CRT outlines the socio-political constructs of race and racism as experienced by young SSAs and other culturally and linguistically diverse people (Stefancic 2014). Whilst young SSAs may not be familiar with or articulate that they are a part of a New Social Movement per se, NSM theories (Buechler 1995) outline concerns with representation and urge us to account for the many voices within social movements, the discursive positioning of stakeholders – including the ethnographer – and the complex epistemological and political negotiations at stake (Escobar 1992, 421). These negotiations take place through identity politics, demonstration of political voice, and alternative forms of resistance as they pertain to young SSAs and urban youth culture.

I move to briefly describe my research design in my related PhD research as it relates to co-researching with young SSAs as they explore and articulate their intercultural and diasporic identities using Hip Hop to resist racialising discourses. Under the umbrella of ethnographic inquiry, the specific analysis tools utilised are narrative and arts-based inquiry approaches. Through ethnographic writing on the topics of politics and resistance, each subsequent chapter (3–6) foregrounds analysis of the BTSO artivists' and participants' expressions of political voice through various artefacts.

The sub-questions presented above are used to structure chapters 3–6 of the monograph. Chapter 3 provides background to chapters 4–6, outlining how young SSAs build agency and develop their political voice. The chapter explores the types of systems participants are resisting and introduces the conscious use of the Hip Hop genre, which was chosen by young SSAs to express their political voice.

Chapter 4 addresses the first *consciousness-raising* step of an NSM and unpacks elements of this journey as experienced by young SSAs through the *Culture-centred Approach* (CCA) (Dutta 2020). It explores how individuals conceptualise the consciousness-raising journey within the opportunity that the art form of Hip Hop presents in the Gua Performance and Leadership Camp, the first stage of Footprints' Grounded Project. The analysis identifies stories of young people who became 'woke' (conscious) (Mirzaei 2019)[3] of the socio-political systems operating in the world and their role in it in response to geopolitical events of recent years. Through the application of CRT, this chapter analyses the interplay between identity politics and Blackness as SSAs go through this process. This is explored within a *third culture* context (Bell-Villada et al. 2011).

An examination of young SSA's experiences with racialising discourses (as conceived through CRT) follows in chapter 5. A historical account details the series of events stemming from the murder of SSA Liep Gony and other key events pertaining to SSA communities and concludes with the Apex gang focus from the period of 2007 to 2020 detailed earlier in this chapter in table 1.1. This series of events necessitated the need for a political voice. Therefore, this chapter expands on previous research findings by demonstrating an exploration of the specific counter-narratives that young SSAs identify specifically through the Grounded Project hosted by Footprints in response to media and political perspectives. These are explored as another aspect of an NSM.

The final findings chapter 6 explores young SSAs' stories in relation to the notion of being BTSO. Using the CCA as an analysis tool, the Grounded Project is explored to continue to define the specific site of social change. Through iterating the final step of the beginnings of an NSM, it pinpoints how participants conceptualise a movement-making process of everyday resistance. This is described as an individual process for young SSAs as the findings show the heterogeneity of responses. Considering CRT, chapter 7 also details young SSAs' searches for, or demands for, freedom, and their creative pursuits to demonstrate how they are 'born to stand out'. They are therefore depicted as 'BTSO artivists'.

The topics raised throughout this monograph findings related to consciousness-raising, counter-narrative storytelling, and the impact of racialising discourses for research participants, are critically discussed in chapter 8. This discussion chapter analyses the findings to demonstrate how a political voice for young SSAs manifests in important new ways that conventional theories of activism or resistance do not fully capture. Here, participants describe their thoughts on the effectiveness of their actions of resistance and consider some preliminary next steps.

Chapter 8 concludes the monograph by discussing how young SSAs are carving out space in the face of racialising discourses and identifying opportunities for future research. Overall, the key findings of this monograph highlight young SSAs' visions for a future where they outline and enact their roles in decision-making and display agency. Finally, the privileging of young SSAs' stories about the lived experiences and impacts of systemic racism and integration policies in an urban Australian context is seen to be imperative, demonstrating implications for Antiracism policy and practice.

NOTES

1. All poetry and artist lyrics in this research are represented in a different font to differentiate them from participant quotes or citations (see chapter 3, which outlines thesis formatting approach).

2. Ayuen K Bol (2020) – Poem based on theme 'Born to Stand Out' (used with permission)

> *Tears flowing*
> *Aches in streams*
> *Yet I forget the water*
> *That level this body*
>
> *I miss the laughter*
> *I miss the way we'd climb trees*
> *Sitting at the very top*
> *Views of shrunken people and huts*
> *Cradled amongst falling asleep*
>
> *I miss the food*
> *Giving me strength*
> *Uncle hurt, memories of dis-total rage.*
> *All our mother magic*

Using porridge to heal
I strayed far
Distanced to a new land
Leaning in language that binds me
Forgetting what I was sent here for

I was convinced to shed my skin
And wash my mind
The mirrors told me I was one of them
Shrinking even smaller, in this height

A familiar knock at my hears door
I open again and again with caution
They took me away
Unfamiliar to words of healing

I've never been here
Silenced and still
This Land of a people
Mothered my tong, speak through me
My name is Ayuen Kuol Bol
Regaining pain of a child's longing
Land, this Land of a people
Strengths in magic, that drew mine

Holding me, speaking truths
Bringing back a smile
One I didn't practice in the reflection
A child that waited years to escape

Wëk chäkë lëëć, ë riel ëya Piou
I appreciate you all, in my hearts strength
Koć theer kuä atö etenë kën wök
Our old people are here with us

3. 'Woke' history: Black Americans in their ongoing fight against racism and social injustice have used the term 'woke' at key moments in history.

In literal terms, being woke refers to being awake and not asleep. One *Urban Dictionary* contributor defines woke as 'being aware of the truth behind things 'the man' doesn't want you to know'. Meanwhile, a concurrent definition signals a shift in meaning to 'the act of being very pretentious about how much you care about a social issue'.

The Oxford dictionary expanded its definition of the word 'woke' in 2017 to add it as an adjective meaning 'alert to injustice in society, especially racism' (Mirzaei 2019).

Chapter 2

Freedom to Enact Political Voice and Develop Forms of Resistance

SITES FOR SOCIAL CHANGE

Throughout this monograph, I suggest that sites of social change can be created if young SSAs build their political voice and forms of resistance. Reflecting the interdisciplinary nature of the PhD research reflected in this monograph, table 2.1 depicts how theories and perspectives informed by *Critical Race Theory* (CRT) and *New Social Movements* (NSMs) were selected to discuss this hypothesis and are presented as theories that inform each chapter. CRT helps to frame young SSAs' experiences in relation to racism and racialising discourses. Racism and racialising discourses are the social conditions identified that necessitate the need for the expression of political voice, primarily expressed throughout by the modality of arts-based resistance to racialising discourses. NSM theory explains how the formation of any identity-based social movement is a process involving various actors – in this case, urban young SSAs. As Hip Hop is considered to be an NSM (see chapter 4), two further concepts augment NSM that supports understanding of young SSAs' involvement with NSM formation or practice: (1) Critical Hip Hop Pedagogy (CHHP) highlights the importance of starting with a consciousness-raising process amongst young SSA participants; and (2) the Culture-centred Approach (CCA) specifically posits that the process of reclaiming 'identity' has become a site for NSMs. These concepts and theories can help explain resistance and social change and are therefore used to illuminate young SSAs' forms of resistance in response to racism and racialising discourses.

Demonstrating an Afrocentric perspective, U.S. scholar Kendi's (2019) exploration of CRT pinpoints practical applications of Antiracist perspectives. CRT and Antiracism concepts originated in the United States due to the extensive civil rights movement and race analysis. CRT conceptualises societal categorisations of racial groups, which has resulted in black people being Othered through racialising discourses (Crenshaw et al. 1996). Australian scholarship has argued for the application of locally based CRT, which I layer with perspectives from Australian critical race theorists Lentin (2020) and Idriss (2021), as well as Indigenous, cultural and post-colonial scholarship (Moreton-Robinson 2000, 2004a, 2004b).

African Australian scholarship is sometimes critical of conceptual frameworks and popular culture reference points imported from the United States (Zwangobani 2008). When discussing the nuances of the experiences of people of African descent in Australia, I therefore utilise Majavu (2020) and Gatwiri et al. (2022) honouring of a black/African diaspora theoretical framing. By doing so, this approach links this monographs conceptualisation and connection of the lived experiences of black people globally whilst analysing the ways young African Australians draw on primarily U.S. cultural reference points to craft Blackness within a specifically Australian context. This approach has implications for multicultural and urban youth cultures (Dimitriadis 2001, 2007; A. Harris 2013) who might identify with global phenomena on expressions of Blackness. These implications include not feeling isolated in your social cause but connected to a broad network. For example, through their links with global movements on racial justice such as the BLM movement, young SSAs seek to enact their political agency and voice, further imparting their contribution in this space (Gatwiri and Townsend-Cross 2022).

The black African Australian experience has further intersectional nuances regarding the compounded racialisation of this group. Due to the nature of (forced) migration and integration discussed in chapter 1, the relatively recent history of large-scale African immigration means that non-Indigenous Blackness is often migranticised and classed (Gatwiri and Anderson 2020, 2022; Majavu 2015, 2018; Williams 2015). Another aspect of intersectional nuances to black studies in Australia is that the building of political voice for young SSAs to resist racialising discourses could also be read as an investigation into black identity development in a social group that historically has not had to grapple with their Blackness and racialising discourses based on the construct of Whiteness. This is due to coming from a country where the majority have noticeably darker skin (Bulhan 1985; Sullivan 2018; Williams 2015). Attending to this further supports an argument for Australian CRT in establishing how the Australian case is distinctive from, and can talk back to, U.S.-based theorists.

The overarching focus of this monograph is how the arts has the potential to build sites of resistance to racialising discourses and enact social transformation. The steps of resistance are outlined using the theory of NSMs to explain this process. The first stage draws on Freire's *conscientisation* theory through Akom's (2009) conceptualisation in his book *Critical Hip Hop Pedagogy as a Form of Liberatory Practice*. When considering Hip Hop as a NSM taken up in chapter 4, through using components of Hip Hop as an engagement strategy and using teaching tools to unpack a social issue. As a pedagogical tool to empower young SSAs in the Footprints Grounded Project depicted in this chapter, this involves participants first becoming conscious (aware) of their social cause. Activities involve embarking on a journey of breaking down the impacts of systemic violence and the opportunity to brainstorm interventions. Through this process, young SSAs explore the social and political climate for interventions involving the enactment of political voice and agency. This process of consciousness-raising not only ensures that individuals or communities are aware of their surroundings, but also that once you are conscious, it is almost a duty to share this knowledge with others. Once a social issue such as racial injustice is deconstructed, this provides the context where young SSAs develop counter-narratives to racialising discourses through storytelling and performance in the form of standpoint projects. The second stage of NSMs draws on Dutta's (2011, 2012, 2018, 2020) CCA to locate culture as the specific tool to engage broader society in the social cause and as a pertinent site of social change. Finally, the motto of artists being 'born to stand out' is unpacked as it is conceptualised in young SSAs' political voice messaging. Barriers to freedoms for young SSAs to express political voice are also conceptualised through *identity politics* (Moussa and Tony 2017; Bernstein 2005). Table 2.1 depicts the research theoretical frameworks.

OVERVIEW OF THE GROUNDED PROJECT AND CRITICAL HIP HOP PEDAGOGY

Chapter 1 describes the longitudinal focus of Footprints' (2020) YPAR projects, which informed the ongoing mission and vision of Footprints as a not-for-profit organisation and the research design of the PhD research explored in this chapter.

The ethnographic process of Footprints' YPAR project (2018–2019) covered in this monograph analyses the agency of young SSAs to build their political voice, which they explored and enacted through the Grounded Project. This YPAR project consisted of three creative workshops which were hosted at the Gua Performance and Leadership Camp, the first stage of the project. Data collection consisted of two focus groups and arts artefacts collected at the Gua camp, followed up by 38 narrative interviews. Focus groups and interviews explored topics such as identity, culture, and utilising Hip Hop for arts-based resistance. Additionally, Hip Hop artefacts, researcher observations, and

Table 2.1 Research Theoretical Frameworks

Theoretical Frameworks	*Concepts and theories used to explain resistance and social change. They are used in this research to illuminate young SSAs' forms of resistance in response to racism and racialising discourses.*
Critical Race Theories (CRT) – helps to frame young SSAs' experiences in relation to racism and *racialising discourses*.	New Social Movement (NSM) theory – explains how formation of any identity-based social movement is a process involving various actors. - The actors in this research include urban young SSAs. - As Hip Hop is considered to be a NSM (chapter 4), two further concepts augment NSM to structure a detailed theoretical framework that supports the understanding of young SSAs involvement with NSM formation or practice:
	Critical Hip Hop Pedagogy (CHHP) (chapter 2) highlights the importance of starting with a *consciousness-raising* process amongst young SSA participants as the first step of participating in an NSM; and the Culture-centred Approach (CCA)(chapter 4) specifically posits that the process of reclaiming 'identity' has become a site for NSMs. 'Culture' is located as the specific tool to engage broader society in the social cause and as a pertinent site of social change.

project evaluations from similar Footprints' arts-based community development projects from 2007 to 2021 were used to triangulate learnings from the Grounded Project data. This included a range of approaches such as workshops, camps, festivals, and flash-mob or pop-up performances.

This section briefly outlines relevant aspects of my PhD research methodology and analytical framework. Firstly, I discuss my positionality as a researcher and as the author of this monograph. This is followed by a description of the YPAR and CHHP approaches utilised by Footprints for the Grounded Project activities.

Critical reflexivity and an awareness of positionality underpin this research's exploration of young people's stories about themselves and their experiences of forced migration and paving a way in Australia. As such, chapters 4–6 are written in the first person through a narrative inquiry approach as an ethnographer and as an expression of the experience of both creating and conducting fieldwork. I specifically address the experiences of young SSAs in Australia (noting the social, political, and historical context) and how they perceived their articulation of political voice in response to racialising discourses. Figure 2.1 depicts my PhD research design and the triangulation of data depicted in this monograph and how I constructed my framework as a result of my positionality.

Freedom to Enact Political Voice and Develop Forms of Resistance 31

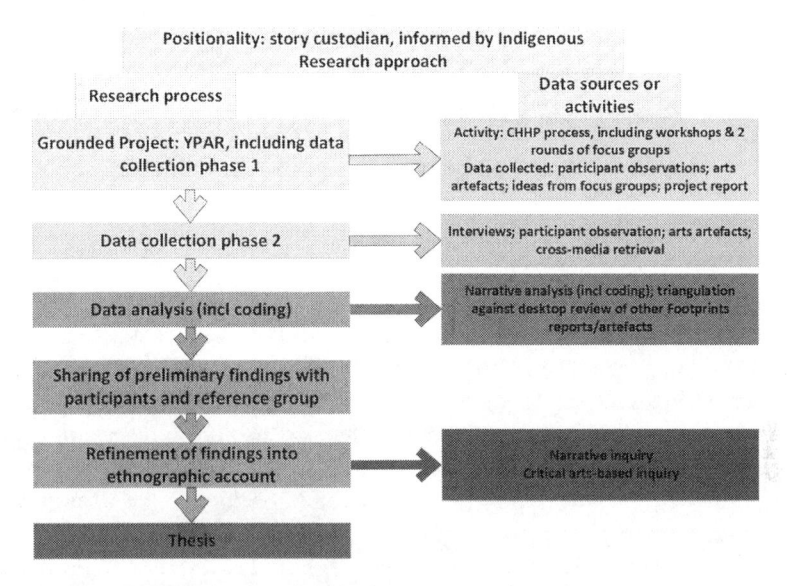

Positionality: story custodian, informed by Indigenous Research approach

Research process	Data sources or activities
Grounded Project: YPAR, including data collection phase 1	Activity: CHHP process, including workshops & 2 rounds of focus groups Data collected: participant observations; arts artefacts; ideas from focus groups; project report
Data collection phase 2	Interviews; participant observation; arts artefacts; cross-media retrieval
Data analysis (incl coding)	Narrative analysis (incl coding); triangulation against desktop review of other Footprints reports/artefacts
Sharing of preliminary findings with participants and reference group	
Refinement of findings into ethnographic account	Narrative inquiry Critical arts-based inquiry
Thesis	

Figure 2.1 Research Design for PhD Thesis. *Source*: Author's figure.

RESEARCHER POSITIONALITY AND CRITICAL-TRANSFORMATIVE PARADIGM

I discuss my positionality as a pracademic (i.e., practitioner-academic) (Gartner 2024), including the philosophical approach I take as an author/researcher. I begin by discussing my personal context and worldview, followed by broader socio-political and decolonising approaches.

I am a community arts and cultural development practitioner with almost two decades of experience as a youth worker, project manager, and team leader in the humanitarian resettlement, youth alcohol and other drugs (AOD), and justice fields in Naarm. The knowledge I have developed from walking alongside migrant and former refugee young people during this time forms the foundation of my current academic interests and is built on a *critical transformative* paradigm which prioritises an Indigenous lens of relationality and critical theory (Romm 2015). I seek to 'bear social justice issues in mind so that their inquiries become intertwined with a political agenda and are action-oriented towards generating increased fairness in the social fabric' (Romm 2015, 411). As such, focused ethnography for research in small community development non-profit organisations such as Footprints is a critical but pragmatic form of ethnography. The process involves a focus on a specific phenomenon whilst conducting short, intensive fieldwork. This form of ethnography can align with community development principles through compatibility with 'bottom-up programming, active participation, locally led action, inclusion of [minoritised] groups and local wisdom, devolved decision-making, and social justice agenda' (Kelly 2022, 1).

I co-founded the grassroots community non-profit Footprint Enterprises Inc. (Footprints) in 2007, in part to combat media portrayals of young SSAs not integrating into Australian society, as I had observed a different reality from that depicted in the popular media. Moved by the racially motivated murder of young SSA Liep Gony in 2007, I saw that many young teenagers his age in my local community wanted to 'rap' (lyrical Hip Hop) and explore who they were and their sense of belonging (or not) in Naarm. In the early days, I met young rappers in my local area in the City of Greater Dandenong (discussed in chapter 1) and it was clear they had chosen Hip Hop to express themselves creatively and somewhat politically when the times called for it. I recognised that they often faced systemic barriers acquiring places to record, practice, or perform for audiences. Alongside other initiatives, Footprints provided a platform to support their self-expression through arts-based projects and led me on a journey of discovery to get to know these young people and the meaning they made through Hip Hop. Due to this process, Footprints project designs have therefore been predominantly based on the following artistic elements of Hip Hop:

> (1) deejaying and turntablism [also known as 'disc jockeying'], (2) the delivery and lyricism of rapping and emceeing [performing Hip Hop lyrics], (3) breakin' [urban form of doing dance tricks commercially known as break dancing] and other forms of Hip Hop dance, (4) graffiti [street] art and writing, and (5) a system of knowledge that unites them all including a knowledge of self. (Morgan and Bennett 2011, 177)

Whilst the core focus has been on rapping and emceeing, other aspects of Footprint's project design are based on Hip Hop's tenets of peace, love, unity, and having fun (Iglesias and Harris 2019).

Whilst I use the language 'walking alongside', I realise that due to power imbalances of my own white-centric background, I can also walk away. I consider this language in the context of the Bantu notion of *Ubuntu* (I am because you are) (Ntibagirirwa 2018), which was emphasised on my first trip to North and South Sudan in 2008. This philosophy and metaphysical framework draws on the mutual relatability of humanity in terms of being bound with one another's liberty. For example, if my black siblings are free from racial injustice, we are all free (Hart 2020). This relational process was present long before the research process and will continue long after. This is an important component of Indigenous research methodology upon which I drew (described below), which involves maintaining accountability to these relationships. The 'ceremony' of social research involves mutually gifting each other with knowledge and hospitality and sharing grief in the hard times (Wilson 2008).

Throughout this journey, the rate of young SSA deaths have remained high. I recall attending at least ten funerals for young SSAs over the last decade. My first exposure was in 2012 when one of my best friends, young SSA Erjok Nai (to whom this research is dedicated), died tragically and suspiciously. The way in which this occurred is extremely mysterious, and police or security involvement was suspected, although a thorough investigation did not proceed, and this incident was restricted from the media. When I first embarked on my master's research (described in the previous chapter), in 2013–2014 I attended three funerals in Naarm whilst one young person remained seriously injured in the hospital. I am aware of at least another four suspicious, preventable deaths of young people within the broader African Australian communities during 2008–2014 (Green 2013; Cauci 2013; Toscano 2013). At the time of beginning my PhD journey, another young South Sudanese female had suicided, and more occurred throughout the journey, many of whom I had a connection to. In the weeks before the submission of my PhD thesis, I had attended three funerals of African diaspora young adults who participated directly in a number of Footprints' projects, and another when submitting my monograph. Getting to the finish line of this stage of the journey is dedicated to their legacies.

During my fieldwork and PhD thesis write-up for this monograph throughout the COVID-19 pandemic, SSA youth suicides peaked. The deaths of my friends not only elicit emotions such as grief, loss, pain, anger, and rage, but also hope for a better future and hope for developing a new social imagination (Kubler-Ross and Kessler 2014; Milstein 2017; Graeber 2009), which is connected to direct action as discussed in chapter 2. These events and the intergenerational trauma that many young SSAs have experienced (Barlow 2018; Abur and Mphande 2020; Abur 2019) are integral to my work and inspire me to share our story (with permission), see figure 2.2.

My prime concern is to support young people through their journey and identify how we can create forms of resistance together (Kwansah-Aidoo and Mapedzahama 2018). This involves the emancipatory notion of critical praxis:

> where knowledge is not only about finding out about the world, but about changing it. Therefore, not only are participants of an inquiry analysed in terms of their potential for developing group action, but critical researchers themselves engaging oppressive structures and their own inquiries embody praxiological concerns. (Truman, Humphries, and Mertens 2000, 6)

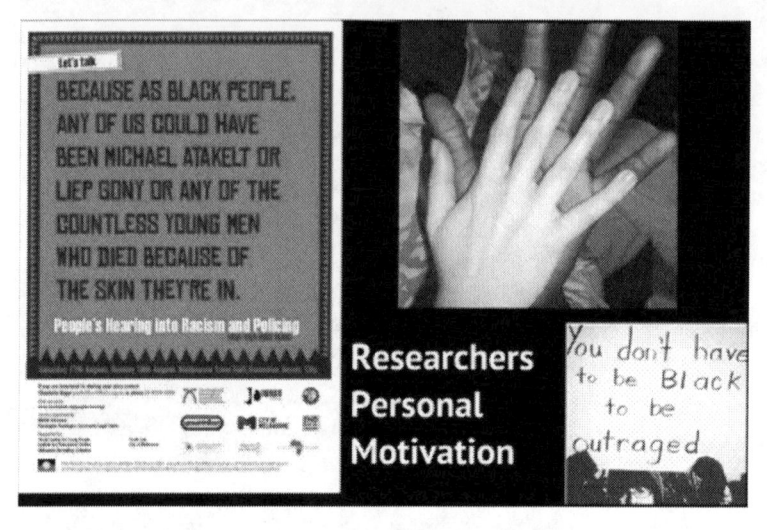

Figure 2.2 Researcher's Positionality Statement. Tribute to Erjok Nai (Eeh). *Source*: Flemington Kensington Legal Service; Footprints; © Tim Pierce.

The socio-political structural disadvantages faced by young SSAs as former refugees in Australia are expanded in chapter 1. This context interacts with and influences my philosophical approach to research, which involves an intersectional, decolonising, Antiracist, and Indigenous inquiry research approach.

TOWARDS DECOLONISING, ANTIRACIST AND INDIGENOUS RESEARCH

I have drawn upon the key idea from Indigenous methods of attempting to authentically include the voices of primarily BIPOC without presuming to speak for them (Wilson 2008; Chilisa 2020; Tuhiwai-Smith 2021). Traditional social research in Western communities does not always adequately engage or represent minority communities or young people (Truman, Humphries, and Mertens 2000; TASA 2021; Ayala 2017; Burke, Greene, and McKenna 2017). Tuhiwai Smith (2021) urges researchers towards practices that are more respectful, ethical, sympathetic, and useful rather than racist, ethnocentric, and exploitative. In line with this, I sought to ensure that subaltern (sidelined) and minoritised voices of young people were at the forefront through their own forms of storytelling without further perpetuating deficit discourse (Dutta 2011; Hickey-Moody 2013; Spivak 1999).

Due to the dual role as co-founder of Footprints and primary researcher, it is important to note that as the author, I am a central agent in the cultural policy ecology that supports the project, performances and individuals who are being discussed. For example, the intrinsic nature of being the co-founder of Footprints, alongside South Sudanese counterparts, I conceptualised the Grounded Project, developed the project infrastructure through seeking funding and was one of the key project managers. As a researcher, I observed Footprints' YPAR project, which employed young SSAs to co-design and carry out the project. The additional interview process and observation of extensive artefacts with young SSAs was possible due to the relational process and the concept of friendship as a method (Cann and DeMeulenaere 2012; Tillmann-Healy 2003). As the role of community cultural development practitioners and youth workers are often tied to cultural policy and practice (Clammer 2015; Stephenson Jr, Tate, and Goldbard 2015), one limitation of this research, however, is limited analysis of the role of the white researcher's involvement in the power and decision-making, and examination of potential biases in the research project.

Another feature of Indigenous methodology utilised in this research is storytelling, which attempts to embody the slogan 'nothing about us without us' (Boulet 2018). I therefore take on the role of 'story custodian' where I have participated in and been gifted stories through my relational process embedded in communities (Kelly and Rogers 2022). Due to this role, my researcher positionality and participant engagement processes described below discuss how I enact relational accountability with motives made as transparent as possible (Boulet 2018; Boulet and Hawkins 2021; Lane et al. 2013; Macmillan 1995; Wilson 2008). Like Nigerian writer Chimamanda Ngozi Adichie (2021), and in line with a constructivist perspective engaging social discourse and developing new meanings together, I recognise that there is not one homogenous or 'single story' to be told.

As a community cultural development practitioner who curates artsprojects for social purposes, I position myself as an 'Antiracist ethnographer' and 'artivist' (activist-artist). The Antiracist aspect involves attempting to be aware of my ethnocentric lenses and seeking my own conscientisation regarding cultural appropriation and white privilege (Yo 2006; D. Harris 2017; Howley 2008; Juris 2007). In social movement scholarship, Escobar (1992) and Bevington and Dixon (2005) suggest that activist ethnographers are embedded amongst actors of social movement practice. Through this process of being embedded, they face new questions concerning unprecedented social processes, such as negotiating identity politics on a local and global scale. A critique of social movement literature suggests activists are often disappointed by what they find in social movement theory – it often fails to address practical concerns and is pitched to academic audiences. The recent 'activist turn' in social movement research seeks to remedy this by providing useful knowledge for those seeking social change (Sutherland 2013). This includes being interested in accounts of how young SSAs have responded to media and moral panics in new and creative ways. Activist ethnographers are better positioned to capture the immediate mood, tone, emergent direction, and impact that is often missed by external observers (Escobar 1992; Bevington and Dixon 2005).

Though attempting to utilise an Antiracist perspective (Kendi 2019), I recognise this is an ongoing process fraught with potentiality to make mistakes and requires uncomfortable inward gazing (Williams 2020; Land 2015; Milstein 2015; Okun 2014). The implications of this approach are discussed in chapter 8 regarding future research considerations and suitable research design frameworks. My mode of praxis, theories, and decolonising methodologies are located within a broader paradigm of liberation-oriented work, which seeks to emphasise our common humanity and bring racial injustices experienced by BIPOC communities to the fore (Hart 2020; Montero 2009; Crenshaw et al. 1996; Carroll 2017; Gillborn and Ladson-Billings 2019). Utilising these approaches, I seek to

> make visible the workings of power and to develop ways of knowing, doing, and being that are empowering and socially inclusive with an understanding that culture is always in the making. (Sonn and Baker 2016, 222)

ARTIST REPRESENTATION

The Footprints Grounded Project (a YPAR process) involved 35 participants. Following this, I conducted 39 narrative interviews, the majority of whom had participated in the Grounded Project. Participants primarily live in the Southeastern and Western suburbs of Melbourne (see figure 1.3) and were divided into three categories: primary, secondary, and generalists – critical reference group.

The primary participants consisted of 28 young adults and adults aged between 18 and 40 from a South Sudanese cultural background. They identify as first-generation Australians and as African diaspora, as they had fled South Sudan as children or were born in transit countries (some in refugee camps) such as Kenya, Egypt, or North Sudan. They identify as urban artists who were either involved in the Grounded Project or were known through Footprints' networks to have broad influence in their communities. One participant identified as an International Hip Hop artist, whilst the others primarily identified as Hip Hop artists, with a small few being Hip Hop enthusiasts and subsequent community leaders. To ensure confidentiality, when participants are quoted from their interviews, they are de-identified with a participant alias.

As urban artists, the participants in this research indicated that they wanted their public art acknowledged. Although they are also represented as de-identified participants with aliases when discussing their individual opinions and beliefs, table 2.2 depicts how they have been represented as 'born to stand out' (BTSO) artivists when discussing communal claims and themes. It is acknowledged that BTSO artivists, as a collective however, have unique voices/opinions individually. Therefore, throughout chapters 3–8, their artist names are depicted in *italics* when citing a public quote or artwork representing an individual approach. When referring to 'BTSO artivists' as a collective in this monograph, I am therefore referring to this group of artists in figure 2.3a to 2.3i and not all research participants.

Interviews with this primary group were followed by interviews with 10 secondary participants who identified as community leaders, professionals such as teachers, filmmakers, community arts managers, social worker or community development practitioners, and a select few professionals affiliated with Footprints' projects or those who identified as audience members (x3). Four of these participants identified with various white cultural backgrounds. Two of these were included to gauge an audience perspective, although this was not the focus of this research. Three participants were project consultants to Footprints and were from various ethnic backgrounds. These interviews were conducted to further understand the impact of the Grounded Project in terms of young SSAs' resistance to racialising discourses.

This research provided an opportunity to build partnerships and integrate the knowledge systems of the young people involved (Chilisa 2020). The additional six generalist participants who formed a Critical Reference Group (CRG) are primarily SSA adults known to Footprints as colleagues. They consist of co-founders of SSA youth initiatives and Elders of the South Sudanese communities in Naarm, legal advocates, researchers, mentors, project partners, arts-practitioners, and other professionals who have worked alongside the participant group in the Grounded Project. These SSA participants consulted on the research design, data analysis and final drafting process but did not participate in narrative interviews.

Participants were already known to the researcher and were recruited through Footprints' networks coordinated by Footprints' President (i.e., not me). Due to the nature of the research question, the primary research participants needed to be of South Sudanese cultural background and Hip Hop artists or affiliated with Footprints' Grounded Project. Footprints sought to achieve a gender representation amongst participants.

Table 2.2 Born to Stand Out (BTSO) Artivists. Images Provided by Artists

BTSO Artivist Name	Music Biography and Link
Titan	Titan is a 21-year-old recording artist who moved to Australia from South Sudan in 2004. Social-activist, rapper and music curator, Titan Debirioun, is a Naarm Hip hop artist producing fierce boom-bap and trap offerings. Working within the South Sudanese and broader Australian communities, Titan creates funky political conscious Hip Hop, paving the way for black and Indigenous artists in Australia. He also co-designed drop-in music programs in Tarneit; a podcast; other pop-up installations and his own tv channel. https://soundcloud.com/msgtitan; https://www.youtube.com/channel/UCjvKPBWtA3i5Rb7WzvkgTkw; https://www.instagram.com/titan.debirioun/?hl=en.
Amac Don	Formerly a member of Future of Rap, Amac Don (Aluong Majok Mac) is a South Sudanese Australian artist based in Naarm. He made his international debut with the album *Dinka* in 2014. https://open.spotify.com/artist/4A7cij7uJefkpKPWFyVDxb?autoplay=true; https://www.facebook.com/amacdon100; https://www.instagram.com/amacdon100/?fbclid=IwAR0N3KxonaqqFIC-hAEpUzYKYwCzHDPAvTp6j5tPxXlll2nwdEDbM_tqjkI.
Burn City Movement (BCM)	Burn City Movement (BCM). identifies as an arts-based movement with the focus of starting arts facilities. Consisting of multicultural young people, they are an arts-collective of producers, songwriters, and creatives. BCM's aim is to ignite the growth and development of arts-culture in the South-east of Naarm through the leadership of a movement. Their energy-filled live-shows garnered a lot of attention in the lead up to the release of their debut album *Realness for Sale* in 2020. https://www.facebook.com/bcmthemovement; https://linktr.ee/bcmthemovement?fbclid=IwAR357HCD-w_HHW_uMgCtyS6ztFPZqLzKyVqLtUg3xKVV_bCnscSwAAmCFciM.
Élkato	Lily Kato also known as *Élkato* is a South Sudanese, emerging Naarm-based rap artist. Through political and conscious Hip Hop she has a 'message for the youth'. https://soundcloud.com/user-940608762/lkato-matrix.

Freedom to Enact Political Voice and Develop Forms of Resistance 39

Malesh P	Malesh P is a proud South Sudanese Hip Hop artist currently residing in Naarm. His wish is to inspire all to respect differences, embrace diversity, and stand proud of living with two cultures.
	Malesh P expresses feelings in an honest way that sparks mindfulness. His music shares life stories providing insights and social awareness. Malesh P started writing music in 2004 and released his first solo project in 2013. In 2015, Malesh P released his debut album *Dreamer	Believer* sharing real stories and hope for the future. Accompanied by a vibrant live band, Malesh P has performed at various events and festivals across Melbourne over the past 10 years.
	https://www.facebook.com/OfficialMalesh/; https://maleshp.com/
Queen P	Formerly known as P Unique, Queen P's music is raw, unique, genuine, and heavily shaped by strong personal experience. Her words flow with relentless speed and sharp lyricism, floating across futuristic bass-heavy beats and rippling hi-hats. Queen P writes from the heart and speaks her mind, expressing her perspectives confidently via spoken-word and Hip Hop.
	Adding a dark and powerful element to her music whilst highlighting her ability to bring word play and impeccable speech together, this Queen's music is highly danceable whilst maintaining its authentic underground sound and feel. Stepping on the scene in August of 2017, this young and vibrant rapper has been rapidly gaining attention and making a name for herself.
	https://www.facebook.com/QueenP; https://linktr.ee/itsmequeenp.
Krown	Born in South Sudan, Krown is a rapper/songwriter now based in the Western suburbs of Naarm. His first EP *Wake Em Up* debuted in August 2017. Krown's second music project was a 17-track conceptual EP highlighting current struggles and reality of his people and wider Australia. *Hold The Flag* released July 2018.
	As an emerging artist and recognised as one of Triple J radio station Hau Latukefu's 'Artists to Watch', Krown aspires to inspire by means of making impactful, storytelling music and being a mentor and leader for young people.
	https://www.facebook.com/militarykrown; https://www.abc.net.au/triplejunearthed/artist/krown/

(Continued)

Table 2.2 (Continued)

BTSO Artivist Name	Music Biography and Link
Daniel Elia	Producing music with a strong political and spiritual message, *Daniel Elia* encapsulates the trials and tribulations faced by the Naarm South Sudanese community, and what it means to be black in Australia in one of the most hostile periods in Australia for African youth. Taking the mantle of 'Conscious Rap', *Daniel Elia* is striving to make a difference with his art. *Elia* shares stories of his experience as a Sudanese immigrant. At age 19, he began writing lyrics and recording his tracks on his laptop. With an extensive background in dancing and touring, it became apparent that his natural creativity and emotional intelligence was able to thrive through the creation of music. *Elia* captivates his listeners with lyrical poetry and unique instrumentals. The recognition of his talent provided him with opportunities to perform at St Kilda festival 2019, Thando's EP launch (part of Brunswick Music festival) 2019 and Groovin The Moo 2019. *Daniel Elia* spoke with *VICE* magazine about his conscious lyrics in collaboration with Hennessy. The article described Daniel Elia as being 'at the vanguard of conscious rap in Australia, embedding a message of positivity and community spirit'. https://www.facebook.com/iamdanielelia; https://www.aliarecords.com/.
Emmanuel Jal	From his start in life as a child soldier in the war-torn region of South Sudan in the early 1980s, *Emmanuel Jal* has come through huge personal struggles to become a successful and acclaimed recording artist and peace ambassador now living in Toronto, Canada. He has toured Australia a number of times and remains an inspiration to many Hip Hop artists globally. 'I share my story for social-emotional learning through the arts, business and philanthropy. I offer experiences with music, healing, education and healthy living – so that together we can create positive, global awakening'. – *Emmanuel Jal* https://www.emmanueljal.com.

Figure 2.3a to 2.3i Born to Stand Out (BTSO) Artivists. *Source*: 2.3a–Titan, 2.3b–Amac, 2.3c–Burn City Movement (BCM), 2.3d–Élkato, 2.3e–Malesh P, 2.3f–Queen P, 2.3g–Krown, 2.3h–Daniel Elia, 2.3i–Emmanuel Jal.

Additional fieldwork consisted of attending Youth Support and Advocacy Services' (YSAS) Empower project one day per week for one year across 2019–2020 at YSAS Dandenong. This fieldwork ensured long-term immersion with disenfranchised young people (of various cultural backgrounds) engaging in Hip Hop. This process, therefore, provided the opportunity to capture any voices of dissent. YSAS is an agency working with young people with experiences of the youth justice system or who have substance concerns. The next section discusses the Grounded Project's community engagement process through CCHP and the interplay with the YPAR approach.

PHD RESEARCH METHODS

Utilising multiple Indigenous ways of knowing, multiple data collection sources and analysis tools were utilised to paint a broad picture/oral canvas with threads being woven through discussions of theoretical frameworks and empirical applications (Holbraad et al. 2018). Therefore, the following sections detail the layered approach of how Footprints' YPAR is coupled with CHHP to demonstrate an experimental guide to how action might occur in response to a social issue of racial injustice through the Grounded Project. CHHP framework also helps guide Footprints overarching mission/vision and pedagogy/praxis used. Footprints YPAR process described below is one example of this and is the first step of an ethnographic account of this process.

Youth Participatory Action Research

Youth Participatory Action Research (YPAR) involves developing projects with young people, reflecting/learning, then altering practice on a continual basis (Burke, Greene, and McKenna 2017; Wadsworth 2016). YPAR has the potential to foster hope, develop radical collective imagination for what can be, and prompt action in communities (Ginwright cited in Bautista 2018, 194). Footprints (2020) identifies four core aspects of their collective vision in enacting YPAR projects. The first is to educate young people about the importance of cultural history and identity, the joy of being creative and focused, and the empowerment of connecting as a community. The second core aspect is to promote mutual respect, open-mindedness, and social equality in order to reduce violence, substance abuse, and discrimination. The third is to challenge social and institutional racism that exists in Australia. The fourth and final tenet is to bring diverse people together and build strong relationships through music and performing arts. Footprints seeks to achieve these goals by

> encouraging young people's exploration of their identity through the use of creative arts in a supportive, like-minded community. By using the tool of creative expression as a bridge, we hope to inspire and educate – addressing racial tensions in Australia. (Footprints 2020, 1)

This iteration of Grounded in 2019 involved collaboration between five community organisations. These were Footprints Enterprises, Springvale Neighbourhood House, Jungle City Projects, South Sudanese Australian Youth United (SSAYU), and Borderlands Cooperative.

The critical praxis (cyclical action-plus-reflection) process was conducted by Footprints using YPAR, where a problem (racism) was identified, with young people as co-researchers. Practically, Footprints' role in this process was to support young SSAs in mobilising on the topic of racism by providing additional resources through the infrastructure of the project (the set-up of performances and events, public liability insurance, etc.).

The Grounded Project[1] serves as an example of a series of arts-based activities. Through a decolonising social movement model, the Grounded Project was developed as:

> critical youth praxis in a transformative youth organising framework which represents the opportunity for young people to build on their reflections on the dialogues that engage the various dialectics that are interrogated in counter-hegemonic spaces and to participate in intentional action. (Bautista 2018, 245)

The very first Grounded Project was conducted in the CGD in 2009 and has evolved into three iterations: 2016–2017, 2018–2019, and 2020–2021 (Footprints, Grounded Project evaluation 2009). The need for this project was identified after Liep Gony's murder, with Footprints noting negative media and political attention focused on the South Sudanese communities' alleged inability to 'integrate' into Australia (Farquharson, Marjoribanks, and Nolan 2018). Each iteration of the Grounded Project consists of a performance and leadership camp, followed by a series of public performances culminating in a one-day festival. The camp is the consciousness-raising component where CHHP is utilised to discuss the issue of racism and issues surrounding identity politics (discussed in chapter 4).

To conduct YPAR in line with a strengths-based approach, Footprints draws on the *Asset-based Community Development* (ABCD) model. ABCD is oriented to identifying assets in a community and recognising existing skills, knowledge, talents, resources, networks and experiences that can be pooled and built on to make their communities better places to live (Kenny and Connors 2017). Whilst Footprints holds the vision and accountability for the YPAR process, Footprints sees its role as a mixture of external practitioners embedded in communities, and practitioners and peer mentors who are also from the cultural communities they engage (Footprints Constitution 2007). Practically, this involves:

> *transformative youth organising* spaces which cultivate the agency of youth by engaging in critical youth praxis as reflected in the application of critical pedagogy, critical/youth participatory action research (CPAR/YPAR), and other forms of critical youth studies. (Bautista 2018, 245)

Primarily, young SSAs are employed to facilitate and engage camp participants to discuss the project aims, to consider joining the project management team in each iteration of the project, and to decide on the artists and content that will be performed at the pop-up performances, school tour and the Grounded Youth Stage (discussed in chapter 6). These community engagement strategies were structured this way so that participants could identify key people who could play roles in this process of counter-storytelling and further consciousness-raising through the artists and topics they selected (Fieldwork notes 2019). Young SSAs involved then implement the project action plans with my support for the curation process. This was followed by analysis and evaluation phases, which then followed more reflection or implementation depending on the ongoing analysis (Levin 2012; Wadsworth 2016; Bourke 2009).

Critical Hip Hop Pedagogy

The theoretical outline of CHHP discusses Freire's conscientisation theory through Akom's (2009) conceptualisation. The application of CHHP is detailed in chapter 4. Akom (2009, 2011) describes CHHP as a form of *liberatory and emancipatory praxis* which starts from the premise that Hip Hop is an important lens for socio-political analysis and representation of subaltern/minoritised communities. It was chosen due to the cultural practice of Hip Hop as an engagement activity to which young people relate to and as an avenue to reflect the political principles they hold through the development of public pieces.

As it also pertains to research design, CHHP works as the framework to enact YPAR in this research. Engaging young people in CHHP activities first starts with consciousness-raising activities, such as discussing and analysing Hip Hop lyrics and content with the purpose of identifying social messages. The second stage involves participants creating new Hip Hop content. Both stages involve young SSAs building artivist skills to develop their political voice and forms of resistance. In this context, CHHP utilises the following elements: (1) The centrality of race and racism and their intersectionality with other forms of oppression; (2) challenging traditional paradigms, texts, and theories used to explain the experiences of BIPOC; (3) the centrality of experiential knowledge of BIPOC; (4) commitment to social justice; and (5) a transdisciplinary approach (Solórzano and Delgado Bernal cited in Akom 2009).

The significance of this approach is that

> through reading the world, young people begin to meaningfully develop strategies for pursuing social justice, and take increasingly public roles in advocating, organising, educating . . . in an effort to create positive social change. (Yang cited in Akom 2009, 55)

This occurs through collective voices being heard following the development of counter-stories. These counter-stories were expressed through Hip Hop performance workshops discussing elements of CHHP at various stages of the fieldwork journey described in the Grounded Project.

The Grounded Project

The Grounded Project 'represents diverse young people in Melbourne's West and Southeastern suburbs uniting through grassroots youth culture to pursue positive social change for our community' (Grounded Project 2019: Media Release). In 2019, the Grounded Project engaged approximately 35 young SSAs, along with young people from other cultural backgrounds in Naarm. A key element of the project was the Gua Performance and Leadership Camp, which ran from 29 to 31 January 2019. The camp included two focus groups and three artistic workshops that used CHHP prompts to guide discussions and practice (Akom 2009). Two of the workshops centred on writing and recording whilst the third focused on dance. Participants were mentored by professional artists *Malesh P*, Jungle City Projects[2] and Akimera[3] alongside the Footprints team. These activities are detailed in chapter 4 and are called the Gua focus groups throughout the monograph. *Gua* is translated as peace, power, and strength in Arabic and Nuer, a South Sudanese tribal language. Chapter 4 outlines the specific processes of engagement in more detail as I relate the findings of the consciousness-raising process around cultural strengths and maintaining dignity despite adversity.

In the 2019 iteration of the Gua camp, attendees were aged 15–30 and were predominantly from African diaspora and young SSA cultural backgrounds. The young people were identified through Footprints (primarily Southeastern suburbs of Naarm) and project partners Jungle City Projects' (Western suburbs of Naarm) activities/projects and through YSAS and South Sudanese Australian Youth United (a young SSA youth-led organisation). The participants were invited as it was recognised that they already had emerging skills in art forms such as dance, spoken-word, and Hip Hop or were identified as leaders or influencers in their community. Many participants often cannot afford to pursue their artistic talent or have competing responsibilities, such as family commitments. Project partners identified that young people might share their music with their friends but recording time, performance opportunities, and practice venues are scarce (Footprints, Grounded Project Acquittal 2017, 3).

The masterclasses that the participants attended provided exposure to industry professionals with experience in performance, event/stage production, making public statements with the media, social networking strategies, and promotion and marketing. The camp environment gave participants and facilitators time to get to know each other. Participants advised camp organisers that they continue to meet with this support network and collaborate post-camp (Footprints, Grounded Project Acquittal 2019, 5).

Approximately 35 young people from culturally diverse backgrounds (predominantly young SSAs) attended the Gua Performance and Leadership

Camp. Through this phase of the YPAR, the CHHP process was utilised to encourage participants to discuss black immigrant identities to analyse the extent to which Hip Hop can be used as a tool for social justice (Akom 2009) and the key messages that Hip Hop tracks might convey. This was achieved through a consciousness-raising process where participants wrote Hip Hop lyrics about their life experiences after group discussion or hearing from artistic mentors from primarily BIPOC communities.

Figure 2.4 depicts Gua camp participants planning the next stages of the Grounded Project discussed in chapters 5 and 6. This included camp participants planning for the two pop-up performances at the Brunswick Street Parade and the Southern Migrant Refugee Centre Dandenong market tent, and one school performance at Dandenong High School's Harmony Day lunchtime performance. These stages of the project were conducted during Cultural Diversity Week (CDW)[4] 17–24 March 2019. Dance and spoken-word practices as part of the community development process occurred at YSAS's drop-in space in Dandenong, February–March 2019. Beyond the intended positive impact on participants, this project aimed to engage members of the public (i.e., audiences) in an alternative narrative to deficit-based racialising discourses and depictions of SSAs.

This collaboration culminated in the Grounded Youth Stage on 17 March 2019 which was a part of the Harmony Festival at Harmony Square in Dandenong. The Grounded Youth Stage gave camp and workshop participants the 'opportunity to perform their original work alongside well-known and highly respected performers' (Footprints, Grounded Project Acquittal 2019)

Figure 2.4 Grounded Project Planning Meeting at Gua Performance and Leadership Camp, 2017, Featured in the *Grounded* Documentary, 2018. *Source*: Footprints.

who were selected to fulfil the BTSO theme (discussed further in chapter 6). I captured interactions and incidents by documenting each stage of the project and monitoring social media hits on project-related photography, film, and short clips that were distributed by project partners on social media and in public spaces. This ensured public awareness and momentum leading up to the Grounded Festival, the final stage of the project (Footprints, Grounded Project Acquittal 2019). This monograph is therefore presented as an ethnography that tracks the development of political voice and forms of resistance amongst young SSAs.

ARTS ARTEFACTS FEATURED

Hip Hop and spoken-word lyrics from artists are presented through this study as artefacts, with weblinks or lyrics provided in appendix iv-cxxxiii. During this process, political Hip Hop tracks were developed that were later presented in flash mobs, at school-lunchtime performances, and on the Grounded Youth Stage (March 2019). Participant observation occurred during the development and performance of these tracks.

Arts artefacts including photography and video were collected through cross-media retrieval methods (Peng, Huang, and Zhao 2017) capturing relevant social media commentary (posts of participants pertaining to the project) and news reports about the project. The core arts artefacts displayed throughout this monograph are the song lyrics and artefacts created/retrieved from the Grounded Project (such as performance images). Additionally, I have presented samples of artists' artefacts (their tracks) throughout the monograph as it relates to the topic of political voice, forms of resistance, and Hip Hop in Australia. A total of 39 selected tracks were collected alongside artists' pre-existing public tracks, and I obtained their permission to analyse these tracks for specific themes. The full representation of lyrics of these tracks and PhD thesis music data are presented in Footprints' blog:

https://footprintenterprisesdotorg.wordpress.com/2022/11/04/born-to-stand-out-thesis-hip-hop-music-data/?fbclid=IwAR3DJGt8tVQnq1RBtYirr3YJGIOvFhBOOsg8Dna--mpRUzK-kCKDWP_LVZE). The specific link to each BTSO artivist's track lyrics are linked in the 'Notes' of each chapter.

Each appendix reference to the public track also cites the track number in the blog. Where participants identified that they wanted their artistic name to be mentioned, biographies and links to their art have been shared where relevant (see table 2.2). When citing artists' lyrics or poetry, I have used a different font (Calibri). Artists' tracks are cited in the bibliography and the public weblink to the music data blog is included in appendix. When a public link to a track is not available, I have attached the full lyrics in the appendix.

This also credits the intellectual property of artists and acknowledges their important creative contributions.[5] When citing an artist's quote from a publicly sourced and identified artist media interview, I use single quote marks and cite the source. When citing a participant's quote with an alias, I use single quote marks and *italics* to differentiate from other citation styles. The final aspect of data collection was cross-media retrieval.

A desktop review was conducted, which involved collecting evaluation material, media interviews, policy documents, research papers, and minutes from public forums in order to review social indicators regarding young SSAs' interactions with, or countering of, racialising discourses. Other mixed-media was collected through social media and websites. The data from observations, interviews and artefacts are triangulated against this desktop review to provide a multi-dimensional picture of actions, behaviour, interactions, and beliefs (Reeves et al. 2013).

DATA CODING AND ANALYSIS

A self-reflexive and deductive analysis was utilised to explore themes within qualitative data as it moves beyond the scientific idiom that 'the facts speak for themselves' and frames data and facts as constructions, as results of interpretation (Alvesson and Sköldberg 2018). This was followed by an emergent analysis process. Whilst *ethnographic inquiry* formed the foundational approach to research and analysis for my PhD thesis, *narrative* and *critical arts-based inquiry* enhanced the analytical framework for understanding and interpreting the research data. In line with the methodological underpinnings of *Indigenous inquiry* described previously in this chapter, narrative inquiry was chosen to consider the 'storytelling' aspects of data analysis (Connelly and Clandinin 1990), providing an opportunity to explore the actors, the narratives surrounding participants experiences and their ambitions, such as what it means to be 'born to stand out' (Bruner 1991). The second approach to inquiry is critical arts-based inquiry, which is particularly interested in the performance of resistance politics. It is structured on the 'notion of possibility, the *what might be*, by describing the functionality within the liminal spaces between heterogeneous projects and social transformation' (Finley cited in Denzin and Lincoln 2017, 971). Key themes identified in the data-coding process note the social, political, and historical contexts in order to explore the narration of political voice in song lyrics. These themes are additionally analysed across shifts in themes throughout the workshops/focus groups. This is to assess what participants learned/retained, to discern how their political voice for resistance developed, and how they perceived the interplay with this term. The degree of dialogue within counter-storytelling through Hip Hop lyrics is explored through *narrative inquiry* (Wadsworth 2016; Bhattacharya 2017; Bruner 1991) and *counter-narrative arts-based inquiry pedagogy* (Bhattacharya 2017; Sonn and Baker 2016). These two analysis tools are chosen to describe and analyse the impact of arts-based interventions briefly taken up in chapter 1 through the perspective of participants (Goessling et al. 2021; Ware and Dunphy 2020; Leavy 2015; McNiff 2013).

Critical arts-based inquiry occurred at a later stage, which also involved determining where arts artefacts and BTSO artists' Hip Hop tracks would be placed during the refinement of findings into an ethnographic account. Presented across chapters 4–6, multiple forms of data such as interviews/focus group/arts artefact data from the Grounded Project were examined to identify and categorise the themes and key issues that emerged (Reeves, Kuper, and Hodges 2008; Braun and Clarke 2012). In this format, rather than focusing on one analytical framework systematically in data chapters 4–6, the three analysis tools of *ethnographic, narrative* and *critical arts-based inquiry* were selected to enhance and provide glimpses of a multi-modal analytical framework by complimenting each other and weaving a story or a cultural tale of the Footprints YPAR project. Through this presentation of ethnographic data, qualitative work carries its meaning in its entire text (Denzin and Lincoln 2017). This is through a thick description of the data-sets, for example, participant quotes, artefacts, or artist tracks (Reeves, Kuper, and Hodges 2008). The research data was triangulated against artefacts and evaluation reports from other similar projects run by Footprints 2007–2021. When analysing the data sets, the key themes I sought were those exploring the particular identities, desires, interactions and struggles of young SSAs in relation to the BTSO theme and their forms of resistance through alternative forms of artivism. Here, observations of social movement practice are analysed through critical anthropology, social movement theory (Escobar 1992; Jasper 2010), and my own process of critical praxis as an actor amongst participants (P. Freire et al. 2018[1968]) to generate a rich understanding of social action.

To ensure theory triangulation (Reeves, Kuper, and Hodges 2008), four frameworks and theories of consciousness-raising – CHHP, the CCA, New Social Movement (NSM) theory, and CRT – were chosen to review social indicators identified as relevant to each analytical approach. These are outlined in detail in chapter 2. Detailed below is how they are applied in each chapter.

Defining the epistemological terrain of key concepts is fundamental to enacting the project and analysing the data. In chapter 4, the description of consciousness-raising through CHHP is used to describe the precursors to political actions that young SSAs take when involved in an NSM. This is through discussions about forms of Blackness identity which counteract racialising discourses claims. Chapter 5 discusses the implicit biases of racialising discourses in 'what they are saying' and 'what are they not saying' within the framework of CRT. For example, the crux of racialising discourses is that Whiteness is centred, and Blackness is Othered. It plays out in young SSAs being identified as criminals or as not 'integrating' into Australian society. NSM theories explore how the key themes capture the conditions of political opportunity in response to this, mobilising structure and a more dynamic analysis of the reoccurring mechanisms and processes of contentious politics (Bevington and Dixon 2005; Giugni 2009). In chapters 4 and 6, Dutta's CCA (Dutta 2015, 2020) acts as a conceptual and evaluation framework to capture the YPAR process where young people are the initiators and drivers of their own resistance projects (Akom 2009, 2011; Dutta 2018; Gatwiri and Anderson 2022). Fitting within the broader field of communication for social change, the goals of the CCA relating to this project are to understand and review:

(a) the location of communication with the complex interplay of structure and culture,
(b) the ways in which individual and collective agencies are enacted within, and in resistance to, structural constraints, and
(c) the interactions of human agency and communicative processes in bringing about social change and structural transformation. (Dutta 2021, 1)

Whilst utilising examination of the CCA, I explore the way in which the youth and arts-based development project, the Grounded Project, has made a change or set of changes through observation of the YPAR process. For example, three audience members were asked their perspective amongst participants. Here, the theory of change tested was the degree to which Hip Hop arts interventions developed young SSAs' political voice and enabled them to live the lives they want through the motto 'born to stand out' with no need to 'fit in'. As it is not a major focus of this research, in chapter 9, I detail how the question of 'audience impact' could further be explored in future initiatives through a process of *Communication for Social Change* (Dutta 2015).

It is important to note that all stages of the PhD research process involved a continuation of relational accountability, which provided research participants and the CRG with opportunities to co-construct the evolving themes and review interpretations of the data and drafting process. This iterative process was seen to be important when presenting voices and forms of storytelling and discerning findings (Wadsworth 2016). As Bevington and Dixon (2005, 186) note, the 'central problem with the dominant social movement theory: it is not being read by the very movements that it seeks to illuminate'. The reflexive researcher as interpreter consequently explicates themselves in a journey of reflection; looking at the perceptual, cognitive, political, cultural, social, and personal circumstances that 'impregnate', and thus form the conditions, of all analysis (Alvesson and Sköldberg 2018; Mauthner and Doucet 2003).

ACHIEVING FREEDOMS AND ASPIRATIONS

Rather than being conceptualised as the Other or at the bottom of the racial hierarchy, BIPOC prefer not to emulate Whiteness, but rather to be proud of their dialects, hair, bodies, and 'doing their own thing' (Eyerman and Jamison 1998, 78). Art and music – predominantly Hip Hop – are central to this process of achieving freedom (Sen 2001[1999]; P. Freire 1972; Fanon 1968). This is due to Hip Hop being a major player in black consciousness as a tool for resistance. It is such 'upgrading of the black experience' that this research addresses as it is relevant for young SSAs utilising their artistic agency to express their political voice through Hip Hop. Utilising CRT and NSM theories, this chapter has described how the purpose is not merely for young SSAs to 'fit in' but to live as if 'born to stand out'. This is defined as demonstrating a sense of vibrancy and being proud in culturally diverse communities across Naarm and Australia.

By employing critical race perspectives to understand the subjective experiences of black-African migrants in Australia, Gatwiri and Anderson (2020, 1) capture my stance that 'migration is more than just the movement of bodies, it is a phenomenon solidly tied to global inequality, power, and the abjection of black bodies'. Following this assertion, and as participants in the findings chapters that follow rightly point out, research in this area must also incorporate 'histories of colonialism, racism, marginalisation and their impact on the lived experience of black people in predominantly white countries' (Gatwiri and Anderson 2020, 3). Only then can a discussion of freedom be contemplated in the context of identity politics, which this research seeks to address.

The theoretical foundations noted in this chapter support the generation of storied and creative storytelling expressed in the following chapters that speaks of meaning-making and identity. Specifically, young SSAs express alternative forms of artivism and utilise their political voice presented in chapters 4–6, explored as entry points to gaining a deeper and more nuanced understanding of the ways young SSAs conceive of themselves within their artistic experience. This is in response to media and political moral panics and racialising narratives. Furthermore, agency and resilience are examined within the challenging circumstances young SSAs navigate during their journey to and settlement in Australia. I explore how they contend with positions of anger, confusion and sometimes hopelessness alongside the more positive perspectives of agency and achievement. These accounts are positioned against African gangs narratives and the 'Whiteness regimes of multiculturalism' to present dissenting voices against the dominant pathological and deficit models that embody the forced-migrant identity (Majavu 2015, 2018, 2020; Gatwiri and Anderson 2020) whereby young SSAs forge their own pathway.

The shared strength of YPAR and the ethnographic approach is the opportunity for collective identification and critical analysis of the building political voice for young SSAs. Layering their experiences and documenting these between their interplay within systemic structures underpinning their experiences is seen to be crucial (Nichols and Ruglis 2021). This monograph synthesises multiple sources of information to answer complex social questions. The information gathered provides the basis for an ethnography about the impact of racialising discourses on young SSAs and their counter-narratives. The following chapters move on to explore how the political voice of this group of young SSAs manifests in important new ways that conventional theories of activism and resistance may not capture – namely, through participation in Hip Hop as an NSM and through creating alternative subcultures. Exploring this topic alongside amplifying young SSAs voices points us towards ways of thinking and acting differently in the world (Dimitriadis 2016). Chapter 3 transitions to detailing the context, presenting broad metanarratives of young SSAs experiences with racism and systemic injustice in Australia, and how they formed and built their sense of political voice in response.

NOTES

1. Funded by the City of Greater Dandenong Community Grants, the Victorian Multicultural Commission Festival and Events grant, and by Stairway Church (Grounded Project Acquittal 2019).

2. https://junglecityprojects.com/.

3. https://www.facebook.com/akimera/.

4. http://www.multicultural.vic.gov.au/projects-and-initiatives/cultural-diversity-week

5. For a further contextual immersion into participant voices through their tracks and Footprints mixed multimedia artefacts, listening/viewing is highly encouraged as Hip Hop expression is better witnessed this way.

Chapter 3

The System

AN EXPRESSION OF POLITICAL VOICE IN THE 'HOOD'

It is the eve of the 2020 Aria Awards, Australia's high-profile music industry event. Zambian Australian artist Sampa the Great is nominated for six awards and the winner of three categories – Best Female Artist, Best Hip Hop Release, and Best Independent Release (Harmon 2020). At the beginning of Sampa's virtual performance of her song 'Black Power' before accepting the ARIA awards, she looks down the lens of the camera and states in spoken-word poetry:

In a country that pretends to not see black. To not see its origins
   and its past. Not only did black visionaries make you see
   but made it known who created human history.
And when you win awards they toss us on ad breaks of course but
   is that history lost. Can't remember what you forgot.
Is it free, this industry, for people like me?
Diversity, equity in your ARIA boards, To my people I say . . .
WE. ARE. OUR. OWN. FREEDOM! (Sampa-the-Great 2020b)[1]

Sampa is noted for 'calling out' systemic racism in the Australian music industry (Vrajilal 2020). Arguably, this has broader implications for calling out systemic racism in Australia due to the influence that popular culture has on society. Recent trends in the study of popular culture contribute important 'clues and methods to explore further the relations between daily life, cultural resistance, and collective political activity' (Escobar 1992, 409). In addition, Sampa's Afrofuturistic themes in her Hip Hop videos (stating the future that

Afro diaspora visualise through futuristic cues) have placed her on the map in Australia and globally (Sampa-the-Great 2020a). Whilst presenting Afrofuturistic themes, Sampa's lyrics also depict Afrocentric identity politics, discussing race, identity, and Hip Hop politics. Sampa's bold statement *'we are our own freedom'* (Sampa-the-Great 2020b)[2] reflects a type of political voice expressed by Hip Hop artists that sets the scene for this chapter. It aligns with the overarching research theme and motto 'born to stand out' (BTSO) that young SSAs voice for themselves – to seek freedom and a future through their own self-determination.

This background chapter begins by elaborating upon the oppressive sets of contextual circumstances outlined as a 'war on Blackness' that young SSAs experience through structural racism. Examples of the 'war on Blackness' detailed in this chapter are considered to be forms of *necropolitics* (death-dealing regimes) (Mbembe and Corcoran 2019). Through the lens of Critical Race Theories (CRT), it demonstrates how race can be theorised as a political project with ongoing effects (Lentin 2020). This is followed by a depiction of the interplay with the ways in which Hip Hop features in urban youth culture and urban vernacular, often in response to dangerous racialised narratives directed towards their communities. A rich description of a selection of Hip Hop lyrics demonstrates participants in dialogue with the structural challenges participants label 'the system'. These include challenges with urban zoning, employment, and other life pressures that have profound effects on young people (Dimitriadis 2007c, 111–119).

Following this depiction of interplay with Hip Hop lyrics and context, this chapter elucidates urban young people's creative impulses to express their political voice in response to rhetoric directed towards them (Dimitriadis 2007b, 110). Specifically, this chapter explores how young SSAs identify how their political voice develops. Finally, the chapter shows how young SSAs respond by turning to conscious Hip Hop to portray an alternative response to these narratives that question their Blackness and visibility in public spaces. They alternatively demonstrate their *'visions from the kitchen'* (Elia 2016, 2017a)[3] their hopes for their communities and the broader Australian society. This chapter therefore answers the first research sub-question: *How do young South Sudanese Australians build agency and develop their political voice?*

'RACE' AND 'RACISM'

The application of CRT helps to understand the structural conditions that underpin young SSAs' experiences, including explicit racism and situational analysis of the Australian context. The term *racialising discourses* is used to describe the specific discourses circulated through media and political moral panics. Thus, the focus of this monograph is on discourses that present young SSAs as allegedly failing to integrate into Australian society and as enactors of antisocial behaviours resulting in criminality. These are the discourses that young SSAs actively resist.

CRITICAL RACE THEORY AND THE 'R' WORD – RACISM

Critical Race Theory describes the structural nature of racism (Delgado and Stefancic 2000). Under the umbrella of CRT, identity has many implications for inequality, exploitation, and oppression despite it largely consisting of cognitive or social constructs (Bernstein 2005). As such, nuances of Australian forms of Blackness are identified as they pertain to young SSAs' experiences of racialised and socio-political group disadvantage and necessitated the need to build political voice through forms of Hip Hop expression.

The formation of CRT is attributed to historical accounts of systemic racism, such as through the trans-Atlantic slave trade. Through religious doctrines marking 'black' peoples as inferior to 'superior whites', notions of what it meant to be 'white or black' were established, and this provided the ideological basis for slavery and oppression which was then legislated (Kendi 2019, 38). As the 'first race maker and crafter of racist ideas', these terms solidified into hard attitudes that are perpetuated, ensuring the 'ultimate goal of the economic and political supremacy of white elites' (Oluo 2018, 11). Whilst the concept of race has 'no bearing in reality' – that is, race is not a genetic feature of humans – it had to be 'invented' and 'needed to be constantly secured' to provide legitimacy for oppression and exploitation (Kendi 2019, 52, 56). Antiracist educator Channing-Brown (2018, 114) poignantly describes the significance of such narratives, pointing out that 'slavery and black subjugation was not an accident', it was 'on purpose'.

The notion of the 'racial hierarchy' was further solidified by taxonomists, anthropologists, and eugenicists who used ideas such as phrenology to describe human skulls, placing them in four 'race categories' – Caucasoid, Mongoloid, Australoid, and Negroid. The Caucasoid skull structure was identified as having superior qualities to that of the Negroid. Despite being thoroughly discredited, these race classifications resulted in what was described as lower (darker) races needing to assimilate or adapt to achieve the ultimate goal of becoming 'more white' (Kendi 2019, 51). The basis for CRT, of which there are multiple variants, was established in the United States after acknowledging the racialisation of identity and the expectation of racial subordination of non-whites. The origins of the terminology emerged out of critical theory analysing power structures in society in the 1970s. Initiated by U.S. legal scholars such as Crenshaw (1996), CRT developed as a movement in the 1980s instigated by activists, civil rights leaders, and scholars to specify racial injustices that led to systemic oppression, notably around ethnic disparities in the legal system. These inequalities and continued disproportionate black and brown deaths instituted by the state led to the resurgence of the civil rights movement BLM in 2020 and catalysed global discussion of CRT. It also resulted in Australian-based responses (Guardian 2020; Henriques-Gomes and Visontay 2020; O'Brien 2017).

In order to continue highlighting socio-political disadvantage, the basic tenets of CRT include that racism and disparate racial outcomes are the result of complex, changing social and institutional dynamics rather than explicit and intentional prejudices on the part of individuals (Gillborn and Ladson-Billings 2019). Additionally, Mbembe (2019) stipulates that racism (as conceptualised in CRT) is the prime driver of *necropolitics* ('deathworlds'), stating that racialised people's lives are systematically cheapened and habituated to loss through forms of violence instituted often by white elites. The specific forms of *necropolitics* represented in this monograph are described as almost two decades of media and moral panics directed towards and brutalising young SSAs (detailed in chapters 3 and 5). Whilst exploration of this history could fill multiple books, it is briefly outlined here to establish the historic significance and implications of notions of Whiteness (superiority of white identities). It is important to note that, whilst using the terminology of Whiteness to describe this phenomenon, this explanation is not to be conflated with the overt racist hate directed towards people with white skin colour (Kendi 2019). What it does highlight is that it is not possible to talk about racism without explaining the genealogy of race as a system of control that has been continually reproduced in various forms for several centuries (Lentin 2020; Kendi 2019).

Acknowledging the power imbalance, CRT recognises that systemic racism is ingrained in the fabric of social structures and reveals itself through unconscious and conscious socio-cultural attitudes. As an analytical lens, it examines existing power such as the domination of Whiteness in society, which perpetuates the marginalisation of BIPOC communities (Dei 2018). Relevant is the notion of how race intersects with identity, particularly for the South Sudanese diaspora in Australia. Despite race being described as a 'mirage' and a false paradigm that humanity continues to 'organise itself around in very real ways' (Kendi 2019, 37, 54), it is a pervasive social construct that has everyday impacts (Elias, Mansouri, and Paradies 2021). These impacts poignantly affect young black SSAs (Abur 2018; Majavu 2020; Gatwiri and Anderson 2022). Building on the 'plethora of research that attests to the media's role in (re)producing racist narratives, influencing public opinion, perception and discourses around race' (Elias, Mansouri, and Paradies 2021, 211), the focus here is on excavating some of the impacts these phenomena have on young SSAs.

I have highlighted that 'race' remains an 'inescapable marker of differences', where a perpetuated 'black-white' continuum defines assimilation models in settler-colonial societies such as Australia and the United States (Tuan 1998, 5). I now move to how CRT allows for an analysis of contemporary everyday racism in the Australian context. Despite a lengthy First Nations history of activism resisting the settler-colonial context (Moreton-Robinson 2015; C. Land 2015), until recently, open discussions about racism have been silenced through quietly coded references to the 'R' word (Parter et al. 2021). Even though BIPOC communities speak out about these experiences, they find themselves 'policed for "making it about race", as though they – not the persistence of racial rule – were responsible for their own oppression' (Lentin 2020, 15). Everyday racism is experienced in more subtle forms such as through microaggressions involving constant verbal and non-verbal abuse directed at BIPOC communities on a daily basis (Kendi 2019, 46–47). The cumulative effects of these constant jabs that you are '"less than" does real psychological damage' (Oluo 2018, 173).

Racism in Australia has many complex and localised nuances beyond the scope of this monograph but detailed elsewhere (C. Land 2015; Cole 2016; Moreton-Robinson 2004a; Elias, Mansouri, and Paradies 2021). As it pertains to the application of CRT in Australia, put succinctly, eugenics projects throughout the early twentieth century were committed to politics that aimed to fend off alleged 'pathogenic coloured races' (Anderson 2005, 120). The racist project of 'the breeding out of colour' was taken up enthusiastically by Australian scientists promoting a 'scientific breeding programme' that aimed to remove Aboriginality and Blackness without 'throwbacks' resulting in the Stolen Generations phenomenon (Anderson 2005, 237, 255). What this history reveals is that the Australian national identity is founded on the ideology of Whiteness expressed through the racist idea of the 'white man's country' and 'white Labourism' which eventually became the White Australia Policy (Anderson 2005, 15, 86, 193, 239). This context sets the backdrop for how SSA communities develop their political voice to resist racialising discourses.

Kendi (2019, 18) elucidates racism's function in society as an essential structure of power and control, which demonstrates why there has been limited change. Rather than simple understandings of racism as prejudice towards another 'out-group', racism from a CRT perspective acknowledges inherent power imbalances that are a 'marriage of racist policies and racist ideas that produces and normalises racist inequities' (Kendi 2019, 18). Therefore, CRT defines racism more broadly and deeply than reductionist mainstream conceptualisations. Instead of perceiving racism as an 'individual manifestation of hatred', CRT explores 'the social structuring of racism as a complex, changing, and often subtle aspect of society that operates to the benefit of white people, especially white elites' (Gillborn and Ladson-Billings 2019, 1). However, Kendi (2019, 18) elaborates on the limitations of terms such as 'structural and institutional racism' and instead prefers the concept of 'racist policy', which produces and sustains racial inequity between racial groups. From this viewpoint, he describes racism as less about white people against black people (as he also acknowledges the existence of intra-racial class differences) but raises the importance of considering who benefits from racism. CRT also highlights that 'how we define racism determines how we battle it' (Oluo 2018, 29). Ture and Hamilton (1969) confirm that it is important to frame the critique and analysis of the critical incident/ces before taking action in calculated ways. Due to this observation, it is important to explore how CRT is adopted as a critical tool to analyse conditions in the Australian context.

CRT IN AUSTRALIA

Critical race theorists Lentin (2020) and Idriss (2021; 2021) also highlight the pertinence of the social construction of race and have shaped CRT in an Australian context. Through a critical analysis of Australian racism, what is most relevant here is the way that colour-coded and imperial racism has continued to perpetuate the Othering of African migrants in blatantly racist ways (Cole 2016; Majavu 2018, 2020; Matereke 2009). Henry-Waring (2008) suggests that social policies of multiculturalism, which are supposed to encourage the embracing of diversity, do not match Australia's rhetoric of a cohesive multicultural society. Rather, different iterations of Australian multicultural policy are linked to other factors like the troubled historical, political and social legacy of settled Australia bound up within the discourses of Otherness and Whiteness. She therefore coined the term 'metadiscourses of Otherness' that simultaneously normalise Whiteness yet fix and essentialise difference as negative Otherness. In practical terms, this involves 'reckoning with the ways that Whiteness – even as a construction and mirage – informs nationalistic undertones and notions of the privilege of white identities as being inherently normal, standard, and legal' (Kendi 2019, 38). These settler-colonial multicultural conditions that shape race politics in Australia have generated an Australia-specific CRT.

Rather than just discussing race as a social construct in an abstract way, there is an urgent need for race literacy which points towards localised and practical applications of dismantling systemic racism. One poignant way of doing this is by demonstrating that race continues to matter (2015, 2020). We cannot claim a post-racist society or the end of racism until we understand what race is really about (Lentin 2015; Kendi 2019; Oluo 2018). Further, Australian CRT contributors demonstrate the need for language and skills to challenge the contemporary local and global flows of inequality that perpetuate structures by processes of racialisation and racism (Idriss, Butler, and Harris 2021; Moreton-Robinson 2015; Lentin 2020). Australian society in general lacks maturity around conversations about race, social, and power constructs and how these might be addressed in practical ways (Gatwiri and Anderson 2021; Knowles 2021; Elias, Mansouri, and Paradies 2021). Prentis (2017) does not believe we can begin to speak about a post-colonial world (particularly in the lands we now call Australia) unless a *truth-telling* process occurs. This involves reckoning with the conditions and legacies that made forms of colonisation possible. Proponents view the possibility of CRT as including revolutionary concepts that outline what a 'post-racist' future could look like, acknowledging that a truth-telling process is the first step (K. Quinn 2020). In a recent Australian backlash against CRT narratives, NSW Police Minister David Elliot states he does not believe that Australia has a 'race issue' (McPhee and Chrysanthos 2021). Lentin (2020, 10) alternatively suggests:

> [There is a] growing number of white supremacists in Europe, North America, and Australasia, [therefore we are in the] throes of a race war. They are armed and ready to act. However, many more people of colour die, are physically or mentally injured, or suffer in other ways at the hands of the state.

Engagement with the intersectional nature of the racialisation of young SSAs categorised as black-Africans and this 'race issue' is therefore crucial. Whilst it particularly relates to the construction of Indigenous difference amongst Australian critical race theorists, Moreton-Robinson's (2004b; Briese and Menzel 2020) utilisation of *Indigenous standpoint theory* is also illustrative of Australia's settler-colonial and multicultural racial politics which set the scene for the application of a locally nuanced CRT. She contends that race is the operationalising paradigm undergirding the signification and construction of Indigenous difference under the guise of cultural difference. For example, anyone that does not fit into the category of being of Caucasian background or under the construct of Whiteness is often 'lumped together' as having the same experiences of Bla(c)kness and cultural diversity in the Australian context. That is one reason terminology such as POC (People of Colour) was extended to BIPOC (Bla(c)k, Indigenous, People of Colour) and as chapter 1 suggests, these terms can be contentious (BICOC-Project 2020). Therefore, when broad terms such as multiculturalism or multicultural policy are invoked, it is assumed that Indigenous Australians' voices fall under this broad grouping of diverse peoples with nuanced experiences. The point here is to restate that Indigenous and African migrant experiences cannot be conflated. Chapter 1 described how the relatively recent history of large-scale black-African immigration means that non-Indigenous Blackness is often migranticised and classed. Removing the façade of cultural difference, that is, black Africans are not integrating into Australian society and therefore the social construct of Whiteness, this example of *Indigenous standpoint theory* is used as it resembles the experiences of the African diaspora in Australia. Specifically, determining their own nuanced experiences of Blackness, Africanness, and living in a settler-colonial context (Gatwiri and Anderson 2022).

The example sets the tone for allowing a more effective means to disassemble the rhetorical mechanisms of colonisation and oppression. Additionally, there has sometimes been alignment, but also distance between BLM movements in the United States and elsewhere, and between First Nations struggles and Afrodiasporic struggles where issues of sovereignty for Indigenous Australians are centred in the Australian context. Race talk in Australia, therefore, has a different history and distinctive contemporary manifestations and silences. The various theoretical threads in this section are based on sometimes contrasting epistemological stances.

The significance of race and racism as it pertains to Australian applications of CRT highlights the 'need to theorise race as a political project with ongoing effects' (Lentin 2020, 16). As such, CRT provides a framework to understand the intersections with Whiteness and the development of political voice, for example, through Antiracist approaches. This understanding of Whiteness is used now to discuss the specific impact that Australian media and political and moral panics (as a form of perpetuated racialising discourses) have on young SSAs.

EXPERIENCES OF EVERYDAY AND SYSTEMIC RACISM

Before discussing forms of political voice expression specifically in response to racialising discourses (discussed in chapters 4–6), it is important to further understand the incidences of racism present as a result of *necropolitics*- racist policies and practises which result in 'deathworlds' which this section depicts. Sampa's (2020b) lyrics – '*In a country that pretends to not see black*' – are a nod to Australia's *war on Blackness* (further described in this section) and therefore suggests a framework for the alternative form of artivism described as arts-based community development discussed in chapters 4–6. Through a CRT lens, this section demonstrates how young SSA participants experience racism in a number of ways through *systemic, interpersonal* and *intrapersonal racism* (Priest et al. 2021). *Systemic or structural racism* is described as the totality of ways in which societies foster racial discrimination through mutually reinforcing inequitable systems. It can also be referred to as *institutional racism* referring specifically to racially adverse discriminatory policies and practices carried out within and between individual institutions based on racialised group membership. *Interpersonal racism*, however, refers to discrimination between people. For example, it can include racially motivated assault to verbal abuse, ostracism, and exclusion, which can involve varying degrees of frequency and intensity. *Internalised (or intrapersonal) racism*, on the other hand, refers to attitudes, beliefs, or ideologies within communities often founded on understandings of innate superiority/inferiority held primarily by members of dominant social groups (Priest et al. 2021).

The first example of intrapersonal racism can be seen in the intent behind young SSA Liep Gony's murder due to perceived racial superiority (further discussed in chapter 5). From September to October 2009, the Supreme Court of Victoria heard the account of Gony's death, where it was alleged that prior to Gony's murder, one of the perpetrators (then 19 years old) sprayed racist graffiti on a wall of a rented house and was heard to say he was 'going to take the town back by killing blacks' (AAP 2011). In her article 'How Racism Diminishes Humanity', South Sudanese lawyer and community advocate Nyadol Nyuon (2018, 1) notes that people who experience racism are just 'pawns in a larger game' where some people are viewed as 'means to an end'. Nyuon was referring to the effects that the Victorian state election in 2018 had on herself, her family, and her communities, specifically with the 'Apex saga' portraying young SSAs in gangs (see table 1.1) being used as political bait to win votes. She also refers to a broader systemic analysis, noting the coercive ways racist power yields attention (often on purpose) which is a focus of CRT (Hohle 2018). Therefore, the aspects of CRT that this chapter addresses specifically focus on race as a social construct and that race can be theorised as a political project with ongoing effects (Lentin 2020).

Emmanuel, Lizzie, Ajur, Tito, Amina, Felicia, Nyok, Jikany, Jacob and the *BCM* crew asserted that '*racialising discourses are racist*' and they shared scenarios from their experience. A few accounts of their experiences of racism, where racialising discourses are most strongly asserted are explored below. Alongside scholarly accounts (AHRC 2010), they acknowledge that they experienced racism early in their resettlement journey in Australia. Due to their noticeably darker skin, this was equated with 'colour-coded racism' (Cole 2016). In terms of tying this in with commentary on multiculturalism, the paradox is that Australia is portrayed as a 'success story of multiculturalism', despite the fact that 'rampant racism persists' (BBC 2017, 1).

As discussed, these experiences necessitated the need for young SSAs to build political voice through Hip Hop expression. A narrative analysis of BTSO artivists tracks reviews the types of discourses present and pertinent for young SSAs. In the 'AfriCAN track (2018)'[4] developed as part of the Gua focus groups and workshops (discussed further in chapter 4), *Burn City Movement* (BCM) artist *i.OG* admonished listeners, asking them not to *'dirty my skin. I meant it'* in response to experiences of socio-political disadvantage and perpetuated media and moral panics spanning decades. As an example of intrapersonal racism, *i.OG* is referring to the treatment his community experiences due to the colour of his black skin and reminds us that *'racism is still cemented within the minds of generations'* due to racist ideologies. Further on in the track, Karabo (also a dancer) shares her spoken-word ad lib reflecting her accounts of the effects of racism:

She approaches me with hate
Bringing generalisations, stereotypes, violence to my Blackness, my soul
He brings with him sorrow, anger, confusion, darkness
Molten lava seeping through my veins
Something I cannot escape
They take away my ability to love, to feel harmony
Surrounding me with rain and thunder
Cautioning my step
Their name is RACISM. (Karabo, 'AfriCAN' (2018))

Whilst the broader 'AfriCAN' (2018) track is about black excellence and power, this ad lib was included in the track to remind the listener that despite the way African diaspora young people wish to present themselves through their strengths framed by the BTSO motto, the reality is that they face these brutal attacks on their well-being constantly. Whilst this track portrays the debilitating effects of racism, the following encounters pertain specifically to this research's exploration of media and moral panics portraying young SSAs as criminals or failing to 'integrate' into Australian society which are a form of racialising discourses and necessitate the need to build political voice through Hip Hop.

In terms of an example of interpersonal racism and the discourse of portraying young SSAs as criminals without reform, SSA artist *Queen P* (2018) described how she had *'never been called a n**** until the break of the Apex narrative'*.[5] Gua focus group participants also frequently discussed this discourse, noting the time they were first called a *'black c***'* by an angry bystander. This caused real *'body affects'* including internal angst and turmoil, forcing victims to hold significant trauma in their bodies. These statements are crucial for linking back to the effects of racialising discourses, as racism and racial discrimination are fundamental causes and determinants of health and health inequalities globally (Priest et al. 2021).

SSA artist *Titan* outlines that it was common 'being treated with suspicion' after a local festival, Moomba, where young SSAs were labelled as violently rioting in Naarm. This was at the peak of the Apex gang narrative, and one of the frequent topics reported alleged that young SSAs are commonly involved in 'gang behaviour'. *Titan* shares that, as a result of this discourse, 'everyone is staring at you like you're about to do something' (Vice-Australia 2018, 1). When newly arrived in Australia, participant Suleyman shared similar experiences when walking down the street with a group of ten friends and observing people's reactions regarding unspoken expectations to assimilate to white cultural norms.

Although this kind of treatment has systemic causes through forms of socio-political disadvantage and in some cases preference for white nationalism, these accounts demonstrate further interpersonal effects. Suleyman felt cautious about being out at night because he was *'scared for himself'* due to other's perceptions of him at night. As a result, he was the one to cross the street so that others might not feel scared. He commented that the *'racist Apex narrative'* meant that young people had to walk around in school uniform so that people on the street did not think they were part of Apex or confront them. Some also noted teachers asking siblings if they were part of the Apex gang (Gua focus groups, 2017/19). Amir described how, after Gony's murder, he was chased down the street by a group of four young hostile men in a car, yelling out obscenities such as *'go back to where you came from you black c***'*. This is an example of interpersonal racism based in forms of nationalism perceived through the racist lens of skin colour, which was identified through a CRT analysis. He recalls safely arriving home and his Mama asking him what was wrong as he appeared flustered. Amir reflected on this experience: *'I'm not gonna lie, sometimes I look back then. As a young teenager, you'd be afraid. And of course, like that sort of made us stick to ourselves'.*

Suleyman also described how racism was experienced *'behind the scenes'* in further interpersonal and intrapersonal ways experienced as microaggressions (daily subtle and implicit comments). These include not being able to get work or finding out that things are said about you. Suleyman describes how he feels this is considered *'the worst type of racism'* as it is difficult to combat:

> how do we face it when we have no control over it? . . . like how do you change something about yourself . . . like my DNA [melanin] is something you can't change . . . and other people are the ones who have power over it.

These incidences describe some of the experiences of everyday racism (Lentin 2015, 2016, 2018) and demonstrate what CRT theorises as forms of biological racism. Kendi (2019, 44) distinguishes that biological racism:

rests on two ideas: that the races are meaningfully different in their biology and that these differences create a hierarchy of value. Biological racial difference is one of those widely held racist beliefs that few people realise they hold – nor do they realise that those beliefs are rooted in racist ideas.

Combating these often-subconscious attitudes requires people to strive towards being a biological Antiracist. In order to consciously respond, Kendi (2019, 44) outlines the definition suggesting that this involves 'one who is expressing the idea that the [social construct of] races are meaningfully the same in their biology and there are no genetic racial differences'.

Other significant encounters of systemic racism discuss racial profiling of young SSAs. *Titan* shared his account of when he and his friends (who happened to be black) were playing basketball in his neighbourhood in Wyndham in southwest Naarm. He described how all of a sudden, a police helicopter and a riot squad, including police horses, surrounded the court. This experience was understandably 'very intimidating!' (Vice-Australia 2018). Despite this not being the main topic of interviews, participants continued to describe numerous experiences. This demonstrates the importance of wanting to 'vent' or detail their experiences of racism.

Suleyman also shared about the time he was sitting with his friends in his friend's apartment in South Yarra (an affluent suburb in inner-city Naarm). They joked about the possibility of police or neighbours thinking because they were black people in this fancy property that they had broken in. He described that what occurred next was that these jokes eventuated into a '*whole bunch of police jumping the back fence*' ready to interrogate them for being in the property. They began pulling out their phones to record, which de-escalated the police response as his friend explained it was his property and he just had friends over. At this point of the interview, Suleyman leaned over and showed me the footage they had uploaded on social media. We began discussing together what might have happened if this scenario occurred in Turtle Island (U.S.) due to critical incidences of police brutality and were thankful the police disengaged and went back over the fence after being embarrassed by their conduct.

Through my profession as a youth worker and from observations during YSAS fieldwork, I have witnessed young people's incidences of police brutality (cases of young people being assaulted by police behind closed doors and adverse treatment before my eyes); I also covered this topic in my master's thesis (Williams 2016) (outlined in chapter 1). This sort of treatment has been extensively documented (Smith 2011; Grossman and Sharples 2010). These scenes described sound like they are out of a movie, and yet it was experienced specifically by South Sudanese males who remain under constant surveillance by police, often through mistaken identity. Whilst we do not have the same incidences of police shootings or killing BIPOC people in public as in the United States, these accounts indicate that we also have some serious systemic issues of institutional racism and individual 'bad apples' (discussed below) in public professions in Australia. It appears these 'bad apples' buy into the rhetoric of racialising discourses and contribute to systemic racism through perpetuating forms of socio-political disadvantage.

Most worrying to participants were forms of interpersonal racism. Citing a series of growing right-wing gatherings in 2018 (Vice-Australia 2018), Suleyman expressed his distress: *'the fact that there can be a neo-Nazi fucking riot that happens in Australia in Saint Kilda and you see how many people actually showed up for it!'* Commentators in Australia have continued to note concern for growing armed neo-Nazi and white supremacist groups present in Australia due to the security and terror threat this extremely racist behaviour poses on BIPOC civilians (Cooper 2021; McKenzie and Tozer 2021; Hage 1998).

A series of tracks written by Naarm-based rappers from the period 2017–2021 further demonstrates the significant impact the Apex gang narrative had on young SSAs. SSA artist *i.OG* raps in BCM's 'Trials n' Tribulations (TNT)' track (Burn City Movement 2020c)[6] that being stereotyped as African gangs has been like *'a little too many speakers louder than a stereotype'*. In this track, he suggests that *'it's standard for the black man how they devalue and label us'* (Burn City Movement 2020c). Whilst in his track 'Lonely' (2017b)[7] SSA artist *Daniel Elia* raps, *'like watching the news you think my skin Apex'*. *Titan* in his 'Ghetto Tears' spoken-word poetry highlights that *'the colour on the TV is what they call me. . . . It sad how I am treated'*[8]. As a result, this amplified narrative of what comes across as non-acceptance and intolerance towards SSA communities from a broad range of Australians has had long-lasting mental health effects (Abur and Mphande 2020). When listening to these tracks, you can almost hear the sounds of lament, anger, and despair hidden in their voices as *i.OG* describes how the *'pressure on us is dripping out'* (Burn City Movement 2020b)[9] in response to racialising discourses.

The impact of these racist terms and narratives are described in Karabo's verse in the 'AfriCAN' track but also through participants' assertions that racialising discourse *'affects everyone individually in different ways'* (Emmanuel) and on *'multiple levels'* (Malual). This can include on a personal emotional level, on a societal level, and by seeing your community affected (Everest 2019). Young SSAs continue to articulate how experiencing forms of racism have long-term and everyday impacts (Mushroom-Creative 2017). Jamal, Lizzie, Ajur, Abdul, and participants in Footprints longitudinal Gua focus group in 2014 detail specifically what these are which include feeling *'victimised'*, *'treated differently'*, *'drained'*, *'alone'*, *'judged'*, *'violated'*, '*traumatised*', '*frustrated*', '*triggered*', '*burned out*' '*heartbroken*' or like you have '*identity crisis issues*' or experience a '*gunshot to your heart*'. Gabriel, Akra, and Akur note how part of the heartbreak is young children experiencing interpersonal racism as '*comments can really have an impact*'. The most alarming impacts include a tragic string of suicides and stress-related deaths of young SSAs (TACSA 2020) spanning over a decade. Experiences of systemic racism are highlighted as a leading cause of death (Rosenblatt and Wallace 2005; Kwansah-Aidoo and Mapedzahama 2018).

Whilst this chapter demonstrates significant pain amongst young SSAs, BTSO participants, and community members present their own solutions to community concerns which are not yet a feature of any existing study (TACSA 2020; Abur and Mphande 2020; Elston 2019). Overall, there was a general consensus that research participants felt that they had been '*dealing with racism*' in Australia to varying degrees '*since a young age*' (Akra). However, it was acknowledged that racism is '*basic*' and '*not founded by an intellectual reasoning for its necessity*' (Ibrahim). One of the main tenets of CRT argues that race is a social construct, hence making racism a byproduct of this illusion (Kendi 2019; Moreton-Robinson 2004b). The sentiments of most participants aligned with Malual's wish to '*move on*'. Through a crowd refrain '*Fuck Channel 7*' at his performance at Yah Yah's bar in 2019,[10] Titan wished he never had to organise a Channel 7 protest in response to the African gangs narrative perpetuated by mainstream Australian media again (see chapter 6). Before being able to 'move on' from extensive detailing of various experiences of Australian racism, it is important to address the debilitating effects of this social construct of Whiteness, which perpetuates and recycles harmful narratives to maintain the status of white elites. The following topic, therefore, addresses how young SSAs challenge perceptions of their communities whilst also describing structural barriers.

Participants described how the murder of Liep Gony in 2007 and perceptions of youth culture put young SSAs in the public eye for all the wrong reasons. This led to challenging societal perceptions of young SSAs as predominantly involved in crime. In her Voice for Change interview with MoMo from Diafrix, SSA rapper *Queen P* pleads for people not to generalise her whole community. Like any community, she uses the analogy, 'when you have a few bad apples you don't throw away the whole tree' (Mushroom-Creative 2018a, 1). She goes on to describe the many frustrations of how 'Aussie kids' (whom she conceived of as white youth) do the same things as African Australian youth. However, it is not reported to the same degree in the media (Mushroom-Creative 2018a). This was a sentiment shared by many participants and was frequently reported as frustrating. Another frustration reported by BTSO participants as a type of double standard is the fact that many non-black young people enjoy black culture or are seen to benefit from it when it comes to musical preferences. Ezra, Jesko, and SSA artist *Daniel Elia* (2017a)[11] detail a specific example of this is when club owners or security sometimes exclude black people at the door whilst simultaneously playing black music inside the club.

The track 'Memories Lane' by SSA rappers Sudo Boiz (2010)[12] which featured a *'lost homie'* (friend who passed unexpectedly), is described as the journey of *'us being here and different stereotypes that were thrown towards us as kids growing up here . . . how we're perceived. We're still seeking validation here which makes it really hard'* (Shaker). Continued frustration occurs when young people struggle to find facilities to participate in activities they enjoy. As one example, 'studio time' can be an opportunity to make Hip Hop tracks and beats or find a freedom of expression or a sense of belonging when hanging with 'homies' (friends). Participants suggest that young people might get up to mischief where opportunities for such positive interactions are lacking. Participants considered the lack of such opportunities extremely unfortunate because:

> *there's a lot of kids with a lot of artistic talent inside of them. They have a lot inside that can't really be expressed. There's a lot of frustration. There's a lot of avenues of trying to express yourself in different ways. So you kind of start acting out just to kind of feel wanted.* (Ibrahim)

This idea goes against misconceptions of young people, who are often described in public discourse as perhaps lazy, unmotivated, disinterested, or apathetic towards society (Micoleta 2012). On the contrary, young people in this research, who are successfully running their own initiatives, suggest that *'we have a lot of people who just want to contribute to the success of our community as a whole'* (Ibrahim). This may take other avenues than traditionally explored forms of activism or community development initiatives. For BTSO artivists, making music inspired by Hip Hop as a culture is a way to engage and further inspire peers, the public (anyone who chooses to engage with the message), and future generations. These initial responses are described as a precursor to young SSAs being able to build agency and develop their political voice, further outlined in chapters 5–7.

URBAN YOUTH CULTURE – HIP HOP MUSIC AS A WAY TO ENGAGE AND INSPIRE

Whilst critique is present (Andrews 2020), scholarship still broadly uses the term *urban youth culture* to describe how young people are crafting new identities and social networks using a range of globally generated and proliferating resources . . . moving both literally and figuratively, crossing national borders with their bodies as well as imaginations, constructing new and unexpected kinds of identities. (Harris 2017, 139)

This section outlines how young SSAs describe the set of circumstances they experience living in suburban parts of Naarm. This sets the scene for how young SSAs who identify with urban youth culture in Naarm depict their political voice, influence, and discuss topics affecting them. This is primarily through their own unique forms of expression through the modality of Hip Hop as a culture. The linkage made here is that Hip Hop as an NSM has historically addressed systemic racism and provided minoritised communities a voice (Iglesias and Harris 2019).

This topic was identified through three themes that emerged in their lyrics, interviews and focus groups: namely, the influences of youth music culture and fashion, the ways in which young people prefer to pass the time or motivate themselves, and how they begin to define how they respond to key structural barriers for young SSAs described above.

EXAMPLES OF URBAN YOUTH CULTURE MUSIC ENGAGEMENT AND ARTIST TRACKS

One example of urban youth music culture is through *Titan's* track 'Cheques and Balances' (2020):[13]

> *Nikes [branded shoe] on my feet that's a cheque, they [politicians /media] be throwing threats. I ain't never getting touched, see me on the street show respect. Let's do it for the block.*

Titan uses urban vernacular to discuss his fashion choices influenced by U.S. music styles and fashion as a form of expression. This is common in Hip Hop lyrics as a kind of 'hype' lyric (hyperbole) to show people who is 'boss' (not to be messed with) or positioning his 'swagger' (sense of style) on the streets (Mason 2018). These aspects demonstrate the identity establishment and engagement process of young SSAs as they seek to 'carve out' and define their own space in Australia. This theme is now explored through the way in which Hip Hop, as a part of urban youth culture, was chosen by young people.

African diaspora artists including Sampa, Diafrix, Tkay Maidza and Remi (alongside their First Nations counterparts) have changed the face of Australian Hip Hop, making new claims on the original black cultural form (Cleland

2016). This leads to the claim in this study that a selection of young SSAs turn to Hip Hop to give voice to their need for understanding and justice, and it was chosen *by* them, not for them. Young people in this research passionately discuss their love for music, explaining that 'music is a way to engage young people and inspire' (Mushroom-Creative 2018a). Similarly, Lizzy poignantly states that *'music is the way we express ourselves. You've got to listen to the lyrics'*.

Hip Hop has always been a formidable force of political voice (Hill-Collins 2006; Reiland 2013; Asante 2008; Bonnette 2015). Its origins stem from an Afro-Caribbean black cultural form describing 'life in the hood' (or the streets) in the Bronx, NYC (Morgan and Bennett 2011; Black 2014). This legacy now extends to being a commercial, worldwide subculture where artists continue to rap about daily experiences within an oppressive system, which can include interactions with police (Oware 2018; Bonnette 2015). Block parties were hosted to celebrate 'freedom of expression' or 'black joy' if only for a minute (Morgan and Bennett 2011; Bonnette 2015). Being young and black had its highs and lows as Hip Hop peaked as a cultural phenomenon, particularly during the Hip Hop generation (1985–1995) (Asante 2008). Considering the historical roots of the inception of Hip Hop, those who relate to these roots consider it has always existed to be a form of resistance and as a *consciousness-raising* tool (Akom 2009; R.R. Land and Stovall 2009; E. Quinn 2003; Porfilio 2015). From the viewpoint of those who were excluded from the discos in Manhattan, NYC and wanted to be able to party freely in their own boroughs of NYC, the cultural expression of Hip Hop can also be a *consciousness-numbing* mechanism. That is, if you just wanted to 'tap out' and get lost in the music or the 'bangers' (consisting of heavy bass tones, catchy beats or lyrics and up-tempo style) (Oware 2018). These early roots of Hip Hop are not too dissimilar to young SSAs' experiences in urban parts of Naarm.

Current generations of Hip Hop artists are now in the throes of creating their own style and deciding the imprint they wish to make in their artform and broader impact on culture. Asante (citing Fanon 2008, xii) reminds us that 'each generation must out of relative obscurity, discover its mission, fulfill it or betray it'. A schoolteacher, Bella, based in the most culturally diverse LGA (CGD) in Australia, shared her observations of students. She suggests that for culturally and linguistically diverse (CALD) young people *'culture isn't necessarily the primary thing. Young people find a way of working out who they are through music or different ways to position yourself'*. This speaks to the ways in which art informs identity expression. One former child soldier, Khalid, also described it as *'a way for the human brain to start healing, to be able to concentrate'*.

A key theme explored is that young SSAs started taking their Hip Hop artistry seriously after some of the issues occurred in the community or within Australia, and the racist discourses directed towards them meant that they wanted to voice their concerns more publicly. For example, one artist references starting to write rap lyrics after the murder of young SSA Liep Gony when his crew wrote a track describing their frustrations with how his death and their community were portrayed in the media (Amir). Shaker similarly contributes: *'You know we experienced a lot of discrimination, a lot of prejudice towards my community so that's why I started Hip Hop'*.

Referencing how the word 'Apex', originating from the Apex gang narrative, has now been equated with black, South Sudanese young men in Australia, *Titan* (2017)[14] situates these narratives in the ongoing

. . . struggle of the black man
Living by the goddamn rules of the white man
With plans for his white fam
It's sad how I am treated.

Liep's murder and details about depictions of the Apex gang are further discussed in chapter 5. These references to racialising discourses, being expected to live by the rules of Whiteness, is a key theme of this study discussed in chapter 6. *Titan's* track portrays how many black males feel about daily life in the 'ghetto' – that is, they feel like they are treated unfairly, differently or badly by society. Throughout the 'Ghetto Tears' track, *Titan* (2019)[15] describes some of the tragedies he has observed throughout his time in Australia as a result of this treatment. He mentions poverty; what he and other participants describe as profiling by teachers (singling out black students, having limited expectations of career goals or academic achievements, or having no teachers who look like you) and his tears for the daily treatment he and his family endured. Other participants also drew on these themes. This situation is described in the hook (bridge of the track):

Everywhere we seem to go
Ghetto tears on my lowest notes
Tears for my little bro
Tears for my Mama too
Pray for a miracle

(Debirioun 2017).[16]

Titan's purpose is that he sees himself as doing music *'for the culture'* (Debirioun 2017)[17] (a term referencing Hip Hop/street/urban culture and people who associate with it and his own personal cultural links); for his *Gs* (homies or friends) and *OGs* (a term which has a literal meaning of 'original gangsta' but is also fondly used for elders or those who have gone before to pave the way). Despite his best efforts, *Titan* mentions the unfortunate truth for him and many of his counterparts that *'no one sees greatness when I finally make it'* (Debirioun 2017).[18] This is because: *'it seems like we overlooked. And these demons got us really shook'* (Debirioun 2017).[19]

This links back to Sampa's point about being overlooked in the music industry. This is something BTSO artivists are also beginning to change through their art and influence. Through artistic expression in the form of Hip Hop culture, they also showcase the ways in which they choose to express themselves, which may be different from traditional approaches. An embedded approach and taking the time to listen to their lyrics provides insight into the process of relationship development with these communities of young people and construction of historical knowledge (Dimitriadis 2000).

Whilst Hip Hop initially reflected U.S. styles of music (Shaker), it has branched out into new sub-genres due to the ways in which new generations put their own spin on the artform (Gua camp focus group notes 2019). This study specifically focuses on the sub-genre of *conscious Hip Hop* in order to demonstrate how participants of this research go on a consciousness-raising journey (described in chapter 5, which begins the discussion of how this process is linked to an NSM). A community cultural development specialist, Niki, shared learnings from her extensive career engaging young people, which started in the North Richmond housing estate (inner city of Naarm) in the early 2000s when SSA communities started arriving in Australia after being displaced by long-term civil war. She shared how she and many colleagues worked in close proximity to Hip Hop culture for a long time as it was *'the form of choice for young people'*. Niki describes how, as workers, they were interested in language and issues of power and they identified how urban cultures such as Hip Hop are a highly accessible art form. She recalled young people who started their Hip Hop 'crews' (music groups) or wrote tracks after Gony's death and some of the socio-political circumstances at the time. Young SSA artist Anyaak (William) Manhoum was one such artist (Dwyer 2018). Niki highlighted how *'young people are on the receiving end of very blunt instruments both in the education system and policy. Lack of opportunities for employment are forms of structural discrimination'*.

As U.S. Hip Hop artist J Cole points out in the track 'No Role Modelz' (2014),[20] there are few positive role models for BIPOC young people. This can be due to the reasons described above; for example, in an Australian context, the music industry elite is filled with people who do not necessarily reflect the broad multicultural demographics of Australian young people (Australian-Council-Arts 2020; Diversity-Arts-Australia 2018, 2019). At 21 years old, one way *Titan* has been able to influence other young people by his mentorship model is by hosting the Off the Grid project in the City of Wyndham (MAV 2019) to upskill the next generation in music production and emceeing (being a Hip Hop performer), teaching them to write, record, and perform their own compositions (SBS 2020). Footprints (2019) and other BTSO participants hosted similar projects, noting that particularly after being released from a youth justice precinct (a youth prison), having access to a studio is '*a way to express themselves, they can't hide away from [systemic pressures] and have to make something of themselves through music*' (Jamal). One way to do this is through live performances and shows to attract a younger generation and a new fan base (Marley). The *BCM* crew (Burn City Movement 2020a; The-Drum-Theatre 2020) sees this as an opportunity to '*get young people to look at better role models, see something and say, I can believe in that too once they see everyone involved*' (Marley).

In addition to being a successful engagement activity, participants describe how in music, sports, and even in the fashion industry, you see a lot of African diaspora young people representing the Australian community on a larger international or domestic level. Whilst they showcase their talents, they have the opportunity to '*hold two identities proudly*' (Emmanuel), as discussed further in chapter 5. Participants urge the community to continue to work with them as '*with a lot of young people we have different levels of engagement but there's still hope*' (Emmanuel). Malek, Shaker and Felicia described this in their Hip Hop journeys noting the power of Hip Hop as a tool to engage young people. Shaker noted that in his earlier years he could have been swayed by different forms of U.S. gangster rap. However, as he contemplated his journey, he identified that he also acknowledged the power of a social message through lived experience. He suggested that as a result '*we started creating more awareness through our music*' (Shaker). This journey is a key theme discussed in the following findings chapters by highlighting various forms of Hip Hop culture expression: through artivism, expressing political voice in rap lyrics, or through various forms of community-building activities consisting of Hip Hop performances.

'VISIONS FROM THE KITCHEN' – MOMENTS OF CLARITY FOR THE FUTURE

Despite these significant challenges, BTSO artivists take enormous pride in their artistry and their ability to cook up '*visions from the kitchen*'[21] (Elia 2016, 2017a).[22] Hip Hop and soul artists *Malesh P*[23] and Tébir in the track 'Why Are We?' (Junub-Television 2016)[24] acknowledge their frustrations with the choices some young people make. However, *Daniel Elia's*

(2017a)[25] idea of being like a hero, *'spreading all the gold through the hood with an arrow'* [with his rhymes like a black Robin Hood], showcases how BTSO artivists are 'here to make a difference' (Mushroom-Creative 2018b). Through *'making a change off of these bars [lyrics]'*, they are here to bring *'hope'* (Malesh-P 2015)[26] or to 'inspire' (Mushroom-Creative 2018a).

Malesh P and *Tébir* (2016)[27] also try to communicate a vibrant and upbeat feeling through their tracks, by encouraging *'the youth'* whilst sharing about the process of leaving the *'Motherland'* of South Sudan due to *'education being a problem; dead bodies piling up; mothers being beaten and left crying'*. This attempt to communicate to the next generation that *'we are the future, we all know why we are here'*, the reason being *'we promised on arrival to be entrepreneurs'* (Junub-Television 2016).[28] I met artist *Malesh P* as a teenager after his performance in 2008 and have seen him develop and become an innovator. Through his own demonstrated experience, *Malesh P* (2016)[29] implores young people to *'quit messing around'* as *'time is very crucial'*. He encourages young people to *'keep your pedal to the metal'* as they *'are the future'*. Starting in high school in one of Melbourne's first South Sudanese Hip Hop groups – the African Mic Controllers (AMCs), *Malesh P* has been described by many participants as a role model for budding artists and youth workers as he has dedicated his life to paving the way for other young people to participate in Hip Hop when it was not popular or accepted in his community, particularly amongst elders. He has reached all kinds of young people and other audiences through his music and performances and through his role as a youth worker and educator in the youth justice system, whilst at the same time, supporting Footprints as a workshop facilitator and performing at the Grounded Youth Stage on multiple occasions.

When running workshops or asked to give advice to young people, BTSO artivists take a pragmatic approach to giving advice to the next generation whilst encouraging them to inspire and educate broader society. *Malesh P* and *Krown* encourage young people to 'find their passions', 'even if it means switching off social media to think about what you want to achieve in life' (Beat-Magazine 2017). Others take the approach of 'being real' (sharing their experiences openly and honestly) with young people, as they see themselves 'equipping more young people to tell their own truth' (SBS 2020), which aligns with the idea of being 'born to stand out' (BTSO) (discussed in chapter 6).

BTSO artivists' main message in this section is to ask: 'When are we able to say enough is enough?' This points to young SSA artists' desires to present a solution to community concerns. This involves unifying people whilst 'challenging negativity' (SBS 2020). BCM artist *i.OG* in his verse raps, *'within the minds of the generations we've got to spark the change so the change can be amended'* (i.OG, *AfriCAN* track).[30] Workshop facilitator and filmmaker

Izzy Films expresses that the key point of art or Hip Hop and the reason he writes scripts is to *'protect the future'* (Gua camp focus group notes2017). This research showcases that whilst there are already a lot of young people *'contributing to the success of the community as a whole'* (Marley), the future is looking bright. With young SSAs, there is *'a lot of greatness rising up, the next generation are doing some good stuff'* with a focus on *'eventually bringing artists together from around the world'* (Abdul). The following sections address this future and responses led by young SSAs.

PUBLIC PEDAGOGY – PLACES, SPACES, 'LITTLE PUBLICS' – YOUTH-LED RESPONSES AND STANDING OUT FOR THE RIGHT REASONS

Whilst around 24,000 South Sudanese people live in Australia, totalling only 0.1 per cent of the population (RCOA 2018), this research is interested in how South Sudanese communities have featured heavily in the narrative of a nation (discussed as racialising discourses). It details how they form *little publics*, a term Hickey-Moody (2013b) uses to portray different expressions of heterogeneous youth culture. This is a term derived from Dewey's (1927) concept of *public spheres* and is used in this monograph to describe the way in which young SSAs express themselves through art (in this case, Hip Hop) as a public pedagogy to develop their political voice. Before delving into this further below, this section explores the theme of what it means to be 'visible' in public, a phenomenon experienced by young SSAs after decades of targeted media and moral panics directed towards their communities, with a focus on the Southeastern suburbs of Naarm.

Hanging out in public places is also a sign of youth culture. Young people like to be visible and express themselves in a myriad of different ways and on different platforms, including via social media. In fact,

> young people around the world are carving out new, unpredictable, and in some ways rhizomatic forms of cultural identification. . . . Sometimes these forms are defined by taste. Sometimes they are defined by race or ethnic identity. Sometimes – often – they are marked by both. (Dimitriadis 2007b, 119)

The concept of being 'visible in public' as young SSAs with 'noticeably darker skin' was explored in my Master's thesis (Williams 2016) (described in chapter 1). Whilst not covered extensively here, participants noted a few stories because the concept of 'being different in public' is a pervasive theme in their everyday life, particularly as it draws out racist racialising discourses (the counter-narratives to this are explored in chapters 5–6). During a media interview, the BCM Hip Hop crew tried to debunk some of the myths about the 'African gangs' crisis' over coffee in an inner-city café. The journalist Johnson (2019) notes how the BCM boys stand out with obvious stares from the patrons referring to a group of young black males in a predominantly white demographic.

Linking to moral panics about young people congregating in public space (White and Mason 2006), a fight instigated by black spectators at a local soccer game in CGD instantly made it to national news (Precel 2019). Nyok suggested that media leaks are often reported by a *'narrow-minded white person'*. Additionally, young people's social media pages are trolled and reposted by the media. These contributions of scenarios discussed by participants provide further insight into the processes for community groups to further interact with the public sphere when considering biases that may have formed. Often, debunking of moral panics is required when considering the contestation of public space. I now address how young people may interact in this space when facilitating their own youth-led approaches to debunking the narratives portrayed.

Whilst instances of concerns for public safety are noted (Eddie and Zhuang 2019), this research aims to delve deeper into the actions of young people in public spaces when expressing themselves. Participants overwhelmingly noted the lack of youth-friendly spaces to hang out in the southeastern suburbs of Naarm, particularly after hours. This is one reason young people choose to congregate in streets, parks, shopping centres or outside train stations (Furlong 2013). Other than catching up with friends, the other main reason for meeting in groups in public (for predominantly BIPOC young people) was to feel safe (Grossman and Sharples 2010, xii). Kendi (2019, 172) additionally notes how access to resources defines a space, which is more noticeable in some neighbourhoods than others.

The *BCM* crew highlighted how *'one of the biggest hassles was not having a facility [a studio]. There was art we wanted to create'* (Ibrahim, Kiir, Marley, Gua focus group notes 2019). After knowing each other for some time, they pooled their own money to hire a studio in CGD with a view to *'open up the community to involve other people in it'* (Marley). The Noble Studio (Burn City Movement 2020a) was therefore created as a way to acknowledge that *'community plays a big part'* and ideally, having such spaces available is *'about inspiring these kids [some of the ones getting in trouble], that they can do better. See a better way out'* (Kiir). The studio helped fill a gap in music production but recognised gap in the ability to produce live public performances across Naarm remained (Marley).

Excessive risk-management processes such as having to pay a larger bond or maintain an increased police presence meant that African diaspora groups found it difficult when hiring venues. Many of these groups feel frustrated at the generic responses when not all African communities in Australia have been involved in media and political rhetoric, which they blame for these reactions. These processes are a result of racialising discourses questioning whether large groups of young SSAs can be present in public space due to discourses of criminality and the contestation of public space. BCM have the vision that *'if we want change we have to do it ourselves'* (Marley).

At the same time, they wish to address the view of their parents, elders, or guardians and the broader community that participating in Hip Hop as a hobby or a career is a waste of time (Marley). Marley, in a group interview with his BCM artist crew, envisages as an aim of their artivism having *'people of all different cultures and backgrounds, and different ages, being together and just enjoying the sense of belonging'*. Creating a space like this studio space was necessary as 'Melbourne culture would have to find a way to welcome people of all backgrounds' for them to 'feel comfortable utilising . . . spaces to use together' (Johnson 2019). Sadly, during the onset of the COVID-19 pandemic in 2020, *BCM* had to give up the lease for the studio, and all live performances and projects were cancelled. This experience typifies the ongoing struggle for artists in the community. This demonstrates the significant challenges that African diaspora communities in particular face when engaging in and leading 'pro-social activities' in *little publics*. The following section outlines how this setting led to the building of political voice for young SSAs through forms of Hip Hop expression and the development of counter-narratives explored in chapter 5 regarding 'being different in public'.

DEVELOPMENT OF POLITICAL VOICE

Dominant hegemonic practices attempt to normalise a set of categories to understand reality in social contexts. Essentially, this results in various antagonisms emerging, which have been described in this chapter. These antagonisms necessitate the 'need for new actors and discourses to present a more well-rounded view of society in its multiple representations' (Escobar 1992, 404). In response to these phenomena, social agents are left to embark on a meaning-making expedition through the building of collective identities that can articulate what these experiences mean to them (Escobar 1992). I was awed by the intellectualism and charm of BTSO artivists who have 'beautiful mind(s)' (Jenkins 2011, 1). Some of my interviewees posed thought-provoking ideas when discussing their own conscientisation journey in relation to this process. Because of the inspirational, wise, and thought-provoking content I was hearing, I wondered, 'was I just meeting with Tupac?' (Fieldnotes 2019).

Whilst there are many sub-genres within Hip Hop, this research conceives of 'political voice' as demonstrated through the social agency of young SSA Hip Hop artists. The two sub-genres focused on in the next few chapters (4–6) are 'conscious Hip Hop', also known as 'message Hip Hop', and 'political rap Hip Hop', which came about because rap gave marginalised groups the opportunity to assert their voices (Oware 2018; Bonnette 2015).

Throughout the following, I use Bonnette's (2015, 25) method of identifying a demonstration of political voice in Hip Hop for the criteria I use to analyse the Hip Hop tracks that BTSO artivists' produce and whether they are relevant to my research topic. This includes whether there is a reference to either a 'social issue', a 'political reference' or whether the track poses a 'solution' (see figure 3.1 below). Specifically, the issues referred to are relevant to black communities in Australia and provide information about injustices community members face.

With this in mind, the next section explores research participants' opinions on whether they feel they have a political voice and how they developed it.

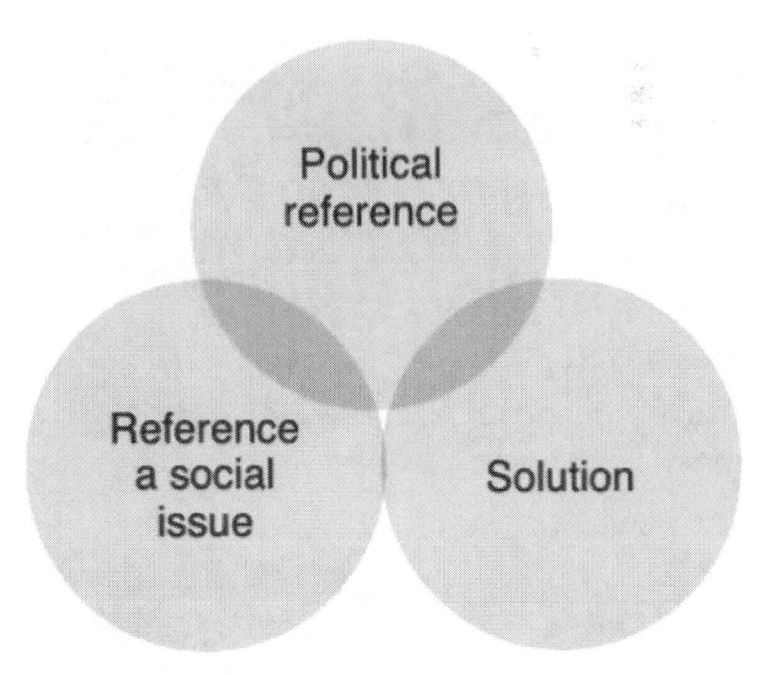

Figure 3.1 Categorising Political Rap Songs. *Source*: Bonnette 2015.

DO YOUNG SOUTH SUDANESE AUSTRALIANS HAVE A POLITICAL VOICE?

My synthesis and analysis identified that there were three key themes discussed about the status of young SSAs' sense of voice. Firstly, *Titan* (cited in Moyo 2019, 1) pinpoints that in his community:

> we realised, we do not really have a voice. Every time we wanted to say something, or every time something happened within the community it had to go to another person's platform and they controlled what we said. They controlled our voice and they took away our stories.

In recognition of this, *Titan* advocates for local voices to be heard in his community. Alternatively, Emmanuel appears frustrated at often being asked to be a spokesperson for his community:

> *I believe and I think we all do . . . have a voice. It's just that some people are placed in the position where we don't want to be the ones who are having to justify what's happening within the community because there's a lot of (I hate saying it but) ignorant people in society yeah and there's people who do believe everything they see in the media.*

Finally, Gabriel appears to take a pragmatic approach and believes that it is possible to have a voice in some spaces but not others:

> *Social media has allowed us to have a voice, because if you have a strong message . . . people can hate but you can't ignore it. . . . Before the social media era it was hard because you had to get an audience to listen to you. . . . But as far as amongst the powers that be, I do not think we have a voice on some platforms such as A Current Affair [mainstream news program].*

Participants' senses of voice, which involves freedom of self-expression and evolvement into political voice, was developed through several means, as captured in table 3.1.

In order to project one's voice, music was chosen by Emmanuel as '*the most powerful tool and effective way*' to be able to '*touch people because so many people, regardless of the age, ethnicity, listen to music*'. He shared why he chose Hip Hop in particular:

> *I do it because it enables me to express myself. At the same time being an artist, I am able to put myself in an environment or space where I normally wouldn't, or people wouldn't usually put me in that place. When I'm doing things on stage,*

I'm expressing myself, but sometimes artists are also there to entertain people. That's where Hip Hop comes in as an art form to be able to express myself.

The majority of BTSO artivists did not see themselves as political rap artists; however, they produced music with a political or conscious message when experiences in life or society meant they felt they needed to speak out about

Table 3.1 Participants Development of Their Sense of 'Voice' and Political Voice

Development of Voice and Political Voice	Application
School	Malual was encouraged by his teacher to write haikus (a type of poetry) in year 5.
	Emmanuel's teacher suggested he do music as a career after seeing something special in him.
	Gabriel developed his voice in high school, sticking up for himself and other young people from similar backgrounds. He educated himself on his rights.
Youth Programs/ Mentorship	Amina got out of her comfort zone, started writing music and poetry, and joined some of Footprints' projects during high school.
	Nyok started attending youth programs where he started to learn how to rap. He was taught by a mentor.
	Sam and Akra noted as youth workers, that many young people do not conceive of themselves as having a political voice.
	Political voice is not necessarily the terminology they would use. They do observe young people expressing themselves through Hip Hop.
	Veronica suggests that youth services host many programs focused around 'youth voice'.
Strategic settings	Abiel considered using his political voice diplomatically and strategically when working in state government and co-leading a youth organisation.
	Malek spoke about the necessity to 'control' his political voice. He shared how he started using it before he really understood how to strategise with it. He now understands that if he has the heart to create change, he will use it.
Through creativity	Mumor found his voice through creativity and making films.
	Amir started listening to U.S. artist Immortal Technique, a political rap artist, and went on to study politics at university.

(Continued)

Table 3.1 (Continued)

Development of Voice and Political Voice	Application
Community issues	Jamal noted that a lot of artists write from their frustrations to create change. He points to the consciousness-raising journey he went on as an artist before he was able to simplify key messages for his community and audience to understand.
	Felicia saw how issues affected her community and wanted to be heard.
	Khalid was focused on finding a solution for his community in South Sudan and creates global awareness around well-being and conflict resolution.
Developed over time	Akur grew up 'minding her own business' but developed her political voice over time. Now she runs workshops at schools to help other young people understand their importance.
Developed leadership capacity/ philosophical approach	Shaker once ran for the local Council. As he identified as a leader, one example he recalled was that there were always people following somehow including many of his peers.
	Abdul believed he must be true to himself, and no matter what he does, it has a consequence.

it either for personal or public purposes. This falls within the more common understanding of this genre. Because of its 'underground nature' (i.e., not often performed in mainstream settings), political rap represents an information source that

> many segments of the population do not have regular access to. Therefore, minority rap fans may possess first-hand experiences that give them the perspective to understand and interpret the information presented. (Bonnette 2015, 27)

Participants such as Tina saw the influential value of Hip Hop, as once a 'beat' or a 'lyric' hits your ears, it can be like an '*earworm*' that never goes away. Likewise, political rap music assists in an 'information transference by providing political information and social commentary' (Bonnette 2015, 27). The information is in turn 'received and interpreted by listeners' (Bonnette 2015, 27).

Tina loved the way that forms of Hip Hop can be used to not only express oneself but '*it can be offensive to authority, it can be brash, it can be outspoken*'. Participants spoke extensively about the challenges of developing their political voice. The most common challenges include knowing the most suitable and safe forum to express oneself authentically, facing significant backlash and race-based gaslighting (making someone question their own reality) through societal responses; personal challenges, facing hardships, and rising above; and internal challenges within cultural communities. Some of these challenges are also depicted in BTSO artivists' lyrics. Whilst there are many messages that Hip Hop lyrics might portray, the next section details a topic *'the system ain't playing'* which is a lyric from SSA artist *Krown* (2018).[31] This lyric and topic establish a relevant setting for all subsequent chapters in understanding young SSAs' experiences of racialising discourses.

MESSAGE TO THE SOUTH SUDANESE YOUTH – 'THE SYSTEM AIN'T PLAYING'

Critical Race Theory is a derivative of critical theory, which uses Marxian analysis, amongst other sociological and philosophical traditions, to challenge power structures by arguing that social problems are influenced and created more by societal structures and cultural assumptions than by individual and psychological factors (Ritzer 2005; Habermas 2007[1987]). Modelled on the work of critical theorists such as Freire (2018[1968]), who drew from African thinkers and political actors, the social movement of *critical pedagogy* allows oppressed peoples to depict a counter-story to experiences of systemic oppression by naming one's own reality. In the case of this monograph, Hip Hop as a form of storytelling illuminates lived experiences of racial oppression (Gosa 2011). It is not enough for the artist to analyse societal power structures and hierarchies, to merely recognise imbalance and inequity; critical pedagogy must also empower the listener to reflect and act on that reflection to challenge an oppressive status quo (Akom 2009; Freire et al. 2018[1968]).

This section explores the response of SSA Hip Hop artists to racialising discourses, their interactions with 'the system', and the message they would like to share with BIPOC young people. In this case, the focus is on the youth justice system but extends to other aspects of society. In his track 'Let Us Live', SSA artist *Krown* (2018)[32], expects the listener and his peers to mark his words.

To my young n***a's play your cards right
Because the system ain't playing.

Krown's claims that the *'system ain't playing'* is referring specifically to mainstream right-wing-leaning media and politicians, the influential perpetrators of racialising discourses (see chapter 6), who form what he sees as the main power structures in a neoliberal society. As described in this chapter, 'the system' (to which Whiteness and racialising discourses are significant contributors) has a profound impact on young SSAs' lives and is therefore 'not playing [fairly]' due to necessary strategic intent (Williams 2022). In this system, the elite whites are the powerholders, and they need to maintain that level of power to keep control, which necessitates that power be taken from others. Thus, inequity is a necessary part of maintaining privilege for certain groups (Hohle 2018). This aligns with a CRT analysis, showing how forms of racism are created on purpose for the elite (Kendi 2019).

In consideration of strategic benefits for elites, this lyric *'system ain't playing'* and the theme of the track *'Let Us Live'* (Krown 2018)[33] display similarities to an early Hip Hop song with conscious lyrics 'The Message' by Grandmaster Flash in 1982.[34] U.S. artist Grandmaster Flash reflects on the systemic imbalances for BIPOC when living in the boroughs of New York and his experiences of facing the system. He states in the chorus: *'It's like a jungle sometimes it makes me wonder how I keep from going under'*. This track marks the change in sensibility from party tracks to political ones that depict 'ghetto life' as 'profoundly desolate' (Jenkins 2011, 2).

For urban youth living in Naarm who may relate to these experiences, figure 3.2 depicts SSA artist *Élkato* (2019)[35] standing in the centre of Naarm CBD. *Élkato* has a similar *'message to the youth'* where she advises, *'don't get stuck in the Matrix'*. These lyrics refer to the 'system' and insert extracts from the popular film *The Matrix* such as *'you've got to decide which pill to take'* (e.g., whether to stay ignorant or become 'woke' to the truth that this system exists and we have a role to play in it). In figure 3.2, *Élkato* is depicted in the city of Naarm wearing a black outfit like the character Neo in the film; she has a message for society. In her track, *Élkato* suggests that *'living in the Matrix is like a simulation of the mind'* whereby *'they only televised what they want us to know. It's part of their tactics. They don't want us to grow'*. She describes the ways she sees society play out in the system to *'exclude and divide'* whilst *'brainwashing the youth'* (Élkato 2019; Mills-and-Boom 2020).[36]

Drawing on her experiences, the systems and institutions described by *Élkato* in 'The Matrix' track include the education system and the youth justice system, which can involve the *school-to-prison pipeline* and the *prison-industrial complex*. These criminalising processes involve black and brown children or teenagers being exposed to marginalising practices in predominantly public-school systems. Exposure to these practices commonly results in what is claimed to be deviant behaviour, suspensions, and a one-stop or revolving trip to the prison system. This results in an over-representation of black and brown people in the prison system (Oluo 2018, 124–133). In addition, in her power analysis of 'the system', *Élkato's* lyrics refer to *identity*

Figure 3.2 Artist Élkato Standing at the Intersection of Federation Square and Flinders St Station, Naarm CBD. *Source*: Kimberley Summer.

politics playing tricks (Williams 2022). The notion of identity politics playing tricks was also derived from further findings of the PhD research explored in this monograph (addressed in chapter 4), which observed young SSA Hip Hop artists' discernment of their diaspora identities against the backdrop of a nation that often displays a political agenda about their presence (Williams 2022).

Élkato (2019) further elaborates on her own experiences of identity politics through how the rules of the system in the context of socio-political disadvantage apply to some and not others; these include the politics of privilege from those who benefit and perpetuate this system which are *'blind to oppressions'*. Other examples under the context of necropolitics include Australia's immigration and citizenship system, which she likens to *'assimilation of the mind'* or *'being imprisoned'*. Her lyrics outline that the everyday roles played by people living in this system involve what might seem to be mundane lives as *'robots'* or as *'mental slaves'*. Along with other institutions that claim a lot of power, this study highlights the influential power of mainstream media as a force of control. As such, artists refer to the *'cruel world'* and highlight that the might of the systems that oppress them is *'leading to depression'* (Élkato 2019; Mills-and-Boom 2020).[37]

The lyric *'the system ain't playing'* (Krown 2018)[38] has wide implications for what this study asserts are some of the root causes of 'defiant and antisocial behaviour in black and brown youth' (Oluo 2018, 132). With this in mind, *Élkato* warns future generations about *'being controlled'* or not following *'misleading dreams'* where she claims you might be considered the enemy of wider society if you are *'spitting the truth'* (Élkato 2019; Mills-and-Boom 2020).[39] Through her need to develop her own political voice through Hip Hop expression, she urges young people to become 'woke' (conscious) by understanding:

They're trying to tame our souls
They want to chain us all
We need to claim our souls.

(Élkato 2019; Mills-and-Boom 2020)[40]

Élkato's track 'The Matrix' explains her consciousness-raising journey by examining social relations of daily life. Her conscious Hip Hop track has implications for exploring the 'question of the meaning of political practice in daily life' and 'how and where systems of social and cultural relations are articulated with mechanisms of power and what are the mechanisms of inter-mediation' (Escobar 1992, 408). Utilising Hip Hop as a form of expression, this track in effect applies critical social theory (Ritzer 2005; Habermas 1987) to present a counter-narrative or 'truth-telling' process through critiquing social constructions and postmodern society (Hill-Collins 2002, 2013; Gosa 2011). This has further implications for the development of political voice through processes whereby young people individually and collectively go on a consciousness-raising journey to articulate their resistance to the system, shape their own futures, and display alternatives through self-determination. This chapter has defined the conditions that young SSAs face in relation to racialising discourses which have led to a range of responses explored in the following chapters.

URBAN PORTRAYALS OF YOUNG SOUTH SUDANESE AUSTRALIANS IN RADICAL CONTEXT

This chapter has presented urban portrayals of young SSAs described in the *radical context* when considering a critical and system's analysis of their experiences in Australia (Dimitriadis 2007a). I have pointed to the need to look at larger social constructs (such as systemic racism) and question why broader social issues form as a result (Dimitriadis 2007c). Yet, at the same time, I acknowledge that to find freedom, one must locate oneself in the 'struggle'. This work is important for understanding the social landscape of young people who identify with urban youth culture in Australia. The significance of this is the study's ability to address the research aims of better understanding how young people conceive of and navigate this experience, specifically, how they enact and maintain agency and resilience in response to racialising discourses.

This identifies the need to 'untangle the traditional isomorphic relationship between space, place, and culture when addressing the needs of [potentially] disenfranchised youths' (Dimitriadis 2007b, 117). Hickey-Moody (2013a) discusses how *little publics* can be spaces very much aligned to social or political norms and hegemonic agendas. Kendi (2019, 167–169) notes that some of these agendas can include outdated notions such as 'integrationist or segregationist strategies' or they can be 'spaces of resistance; or indeed conflicted political sites brought together around shared aesthetic or intellectual concerns that unite politically divergent communities'. He also warns of 'racialised spaces', which include holding racist ideas of the dangerous black neighbourhood or maintaining resource inequity through creating a racial hierarchy of space (Kendi 2019, 167–169).

Through the presentation of young SSAs' complex interpersonal, political, cultural and personal narratives growing up in urban youth culture, this chapter has explored the diversity of experiences and has created space for multiple and competing viewpoints to emerge simultaneously. The Hip Hop lyrics and BTSO artivists' viewpoints presented in this chapter have identified new knowledge about young SSAs' sense of agency that extends and complements current urban youth scholarship by presenting anti-deficit narratives. It also points to policy and best practice reform in several key areas, such as the application of culture-centred approaches to youth work practice and urban youth studies with a system's analysis in mind.

This chapter has demonstrated that 'questions about daily life, democracy, the state, and the redefinition of political practice and development are closely interrelated' (Escobar 1992, 408). As a result, a range of responses is evident, such as requests by young SSAs to have the freedom to live their lives in peace, or as this research demonstrates, a range of creative responses derived from the overall themes of being BTSO and alternative forms of artivism, which I will explore in subsequent chapters.

Chapter 4 builds on the contextual base provided in this chapter and examines how young SSAs reclaim their identities in response to, or through bypassing racialising discourses by going on a consciousness-raising journey. Through this process, they find meaning and comfort within their African diaspora cultural roots and by exploring their Blackness.

NOTES

1. Sampa the Great (2020) performance of 'Black Power' at her Black Atlantis set at Planet Afropunk, Anastasia Tsobanopoulis: https://www.youtube.com/watch?v=Mx2a9s3mOgU. See blog post #1.
2. See Notes '1'.
3. Daniel Elia (2017) 'Shook' (official video), ALIA Records: https://www.youtube.com/watch?v=R7jriGuHdk0. See blogpost #10.

4. 'Afri–CAN' (2019) produced by *Malesh P* - GUA Project - AfriCAN.mp3. See blogpost #2.

Created by workshop facilitator Malesh P at Gua Performance and Leadership Camp hosted by Footprints in January, 2019.

(*Ululating in background)
Intro:
Descendants from the land of jewels
Diamonds and pendants
God's gift in the presence of Kings and Queens

Chorus: (layered chorus with everyone's voices x 2)
I'm always trying to do the best I can
Gotta represent for the Motherland
Pure blood running through my veins
Oh yeah, I'm an African

Verse 1: (Élkato)
I just do it for South Sudan
I just do it for the Motherland
Pure blood running through my veins
Because I'm an African
My identity defines who I am
A black female who's misunderstood
I know about the struggles because I grew up in the hood
I'm trying to get our message through I hope it's understood
We represent the people and we know we're doing good
Ah, yeah we know we're doing good!

Verse 2: (i.OG)
I'm an African descendant
Don't dirty my skin, I meant it
Racism is still cemented
Within the minds of the generations
We gotta spark the change
So the change can be amended, so the change can be amended
Check my identity, power through poverty
Always tell the truth so they never could bother me
Look at the modesty, check the reality,
take a look at the mirror and see who is the minority

Chorus: (layered chorus with everyone's voices x 2)
I'm always trying to do the best I can
Gotta represent for the Motherland

Pure blood running through my veins
Oh yeah, I'm an African

Verse 3: Spoken-word Adlib (Karabo)
She approaches me with hate
Bringing generalisations, stereotypes, violence to my blackness, my soul
He brings with him sorrow, anger, confusion, darkness,
molten lava seeping through my veins
Something I can't escape
They take away my ability to love, to feel harmony
Surrounding me with rain and thunder
Cautioning my step
Their name is RACISM

Verse 4: FLEXX
Well check the veins
A trail of the Motherland
Got a big heart, soul and ambition
Way too persistent
You hate us, that's basic
We got love for all faces
Damn, we're amazing
Melanin be poppin'
If you're 20/20 with your vision
If you look at us, black excellence
My style you took that
My skin you check that
But one thing, for a fact, you were never going to take Black
Blessed

Chorus: (layered chorus with everyone's voices x 2)
I'm always trying to do the best I can
Gotta represent for the Motherland
Pure blood running through my veins
Oh yeah, I'm an African

Verse 5: (Wiaa)
My blackness precedes me
We were destined from the start
With persistence we bring resistance, revolutionary at heart
Through culture and history, we march on to victory
You are limitless to all my sisters, lets break prejudice through art

Bridge: (Akimera)
Yeah, yeah, yeah, yeah,

Yeah, yeah, yeah, yeeeeeeaaah

Verse 6: (Malesh P)
Ah, no road is long enough for me to not take
No word is strong enough for me to not break
For many years my Africans have been excluded and denied of our rights
But the same people we influence

Marginalised, in the band my accessories
You can hate on me but you cannot get rid of me
I carry my flag so I can represent for my ancestors
Who hung up their soul so we can hang our Masters up!

Chorus: (layered chorus with everyone's voices x 2)
I'm always trying to do the best I can
Gotta represent for the Motherland
Pure blood running through my veins
Oh yeah, I'm an African

Verse 7: Spoken-word Adlib (Sarah)
We all need to be aware of the space that we fill
I really want to be a person that's kind of chill
I want to use my resources for good
But with permission
To join in the vision and future steps
But to be able to listen

Outro: Ululating

5. Queen P (2018) 'Black Panther', from her Bring Black Back EP, Queen P: https://open.spotify.com/album/5jKDhvX8Yt2iHXdRUlFHnd?si=iEgYAou-QCqagcp0eY8Ohg.
   See blogpost #3.
6. Burn City Movement (BCM) (2020) 'Trials n' Tribulations (TNT)' featured in Burn City Movement's Realness for Sale EP, Noble Studios: https://tidal.com/browse/album/131189065.
   See blogpost #4.
7. Daniel Elia (2017) 'Lonely' (Remix), ALIA Records: https://www.youtube.com/watch?v=Qb4gzkFKQI0.
   See blogpost #5.
8. Titan (2019) 'Ghetto Tears', performance at Yah Yah's bar, Titan Debirioun:
   See blogpost #6.

*Ghetto what? *[crowd responds] Ghetto tears*
Ghetto what? Ghetto tears

Ghetto what? Ghetto tears

I spend my life with the wisdom
It's the plate I was given
It seems every situation I was in I was sinning
Don't you . . .
Don't you look at me different
I've had the Masters since the beginning
This ain't the life I've been living
All our rhymes have been taken
My life has been taken
But no one sees greatness when I finally make it
and live my life educated
So please won't you try
All you teachers are biased
All the lessons I learned are like David and Goliath
It's funny how they treat me
The colour on the t.v. is what they call me
I do it for my culture, my music is for my RiRi
I'm dancing for my young G's
I'm realer for my OG's
The struggle of the black man
Living by the goddamn rules of the white man
With plans for his white fam
. . .
It's sad how I am treated
Got a plan for you n****'s who can't be defeated
It's sad how I am treated
Got a plan for you n****'s who can't be defeated

[Hook]
Everywhere we seem to go
Ghetto tears on my lowest notes
Tears for my little bro
Tears for my Mama too
Pray for a miracle
Everywhere we seem to go
Ghetto tears on my lowest notes
Tears for my little bro
Tears for my Mama too
Pray for a miracle

My . . . was strong
That's what tragedy does

Pretend I don't see you
But tragedy look
Imagine you love
Poverty look
Because that's what helps you to breath
Like I carry these lungs

This is how I do
Straight to rushing through these days
Progressing through the cave
If I don't give you a dime you could soon look away
God never sees us when we pray so we gotta be like in Jesus
. . .

But it seems like we overlooked
And these demons got us really shook

[Hook]
Everywhere we seem to go
Ghetto tears on my lowest notes
Tears for my little bro
Tears for my Mama too
Pray for a miracle
Everywhere we seem to go
Ghetto tears on my lowest notes
Tears for my little bro
Tears for my Mama too
Pray for a miracle
*Ghetto what? *[crowd responds] Ghetto tears*
Ghetto who? Ghetto tears
Ghetto what? Ghetto tears
You're all lit

    9. Burn City Movement (BCM) (2020) 'Scary Hours' feat. A1 Krashn, featured in Burn City Movement's *Realness for Sale* EP, Noble Studios: https://tidal.com/browse/album/131189065.
    See blogpost #7.
    10. Titan (2019) 'Fuck Channel Seven' [news network], performance at Yah Yah's bar, Titan Dibirioun:
    See blogpost #8.

[Titan] Fuck Channel Seven
[*crowd responds] Fuck Channel Seven
[Titan responds] Fuck Channel Seven

11. Daniel Elia (2017) 'Shook' (Official Video), ALIA Records: https://www.youtube.com/watch?v=R7jriGuHdk0.
See blogpost #12.
12. Sudo Boiz (2010) 'Memory's Lane', Sudo Boiz: https://www.reverbnation.com/sudoboiz/song/8938324–memorys-lane.
See blogpost #9.
13. Titan (2020), 'Cheques and Balances', GRID Series: https://www.youtube.com/watch?v=oBjfFvsdP6w&feature=emb_logo;
https://open.spotify.com/album/4mNPnY2Tl2WomjI9FircUe?si=BN6QKnBXQcaUBZrXGFBrGw.
See blogpost #10.
14. See notes '8'.
15. See notes '8'.
16. See notes '8'.
17. See notes '8'.
18. See notes '8'.
19. See notes '8'.
20. Cole, J. (2014) 'No Role Modelz', Roc Nation: https://www.youtube.com/watch?v=S8N92GGzfLY&list=RDLuRa25RSwyQ&index=8.
See blogpost #11.
21. *Vision from the Kitchen:* This phrase is used to 'describe a mental place where your brain is running at its highest level of power. In the zone x10. After marinating on something, you find yourself IN THE KITCHEN!' https://www.urbandictionary.com/define.php?term=In%20the%20Kitchen.
22. See Notes '2'. Elia, D. (2016) Visions from my kitchen (Feat. Wantu ThaOne) [Explicit]. ALIA Records: https://www.youtube.com/watch?v=9cWgnlCyF3A.
23. After their launch in 2007, the African Mic Controllers (AMCs) were one of the first well-known South Sudanese Hip Hop groups in Naarm. They formed the AMCs group to express themselves through music. They describe how this is the only way they can tell the world who they are and what they are facing in their new country, Australia.

https://myspace.com/africanmiccontrollers; https://www.youtube.com/watch?v=4CDM234i3us; https://www.youtube.com/watch?v=Vs9mOWxlk9Q&fbclid=IwAR34FNc3oUI87ytnkeIE-4-UWviUR-hv6GFczfuG8gY14d3JDMsfVnbTn1k.

After their debut, they then became the Esenadus Squad in 2011–2012. https://www.facebook.com/esenadussquad/; https://vimeo.com/47992451; https://www.youtube.com/watch?v=2_LaNCDX5Cg; https://www.youtube.com/watch?v=KNZr6GzpAmw

Malesh P was a member of these groups and is now a solo artist: https://www.youtube.com/channel/UCHWHInT-L5reQ27Q5so47oQ; https://maleshp.com/about.
24. Malesh P and Tebir (2016), 'Why are We?', Malesh P: https://www.facebook.com/junubtv/videos/1828025160800691.
See blogpost #13.
25. See Notes '3'.
26. Malesh P (2016) 'Hope', Malesh P: https://soundcloud.com/malesh/10-hope.

See blogpost #14.

27. See Notes '24'.
28. See Notes '24'.
29. See Notes '26'.
30. See Notes '4'.
31. Krown (2018) 'Let us Live', Military Mind: https://www.youtube.com/watch?v=lxjsHiLgFJs.

See blogpost #15.

32. See Notes '31'.
33. See Notes '31'.
34. Grandmaster Flash (1982) 'The Message', Sugar Hill Records: https://www.youtube.com/watch?v=PobrSpMwKk4.

See blogpost #16.

35. Élkato (2020) 'The Matrix', YSAS Studios: https://soundcloud.com/user-940608762/lkato-matrix.

See blogpost #17.

36. See Notes '35'.
37. See Notes '35'.
38. See Notes '31'.
39. See Notes '35.
40. See Notes '35'.

Chapter 4

'Oh Yeah, I Am African'

Identity Politics and Celebrating Blackness in the Consciousness-Raising Journey

Hip Hop artist Sampa the Great's line: *'We are our own freedom'* (Sampa-the-Great 2020c)[1] discussed in the previous chapter sets the tone for this chapter and aligns directly with the 'born to stand out' (BTSO) motto and central theme of this study. Sampa's music video for this track responds to the concept of Afrofuturism (Barber et al. 2018). As mentioned briefly in chapter 2, Afrofuturism is a cultural aesthetic envisioning the liberation of black futures stemming from Afrodiasporic experiences in urban contemporary music and visuals. Sampa's music video is an example of how both popular and underground cultures feature forms of identity politics in art (Potter 2012). One of Sampa's social media posts following her ARIA win and her livestreamed performance boldly states, 'we not walking back [*sic*], the future has been here' (Sampa-the-Great 2020a). This statement along with Sampa's carefully curated music videos and live performances are a nod to Afrofuturism in that they present futuristic science-fiction visuals and allude to the hopes and dreams of the black-African diaspora and pride in culture (Yusuf 2018; Sampa-the-Great 2020b).

Focused on black nationalistic intercultural identities amongst young SSAs who discuss some of these themes, this chapter utilises Dutta's (2011, 2012, 2015a, 2015b, 2018, 2020) CCA to discuss the first step of participating in an identity-based New Social Movement (NSM) – the consciousness-raising journey. Research participants conducted this step through the Gua Performance and Leadership Camp as part of Footprints' Grounded Project. Dutta (2015a, 2015b) insists that theorising about communication ought to locate culture at the centre of the communication process such that the theories are contextually embedded and co-constructed through dialogue with the cultural participants. Dutta's recommended approach informs the pivotal process of consciousness-raising, in which research participants discuss their experiences with identity politics and racialising discourses.

Secondly, the ways that young SSAs determine their own pathways through articulating their own black identity development leading to Black Consciousness is analysed through Bulhan's (1985) three stages of *black identity development* and cross-referenced with Cross' (1971) *black consciousness development theory*, which, on the other hand, has five stages discussed in this chapter.

This chapter addresses the second sub-question – *What role does Hip Hop specifically play in building political voice?* Furthermore, through narrative and arts-based inquiry, this focus points to a more nuanced understanding of their identity politics and development of political voice, whereby research findings point to more implicit and subtle expressions of political voice through celebration of Blackness and culture. Hip Hop tracks identifying identity politics are featured in this chapter to demonstrate how young SSAs negotiate the everyday scenarios depicted in chapter 4 in relation to the system, and what messages they wish to share regarding their aspirations for the future.

After briefly surveying social indicators setting the scene for the need for young SSAs to develop their political voice, the next section details two focus groups and three artistic workshops utilising CHHP in order for Gua camp participants to go on a consciousness-raising journey. Following this, the subsequent sections draw on participant interviews, BTSO artivist quotes, and artefacts as I sought to understand young SSAs communities' views on the many facets of their social identities through their Hip Hop personas. This chapter therefore discusses one of the key findings from the CHHP workshops: that the BTSO artivists featured in this research see themselves through the lens of 'identity as calling' (Sawyer 2006). Understanding this facet of their identity, developed primarily through consciousness-raising activities, helped me to understand how participants instigated alternative forms of artivism, which are presented in chapters 5–6.

RESISTANCE – NEW SOCIAL MOVEMENTS THROUGH CRITICAL HIP HOP PEDAGOGY

Forms of resistance and youth political voice that challenge race politics as defined through CRT are deployed to investigate how young SSAs are critically negotiating and resisting these conditions via arts-based expression of political voice through the sub-genre of conscious Hip Hop. This section details how the concepts of NSM theory and CHHP advance CRT perspectives and are used to analyse the forms of political voice that young SSAs express. The CCA is examined as the site of social change in the context of the YPAR hosted by Footprints and outlined further in chapter 2. Barriers to free expression of political voice are also outlined with the discussion of the notions of identity politics.

My interest lies in exploring what happens when young SSAs utilise their creative agency and political voice to influence society through a public art project, using Hip Hop culture as a vehicle to express their individual and collective cultural identities. This artistic process allows opportunities to bring others into the collective space. Alongside Dimitriadis (2007b), I focus on the political agency of urban youth (namely SSAs) and the ways in which they negotiate the complexities of race, class, gender, and the broader politics of alleged difference. In the next sections, I describe their actions (whether conscious or not) as being involved in an NSM and what the nature of an NSM looks like, articulating a gap in knowledge around how urban youth choose to articulate their experiences. This is achieved through their own self-determination and sense of agency and through further identifying their aspirations and anxieties via creativity, imagination, and alternative forms of artivism by means of their Hip Hop personas.

This monograph draws on the story of civil rights for BIPOC around the globe, including Australia, using a strengths-based and self-determination approach. It asserts that young people have the agency and skills within themselves to determine their own futures whilst discussing the practical applications of young SSAs seeking to build their political voice to actively resist racialising discourses through participation in an NSM. Dimitriadis (2007b) and Green (2016) pinpoint 'urban youth agency' amongst structural forces such as racial segregation and economic development that attempt to push them to the sidelines of social discourse. Rather than being pushed to the sidelines, the BTSO artivists participating in this research demonstrate how they build their power to resist racialising discourses.

As young people move to build and enact their voice, Dimitriadis (2007b, 114) highlights the complexity of needing to 'understand more specifically how they are negotiating their way – or not – in these new economic times'. He determines that a myriad of actions could be taken by young people as a result. These can include undertaking the notion of 'resistance' or forms of 'dissent' in what he classifies as 'gang culture'. An alternative could be demonstrating more creative ways to 'resist dominant culture and its logics' (Dimitriadis 2007b, 114). This monograph aligns with Dimitriadis' (2007a) quest to understand the long-term implications of this resistance and the ethical obligations we owe to young people as a result.

The idea that young people have agency despite apparent disenfranchisement is now well-established amongst social scientists (Allan and Duckworth 2018; Checkoway and Gutierrez 2006; Wyn and Woodman 2006; Greene,

Burke, and McKenna 2016). However, much less is known about what types of agency young people might demonstrate (Wray-Lake and Abrams 2020) and what barriers to participation and freedom they might face (Burke, Greene, and McKenna 2017; Sen 2001[1999]). Rather than deficit approaches depicting young SSAs as apathetic to their cause (Majavu 2018), the following sections explore how the concept of NSMs is used to describe how BIPOC young people, specifically young SSAs, enact agency by challenging representations made about them. For example, through the umbrella of NSM, CHHP was chosen to help analyse the first step of building an NSM and political voice. This is followed by the CCA which details the second step of building an NSM through arts-based community development initiatives as another form of resistance. Finally, the goal of participation in this iterative NSM is to address the topic of how being BTSOmanifests through Hip Hop artivism. The process of BIPOC youth empowerment and self-determination can lead to community change but also present some challenges to which I shall now turn.

HIP HOP AS A NEW SOCIAL MOVEMENT – SITES FOR SOCIAL CHANGE FOR URBAN YOUTH

Individual and collective processes of consciousness-raising for young SSAs around cultural, national, and social identities may lead to the formation of social movements. It is important to address the causal role of identity in determining a variety of movement outcomes, such as the ability to form coalitions, which can develop due to inequality, exploitation, and oppression (Bernstein 2005). This sets the scene in terms of how young SSAs conceive of themselves, articulating a counter-narrative to racialising discourses or setting alternate narratives for themselves.

New Social Movement (NSM) theory attempts to explain mobilisation in terms of why and when people act (Bernstein 2005; Buechler 1995). Social movements that flourished in the 1960s and 1970s, such as the American civil rights and women's movements, were geared towards being more concerned with culture and identity than with challenging the class structure (Bernstein 2005, 49). NSM theory suggests that amongst the new swell of identity-based movements, participants 'fight to expand freedom, not to achieve it; they mobilise for choice rather than emancipation' and focus primarily on expressing identity to seek 'recognition for new identities and lifestyles' (Cerulo, Polletta and Jasper cited in Bernstein 2005, 54). Carroll (2017, 601) demonstrates that social movements are a 'productive site to examine race both as a lived experience and as a metalanguage of power' as they reflect an 'opportunity to embrace an intersectional understanding of identity and pursued coalitional politics'. Through focusing on the political practice of collective social actors, today's social movements are seen as 'playing a central role in producing the world in which we live, its social structures and practices, its meanings and cultural orientations, its possibilities for change' (Escobar 1992, 395–396).

Portrayed here are the cultural aspects of politics and resistance by depicting the ways in which Hip Hop artists shape their world through types of 'political activism' that include the 'fashioning of visions, symbols, and alternative meanings as much as concrete forms of mobilisation and organising' (Escobar 1992, 420). Rather than detached scholarship, this research aligns with the emerging direction in social movement scholarship which prioritises the praxis of movement-related work (Bevington and Dixon 2005). It therefore unveils a 'profound transformation in the structure of collective action and political practice, one that requires new concepts and modes of understanding' (Escobar 1992, 420). The following section on Hip Hop and NSMs addresses ways arts-based development projects can therefore position themselves amongst NSM-related work through dialogic spaces and whilst presenting counter-narratives to racialising discourses.

Focusing on everyday forms of resistance, NSMs are not always large social gestures (Touraine 1998; Scott 1985). For young SSAs involved in this research who may not be familiar with this theoretical terminology per se, they are aware of or have been involved in social movement practices such as the BLM movement protests; they do have or are building their political voice; due to the very nature of their political identities, they demonstrate a focus on issues related to human rights (a feature of an NSM); are interested in collective action for a social cause and have demonstrated affinities with norms of close social networks who discuss and participate in civil rights movement practices (E.M. Smith, González, and Frigolett 2021). This monograph demonstrates that young SSA Hip Hop artists have chosen Hip Hop culture as a form of expression, this takes the form of writing lyrics or performing insights into their day-to-day lives, dreamsdreams, or articulating another world is possible. From this perspective, social movements embody a 'new understanding of politics and social life itself' whereby they 'take place at the intersection of culture, practice (collective and everyday), and politics' (Escobar 1992, 396).

Of particular importance is the way in which young SSA artists have created individual Hip Hop tracks that represent their political voice through expression in conscious Hip Hop and joined an arts-based community development project – the Grounded Project (introduced in chapter 2). This project is considered as the framing of Hip Hop artivism and culture as an NSM as actors involve artivists with a political message based on their identity politics, organising together to create social change. This chapter addresses some of Hip Hop's long history with identity politics and necessitation for political voice and expression originating in the 1970s. This is a similar time period when NSMs based around racism and systemic inequity for BIPOC communities also evolved from civil rights movements in the United States. The determining factor between utilising Hip Hop culture to create awareness or becoming conscious of social causes and the cultural forms of Hip Hop being utilised for NSM purposes is the way the Grounded Project is constructed and the way Hip Hop artivists use their Hip Hop personas to organise forms of protest or forms of dissent (i.e., this could be through visuals in a music video, etc.). Other examples of young SSAs' participation in an NSM through forms of protest and dissent are explored in chapter 5. Specifically, the Grounded Project is a *standpoint project* stemming from a social position on racism and involving *transformative youth organising* (Ritzer 2005; Bautista 2018). Young SSAs' involvement demonstrates one aspect of their participation in an NSM utilising Hip Hop. The limits of their participation, discussing the tenets of transformative youth organising, are discussed.

Focusing on the everyday *consciousness-raising* activities (activities which inform participants in 'awakening' to issues of social injustice) results in the formation of individual and collective identities which foster social and cultural forms of relating and solidarity. These collective responses are developed in relation to the crises of meanings and economies circulating through world issues (Escobar 1992). Furthermore, young people are captured as the actors or everyday 'artivists' (artist + activist) in this research, disrupting the misconception that it is only the traditionally conceived activists (such as protesters) who participate or initiate social change (Bevington and Dixon 2005). MK Asante, a passionate poet, professor, filmmaker and activist, suggests that artivism in this case is conceived as the way in which Hip Hop culture is utilised as a vehicle to explore important social and political issues predominantly facing young Hip Hop generations (Asante 2008).

The artivist uses their artistic talents to 'fight and struggle against injustice and oppression – by any medium necessary' merging commitment to freedom and justice with the 'pen, the lens, the brush, the voice, the body, and the imagination' (Asante 2008, n.p.). The artivist knows that to 'make an observation is to have an obligation' (Asante 2008, n.p.). This definition fits into the developments of the Black Arts Movement, which erupted in the 1960s and 70s. This movement contributed to the development of revolutionary and cultural nationalism and politics whilst also changing American attitudes to the relationship between popular culture and 'high' art (Smethurst 2005; Colbert 2017; Fenderson 2019). This led to the conditions for the development of 'urban music' which was established through the foundation of Hip Hop.

HIP HOP CULTURE AND POLITICAL VOICE
EXPRESSION AS A FORM OF RESISTANCE

Hip Hop culture emerged in the 1970s from the experiences and practices of economically disadvantaged, historically oppressed, and marginalised African American, Latin, and African-Caribbean young people who formed a culture distinct from that of the dominant order in under-resourced urban communities in New York (Dimitriadis 1996; Oware 2018; Womack 2013; Morgan and Bennett 2011; Asante 2008).

On one level, some people of influence who contributed to the cultural form of Hip Hop demonstrated messaging of alternatives to gang violence. This is such as with Afrika Bombaataa and his formation of Zulu Nation after his exposure to the Black Liberation Movement and a trip to Africa where he witnessed communities of solidarity amongst Zulu tribal traditions (Rose 1994; Chang 2005). Similar to Bombaataa, who hosted parties in the Bronx bringing people together, another person of influence often recognised as the 'Father of Hip Hop' is DJ Kool Herc. Herc developed Hip Hop for entertainment purposes to provide a physical and often spiritual release (Dimitriadis 1996, 2001, 2015). The lyrics created a space to 'resist and challenge social ideologies, practices, and structures that have caused and maintained [an artist's] subordinate position' (Land and Stovall 2009, 1).

On another level, Hip Hop culture has not necessarily addressed or reduced gang violence with some records showing that gang violence along with violent crime increased. This is such with the introduction of sub-genres known as 'gangsta' or 'gangster rap' or the most recent variant of Hip Hop known as 'drill' or 'drill rap'. Lyrics in these sub-genres do often deal with street life and sometimes violent crime, using a particular street or urban vernacular (Lee et al. 2022). Many pioneers did not leave their gangs or end their gang involvement. The earliest recognised Hip Hop scholar, Rose (1994, 119), has, however, articulated that due to the social and economic conditions faced predominantly by communities of colour, Hip Hop artists are often recognised as 'prophets of rage'. This is through their predominant politics of black cultural expression by responding to forms of oppression in various ways. Overall, Hip Hop's complex history has demonstrated that the culture has contributed to interventions in cultural knowing and the formation of hybrid identities (Oware 2018; Keyes 2019; Whitaker 2021).

Hip Hop has been described as a dominant language of youth culture (Dimitriadis 2001). The global expressions of Hip Hop artists are seen to represent predominantly minority voices. Current expressions of Hip Hop are not exclusive to black culture and history (originating in the United States) but are intrinsically connected to the culture and history of oppression amongst black peoples, particularly those who identify with urban youth culture (Bonnette

2015), which is discussed in chapter 3. As Hip Hop originated from black culture in the United States and stemming from Afrodiasporic influences, many Indigenous Australians who might identify as Blak may also identify with this artform. This is due to the similarities between shared histories of racism and oppression between African American culture further and demonstrating nuances in combating systemic violence (Minestrelli 2017; Gooding et al. 2016). Young SSAs likewise describe similar but differentiated affiliations of Bla(c)kness with this popular and expressive artform in their creative reconstruction of their migrant identity (Moran 2016). This monograph describes how Australian representations of Bla(c)kness are, however, distinctive from, and can talk back to, U.S.-based theorists and nuanced experiences of racialising discourses. Specifically, the first way is through determining how young SSAs discern their own pathways to articulating their own black identity development (Bulhan 1985) which often is (but not always) Afrocentric. The second way is determining young SSAs' unique journey of developing their Black Consciousness (Cross 1971) through the necessity of developing their own vocabulary to talk back to racialising discourses. Young SSAs borrow the revolutionary black American language of Antiracism and popular culture as expressed through Hip Hop.

Harris (2017), however, warns against reinforcing stereotypes by assuming all African Australian young people like Hip Hop or know how to construct a rhyme or rap. Additionally, it is beyond the scope of this monograph to consider in depth the intersectional nature of Hip Hop which has been predominantly male-dominated since its inception and therefore largely had a focus on black male masculinity (Anderson and West 2011; Majors and Billson 1992). Whilst this is not a gendered study, similarly, chapter 2 details how primary research participants consisted of twenty-four male participants and four female participants who identify as young SSA artists or associate with Hip Hop urban youth culture. Primarily, research participants were chosen due to the fact that various forms of Australian Hip Hop are dominated by the male gender. Whilst there are a growing number of young SSA female emcees (Hip Hop artists), this artform and therefore research study consists of a cohort who predominantly identify as male.

Upon arrival in Australia, young SSA females tended to associate with beauty pageants such as Miss South Sudan (Harris 2017) due to the fact that skin colour is ideologically tied to beauty (Hunter 2005). Whilst the landscape is rapidly changing due to various forms of identity politics, addressed briefly, one of the master values of Hip Hop is to be 'cool', a performance of power that is aimed at making the black male visible (Majors and Billson 1992). According to Majors and Billson (1992, 5), being 'cool' is an 'ego booster for black males compared to the kind white males more easily find through attending good schools, landing prestigious jobs, and bringing home decent wages'. However, the 'cool pose' that Hip Hop encourages black males to adopt as part of their persona is often considered as 'consciously off-putting' or is regarded as 'thuggish' in the white liberal imagination (Anderson and West 2011, 3). Australian scholar Hickey-Moody (2013, 43) therefore warns that reinforcing notions of 'masculinised gangsta-like behaviour', a common theme of Hip Hop whereby lyrics assert the culture and values typical of American street gangs and street hustlers, may reinforce stereotypes of 'moral panic' or social marginalisation.

In this context, like the Black Arts Movement and the long history of message or protest music, Hip Hop was initially seen as the cultural extension of politics in black communities. Hip Hop is also linked to the Black power movement and forms of black nationalistic expression to resist racism, build awareness, increase solidarity, fight injustice, and maintain political and social movements (Hill-Collins 2006; Bonnette 2015). Political rap followed the model of uniting black/African Americans through music by discussing issues relevant to black communities and providing information about injustices the community members face, such as race relations (Pope 2020; Hill-Collins 2006).

The music of the Hip Hop generation, conventionally known as black people born after the American civil rights movement, was seen to be critical for knowledge, awareness, mobilisation, and action as a political agent (Bonnette 2015, 40). Pope (2020, 3) uses the term *Rap and Politics* (RAP) to examine the evolutionary discourse in rap music (the specific vocal delivery) through the frameworks of contextual setting, forms of representation, focus on movement building, discourse banks (collectives and collections of artefacts), and impact. RAP advances our understanding of underground rap music and black politics. Sub-genres of Hip Hop include gangster rap, socially conscious rap, politically conscious rap, and alternative rap. This research focuses on socially or politically conscious rap, which continued to evolve from its political roots in the American civil rights movement declaring racial justice messages, media, and discourse (Pope 2020). The purpose of this monograph is to describe how young SSAs speak and enact agency through forms of conscious Hip Hop expression. Conscious Hip Hop specifically refers to Hip Hop with a social message (Deon cited in Akom 2009; Gooding et al. 2016; Oware 2018). This is important as, although it can be expressed locally, Hip Hop is a cultural phenomenon that needs to be understood in a global context as a tool for affirming identity (Gooding et al. 2016; Dimitriadis 2015).

The presence of the actors in a performative space attaches a sense of urgency and action to performances (Dutta 2011). Clammer (2015, 123) highlights how culture can be used 'as a means of protest and affirmation' as well as a tool for dissent (Oware 2018; McGill 2018). This monograph provides examples of lyrics from young SSA Hip Hop artists featuring political, conscious Hip Hop. This type of music can be a form of popular literacy, a form of artivism, and a voice of resistance. There is a long history of socio-political conscious Hip Hop as a tool for 'illuminating problems of poverty, police brutality, patriarchy, misogyny, incarceration, racial discrimination, as well as love, hope, joy' (Akom 2009, 54). Conscious and political forms of Hip Hop are present in the most recent movements of young people forming in protest to racial justice issues. Examples described in this research include the Channel 7 protest, the #BlackLivesMatter movement, and other Black Power movements. As it pertains to a discussion on alternative forms of resistance through Hip Hop artivism, the Channel 7 Australian TV news network protest was arranged by two young SSA artists known as *Krown* and *Titan*. They used their Hip Hop personas to rally the general public in resistance to the continued targeting of young SSAs as being involved in 'African gangs' (Eddie 2018; R. Smith 2018; Mushroom-Creative 2018b). The Subcultures Network (2014; Gildart et al. 2017) cites several artists who use this artform to answer back to inequality, share their message, and channel their anger into perhaps a more productive form of protest. Their message is clear as they offer solutions to those in control of the system, such as, 'start listen[ing] to the young urban working class; make young people feel like they should care about themselves and their society' (Gildart et al. 2017, 88).

CONSCIOUSNESS-RAISING THROUGH STORYTELLING, PERFORMANCE AND PUBLIC PEDAGOGY

Cultural theorists believe that before an NSM can be initiated, liberation of the mind must be achieved as the first stage (Mpofu and Steyn 2021; Thiong'o 1986, 1993). Therefore, Hip Hop knowledge as a form of liberatory praxis refers to the

> aesthetic, social, intellectual, and political identities, beliefs, behaviours, and values produced and embraced by its members, who generally think of Hip Hop as an identity, a worldview, and a way of life. (Morgan and Bennett 2011, 177)

Hip Hop scholar Akom's (2009) work on educational pedagogy analyses the relationship between Hip Hop and critical pedagogy and how it can be used to promote social justice and youth activism. Akom explores the relationship between Hip Hop culture and the development of critical consciousness (borrowing from Freire's term *conscientisation* [consciousness-raising]

(2018[1968])) amongst urban and suburban youth. Original research findings pertaining to this first stage are presented in chapter 5.

The consciousness-raising process aims to support people in thinking critically and deeply about their access to freedom and power. The original theorist of this approach, Freire (2018[1968]), argued that critical awareness of their situation was the fundamental first step for oppressed groups to pursue greater freedoms. Freire (2018[1968], 47) argues that critical awareness occurs through *critical praxis* (informed, reflective action) to claim 'freedom' as a 'quest for human completion'. This process involves a social commitment to learning by doing (Sen 2001[1999], xii, 255). Whilst critiques of this approach exist, Akom (2009) links the relationship between Hip Hop and critical pedagogy, where participants have the opportunity to go on a consciousness-raising journey through teaching spaces utilising this art form. The

> use of Hip Hop as a liberatory practice is rooted in the long history of the black freedom struggle and the quest for self-determination for oppressed communities around the world. (Akom 2009, 53)

Intellectual debate about Hip Hop art and culture notes that young people worldwide are developing critical thought and applying these skills to every aspect of their lives. The result is the emergence of local Hip Hop 'scenes', where young people practice the elements of Hip Hop and 'debate, represent, and critique the cultural form and their social lives' (Morgan and Bennett 2011, 177–178). I developed the PhD thesis topic exploring the role of Hip Hop in building a political voice for young SSA artists as a result of empirical work with young SSAs. Young SSAs were driven by the opportunity to explore their cultural and socio-political contexts through this artform. Due to the changing nature of the political and the interpretative nature of any empirical approaches (Escobar 1992), the term 'political voice' in this context therefore refers to capturing how young SSA people go through a consciousness-raising process on the journey to becoming 'woke' (aware of their socio-political contexts) as depicted in their Hip Hop lyrics and personas.

CHHP is the application of these ideas of consciousness-raising to a conscious form of Hip Hop as a learning space. The critical analysis that occurs in CHHP as a form of liberatory praxis (Akom 2009), which is also discussed in chapter 2, and begins with the structure and message of the Hip Hop lyrics. When constructing Hip Hop lyrics and key messages, Hip Hop artists go through the consciousness-raising phase, where they analyse their experiences of identity politics and constructed worldviews and develop the political voice they wish to portray in response to forms of systemic sociopolitical disadvantage. The construction of lyrics can be likened to narrative therapy, which focuses on helping the artist/recipient re-author their story and find increased personal meaning in their lives (Heath 2018; Levy 2020). In this context, the artist/recipient

> is seen as the 'expert' as they have already developed a complex story or narrative about their own life which they use to understand their world. There is an opportunity to 'reframe' or re-interpret the story. (Nunn cited in White 2009, 303)

Bell et al. (cited in Clammer 2015, 122) identify that this occurs by developing counter-narratives to

> challenge the normalising or hegemonic stories of the dominant communities, deconstruct the self-interested assumptions of those majority discourses, and allow the experiences of minorities to emerge as the valid stuff of stories.

Clammer (2015) describes three levels of practical application to this process, which includes analysis, the collection of resistance stories, and emerging and transforming stories. The latter category is particularly important for taking the whole process beyond simple critique, which may just occur through the analysis stage. The following stages provide an opportunity for creating and articulating change. This produces the emotional and intellectual capacities for transformation. In other words, 'real alternatives are imagined and expressed' (Clammer 2015, 122).

It is the poetic element, as seen in song lyrics, that is most essential in this experience. Poetry is one of the most powerful and frequently utilised forms of performance through which social change activists seek to raise public consciousness about issues (Dutta 2011). The beat, lyrics, repetitive narratives, and word craft all contribute to the dynamic package that forms a Hip Hop track. More than mere music, Hip Hop is 'literary work in which special intensity is given to the expression of feelings and ideas by the use of distinctive styles and rhythms commonly found within formal poetry' (Gooding et al. 2016, 475). Due to being beyond the control of mainstream media messaging, communities who feel their voices have been sidelined or silenced can use Hip Hop or their poetry as an outlet or form of alternative media (Gooding et al. 2016, 475). Therefore, consciousness-raising through poetry involves the 'juxtaposition of ideas and narratives in order to communicate the message of the movement and to inspire action' (Dutta 2011, 202).

Whilst the audience is not the focus, Hip Hop audiences may also partially experience this consciousness-raising process, resulting in transformation and open-mindedness towards minoritised communities when politically conscious lyrics aim to inform and transform. Harter (cited in Dutta 2011) describes how the poetic nature of Hip Hop and the enactment of performer agency are political. The symbolic expressions of art create possibilities for challenging and reconfiguring dominant structures through the creation of new meaning frameworks, for example, discursive politics. This monograph therefore explores the power of Hip Hop narratives articulated by artists who demonstrate agency and freedom of expression when formulating key messages depicted.

For socially conscious, or 'woke', young people, and from the performer's perspective, the need to speak, to tell one's story, is not only an inner need but also a political one. The writer may happen to 'explore areas that no one has explored before, within [themselves] or outside, and to make discoveries that sooner or later turn out to be vital areas of collective awareness' (Calvino cited in Clammer 2015, 116). It is through the absence of a strict narrative that provides for a 'kind of spontaneity . . . allowing for an open-ended and engaging social experience' (Dimitriadis 1996, 182). Performance opportunities, therefore, disrupt the status quo and create sites for social change through the utilisation of public spaces. Through aesthetic forms of representation, performers embody the politics of representing issues of social injustice, oppression, power, control and resistance (Dutta 2011).

Giroux's (1999) term *public pedagogy* describes direct political action and influence amongst those marginalised from mainstream culture through Hip Hop's 'assert[ion of] itself as a liberating force' (cited in Gooding et al. 2016, 466). It is the intersections of storytelling, art, and social change that demonstrate how alternative conceptualisations of aesthetics direct us towards social transformations. Public pedagogy is enacted through broader cultural narratives that are continually disrupted and reinterpreted (Dutta 2011). Giroux (cited in Gooding et al. 2016, 473) deconstructs this process by stating it is true that

> culture (and in this case public Hip Hop) plays a central role in producing narratives, that exercise a powerful force influencing how people think of themselves and their relationship to others.

This can bring people together by informing us about the human experience. From the perspective of the performer, the onus is not necessarily on them to change public perception. Rather, through the action of Hip Hop performance, individuals have described Hip Hop as the voice they never had and as giving them an identity. This process provides a space for the symbolic language of music and poetry to bring young people together for resistance purposes.

IDENTITY POLITICS – FORMS OF BIPOC RESISTANCE THROUGH CULTURE-CENTRED APPROACH

Whilst the concepts of identity politics (that your identity and intersectional identities are political) (Bernstein 2005) and the terms 'woke' (becoming conscious of identity politics) have undergone a pejorative turn in recent years due to bemoaning the loss of 'free speech' or the rise of 'cancel culture' (ostracising people who have spoken in an unacceptable manner) (Richmond and Charnley 2022), identity politics politicised areas of life not previously defined as political, including sexuality or interpersonal relations (Bernstein 2005; Alcoff et al. 2006). This section defines the CCA to dialogue (Dutta 2011). CCA seeks to combat some of these identity challenges through cultural resistance to build identity and work towards the cultural transformation of racialising discourses through CHHP. This level of work comprises the final (and ongoing) stage of an NSM further explored in chapter 6.

Broadly, culture is understood as the customs, social behaviour, attitudes and ideas of individuals and communities within society. It can also be applied to the concept of popular culture as demonstrated within the arts and other manifestations of human achievement. Additionally, through forms of cultural policy regarding the politicisation of areas of specific cultural activities, as demonstrated through institutional supports that channel both aesthetic creativity and collective ways of life (Highmore 2016; Miller and Yúdice 2002). When considering 'culture' in relation to the fields of anthropology and ethnography, the meaning can be expanded to 'a way of life' (Highmore 2016). Culture as a social construct, has very different meanings depending on the context and worldview of participants in this study. As it is applied here, the definition of culture is connected variously to (pan) ethnicity, identity, life stage, that is, urban youth cultures, and pop-culture, such as through the cultural artform of Hip Hop. Also, it applies through the outward demonstration of South Sudanese ethnic cultures and identities, such as through tribal culture or national representations.

Carroll (2017, 604) suggests it is 'the suppression of difference, rather than difference itself, that inhibited movements for progressive social change'. I suggest that if young SSAs build their political voice and forms of resistance through a CCA, sites of social change can be created. Located in the field of communication and social change, the core components of culture, structure, and agency play out in the goals, configurations, and outcomes of dialogic spaces. Culture is defined in terms of the continuously shifting local contexts and frameworks of meanings defining the dialogic. CCA is outlined by cultural theorists Dutta (2011, 2020), Clammer (2012), and Appadurai (2004), who describe the social challenges that exist in current globalisation politics. They examine the communicative processes, strategies, and tactics through which social interventions are constituted in response to the challenge. They document how those in power, for example, some media outlets and politicians, create conditions for the many. Thus, CCA provides a theoretical base for discussing how these positions of power are resisted through the capacity to aspire whilst enacting agency in promoting an alternative to mainstream discourse. Specifically, looking at the intersection of young SSA identities and the outworking of Hip Hop cultural expression.

This work builds on theories of empowerment and freedom by Freire (1972) and Sen (2001[1999]). Sen's book *Development as Freedom* argues that unfreedoms (barriers to achieving aspirations) can prevent us from living 'lives that people have the reason to value' (Sen 2001[1999], 295). He suggests that 'good' development includes dismantling barriers to help build disempowered people's capabilities to pursue their aspirations. Understanding they have the freedom and agency to develop their own social change initiatives on their own terms has profound implications for young BIPOC in the Australian landscape.

One limitation of these theories of freedom, capabilities, and the ability to enact individual agency is that they do not necessarily take into account the extensive structural barriers that continue to oppress BIPOC individuals and communities. To dismantle such barriers relies on collective, disciplined, and sustained action over time (Hart 2020). This research explores how this may come about through recognition of Black Consciousness, which involves understanding the power imbalances that exist in society and demonstrating cultural pride regardless.

The crux is to create theoretical entry points for the critical praxis of social change (i.e., cycles of action and critical reflection on this action, leading to further action). Resistance in this monograph comes in the form of utilising subaltern (Spivak 1999) and minoritised voices, in this case young SSAs and how they might go about resisting social portrayals of them as 'thugs', as in 'gangs', and as unable to 'integrate' into Australian society. Young SSAs determine projects that adequately display their own forms of cultural pride, which may result in onlookers being informed by more than just mainstream media making use of common persuasive devices such as rhetoric, hyperbole, and propaganda. This specifically occurs through the need for young SSAs to resist and build their political voice through Hip Hop expression.

Clammer (2015, 3) specialises in processes of communicating social change in arts-based development projects utilising alternative media, arguing that through CCA fundamental questions can be addressed such as: 'What kind of humans we would like to be, and in what kind of society do we want to live?' To focus these questions in consideration of young SSAs from the African diaspora, Pan-Africanism, Afrocentricity and Afrofuturism are elaborated on in the following chapters as forms of identity politics that specifically relate to the modes of youth resistance and the political voice that young SSAs identify with.

I discuss identity here, as I demonstrate how this continues to be a site for NSMs amongst young SSAs. The book *Identity Politics Reconsidered* (Alcoff et al. 2006) reconceptualises the scholarly and political significance of social identity whilst focusing on the deployment of identity and how multiple identities within the self play out in everyday experiences. Bernstein (2005) suggests that status identities are understood and/or portrayed as essentialist or socially constructed. Where this is pivotal is amongst the competing theoretical understandings of the relationships between experience, culture, identity, politics, and power. In relation to identity politics, Antiracist educators continue to point out, however, that 'race' (different from ethnicity) is 'a power construct of collected or merged difference that lives socially' (Kendi 2019, 34). Thus, in practical terms, one is 'not born black or African American, Mulatto, Chicana/o, Mestiza, poor, working class, or white' (Harding 2006, 254). And yet Olou (2018, 11–12) points out that 'race' as a social construct with 'no bearing in science' was 'created to keep BIPOC at the bottom'.

To elaborate on the application of this phrase, individuals or communities may perceive themselves as identifying in one way or prefer to self-determine their social identities. Whereas, through bestowal of categories of difference by one group of humans upon another, people might be labelled with certain status identities that are not always self-determined. Having these often-predetermined ideas about societal and identity-based category groups predicates our view of the similarities and differences between us. Kenny (2017, 319) identifies, however, that through political struggles, those engaging with identity politics alternatively accentuate, reclaims or assert difference. Amplified here is the way in which artivists struggle for recognition of and respect for difference. Demonstrated is how young SSA artivists fulfil this role but may instead celebrate difference through artistic forms and subcultures. Difference in art can be profitable or popular and have intrinsic personal fulfilment factors, for example, accentuating unique opinions or flair in expression of personalities. For example, the born to stand out photo (figure 1.1) by artist Ayuen K. Bol uses vibrant colour palettes to express specific identities.

Identity politics are assumed to be 'cultural' (and political) not only because 'identity is putatively unrelated to institutional structures and the political economy', but also because scholars in this field see 'identity groups as advocating for recognition of and respect for their cultural differences, which derive from their distinct group identities' (Bernstein 2005, 49). Scholars assume that activists organised around status identities 'understand these identities with their associated cultures in essentialist rather than socially constructed terms' (Bernstein 2005, 49). Scholars are therefore 'critical of what they view as activists' equating identity groups with a culture, and they question what forms the basis for that culture' (Bernstein 2005, 49). Whilst these are important considerations, Indigenous people's social movements advocate for *cultural survival* therefore ensuring that social disciplines attune to the political dimensions of the cultural (Escobar 1992). As Indigenous peoples and global diaspora go about transforming social and cultural orders, this 'affords important clues for rethinking how groups of people participate collectively in fashioning their worlds in their everyday life, grounded in their own cultures and meanings' (Escobar 1992, 402). The theme 'born to stand out' is therefore an example of how the CCA (Dutta 2020) can be utilised to present counter-narratives to the prominent African gangs narratives. The next section addresses some of the social indicators discussing the phenomenon I coined 'identity politics playing tricks'.

IDENTITY POLITICS PLAYING TRICKS

My article (Williams 2022), drawn from insights gathered throughout the PhD journey featured in this monograph, it details the additional challenges and interplay with identity politics that young SSAs face in their identity formation throughout adolescence (Idriss 2017). As suggested, this monograph addresses the tricks that play out through media, in political and moral panics, whereby racialising discourses associate Blackness with criminality (Majavu 2020). As a result, young SSAs must navigate extensive cultural codes on a daily basis (Abur 2019). As chapter 3 demonstrated through discussion of 'the system', young SSAs face many challenges and pose their own solutions, *'all the while trying to discover who you are as a person'* (Malual). These challenges involve systemic issues such as interactions with institutions; personal difficulties, including forging identity in youth culture; and communal hurdles in terms of being a young person from the African diaspora operating within many cultures (Williams 2022). Hip Hop is identified as one tool for the construction of personal and cultural identities (Nguyen and Ferguson 2019; Moran 2016). Noting the challenges experienced by Sampa as an African diaspora artist in Australia, artist *Queen P* points out that 'younger generations are getting more consciously aware of what they are saying. They use it as an opportunity to speak on behalf of their identity' (Mushroom-Creative 2018a). She notes how the presence of young BIPOC artists expressing themselves this way is what Australia needs: 'The more people that are doing it, it is breaking all different types of stereotypes, genres, and the way that we access and share music' (Mushroom-Creative 2018a, 1).

Through a process of narrating their identity expressions through art and civic involvement, this chapter further explores the themes of diaspora life for young SSAs. Young people reframe and theorise their personal and family histories (Johansen and Varvin 2020), assert their identity formation through their Blackness (consciousness) and African identities, and establish themselves as social agents in the world (Habermas and Bluck 2000). Knowledge of this process through the political agenda of Black Consciousness, therefore, sets the groundwork for new types of artivism and expressions of political voice to form.

This chapter builds on recent Australian youth studies scholarship by incorporating 'race' as espoused through CRT as a central theme (Idriss 2021). Despite Blackness being a social construct, it is a mode of being with which young SSAs strongly relate. This chapter explores 'race as a complex, global, structural phenomenon' and delves into how race 'comes to bear on the development of young people's identity making, life choices and lived experiences' (Idriss 2021, 1). The chapter explores the themes participants raised in terms of the politics of 'reclaiming identity' (Salvídar 2006, 152). These types of identity politics feature in their complex descriptions of lived everyday experiences and in their art. This chapter also details personal and collective narratives in relation to how experiences of oppression as instigated by racialising discourses can be articulated and resisted. These complex narratives begin to describe the process of how social and cultural identity movements are formed (explored in detail in chapters 5–6) by focusing on the key topics of identity formation for black diaspora youth. These key themes were extracted from a detailed ethnography of the Grounded Project hosted by Footprints, which began with a process of consciousness-raising as the first step in the creation of an NSM.

THE GROUNDED PROJECT CONSCIOUSNESS-RAISING JOURNEY

YPAR processes provide a space for young people and adults to study historical and contemporary political contexts of injustice together, examine circuits of dispossession – dispossession that occurs across sectors and intersectional axes of oppression, and provides links between research and action (Fox et al. cited in Bautista 2018, 195). This section describes the first stage of Footprints' YPAR process, which focusses on consciousness-raising through *Critical Hip Hop Pedagogy* (CHHP) as an important precursor to more public forms of resistance to racialising discourses highlighted in chapters 5–6. Consciousness-raising is also identified as the beginning step to the formation of or involvement with an NSM. This process was captured through ethnography, as discussed in chapter 2.

The activities discussed in this section, such as attendance at the Gua camp, included 35 research participants who attended two focus groups. Following the focus groups, participants chose between options of participating in a Hip Hop writing and recording workshop, a writing spoken-word workshop, or an Afrobeat and Hip Hop dance workshop, all utilising CHHP (Akom 2009). These took place at the Gua Performance and Leadership Camp hosted by

Footprints 29 –31 January 2019 at Wilson's Promontory National Park in rural Victoria. This camp has previously been held on three occasions in 2011, 2014, 2017. The tagline for the camp is 'East meets West to promote positive social change', where approximately 35 young multicultural artists are mentored by creative professionals to develop artistic pieces exploring identity, strengths, and the root issues behind racial tensions in Australia (Footprints, Grounded Project Acquittal 2017:5). The Gua camp is modelled on American Freedom Schools, where BIPOC youth from Mississippi attended summer schools 'grounded in a vision of culturally relevant education that advances the liberatory efforts of the Civil Rights Movement' (Hale cited in Bautista 2018, 246).

Utilising CHHP, the two focus groups hosted at the Gua camp consisted of co-inquiry about how Hip Hop can be used as a tool for social justice. At the various Gua camps hosted over the years, participants watched a range of social justice documentaries, including 'Favela Rising', 'Warchild', 'Soldiers of Peace', and the 'Interrupters'[2] at camps hosted in 2011–2018. In 2019, participants watched 'Hip Hop Evolution'[3] (described below). The purpose of watching these documentaries was to provide a space where participants could talk openly about peace and conflict and arts-based ways of exploring alternatives. According to Footprints' approach, Freire's (2018[1968]) *Pedagogy of the Oppressed* has 'been extremely helpful when planning camp activities as he has done a lot of the groundwork in thinking out the implications of social movements' (Footprints, Grounded Acquittal 2017:6). Freire clarifies 'that it is in speaking their word that people, by naming the world, transform it, dialogue imposes itself as a way by which they achieve significance as human beings. Dialogue is thus an essential necessity' (P. Freire et al. 2018[1968], 69).

The specific approach to the focus groups, as discussed in CHHP, involves participants exploring cultural politics; political economy; historicity of knowledge; dialectical theory; ideology and critique; hegemony, resistance and counter-hegemony; praxis, dialogue and consciousness-raising (Darder et al. cited in Bautista 2018). Discussing the themes in the films and how they relate to participants' lives gives participants an opportunity to uncover oppressive ideologies in social structures; explore what is legitimate knowledge; encourage reflective action and guide learners towards liberation through humanising culture and their daily lives (Bautista 2018). As a result of watching the documentaries and discussions about key themes depicted, Gua camp participants are able to articulate the links of how Hip Hop has historically addressed systemic racism and supported minoritised communities to build their political voice.

In consideration of young SSAs discussion of black identity development in the focus groups (Bulhan 1985), the first stage of capitulation is demonstrated whereby young SSAs begin to go through a consciousness-raising journey when participating in an NSM. Whilst not aware of the specific analytical frameworks applied when touching on this topic, participants discussed that upon arrival in Australia and going through adolescent development, they are confronted with the first stage, capitulation, which involves the expectation of increased assimilation into the white dominant culture, whilst, simultaneously rejecting one's own black heritage. This occurred at a very early age through exposure to Western education. Similarly, chapter 1 describes how in the first *pre-encounter* stage of black consciousness development (Cross 1971), young SSAs identify their sense of excitement and gratitude for coming to Australia. Due to not being exposed upon early arrival to notions of Blackness and Whiteness, it is demonstrated that they appear to hold attitudes towards race that range from low salience to race neutrality, apart from their exposure to tribal politics stemming from the long-term civil and national wars in their country of South Sudan.

Upon initial awareness of these various forces of socio-political disadvantage, the specific political economy explored in relation to this monograph is how young SSAs experience racialised inequalities and narratives directed towards them, thus highlighting the inextricable link between culture and class. Whilst the oppressive circumstances of racialising discourses are explored, critical pedagogy provides a medium to analyse various types of tensions in history, and critical cultural agency therefore provides a hopeful possibility for humans to exert agency, relationality, a sense of belonging amongst subcultures, self-determination, and collective societal change (Darder et al., cited in Bautista 2018). The implications of these discussions are discussed in chapters 5–6, where participants considered their own arts-based forms of resistance through Hip Hop expression. The key messages they construct regarding positioning their Blackness as a form of political voice and expression are explored in the remainder of this chapter.

The first focus group at the Gua camp consisted of watching the 'Hip Hop Evolution' documentary, which outlined the origins of Hip Hop, followed by a discussion about the different sub-genres of Hip Hop that have evolved and remain relevant to emerging generations. This discussion was facilitated by Footprints' vice president Jacob Apech and artists *Malesh P* and FLEXX. Specifically, participants discussed how young SSA Hip Hop artists develop their content and messages in their lyrics. The contrasting aspect of this discussion was that there were two generations of artists present (aged 15–21 and 22–30 respectively). Considering the notion of the Hip Hop generation (Asante 2008) explored in chapter 4, I arrived at this generational split because these age groups discussed different Hip Hop sub-genres that they preferred (Fieldwork notes 2019). They also discussed how different generations of young SSAs express their political voice (or not) through conscious forms of Hip Hop or other sub-genres such as trap or drill Hip Hop (which may appear more violent). Through discussions during the focus groups responding to watching the 'Hip Hop Evolution' documentary and considering the history of the formation of Hip Hop sub-genres, debate occurred regarding the viability and content that these art forms produce. This was specifically because exposure to U.S. styles of Hip Hop were some of their first experiences of black culture. Once participants became more conscious about their black heritage and sense of Blackness, the second stage of black identity development (Bulhan 1985), *revitalisation*, took place when young SSAs as BIPOC rejected the ubiquitous Eurocentric culture for their African heritage. Expressing themselves through their own versions of Hip Hop styles and lyric content in Australia was one example of when this began to occur. Whilst this was the case, simultaneously concerns were raised about the caricatures that may be portrayed about their communities as a result. For example, in one sub-genre of Hip Hop, the gangsta-rap era, there were baggy jeans and caps turned backward. In the current climate of hybrid forms of Hip Hop urban youth appear to respond to, drill Hip Hop (another sub-genre likened to gangsta-rap) is perceived as violent (Fieldwork notes 2019) (Lee et al. 2022).

Lizzy and Ajur come from the current generation, which relishes trap or drill Hip Hop which appears at times to depict violent scenes in music videos. However, they identify that, unlike some peers, they enjoy the opportunity to be exposed to more 'conscious-rappers' and to hear more about how artists position themselves in the music industry if they have conscious lyrics with a social message. Ajur discusses the impact of these interactions:

But literally just after that session . . . I went back home that day. There were some lyrics that I read back on and I was just like [laughing]. . . . I thought I'm not writing about that. And I ripped it up. And I was like . . . what do I actually want to write about? You know, actually talk about, like, history. I talked about, like, how can black communities and pretty much like black youth and just everything that happens like all the struggles that we go through. . . . I actually want to turn everything that I want to talk about into music, into songs and just like, pretty much teach this generation. Because most of them, it's not that they're sleeping is like, they weren't taught that specific things. They weren't taught about this history, they weren't taught about themselves.

During this interview, I asked Ajur if that's how she came up with the track 'The Matrix' (discussed in chapter 4).[4] She concluded that this was a significant moment for her and that is what the *Matrix* is all about – *'wake up'*.

The second focus group was hosted by me and *Malesh P* and consisted of a discussion of the challenges young SSAs face in the Australian music industry and in Australian society in relation to racialising discourses. Throughout this discussion, the topic of racism, identified by participants, remained prevalent (as presented in chapter 3). Considering some of the 'feelings and emotions that were felt and expressed' (Reeves, Kuper, and Hodges 2008, 512), participants appeared to feel comfortable speaking about these *'painful experiences'* as participants described the camp as being a *'safe space'*. They identified that this was due, in large part, to the fact that these sessions were primarily led by BIPOC facilitators offering support and advice on how to interact and disarm in such toxic and divisive circumstances (Gua fieldwork notes and Footprints evaluations 2011, 2014, 2017, 2019). This finding is represented through a participant reflection:

> Gua camp was like, forming a sense of identity and being in a safe place to like talk about this stuff with a group of people that were like minded with other artists. (Fieldwork notes 2019)

Noting the essentiality of employing diverse BIPOC facilitators, it was very important that Footprints employed young artists from BIPOC backgrounds to host the Gua focus groups and workshops. Footprints describes how involving mentors has proven invaluable for the success of the Grounded Project, which included the planning and fruition of the Grounded Youth Stage event in 2019. It was evident that:

> relationships between mentors and mentees have repeatedly illustrated how beneficial positive connections with others are for the wellbeing of young people from various multicultural backgrounds. Having positive examples of young people from similar backgrounds who've overcome personal challenges to find success is important. The group's mentors model skills as diverse as project planning and arts management to attributes such as confidence, resilience and persistence. Footprints have witnessed mentoring transform the lives and outlooks of those who feel isolated, marginalised or misunderstood. (Footprints, Grounded Project Acquittal 2019, 18)

Three participants who attended the Gua camp discussed how it is an opportunity to invite *'new audiences'* (i.e., young SSAs and other multicultural communities). This was seen to be possible because it is an *'inviting and welcoming environment'* which *'encourages personal, honest expression'* through topics that are *'deep'*. Another important factor explored is that in this intimate setting, BTSO participants narrated *'we are the black majority'* (not often experienced) whereas later, for example, when performing there could be a *'mixed-culture audience majority'* (Fieldwork notes 2019).

As described above, the camp also involved three workshops where the facilitators were Hip Hop emcees (performing), dance, and spoken-word artists. In each workshop, participants either learned a choreographed dance, developed their own spoken-word pieces, or brainstormed lyrics and then recorded them. One of the facilitators, *Malesh P* bought his studio gear – a microphone, speakers, computer, and recording software. *Malesh P* had also hosted workshops at the Gua camp in 2017 and performed at the Grounded Festival in March 2017, which provided an opportunity for relationships and skills to be built over time (Footprints, Grounded Project Acquittal 2017, 3). Young SSAs present as part of *Malesh P*'s recording workshop began the workshop by describing their arts-based initiatives engaging their own communities in self-expression through podcasts, alternative media channels, the creation of other Hip Hop collectives, or fashion design. Through his songwriting workshop and the spoken-word workshop hosted by Akimera[5], participants chose the theme of 'culture' out of the topics depicted in figure 4.1. to explore (see figures 4.1 and 4.2).

Guided by *Malesh P* and Akimera, they proceeded to write short spoken-word poems and Hip Hop tracks with this theme in mind. A joint Hip Hop track 'AfriCAN' (2018), produced by *Malesh P* and featuring a hook by Akimera, *'Oh yeah I am African'*[6] involved consciousness-raising processes (depicted in figure 4.1) in which participants wrote Hip Hop lyrics about their life experiences in response to the topic of racialising discourses after focus group discussions or hearing from artistic mentors. These art forms were chosen to encourage the building of political voice in response to socio-political disadvantages and provided participants the opportunity to participate in alternative forms of storytelling. One participant from the Gua camp in 2017 eloquently described:

Art is my space to self-determine. Art is expressing myself in a unique way.
Freedom of Expression - What's On Your Mind?
I use my art to be real, to find comfort within myself and to understand one-self.
Art to me is being able to set yourself free through your preferred art form.

(Footprints, Grounded Acquittal 2017, 7)

Both this track and the poems are explored as artefacts in this chapter. Figure 4.1, 4.2 and 4.3 depicts the Gua focus groups process (see figure 4.3).

This chapter represents some unexpected themes, coming out of Gua camp participants' selection of 'culture' as their main theme. This was instead of the anticipated themes of systemic racism or continuing to discuss ways they might amplify their political voice. It therefore pinpoints instead where participants wanted to orient their political voice within their Blackness. In a similar fashion to Anderson Sa, founder of the Afro-Reggae Cultural Group in Rio de Janeiro's favelas (Samuels 2018), Footprints also states that 'we believe that culture is the most powerful instrument of change' (Grounded Project 2019: Media Release). These are the empirical conditions where the

Figure 4.1 Gua Workshop Discussion Topics and Process, 2019. *Source*: Footprints.

concept of the CCA was chosen and led to further exploration in chapter 6, where it was applied to the next stage of involvement in an NSM. The next phase of the Grounded Project involved showcasing public performances of the tracks developed at the Gua camp alongside other young SSA artist tracks.

'Oh Yeah, I Am African' 117

Figure 4.2 Workshops at Gua Performance and Leadership Camp. Featuring artists LEZA, Burn City Movement (BCM) crew members, and Footprints Vice-President Jacob Apech. See hyper-link (Mills-and-Boom 2019a) to view Footprints video highlighting the project. *Source:* Footprints (Mills-and-Boom 2019a)

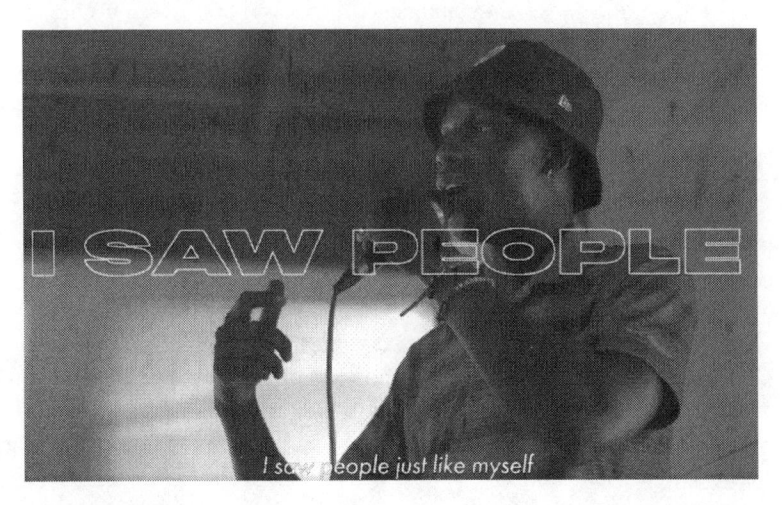

Figure 4.3 Gua Performance and Leadership Camp, 2019. Image featuring artist Wantu ThaOne. *Source*: Footprints 2022b, 2022a.

The Gua camp focus groups necessitated the first stage of being involved in an NSM by exploring how cultural meanings are co-constructed by participants in their interactions with the structures that surround their lives. It is through these co-constructions that young SSA participants discuss the possibilities of resisting racialising discourses and a system that 'continues to locate them at the peripheries of mainstream' (Dutta 2021, 1). Through becoming socially aware, they were ready to 'co-create narratives of social change that transform the silences carried out by mainstream structures of knowledge production' (Dutta 2021, 1).[7]

Footprints member Gabriel elaborated on the significance of the Gua camp experience for participants following a consciousness-raising process:

> *Things like camp are good for tackling topics because it's not just discussing about African diaspora issues you know, topics like integration, there's also a fun side of things.*

He went on to differentiate various stages of political voice and Hip Hop expression depending on the intention of the activity. Gabriel outlined that music and spoken-word poetry are really influential. This is in line with Kenyan scholar and artist Ngũgĩ wa Thiong'o's (1986, 45) emphasis on the importance of song and dance for daily aspects of life in Kenya and other African countries. Through this approach, he highlighted aspects of language for the purpose of storytelling. No longer a 'caged writer', this involves the 'inflexion of voices to add different tones' – 'we therefore learned to value words for their meanings and nuances' (Ngũgĩ 1986, 10–11). One of the nuances Ngũgĩ was referring to was around the topic of culture which varies for Kenyans, as distinct from Western hegemonic approaches. Another purpose of his storytelling was the consideration that 'language brings humans together for understanding' (Ngũgĩ 1986, 15).

When considering similar storytelling approaches and the delivery of your message for a public outcome, Gabriel suggests that *'if there's a pressing issue, that's where something like public place will attract other people'*. Alternatively, if internal *'black issues'* need to be discussed or *'if it's just more about identity'* he believes that *'that's where things like Afro Hub come in'*. Before the COVID-19 pandemic, which resulted in many grassroots venues closing, Afro Hub[8] was a live-music venue in central Naarm whereby the mission of its founders was to curate and produce all things Afrocentric. By doing so, this is a form of resistance and an example of a 'black counter-public' (Bonnette 2015, 12). Specifically, this counter-hegemonic space involves a *transformative youth-organising approach* calling for 'cultivating a haven' that supports the creation of alternative structures, practices, and relationships towards democratic and liberatory aims (Darder et al. cited in Bautista 2018, 63).

Additionally, as an intellectual space, primarily black spaces such as Afro Hub create spaces where 'new readings of the world can unfold, in ways that lead us towards change, both in theory and practice' (Darder et al. cited in Bautista 2018, 63). This occurs through the third *immersion* stage in Cross' (1971) black consciousness identity development theory, characterised by efforts to develop a black identity that is anchored in Black

Consciousness. In this stage, black people often attend political or cultural meetings, the person goes to black music sessions, and attends seminars and art shows that focus on Blackness; everything of value to this person becomes about being black. In this research, participants primarily engage in this via Hip Hop and spoken-word as forms of urban youth culture. The fourth *internalisation* stage marks the point of racial dissonance resolution, and as a result, the person feels calmer and more at ease with their black identity (Cross 1971).

Gabriel then returns to the significance of the Gua camp:

> *If it's more about merging the two, the music, the art, the topic of what does 'integration into Australia' look like whilst considering our African roots. That's where things like camp are great because you learn the art form of it [also referring to the consciousness-raising journey]. You're also networking. And you're also learning and discussing about your [cultural] roots.*

Gabriel explains from an SSA perspective and in terms of engaging young people:

> *It has to always be fun, because not everyone likes these kind of topics [talking about racialising discourses, integration, racism or depictions of SSA communities], you know, because they tear up things. So, we don't like to talk about them unless we have to. For people that want to find their identity, learn what it means to be an African, things like that, Gua camp is good because it's learning, it's not just discussing these hot topics.*

The engagement of young SSAs in consciousness-raising in order to build the expression of their political voice and to flourish speaks to the idea that the discussion of political struggle is understood 'as necessary to generate the kind of group consciousness – subjectivity – that can produce the information and insight oppressed groups need and seek' (Harding 2006, 253). In order to reach this level of 'wokeness' involving becoming awake to issues of racial injustice, great care, and emotional, spiritual, and intellectual labour is involved to reach this level of 'wokeness'. Becoming awake to issues of racial injustice also involves developing respect for unique viewpoints amongst different communities affected. Gabriel's points emphasise that political education should also 'incorporate regular spiritual practices as well as promote physical, mental, and emotional health in its activities and relationship structures' (Bautista 2018, 244). That is why the camp's beach setting, away from the city, was crucial for helping participants process all that they were learning with a 'clear mind/heart' (Fieldwork notes 2019). Gabriel further articulated this experience:

> *So you have all that fun, go on that learning experience and you put everything into practice and then later you just have a bit of a sit back and just be like yeah [ponder the experience and the message].*

Specifically, it is the process of dialogue at this phase of an NSM and as a pedagogical tool that allows for conscientisation or 'wokeness' to occur – a process of reflection and action to develop a deep awareness of the social, political, and historical realities that shape their lives (Bautista 2018). This critical stage of Footprints' YPAR process considers that any serious movement towards freedom must begin in the mind (Kelley 2003; Ngũgĩ 1986). This phase supported BTSO artivists to develop an analysis of the historic conditions they live in and are often connected with through various community-organising strategies and tactics to help act on their critical awareness and challenge unjust systems (Bautista 2018, 11).

Rather than 'despair', 'despondency', 'a collective death wish' or 'possibilities of triumph or victory being seen as remote or ridiculous dreams', young SSAs must 'discover their various tongues to sing the song: "A people united can never be defeated"' (Ngũgĩ 1986, 3). Through his critical thought about resistance and repression in neo-colonial Kenya, Ngũgĩ depicts an alternative vision in his collections *Writers in Politics* (Ngũgĩ 1981), *Barrell of a Pen* (Ngũgĩ 1983), and *Penpoints, Guns and Dreams* (Ngũgĩ 1998), discussing art and politics, writing on oppression, liberation, common struggles, and the tools and positionality of a writer.

Hip Hop collective *BCM* came to the first Gua Performance and Leadership Camp as part of the Grounded Project as participants in 2019 and then became Hip Hop workshop leaders in 2020. In the 2020 Gua focus groups, artist *Wantu ThaOne* (depicted in photo 10), a part of *BCM* shared with participants: Hip Hop for me gave me a purpose. I related to it because I saw people just like myself, being able to express themselves. (Footprints 2022a, 2022b)

Whilst focusing on the role of people as 'agent[s] of culture in process' (Fisk cited in Escobar 1992, 409), the 'thick description' of the consciousness-raising journey as expressed through the Gua camps leads to broader questions – what do we learn about whether young SSAs indeed use conscious or political Hip Hop to build their political voice for resistance? What skills have they developed and how do they use them to mark out their own space? This section and chapter 4 have articulated that the first step is to acknowledge that

> power is central to the dialogic process not only in terms of framing the terrains of dialogue, but also and more fundamentally in terms of challenging and changing structures that oppress the subaltern sectors. (Dutta 2011, 178)

This research therefore asserts that important dialogic moments created at the Gua camp serve as entry points for participating in an identity-based NSM and catalysing social change through the vehicle of Hip Hop to 'creat[e] spaces for alternative rationalities, and by narrating alternative stories that bring forth the taken-for-granted assumptions of the status quo' (Dutta 2011, 178). Through CHHP and the CCA, the

> agency of local communities and the organising of local–global linkages are constituted in a framework of resistance, working collectively to dismantle neo-liberal hegemony through the articulation of other materialities. (Dutta 2015b, 133)

The following section begins to draw out what some of these alternative stories are from BTSO participants' perspectives in the Gua camp.

NOTIONS OF 'BLACKNESS' AND AFFIRMATION OF BLACK IDENTITIES

The key theme identified in the previous section was that through a consciousness-raising journey, BTSO participants preferred to orient their political voice within their Blackness. To explore the creativity, imagination, and political agency of urban youth, and how they negotiate the complexities of race, class, gender, and the broader politics of difference in chapters 6 and 7, it is important to first explore 'Blackness' as it relates to identity politics. It is evident that writing about black identity is really the business of and for black people (see chapter 2 positionality statement) (Milstein 2015). However, knowledge of some key themes of black identity helps to understand Black Consciousness and Black Power and the ways in which young people arrive at their responses to black liberation struggles. Kenyan scholar and artist Ngũgĩ (1972) describes this opportunity in his collection *Homecoming* when discussing the influence of culture and politics on questions such as: What is my colour? What is my race? This is whilst also appreciating that from a CRT perspective of colour-coded racism and with considerations of race as a social construct, these questions have led to blurred lines, particularly in the continent of Africa (and for the African diaspora). In his examination of George Lamming's book *In the Castle of My Skin*, Ngũgĩ identifies:

> the confusion in values that has resulted from a drastic historical change of political, economic and cultural ethos; the effect of such confusion on both society and the individual's psyche; and the need to retain what is ours and recreate from it a new set of living values. (Ngũgĩ 1972, xi-xii)

Similar to detailing the specific narratives of racialising discourses explored in chapter 6, this section touches on the concept of Blackness. Following the detailing of the Gua focus groups and workshops in the previous section, this section draws on participant interviews, BTSO artivist quotes, and artefacts including the 'AfriCAN' (2018) track to elaborate on how this key theme was unpacked. It leads to the exploration of two key sub-themes of Black Consciousness and Black power in subsequent sections as identified through the Gua camp, the first stage of the Grounded Project. In *Critique of Black Reason,* Achille Mbembe traces the conjunction of Blackness with the biological fiction of race (originating from the Atlantic slave trade) as described in one of CRT's main tenets: race as a social construct (Mbembe and Dubois 2017). He theorises *black reason* as the 'collection of discourses and practices that equated Blackness with the nonhuman in order to uphold forms of oppression' which served as 'the template for all new forms of exclusion' (Mbembe and Dubois 2017, n.p.) as culminated in forms of *necropolitics* (Mbembe and Corcoran 2019). Participants therefore touched on the positives and negatives of their black-African diaspora identity in Australia in relation to racialising discourses which often further perpetuate this phenomenon. One example that Shaker gives of a negative aspect of identity politics and the constant discourses of not integrating into Australian society or being criminals is that it often includes '*everyone lumped together no matter what you do*'. As a result, you are '*only highlighted [positively] if you have done something extraordinary*'.

Despite these harmful and racist narratives, BTSO artivists and research participants have demonstrated a strong affinity with Blackness. Therefore, their positive experiences of reclaiming African and black identities appear to outweigh the negatives. This is explored in the following sections, where Gabriel states, '*I do identify as an African, a black man and as an Australian*'. In identifying with the black aesthetic, a spoken-word poet at the Gua focus group on culture and identity (2017)[9] performed with certainty:

Black.
Who I am.
Black.
Who I am.
Black.

In order to move towards 'liberty' from a 'cultural bomb' involving the annihilation of a sense of belief in names, languages, unity, in a sense of value in black-African cultural heritage (Ngũgĩ 1986, 3), the verses in the 'AfriCAN' (2018)[10] track developed at the Gua camp have been selected in this chapter to demonstrate a 'conscious' or 'message' Hip Hop track which has the theme *'Oh yeah, I am African'* (chorus).This message fits within the broader theme of this chapter of identity politics, considering the lyrics of an NSM. It is utilised to draw these themes together in this section. For example, in 'AfriCAN' (2018) verse 5, Wiaa from BCM states:

My Blackness precedes me
We were destined from the start.

Antiracism educator Kendi (2019, 38) also identifies as black – 'not because I believe Blackness, or race, is a meaningful scientific category but because our societies, our policies, our ideas, our histories, and our coaches have rendered race and made it matter'. Through a CRT analysis of race hierarchies and the colour-coding of skin colour, this also explains why Blackness is still so important to individuals and communities. Despite experiencing racial vilification, indeed like BTSO participants, Kendi sees his Blackness as a gift. Instead of being 'colourblind' which involves pretending to ignore difference and failing to see the social impacts of skin colour as experienced through identity politics, it allows him to clearly see himself 'historically and politically as being an Antiracist, as a member of the interracial body striving to accept and equate and empower racial difference of all kinds' (Kendi 2019, 38).

Lizzy and Ajur also viewed their Blackness or their African identity as a gift. This was despite discussing themes of African oppression, struggles, and links to slavery or being a *'black female who's misunderstood'* (Élkato, AfriCAN (2018) verse 5).[11] This is a theme mostly portrayed through participants' artefacts where topics of representation were important. Oware (2018) and Bonnette (2015) describe how in rap lyrics, acknowledging one's race or someone else's can act as a form of 'self-awareness' or 'racial consciousness'. Consequently, as a form of liberatory praxis, such lyrics may challenge 'colour-blindness' and 'racial evasion'. They both describe how context guides the analysis. Oware (2018, 125) asks whether mentioning race or Blackness is a superficial allusion in rap lyrics or 'does this identification occur within a larger conversation addressing racial matters? In other words, is racial self-identification politicised?' This theme, however, appears significant for BTSO artivists when in the past they might have been *'forced to suppress Blackness'* (Felicia). Artists like Sampa and other influencers are instead *'teaching love and comfort within Blackness'* (Gua focus group notes 2017). In the face of continued adversity, statements like these lead to the opportunity to 'spark change' or resistance such as the resistance in the struggle through art (Wiaa from *BCM,* AfriCAN verse 5):[12]

With persistence we bring resistance, revolutionary at heart
Through culture and history, we march on to victory
You are limitless to all my sisters, let's break prejudice through art.

This theme of different types of resistance and forms of black joy is further explored in chapters 6–7, highlighting how different iterations of protest movements or personal artistic endeavours display political voice. In the track 'AfriCAN' (2018),[13] bold claims of turning identity politics on its head are identified by detailing the strengths of African communities instead of deficit approaches. This is demonstrated through claims made by artist *i.OG* from *BCM* (AfriCAN (2018) verse 5) that there is *'power through poverty'* or that his *BCM* Hip Hop collective tracks start to *'bring mirrors'* to racialising discourses. This involves starting to present counter-narratives. Through the process of consciousness-raising, participants were able to point towards weakness amongst oppressors and invoke persistence in the revolution. *i.OG* (from *BCM,* AfriCAN Verse 5)[14] goes on to rap about one form of oppression through racism where he claims:

Racism is still cemented
Within the minds of the generations
We gotta spark the change
So the change can be amended, so the change can be amended
Check my identity, power through poverty
Always tell the truth so they never could bother me
Look at the modesty, check the reality,
take a look at the mirror and see who is the minority.

These statements made by BTSO artivists demonstrate the transformational force given to members of marginalised communities by Hip Hop and alternative forms of storytelling across the globe. Through involvement in an NSM, this force is perceived as a *resistance mechanism* and is derived as a result of the power of cultural expression involving participants of an NSM asserting their visibility in arenas whose majority players deemed them invisible (Bonnette 2015). The statements made by BTSO artivists in their lyrics, also spark everyday pride in black identities through Hip Hop. These assertive affirmations, therefore, make it possible to remain visible through the concept of BTSO rather than hiding away and not expressing one's true identity (Hill-Collins 2006; Bonnette 2015). Hanging *'your Masters up'* (degrees, graduations, Masters of music) (*Malesh P,* AfriCAN (2018) Verse 6)[15] or waving your flags in music videos portrays the idea of *'representing what you're standing for'* (Krown 2018a)[16]. These depictions demonstrate that young SSAs are able to hold multiple identities or ideologies proudly despite ascribed depictions of their expression of their identity through racialising discourses (Williams 2022). This comes as a result of knowledge of black identities and young SSAs discovering and creating 'shared histories and visions with others' whilst recognising that for both individuals and groups, 'identities are always multiple, contradictory and partial or incomplete' (Harding 2006, 254).

With this context in mind, the chorus of 'AfriCAN' (2018)[17] where African diaspora artists state in unison that they are here to *'represent the Motherland. . . . Oh yeah, I'm an African'* points to the constant theme of 'representing' (showcasing strengths) that comes through in participant responses and artefacts. This was evident particularly around the tendency to *'represent black skin'* (Emmanuel). The concept of 'representing' involves being *'proud to be who you are'*, *'where you came from' (Malek)*, or *'proud to represent Africa or South Sudan'* (Felicia). Other than demonstrating cultural and self-assurance, these statements were seen to be necessary due to racialising discourses explored in chapter 5 whereby being associated with having dark skin and originating from the African continent has socio-political undertones. As a result, there is almost an underlying expectation or having an inner quality to *'take pride in all things we're good at'* (Esenadus-Squad 2012)[18] as *'we're not as bad as we're painted'* (Krown 2018b).[19]

Like the idea of 'reclaiming your roots' (your cultural background), there is a necessity within this topic of colour to go through the process of re-storying or developing meaning-making by going on a journey to reclaim Blackness through identity transformation (Ndhlovu 2014; Hill-Collins 2002; Moussa and Tony 2017; Morgan and Bennett 2011; Bonnette 2015). The vehicle of Hip Hop provides another example of developing a counter-knowledge to hegemonic discourse (Gosa 2011). Aspiring Hip Hop Producer Lizzie wishes to remind people of the socio-political origins of Hip Hop by stating that *'Hip Hop is black culture'*. Ajur, as a female Hip Hop artist, shared that her vision and message for her music involves *'talking to my own black youth, brothers and sisters in the struggle'*. It also involves *'painting our own images, writing and lifting each other up'*. Élkato raps in Verse 1 of 'AfriCAN' (2018): [20]

I'm trying to get our message through I hope it's understood
We represent the people and we know we're doing good!

This process of affirming black identities through consciousness-raising also takes many steps which are not necessarily always linear in fashion. Instead, they involve praxis – the cyclical nature of action and reflection. It was understood that the liberation journey *'starts with knowledge of self'* where Jacob states *'I am a young positive black male who stands for many positive things'*. Once again, psychological liberation involves *'loving ourselves as black people'* and *'wanting to get to know more about black history* in Australia and about broader black history and culture' (Ezra). It also involves *'educating other people to be seen in a different light and give back'* (Jacob). Following a personal journey, this continuation of CHHP involves educating the broader public that *'black people are not ignorant'* of these themes or the way they are perceived (Lizzy).

Lizzie, however, felt differently about this, stating that young SSAs are not necessarily the ones who should be doing work in this area. From her own experiences of fighting ignorance and daily misunderstandings about her lived experience of black identity politics, she shares that *'if you want to listen, be informed'* and expresses her wishes: *'don't appropriate or be ignorant'*. Having to prove yourself and articulate this in the face of racialising discourses can be a massive burden on young SSAs and adds to the challenge of being a BIPOC young person, a theme which is explored in chapters 5–6. Therefore, this monograph points towards the necessity of staying informed through listening to young SSAs' voices on issues that affect them. The final theme informing young SSAs' sense of Blackness and the reclaiming of Afrocentric identities is addressed through the following more subtle sub-themes of young SSAs' identification with Black Consciousness and Black Power movements.

BLACK CONSCIOUSNESS AND BLACK POWER INFORMING YOUNG SOUTH SUDANESE AUSTRALIANS' SENSE OF BLACKNESS

Alongside Ture and Hamilton's (1992) focus on Pan-Africanism and black liberation, this section begins by further exploring participants' responses to the theme of Black Consciousness and identity. As previously mentioned, some ways that young SSAs involved in this research were able to arrive at these levels of knowledge about themselves or belief in greatness as a destiny was through a consciousness-raising process (Akom 2009). As described earlier in this chapter, an example of this is the process developed in Gua focus groups where young people watched documentaries about black issues, unpacked themes, and spoke in groups about the things that affected them. They then went on to collaborate and develop arts-based responses together (see chapter 7). The arts artefacts such as 'AfriCAN' (2018) and further BTSO artivist tracks represented are a way of capturing their learnings based on participating in CHHP practice and conceptually engaging with a CCA. Some of the themes pinpointed around Black Consciousness are encapsulated in *BCM's* track 'Trials and Tribulations' (BCM 2020)[21] where concerns of *'being devalued'* and *'stereotypes existing'* are *'standard for a black man'*. Despite this, as young artists *'blow up'* (become more famous) with *'instinct'* it is suggested by *i.OG* *'I know the vision. With the [writing] pad I move with wisdom'*.

This displays one example of the key benefits of the consciousness-raising process and the value of the fifth element in Hip Hop: knowledge (Morgan and Bennett 2011). That is, Hip Hop (writing and performing 'message' or 'conscious lyrics') has the potential to develop wisdom and discernment so that young people can articulate their worth and vision for themselves. Rather than epistemicide (the murder of knowledge about oneself due to neo-colonial influences), Ngũgĩ (1986) attests to the power of storytelling. Language is seen as 'a medium of communication, culture, and collective memory' (Ngũgĩ cited in Bautista 2018, 49) which provides an opportunity to reflect a unique worldview.

Other ways participants described their black consciousness-raising journey and the practical steps they took are summarised in the following areas of knowledge of cultural and black history and being assured of personal and communal strengths. Gabriel explains that rather than saying '*I am black or African so I am probably inferior*' he describes how, through his research, he has built up a sense of his identity so '*you know who you are*'. BTSO participants fight these phenomena in the face of racialising discourses whilst living in a predominantly white-centric society and whilst many injustices continue (further explored in chapter 6). Additionally, as demonstrated by many young SSAs in the 'AfriCAN' (2018)[22] track, it might also involve making communal claims such as '*we have greatness within us*' or '*we knew we would win*' (Future-of-the-Rap 2012).[23] These claims refer to the ways in which Hip Hop can provide a counter-narrative to the dominant discourse. SSA communities demand the opportunity to control the narrative about themselves through self-determination (Gosa 2011) (explored in chapters 6–7). I now turn to how BTSO artivists conceive of this process in relation to their experiences of identity politics. Instead of being consumed by Western hegemonic depictions or racialising discourses, they reframe depictions of their identities through their chosen art form. Their conclusions are formed through an understanding that acknowledging the power of your identity can be a type of calling (Sawyer 2006), which suggests that living out your identit(ies) is a way of living one's life, rather than the pursuit of a vocation or aspiration. Defining this calling is crucial in order for emerging leaders to potentially take others on a consciousness-raising journey.

EMPOWER BLACK LEADERSHIP THROUGH SHOWCASING BLACK CULTURE – IDENTITY AS CALLING

Following this process in 'conscious' or 'message' Hip Hop, *Krown* (2018c)[24] is one example of a rapper who has the ability to '*put it into music*' his personal challenges or what is going on in society. This brings a sense of *'empowerment'* and the ability to *'know your narrative'*. For example, he shares that he is a *'native King'* who is able to *'speak truth through a pen'*. You can therefore *'share knowledge'* if you *'don't end up losing'* as not everyone makes it successfully in the music industry (Artefact, Gua focus group 2019). Initiatives like the Grounded Project discussed in this research and other Footprints' intercultural projects renewed participants' importance of their own bla(c)k identities to 'know yourself more' whilst maintaining a connection to people and country (Genetic-Circus-Productions 2016, 1). This has organically and sometimes strategically transpired into many more collaboration and relationship building activities learning from each other's bla(c)k cultures and where cultural practices are reclaimed (Genetic-Circus-Productions 2016).

Finally, a personal journey through consciousness-raising is seen to be much more difficult unless communities are also developing *'black leadership'* where *'dreams are cultivated'* (Felicia). This was due to the fact that developing your political voice alone can be quite isolating. Additionally, a strategic movement also involves a collective focus. Acknowledging black heroes such as those from the American civil rights movement or blak Indigenous rights activists in the Australian context was seen to be important, as those leading a movement had the ability to create a vision for an alternative, more inclusive future.

NSM building also involves knowing where you stand as a black leader. Rapper and dancer *Daniel Elia,* who has built credibility within the arts industry, young people, and the broader community, therefore collaborated with influential spoken-word poet *Tenda McFly* to create a visually stimulating music video, 'Fear' (Elia 2019b).[25] The visuals can be viewed as a 'battle cry' depicting what black artists go through in terms of positioning themselves in their respective fields. This is also depicted in the way in which *Elia* paints himself in gold paint designs, almost as if they were contemporary Dinka tribal markings, to represent his cultural expression in a creative way. In this track, *Tenda McFly* gives advice to the young artist and others listening. He begins, *'Know that the tip of your pen is the scribe to a present which will soon become history'*. He goes on to translate his cryptic message – *'That means that not only do I see you as a black leader, you're an anthropologist and historian'* (*Daniel nods his head in agreement) (Elia 2019b).[26]

The priority demonstrated by all BTSO artivists is to do it for *'black youth across cultures'* in order to *'provide a better image'* and to *'inspire youth and the community'* (Lizzy). Here the mantle of *'teaching and influencing the next generation'* and being *'overcomers leading'* is passed on (Felicia). Across sectors (not just in music or sport) there are young black leaders who are representing in key areas of influence (Cranswick and Wicks 2021).

Many young people are tapping on the door of opportunity, ready to share their voice and be influencers. This involves cultivating young black leaders (explored in chapter 8). Creative Mumor wishes to assert *'Employ me!'* One way this cultivation occurs is through Hip Hop (Payne 2021). Acknowledging once again that Hip Hop is used as a vehicle for identity-based NSMs in creating social change, I now turn to how BTSO artivists specifically see their interaction with this concept.

Through reviewing BTSO artivists' tracks, it appears that Hip Hop music is an outlet to talk about matters of BIPOC representation and influence. In addition to the theme captured in chapter 4 that young SSA Hip Hop artists have 'visions from the kitchen' including dreams and hopes for their communities – the tracks which most strongly represent the theme of 'identity as calling' (Sawyer 2006), a phrase illuminated by Martin Luther King Jr, through conscious Hip Hop music expression, are discussed in this section. Firstly, *BCM's* 'Trials n' Tribulations (TnT)' track (2020)[27] suggests that *'coming up we never had much. That's when music picked us up'*. This provides the context from which identit(ies) are formed. *Daniel Elia's* track 'Lonely' notes the power of rap lyrics to communicate *'that real deep shit'* (2017b)[28] and also provides a context of challenges faced. In a similar themed track 'Trials and Tribulations' (2018c),[29] *Krown* suggests that he uses his *'mic as a weapon'* as he *'came to heal'*. Similarly, *Daniel Elia* (2018)[30] believes he creates *'music that can heal'*. Elia (2017a)[31] sees himself as a kind of *'hero'* or leader painting a *'Picasso'* who has the vision. These BTSO artivists are, therefore, role-modelling for the next generation what it means to use your influence for a social cause whilst facing many challenges in a social context. This is not always an easy path. Demanding respect for all the hard hours he has put in and whist still demonstrating loyalty to his *'n***a's'*, Elia shares his heartfelt plea: *'You should know I put my heart in every single line that I wrote. . . . In every single record I am trying to give you hope'* (Elia 2019a).[32]

This section presents the power of Hip Hop to 'give voice' to young SSA artists' expression of their identities and an outlet to vent concerns facing their communities. Through analysing these lyrics and discussing deep issues with the theme of BTSO, it was clear that for a select few artists following through with the theme 'identity as calling' (Sawyer 2006) takes a lot of persistence in the revolution resisting African oppression. This theme is most strongly highlighted by *Malesh P* in 'AfriCAN' (2018) (verse 6):[33]

Ah, no road is long enough for me to not take
No word is strong enough for me to not break
For many years my Africans have been excluded and denied of our rights
But the same people we influence.
Marginalised, in the band of my ancestors
You can hate on me but you cannot get rid of me.

Overall, the 'AfriCAN' (2018) track is about sparking change in the minds of generations. Through multiple BTSO artivists who are assured of their identity, whilst touching on the notions of identity politics, the track also has a strong truth-telling component. The overall vision is black excellence highlighting skin colour and appropriation of style. This research demonstrates that there are many young SSA Hip Hop superheroes. This theme is presented as a counter-narrative to deficit approaches depicted in the narratives of racialising discourses (Majavu 2015; Gatwiri and Anderson 2022). Returning to the 'visions from the kitchen' theme in chapter 4, artist *Daniel Elia* sees himself as cooking up a dream. He understands that there is more to life where we can reach a higher level of consciousness through leadership. *Elia* requests that people do not underestimate him or waste time. His 'Wake' (2019a)[34] track is a message of hope aimed to uplift his audience. In *Queen P's* track 'Effort' (2018b)[35] she declares *'this girl has risen'* as her social and political messages reach society whilst remaining true to her unique expression of her black-femme image. In her 'Black Panther' (Queen-P 2018a)[36] track, imagery includes her people (also depicted as superheroes) who are also rising, fighting back, or creating black businesses. She envisages a world where there are no more cages, and no more media manipulation in response to Apex gang betrayal of her community. The overall vision is black power, empowerment, or freedom.

Queen P, in her track 'Queen with Colour' (Queen-P 2018c)[37] encourages black royalty where there is no more slavery or chains. Throughout her *Bring Black Back* EP, featuring these black Afrocentric tracks, the meaning behind bringing back black culture showcases strength in community and that bla(c)k people/s in Australia are on the move despite racism and stereotypes. This is a form of resistance and black power. Black people owning businesses, expensive things, or being independent is a type of 'hyphy [hyperbolic] discourse' (Pope 2020) used in Hip Hop lyrics to emphasise certain points. *Amac Don,* in his 'Future of Rap' track (2012)[38] depicts himself and his community rising up, acknowledging that the revolution will not be televised, or the counter-story will not make media headlines. Ideally, *Amac Don* wishes to change or influence people's perceptions. Through a consciousness-raising journey that might take many forms, BTSO artivists like *Malesh P* (Mushroom-Creative 2017) and *BCM* (2020)[39] believe there is an opportunity to *'flip the script'* and challenge people's perceptions by showcasing people doing great things. BTSO artivists see that these are the conversations we need to have and are not afraid to talk about their sense of purpose, noting that 'conscious' can be popular.

Finally, *Ezeldin Deng* makes films consisting of urban youth narratives, where he considers producing films that represent stories from his SSA and other African diaspora communities counter to what is portrayed through racialising discourses. He sees that through creativity, young SSAs have the opportunity to share culture. Similar to Nyuon, who is often called upon to be a 'voice' for African young people, particularly around 'media unfairly targeted African youths' (Cranswick and Wicks 2021, 1) (explored in chapter 6), in his interview with *Voice for Change*, *Malesh P* reiterates the message of African diaspora BTSO artivists – 'we're here to stay . . . watch this space!' (Mushroom-Creative 2017). One final way they are able to do this is through acknowledgement of young SSAs' Black Power.

BLACK POWER – ASSERTING IDENTITIES WITHIN BLACKNESS THROUGH BLACK EXCELLENCE – UNDERSTANDING THAT YOU ARE 'BORN TO STAND OUT'

Under the umbrella of *Black Consciousness*, two other themes emerge, which include *Black Power* (part of a social movement) and *black excellence* (a recurring ideology). They are seen as a reversal of identity politics by instead highlighting strengths amongst black or African diaspora communities. Black Power is not seen as 'elitism' but stems from the idea that black people are not in 'powerless defence'. Whilst fairly short-lived due to systemic state-sanctioned targeting of the Black Panther Party chapters in the United States, this movement left a legacy where 'black minds were awakened to the ongoing reality of racism' (Kendi 2019, 139).[40] The ways in which participants envisaged and portrayed Black Power is through asserting identities within Blackness by portraying black excellence. This section demonstrates that by going on a consciousness-raising journey, participants continued to explore and understand that they are 'born to stand out' (BTSO).

Once again, the 'AfriCAN' (2018) track links to Afrofuturistic themes whereby the idea behind the title of the track is that 'African's can' do anything with sophistication, power and excellence. With *'limitless potential'* it was suggested that black Australian artists or young SSAs can be *'revolutionaries marching into victory'* (Wiaa from *BCM*, Verse 5)[41] which can take many forms. The track also refers to black nationalistic undertones in Hip Hop expression (Hill-Collins 2006). This is seen to be possible if they remain *'influential and persistent'* (*Malesh P*, AfriCAN (2018) Verse 6)[42] and position themselves as people with a message implying 'don't mess with us' (Fieldwork notes 2019). This is implied by the stanza *'don't dirty my skin, I meant it'* (*i.OG* from *BCM*, AfriCAN (2018) Verse 2).[43]

By following this *'destiny'*, Wiaa from *BCM* highlights *'we were destined from the start'* (AfriCAN (2018) Verse 5).⁴⁴ BTSO participants demonstrate hope and a belief that their people can bring about *'real change not just through algorithms'* (Suleyman). What is meant here is acknowledging that people might share a topic on social media and think it brings about change, but this is more referring to systemic organised or grassroots change. In relation to identity politics, this might extend to the way in which BTSO artivists accentuate, reclaim, or assert difference whilst drawing on the commonalities that exist amongst people groups. This is done amidst the struggle for recognition of and respect for difference. This is a key theme outlined in this research narrative, accentuating the BTSO motto elaborated on in chapter 6.

BTSO artivists' description of what is possible through their visions from the kitchen and assertion of their unique black identities point to the ways in which individuals or collectives go through the process of *conscientising* to cultural/national/social identities, which may lead to the formation of social movement (explored in chapters 5–6). Here social movements are a productive site to examine race both as a lived experience and as a metalanguage of power (Bernstein 2005). To achieve this, Ajur suggests again that *'knowledge is power and strength'* where *'half the battle is not believing you are capable'*. Therefore, the theme of illuminating people's attributes in a different light was seen as vital. Instead of stereotypes painted by racialising discourses, participants painted a more diverse picture. Another way to affirm black identities is *'remembering or recovering strength in blackness'* and your *'beauty or worth'* coming to the forefront (Ajur, Felicia, Akur). Young SSA spoken-word artist *Leza* at the Gua focus group (2019) shared her poem with the group after experiencing racial discrimination on the way to the Gua camp:⁴⁵

Stop making me feel any less because of my identity
Bow down to your Kings and Queens
Dipped in melaninated gold
The goldness of skin
I am black and beautiful
My people are black and beautiful
Is my melanin irritating your sunburn?

Similar to the themes above, she is pointing towards all the strengths in her and other African identities by again alluding to black royalty and richness exuding from culture and black identities. These statements could also be attributed to 'hyphy discourses' (using hyperbole in tracks) as featured through Hip Hop expression (Pope 2020). Bonnette (2015) pinpoints these could also be described as black nationalistic undertones in Hip Hop and can be a form of political voice and displaying a counter-narrative of African countries in Africa as weak nations. Holding on to notions of Black Power equips and prepares young people for the journey ahead. Along the theme of Blackness as royalty, the impact these statements have on young SSAs' sense of identity or self-worth alludes to the fact that young black Australians can hold tight to their sense of cultural dignity through alternative forms of storytelling. Table 4.1 summarises the key themes addressed in this chapter.

This notion of making demands in identity politics also fits within the broader 'born to stand out theme' where due to asserting their black, African, cultural and artistic identities they no longer aspire towards Whiteness. Instead, they wish to assert their position of power (Queen-P 2018b)[46] and be known for their own attributes.

Finally, the 'AfriCAN' (2018) track[47] can be seen as an anthem of black excellence which reinforces the theme that 'greatness that is Blackness within us' (SBS 2020, 1). Alongside BTSO artivists, this research depicts that when black people of all backgrounds unite, they can be an unstoppable force (Davis 2016; O'Brien 2017; Poe 2015). But it can also be witnessed in

Table 4.1 Gua Performance and Leadership Camp Key Themes

Gua Performance and Leadership Camp Key Themes	Chapter
1. The consciousness-raising process is an important pre-cursor to more public forms of resistance. This provided participants the opportunity to: • Talk openly about peace and conflict and arts-based ways of exploring alternatives in a trusted environment with peers and mentors who face similar experiences of systemic racism. • Express black joy and self-care in therapeutic and authentic environment. • Co-inquire about how Hip Hop can be used as a tool for social justice. • Collaborate and learn from creative professionals to develop artistic pieces exploring culture, identity, strengths, and the root issues behind racial tensions in Australia.	4
2. Key themes which came out of participating in this process involved participants demonstrating awareness of their selected topic of culture. Therefore, young SSAs preferred to: • Express their political voice through their knowledge of their sense of Blackness and their reclaiming of Afrocentric identities. Sub-themes: • Empower black leadership through showcasing culture – 'identity as calling'. • Young SSAs identification with Black Consciousness and Black Power movements.	4

Table 4.2 Gua Performance and Leadership Camp Key Themes Cntd.

Gua Performance and Leadership Camp Key Themes	Chapter
3. Participation in the consciousness-raising journey as part of an NSM: • This prepared participants to self-determine whether they wanted to continue to engage and plan the subsequent stages of the Grounded Project involving public performances. • As participants understood what it meant to embody the motto of being born to stand out, they chose to continue with this theme at subsequent stages of the Grounded Project.	5–6

everyday interactions, such as how participants viewed black excellence by *'focusing on strengths rather than the negative stuff'* (Amina). The topic of self-determination and featuring strengths-based narratives is a major theme that was often discussed amongst participants at the Gua focus groups and other Footprints' projects. This chapter has demonstrated that overall, shifting the narrative of themselves and their cultural heritage provides an opportunity to be proud of the country they now live in whilst simultaneously being proud of their South Sudanese origins and their Blackness. This understanding contributes to a sense of being able to establish a sense of freedom in what is often described as a 'white-centric' environment (explored in chapter 6). Table 4.2 summarises how the exploration of this key theme of understanding that you are 'born to stand out' made the following stages of participation in the Grounded Project possible (discussed in chapters 5–6).

ASSERTING BLACKNESS AS AN ALTERNATIVE EXPRESSION OF POLITICAL VOICE

Identity politics has been the core focus of this chapter. This chapter answered the sub-question: *What role does Hip Hop specifically play in building political voice?* by detailing young SSAs' involvement in the consciousness-raising through CHHP, which was the first phase of developing an NSM. Rather than being boldly political in the traditional sense of making tracks about systemic racism, young SSAs instead asserted their Blackness as an alternative expression of their political voice through cultural creative artefacts. In relation to this theme, Castells (2009, 425) insists that identity is crucially important because it builds 'interests, values, and projects, around experience, and refuses to dissolve by establishing a specific connection between nature, history, geography, and culture'. Castells (2009, 425) concludes identities anchor 'power in some areas of the social structure and build their resistance or their offensives in the informational struggle about the cultural codes constructing behaviour and, thus, new institutions'.

Kendi's (2019) anecdotes explore how one might begin to profess Antiracist practice in resistance to these constructed cultural codes, which exist within identity politics. Relevant to this chapter, which particularly discusses preferring features amongst racial groups, he describes how a cultural Antiracist is 'one who is rejecting cultural standards and equalising cultural differences among racial groups' (Kendi 2019, 81). In summary, 'whoever makes the cultural standard makes the cultural hierarchy. The act of making a cultural standard and hierarchy is what creates cultural racism' (Kendi 2019, 83). To be an Antiracist is to 'build and live in a beauty culture that accentuates instead of erases our natural beauty' (Kendi 2019, 113–114).

As an analysis tool, Bruner's (1991) functional approach to narrative inquiry explores the roles that narratives serve and the ways people construct and make sense of their reality through self-examination and shared storytelling. The excerpts of lyrics presented in this chapter and artefacts such as the 'AfriCAN' (2018) track demonstrate how young SSAs make sense of their lives by shaping their experiences in Australia into interpreted, coherent and sharable plots often depicted in fragments through their art forms. Through sharing their art form of Hip Hop, young people have constructed narratives that situate them within interpersonal, political, cultural and personal narratives (featured in each sub-section of this chapter). Through narrating the diversity and complexity of individual and communal identity formation, each participant's contributions also spoke of the social and cultural worlds within which they live and construct meaning and a sense of themselves within the broader notion of identity politics. Here, the core focus was to go on a consciousness-raising journey of restoring cultural roots and black histories, reclaim cultural identity and assert Blackness through black power and excellence. This is negotiated through everyday experiences when establishing social identities through popular culture or their specific cultural backgrounds (such as described in Afrofuturism examples).

Together, these collective experiences have further implications when young SSAs join NSMs or showcase themselves in arts-based initiatives. This is further elaborated on in chapters 6 and 7 when further discussing the impacts that the consciousness-raising process has on young SSAs' abilities to live lives they value. As such, the collection and analysis of young SSAs' tracks and perspectives have contributed to this research's ability to address the research aims of better understanding how young people conceive of and navigate this experience and, specifically, how they enact and maintain agency and resilience.

This chapter has demonstrated that knowledge of black power and excellence through Black Consciousness can translate to a *'movement of solidarity and coming together which includes processing challenges together*' (Amina). Specifically, this chapter has demonstrated how BTSO artivists critically re-evaluate history, racism, and the future of humanity (Mbembe and Dubois 2017). With this in mind, research participants assert that there is '*no need to ask for permission*'. They realise that through involvement in the consciousness-raising process through forms of Hip Hop expression that as black people they have the ability to '*organise ourselves, create music and our own subcultures*' (Akur). These ideas are further explored in the subsequent chapters.

The following chapter identifies how NSMs utilising Hip Hop or practices that can lead to social movements, which 'bring about new social practices' operate in part through the 'constitution of spaces for the creation of meaning' (Escobar 1992, 408). Through the journey of finding freedom and Afrofuturistic visions, participants demonstrate the kinds of futures they want to see through their art and civic engagement.

NOTES

1. Sampa the Great's (2020) performance of 'Black Power' at her Black Atlantis set at Planet Afropunk, Anastasia Tsobanopoulis: https://www.youtube.com/watch?v=Mx2a9s3mOgU.

See blogpost #1.

2. Favela Rising: https://en.wikipedia.org/wiki/Favela_Rising; https://www.youtube.com/watch?v=B5_DnxeEkts; https://www.imdb.com/title/tt1172222/; https://www.youtube.com/watch?v=E5sEGU5P76s; Soldiers of Peace: https://www.amazon.com/Soldiers-Peace-Michael-Douglas/dp/B002JPRLXS; https://www.youtube.com/watch?v=7LZ3szvvbP4; The Interrupters: https://en.wikipedia.org/wiki/The_Interrupters; https://www.youtube.com/watch?v=wS5Hjhy1RhM.

3. 3 Hip Hop Evolution: https://www.netflix.com/au/title/80141782.

4. Élkato (2020) 'The Matrix', YSAS Studios: https://soundcloud.com/user-940608762/lkato-matrix.

See blogpost #17.

5. https://www.facebook.com/akimera/.

6. 'Afri– CAN' (2019) produced by *Malesh P* - GUA Project - AfriCAN.mp3
See blogpost #2.

Created by workshop facilitator Malesh P at Gua Performance and Leadership Camp hosted by Footprints in January 2019.

See Chapter 3 appendix 'iv' for full lyrics of the track.

7. The Footprints trailer video (Mills-and-Boom 2019) and camp pictures (Footprints 2019) provide a feel for the essence of this stage of the research process. These are accessible via the links in the bibliography.

8. Afro Hub: https://www.facebook.com/Afrohub/.

9. Nyaruot (Ruth) Ruach (2019) Spoken-word Lyrics – Gua Performance and Leadership Camp,

This poem is written in response to the prompt 'identity and culture'
See blogpost #18.

I question my existence everyday
Where I fit in the stolen land from the bloodstains of injustice
Why does my soul yearn for home
What is home, where is home?
This unfamiliar space of comfort
A place where I felt the meaning of my own existence
Now, here at this displacement
And my chest is heavy
Maybe someday I will have enough courage to speak about it,
You know, the discomfort of my cultural loss
The funeral I never attended
A coffin without a body
A tongue that no longer understands nor speaks the hymns that my great Grandmothers would sing
I introduce myself with a name that sits comfortably on your tongue
Ruth
Not the name that was tattooed inside my Mother's womb
Not the name passed on generations of bloodlines that connect the roots of who I am
Black
Who I am
Black
Who I am
Black
My given name, Nyaruot
The woman who comforts every last drop of tears
I am she
Your mispronunciation washes my existence
But I have found comfort in it, how sad
The repetition of my mispronounced existence has slowly weakened me to be greeted wrongly
But let me assure that
I am Nyaruot Ruthless Ruach
Mispronounce it and I will tell you how Ruthless I can be

10. See Notes '6'.
11. See Notes '6'.
12. See Notes '6'.
13. See Notes '6'.
14. See Notes '6'.
15. See Notes '6'.

16. Krown (2019) 'Hold the Flag', Military Mind: https://www.youtube.com/watch?v=4FsiK_-2pVk.
   See blogpost #19.
17. See Notes '6'.
18. Esenadus Squad Ft Bangs & A-Mac.[Music Video] (2012) 'Esenadus', Esenadus Squad: https://www.youtube.com/watch?v=MU7WymNd7x4.
   See blogpost #20.
19. Krown (2018) 'Let us Live', Military Mind: https://www.youtube.com/watch?v=lxjsHiLgFJs.
   See blogpost #15.
20. See Notes '6'.
21. Burn City Movement (BCM) (2020) 'Trials n' Tribulations (TNT)' featured in Burn City Movement's Realness for Sale EP, Noble Studios: https://tidal.com/browse/album/131189065.
   See blogpost #4.
22. See Notes '6'.
23. Future of Rap (2012) 'The Future of the Rap' feat. Amac tha Don feat. Abe and Chingiling, Future of Rap: https://soundcloud.com/hbkfam/the-future-of-the-rap-a-mac.
   See blogpost #21.
24. Krown (2018) 'Trials n' Tribulations', Military Mind: https://www.youtube.com/watch?v=dZHsb0D0pZE.
   See blogpost #22.
25. Daniel Elia (2019) 'Fear' feat. Elysia Gomez & Tenda McFly, ALIA Records: https://www.youtube.com/watch?v=hDavDgwX22Q.
   See blogpost #23.
26. See Notes '25'.
27. See Notes '21'.
28. Daniel Elia (2017) 'Lonely' (Remix), ALIA Records: https://www.youtube.com/watch?v=Qb4gzkFKQI0.
   See blogpost #5.
29. See Notes '24'.
30. Daniel Elia (2018) 'I Know it Very Well', ALIA Records: https://www.youtube.com/watch?v=ABx2N2ksGcU.
   See blogpost #24.
31. Daniel Elia (2017) 'Shook' (official video), ALIA Records: https://www.youtube.com/watch?v=R7jriGuHdk0.
   See blogpost #10.
32. Daniel Elia (2019) 'Wake', ALIA Records: https://www.youtube.com/watch?v=kRYzbvk_u1E.
   See blogpost #25.
33. See Notes '6'.
34. See Notes '32'.
35. Queen P (2018) 'Effort' (music video), Sara Tonin: https://www.youtube.com/watch?v=-DMKuwgL6ng.

See blogpost #26.

36. Queen P (2018) 'Black Panther', from her Bring Black Back EP, Queen P: https://open.spotify.com/album/5jKDhvX8Yt2iHXdRUlFHnd?si=iEgYAou-QCqagcp0eY8Ohg.

See blogpost #3.

37. Queen P (2018) 'Queen with Colour', Jarrod Chase: https://www.youtube.com/watch?v=VvairPC3tJM.

See blogpost #29.

38. See Notes '23'.
39. See Notes '21'.
40. Some of the responses to this are explored in the Australian context for SSA communities in chapter 6.
41. See Notes '6'.
42. See Notes '6'.
43. See Notes '6'.
44. See Notes '6'.
45. Leza (2019) 'White Privilege', Spoken-word poetry developed at the Gua camp. See blogpost #27.

Privilege, let's talk about privilege
So, let's talk about mental illness
Which you claim to every time you talk about privilege
So quick to understand that which you do not understand
So quick to blame crime, on mental illness
With the wicked thoughts that roam your mind
And the stereotypes such as crime
Would you spend much time thinking about the privilege that we dream to have
That's equality
Identity
Identity, insensitive to my identity
I am my identity
I live and breathe my identity
My identity is made up of my culture
So when you disrespect me
You disrespect my identity
You disrespect my self-discovery
Trying to find recovery
Driving myself to worry thinking too deep
Feeling sorry, carrying baggage
Running around attracting bad energy
Trying to balance
Find synergy
Living in a world today full of hatred
I can't take it, I can't fake it
Trying to break this barrier that has a wall to deep to break it
Making me insecure

Even though I know I am pure
Stop making me feel any less because of my identity
Bow down to your kings and queens
Dipped in melaninated gold
The goldness of skin
I am black and beautiful
My people are black and beautiful
Is my melanin irritating your sunburn?

46. Queen P (2018). Hummingbird. In *Bring Black Back EP*. Queen P: https://open.spotify.com/track/76GoDC8lvnA4bzJgRxv42A?si=3VvbFuLJRmiq4zY29EL7TQ.

47. See Notes '6'.

Chapter 5

'My Skin Ain't Apex'

Presenting Counter-Narratives to Racialising Discourses

Excerpt from 'Let Us Live' track (Krown 2018b)

We're not as bad as you think we are
Let us live why you making our life hard
We're not as bad as we're painted, not at all
Some of us are bad but not as dangerous as you think we are.

Excerpt from '41 Bars of an African gang member' track (Amac Don 2019)

It's been a minute they've been making a noise
They're broadcasting news, divided voice
They downplay the many making a progress
Paying taxes, graduating and all
The newsroom, the public and the authorities
Judging the many
Based on minorities
I'm victimised, my parents are traumatised
I can't even step in a shop without judgement
Like I'm going to take something
'African gangs' is all over the news
Deport them back is all over social media
The whole community judged based on a few
Who to blame? This corrupt media
Mr. Turnbull you should know better
As a Prime Minister you should know better.

Krown's (2018b)[1] track 'Let Us Live' and *Amac*'s track (2019)[2] '41 Bars of an African gang member' – presented above and detailed in chapter 1 – represent two Hip Hop tracks by SSA artists expressing their political voice to resist the African and Apex gang narrative primarily portrayed through mainstream media and political discourse and targeted moral panics. As forms of racialising discourses, chapter 1 detailed how this discourse involved depictions of young SSA's communities in Australia as not integrating, painting a picture that they are criminals and as a result threatening deportation. Chapter 4 outlined the broad metanarratives of research participants' experiences with racism and systemic injustice in Australia as a result of these harmful narratives, necessitating that young SSAs build their sense of political voice in response. This chapter addresses these key narratives by honing in on participants' views of the specific devices used by mainstream media and some politicians to recreate perpetual moral panics. Following a description of the key narratives of racialising discourses, this chapter concludes by focusing on how young SSA participants responded with their political voice through Hip Hop expression in the Grounded Project to develop counter-narratives to resist these mainstreamed discourses.

'Let Us Live' (Krown 2018b)[3] was released at the peak of the African gangs narrative in 2018, a narrative which was described in chapters 1 and 2 as spanning over a decade. The first time I heard this track was at the youth drop-in centre at YSAS in Dandenong. Two young South Sudanese women, Lizzie and Akur, who are spoken-word and Hip Hop artists showed me the music video which depicted SSA artist *Krown* on the train (see photo 11

Figure 5.1 Krown – 'Let Us Live' Music Video. *Source*: Krown 2018b.

below) where he runs into another young SSA Hip Hop artist *Titan* and shakes hands. One of his 'homies' is holding a placard with a message to Channel 7 mainstream news network: '7 is the Fox News of Australia'. *Krown* was referring to the way in which allegedly right-wing conglomorate news networks are the prime perpetuators of these racist narratives. In the music video (depicted in figure 5.1), the scene transitions to the stark image of an elevator with sparks flying out. *Krown* is standing in front with the South Sudanese flag draped around his neck. Drawing on the key themes of BIPOC representation depicted in chapter 4, the message he is sending is that he is proud of his strength in Blackness and that young SSAs are here to stay in Australia.

Krown's words are direct in the hook (bridge of the track): his message is that he and his homies are sick of being misunderstood by society due to misrepresentation in the media.[4] The significance of this track is that through his engagement with a New Social Movement (NSM), *Krown* is now publicly engaging in depicting his experiences with identity politics and presenting his political voice for broader society to hear his message. *Krown* and his homies announce to society that a fundamental problem exists in the given area of the media portrayal of the Apex narrative by stating *'what the fuck is Apex'* (Krown 2018b).[5] The track went viral with over 10,000 views by July 2022. Comments on the YouTube clip from around the world state that this track represents real Hip Hop due to it being a form of political Hip Hop, music with a message that calls for social change (Asante 2008).

This chapter addresses the third sub-question: *What role does political voice play for young SSAs in specifically resisting racialising discourses?* The use of the props, such as the protest placard and flag demonstrate the 'symbolic' or 'prophetic function' describing the future which will come about, a feature of their message and the message of NSMs (Melucci cited in Escobar 1992, 407). The *cultural function*, also a feature of NSMs, is depicted by *Krown* wearing his South Sudanese national flag with pride and dignity. Melucci (cited in Escobar 1992, 407) describes this as a kind of *new media* due to the influence the politically-driven Hip Hop track has in society. The prophetic function refers to the way in which *Krown* and *Titan* using ther Hip Hop persona's also organised the Channel 7 protest the month before this track video release (Eddie 2018; Mushroom-Creative 2018; R. Smith 2018). Whilst chapter 5 outlined the development of political voice through consciousness-raising of participants as a precursor to involvement in an NSM, *Krown* and *Titan's* actions involved 'contemporary collective action', another step in participating in an NSM which assumes the 'form of networks submerged in everyday life' amongst his 'homies' [friends] (Melucci cited in Escobar 1992, 407). Considering that these networks are immersed in urban youth culture, the portrayal of conscious Hip Hop and civic action is considered to be an NSM. The networks involved in this scenario were *Krown* and *Titan's* broader Hip Hop community and like-minded networks which they reached through advertising on social media platforms.

This chapter utilises CRT (Moreton-Robinson 2004; Briese and Menzel 2020) to discuss *Whiteness* and how displays of the social constructs of Whiteness and political discussions about race are operationalised in Australian racism. As outlined in chapter 2, Whiteness is the system that young SSAs are being racialised by, and what they are being measured by and expected to conform to. The discourses about non-integration and criminality are racialising discourses and forms of *necropolitics* – death-dealing regimes operationalised by proponents of Whiteness. Specifically, notions of criminality and racialising discourses are forms of violence young SSAs are navigating and can lead to 'deathworlds' (implications discussed in chapter 3) (Mbembe and Corcoran 2019).

The specific racialising discourses referred to in this chapter are the media and political portrayal of the African gangs narrative in Australia. Two analytical approaches of narrative and arts-based inquiry explore young SSA responses to racialising discourses through their political voice. As part of the ethnographic presentation in this research, two significant timelines affecting young SSAs discuss the death of Liep Gony (2007) and the peak of the Apex gang narrative (2018) as examples of racialising discourses. In this approach, I emphasise the surrounding socio-political considerations, including how media and moral panics operate in Australia. Utilising narrative and arts-based inquiry, I explore these tracks and others from BTSO artivists to discuss how a common set of media practices (described below) interact with the portrayal of SSAs and form racialising discourses.

Through the lens of NSMs (Trapp 2005; Bevington and Dixon 2005; Escobar 1992), this chapter also explores how young SSAs portray their political voice when involved in public performances in the second phase of the Grounded Project fieldwork. These forms of creative expression were initially developed by Footprints to respond to the concept of 'being different in public' or creating 'little publics', which are counter-narrative to dominant public pedagogy explored in chapter 3. This chapter demonstrates a section of the South Sudanese communities' responses to racialising discourses demonstrated through their political voice in Hip Hop, through forms of artivism, and using their Hip Hop persona in public. This is through participation in this project and YPAR hosted by Footprints. This chapter also represents one of the strongest research themes that emerges from the findings, which explains how young SSAs express their political voice in a more explicit manner. Young SSAs' actions and artefacts demonstrate alternatives to the current systems (Dinerstein 2015).

Interviews with BTSO participants were framed around a discussion of racialising discourses, which was necessary to set the scene. The story of Liep Gony's murder in 2007 and other events were discussed to highlight the SSA communities' depiction in the media and public discourse in Australia over a decade since that event. Findings suggest that whilst media moral panics are common tools as media devices, the longitudinal focus on the South Sudanese community extends beyond the cyclical nature of the ways in which racialising discourses profile new waves of migrants to push political agendas. It resulted in young SSAs undertaking new forms of artivism and demonstrations of their political voice through Hip Hop artivism (Asante 2008). The sustained focus on SSAs is therefore pertinent for how we consider racialising discourses in radical contexts. This chapter debunks myths surrounding some of these narratives by presenting the findings of an ethnographic truth-telling approach (Hill-Collins 2013). BTSO artivists demonstrate their political voice through developing counter-stories to the current pervasive narratives (Gosa 2011).

RACIALISING DISCOURSES POINTED TOWARDS SOUTH SUDANESE AUSTRALIANS

The application of the CRT lens illuminates race as a 'technology for human difference' that places Caucasian peoples at the top to create a system of power that perpetuates white supremacy on both a local and a planetary scale (Lentin 2020, 10). The history of Australia's settler-colonial context has linked race to power structures, whereby the notion of Whiteness suggests that the formation of dominant racial groups constructs a type of consciousness that makes up our identities. We continue to group people based on race markers as a result. Under the umbrella of Australian Whiteness studies (Idriss, Butler, and Harris 2021; Stratton 2020), I now discuss racialising discourses in localised contexts primarily through perpetuated media and moral panics targeting the African diaspora in Australia. Through this process, I recognise that rather than being an overall term, 'Whiteness' needs to be deconstructed to acknowledge that Whiteness is the system by which young SSAs are being racialised by, measured against, and expected to conform to. Lentin (2022, 486) connects the work of race and racialisation with hegemonic Whiteness in this way; describing 'race' as a 'technology for the management of human difference, the main goal of which is the production, reproduction and maintenance of white supremacy'. This includes young SSAs grappling with Whiteness as it is theorised in CRT and which is the fundamental concept in the creation of race and therefore racism (Moreton-Robinson 2004; Briese and Menzel 2020).

For SSAs, everyday racism and racist policies that are informed by the social construct of Whiteness are resisted by participants through forms of Hip Hop expression and through their own articulations of experiences of identity politics. In this context, Moran and Gatwiri (2022) suggest that black bodies are organised and structured within systems of racial hierachicalisation and the impact of this within relational contexts. Building on the concept of racial hierarchies as outlined through CRT, the in-group (elite) in this case is 'mainstream culture' whose attributes are depicted as white and safe, whilst the out-group (subjugated) includes SSAs whose attributes are depicted as dark-skinned and violent. Therefore, young SSAs are racialised through discourses about integration and criminality in ways that maintain and reproduce white supremacy, or the system of Australian Whiteness. This leads to white racialising discourses which includes the racist propaganda and messages of media and political moral panics about racialised communities (Scheurich 1993).

Considering the 'problem of the "colour-line"' prioritising white skin colour at the top of the perceived race hierarchy (Du Bois and Alexander 2018[1903], 29), specifically media and political narratives are therefore developed to demonstrate SSAs' failures to integrate into 'mainstream' (white) culture, further ensuring white elitism. The opening section includes table 1.1, describing how racialising discourses persist to target young SSAs. This occurs through producing stories linking SSAs to 'traditions of violence' that is, portraying them as criminals involved in gangs without reform, which becomes a way of characterising young males in particular as part of a larger 'problem group of South Sudanese men' (Windle, cited in Hickey-Moody 2013a, 43). This monograph asserts that these narratives have significant influence on broader mainstream (predominantly white) society, influencing Australians to see these stories as behavioural norms for these communities (who have noticeably darker skin), resulting in fear and disdain towards this group (Khan and Pedersen 2010).

To maintain positioning as an elite group, tools such as media and political moral panics are folded into social and cultural norms. These practices continue to Other communities as a mechanism of reproducing and maintaining systemic power hierarchies (Elias, Mansouri, and Paradies 2021). Misleading media reporting problematises and taints perceptions of the entire SSA community (Farquharson, Marjoribanks, and Nolan 2018; Benier et al. 2018; Macaulay and Deppeler 2020; Weng and Mansouri 2021), which has led to young SSAs feeling Othered in Australian society (Henry-Waring 2008). Therefore, racialising discourses communicate that it is necessary to adopt *white culture* to *integrate* into the Australian way of life (Tuan 1998). This is a form of *colourism*, thta is, we do not see race and we all must look or act the same to 'blend in' or 'not cause trouble'/disrupt the 'status quo'. I now outline two examples to show how the Australian system of Whiteness produces racialising discourses, racism, and racial logic, and how it is resisted by SSAs through building their political voice through Hip Hop expression.

The first example involves SSA David Nyuol Vincent (2013), a former child soldier and Lost Boy.[6] Vincent painted himself in white zinc cream and confronted former immigration minister Kevin Andrews in 2007. His actions were in response to Andrews' claim that the South Sudanese community were failing to integrate in Australia, an example of how racialising discourses are operating in localised contexts. Specifically, Vincent noted that the Australian government only wanted 'white-only migrants' (ABC 2007, 1). Channing-Brown (2018) and post-colonial theorist Fanon (1968) likens this expected adaptation to the cultural hegemony of Whiteness where one's Blackness may need to be disguised in a *white mask*.

Another example of the manifestations of racialising discourses is the way in which localised place-based stereotypes are also reinforced through the supposed 'racial logic' of stereotypes about enclaves. These narratives are depicted as 'self-segregating' migrant communities that 'disrupt the possibility of social cohesion' (Lentin 2020, 11). When the South Sudanese communities were settling in Australia, places such as Noble Park (see figure 1 in chapter 1), located in the CGD, were likened to the U.S. notions of *hood* and *ghettos* when the media misreported the murder of 19-year-old SSA Liep Gony in 2007 (full details explored in chapter 5). Initially, the media claimed a gang of South Sudanese young people were responsible for his death, likening them to Los Angeles gangs. However, very quickly this case proved to be a racist hate crime perpetrated by two Caucasian males. The media did not amend their error and instead led with federal social policy that outright victimised SSAs by challenging their right to exist in large numbers in Australia due to a perceived failure to integrate (Nunn 2010).

This critical incident led to a decade of Sudanese gang discourse (chronicled in table 1.1) that associated Blackness with criminality, whilst anti-gang legislation had a profound effect on young SSAs' mental health and ability to thrive (Majavu 2020; Pittaway and Dantas 2021). Concepts of youth cultural and creative agency through NSMs are now explored as collective expressions of the process young SSAs take to build their political voice to resist racialising discourses.

RACIALISING DISCOURSES AS A BY-PRODUCT OF 'WHITENESS'

Considering social indicators and a CRT analysis, this section explores how Majavu (2018, 187) accentuates the discursive methods of the Australian system of Whiteness. Through a critical lens, this is the system referred to in this monograph and the conditions that necessitated the need for young SSAs to actively resist. To unpack the interplay of how the system operates, *infra-humanisation* is an example of one of its racialising discourses or practices, specifically by portraying 'uncommodified Blackness' in mainstream media and political narratives. *Racist infra-humanisation* is further theorised as the belief that one's *in-group* is perceived as more human than an *out-group.* These discursive methods such as described by *Krown,* continue to inform society about racist narratives and also lead to the 'blatant racist dehumanisation that Africans are subjected to in Australia' (Majavu 2018, 187). The ways in which racist dehumanisation is experienced by SSAs in particular is typified through how mainstream Australia 'regards them as outsiders and perpetual refugees who are failing at integration' (Majavu 2018, 187). This is further explored through the African gangs narrative below. This section briefly sets the scene for how participants construct 'Whiteness and Otherness' and how it pertains to Australian identity politics.

CRT asserts that conforming to Whiteness is a societal expectation. In practice, particular 'white identities' create discourses in particular ways in order to ensure compliance. Ndlovu (cited in Majavu 2018) suggests that discourses perpetuated by white identities occur in subtle and commonplace ways in the Australian context. This section also describes the ways in which participants attribute this to their experiences of being expected to conform to racialising discourses (fitting in or integrating) rather than finding their own self-expression. Sophia, who is a manager in community and arts development in local council identifies that her definition of racialising discourses speaks to her of *'how we shape and talk about culture . . . in primary or dominant Caucasian areas'*. Whilst recognising 'Whiteness' as a social construct but an all-pervasive phenomenon, this sets the tone for how participants acknowledge the impact of racialising discourses that this chapter addresses. I now turn to participants' further descriptions of racialising discourses.

Misreported media and political moral panics, and the problematic and often racist narratives they portray, which perpetuate racialising discourses, can be used as a technique to develop public opinion. The result is that what is portrayed as mainstream public opinion can then be used for legislative purposes. For example, it is acknowledged that the topic of 'ethnic youth gangs' is commonly depicted by predominantly mainstream media in cyclical moral panics every time a new wave of migrant community settles in Australia (R.E. White and Mason 2006; R.D. White 1999). This monograph forefronts however the unprecedented and unique impacts of a longitudinal targeted focus on the alleged inability of the South Sudanese community to integrate into Australian society – the specific discourse addressed.

The extent of the impact of the African gangs narrative has recently been documented (Benier et al. 2018; Macaulay 2020; Majavu 2020; Pittaway and Dantas 2021). The following section features findings from the ethnographic study to explore themes from two time periods within the development of the African gangs narrative. Despite this discourse occurring over a decade, this chapter focusses on when Gony was murdered in 2007 and the following period, 2016–2018, when the African gangs narrative was in the spotlight in Australian media through the depiction of the Apex gang. The focus in this section sets up the more prominent discussion that this monograph aims to tackle, namely, the ways in which SSA Hip Hop artists develop tactics to tackle and resist these narratives.

MEDIA AND POLITICAL MORAL PANICS PERPETUATING RACIALISING DISCOURSES

Chapter 1 described how critiques of Australian politics and media have linked to their depiction of widespread moral panics. When analysed through a CRT lens, this body of research aligns with Majavu's (2018) claims, which link these critiques to suggestions that prioritising Whiteness is specifically responsible for this frenzy. Whilst broader experiences with systemic racism for young SSAs were detailed in chapter 4, this section builds on current knowledge of young SSAs' experiences in Australia by setting the scene for how participants position media and moral panics as efforts to maintain the hegemony of Australian Whiteness, which drive and perpetuate racialising discourses. This section therefore looks at four topics within which participants discuss the impact of media in their lives and the effects mainstream media have on their communities. These themes were developed as part of the analysis exercise that involved mapping participant responses to their perceptions of the literary devices and practices of the media. A cross-section of voices such as youth, Council workers and teachers who were present at the time are featured in order to account for historical context and triangulate the claims of demonstrated impacts on the South Sudanese communities. Specific links were made to the historical account of Liep Gony's murder and the Apex gang narrative. This process led to the findings which suggest that whilst media moral panics are common tools as media devices profiling new migrants to push political agendas, the longitudinal focus on the South Sudanese communities extends beyond the pervasive nature of racialising discourses whereby media spotlights might be commonly fleeting, but for the SSA community, the negative press has continued. A systemic analysis described in chapter 4 discussing state decision-making and the ability to influence public outcomes through a range of practices resulted in unprecedented and profound impacts such as ongoing youth suicide amongst SSA communities, further impacting freedoms within South Sudanese communities in Australia. Understanding how these experiences are linked to a common set of practices espoused by mainstream media and politicians is the crucial link demonstrated in this chapter.

REFERRING TO LIEP GONY'S MURDER – 14 YEARS ON AND THE 'AFRICAN GANGS' NARRATIVE – 'MY SKIN AIN'T APEX'

Whilst Colic-Peisker & Tilbury (2008) describe a growing bias towards what were described as 'African refugees' during a peak migration point in 2004, alongside Windle (2008), this research contends that Liep Gony's murder and the surrounding commentary on this incident largely led to the racialisation of African young people in Australia. Whilst not necessarily a linear process, this series of events led to the second *encounter* stage of Cross' (1971) black consciousness identity development theory (detailed also in chapters 1 and 4), characterised by a dramatic event, such as being assaulted by white racists or watching a televised report of a racial incident (e.g., Liep Gony's 2007 murder), which shatters the black person's understanding of race and Blackness.

Through demonstrating the socio-political context and an overview of participants' perceptions, understandings, and feelings about these historical events, this section outlines some of the myths that surround the African gangs narrative by exploring some of the key circumstances shaping the portrayal of Liep Gony's murder and the Apex gang saga. This section is imperative to understand the specific narratives emphasised in racialising discourses and the grounds through which young SSAs build their political voice through Hip Hop, as depicted later in the chapter. Understanding media and political devices sets the scene to understand the nature of young SSAs' lyrics and actions when they present counter-narratives resisting these forms of racialising discourses.

This section looks at the dominant discourses to break down the insidious nature of how these perceptions come about by going through the steps in the story of how Gony was murdered and the impending impact on the South Sudanese communities in Australia and his family. As this side of the events never made it into the Australian media to the same extent, it therefore pinpoints a history of 'where it all began' in terms of the media and political targeting of SSAs. As suggested, whilst this has been explored in previous research to some extent, this outline depicted in this chapter brings a unique perspective. As suggested in chapter 3, the motivation for this research provides an opportunity to reflect after a fourteen-year period and is presented out of respect for his memory.

Following this timeline, the African gangs narrative continued through a number of iterations in the Australian psyche. Using topic modelling from a corpus of 41,557 items in six Australian newspapers published over a ten-year period, Nur, Farquharson, and Haw (2021) identified in their research on racialised constructions of 'gangs' in Australian news media discourse that focus on gangs as closely connected to discussions on crime, policing and security. Whilst ethnic youth gangs are a frequent moral panic depicted in the media (R.D. White 1999), the African gangs narrative is described in this chapter as a perpetuated racialised discourse (Kendi 2019) which continues primarily from 2007 to the present day (Nur, Farquharson, and Haw 2021) (see table 1.1). As suggested in chapter 1, the period of 2016–2018 after the Moomba riots led to what is known as the Apex gang narrative. This generic terminology used by journalists, commentators and politicians was used to link a series of criminal acts (allegedly by predominantly SSA young people) involving burglary, assaults, carjacking, and home invasion into a particular narrative, often with little evidence, and in some cases clear contradictory evidence that incidents are related to each other or to the Apex gang at all (NEMBC 2016; Baker and Wiedersehn 2018). Participants highlighted that the way in which these stories were portrayed through racialising discourses created media and moral panics. Participants outlined that they believe media entities and editorial techniques are responsible for the one-sided portrayal of SSAs. This therefore limits their ability to seek freedom in Australia.

The following four sub-sections discuss the key themes of how participants envisage media and political discourse linking with moral panics resulting in a perpetuation of institutional biases prioritising and benefiting Whiteness as conceptualised through CRT. This is further evidence, as discussed in chapter 4 that the *'system [which perpetuates* racialising discourses *and the social construct of race] ain't playing'* (Krown 2018b).[7]

THE IMPACT OF TERMS AND FOCUS OF EDITORIALS IN MAINSTREAM MEDIA

One way racialising discourses are developed is through the specific devices and operations of mainstream media. This section discusses the profound effects that the use of these devices have on young SSAs. Participants attribute a range of media tactics to media tycoons such as Rupert Murdoch and his *News Corps*, including featuring sensational, alarmist news stories and chasing ratings. Malek described how *'terms can be problematic'* as *'words/definitions have the power to create the future. Terms can manifest into things and become life'*. It has been identified that News Corp has the potential to monopolise the way in which news stories reach audiences (Cassell Jr 2020).

For example, News Corp owns the Australian tabloid newspaper Herald Sun, which employed Andrew Bolt, a conservative social and political commentator known for propagating hate speech and vilifying ethnic and religious minorities (Muller 2020). Attempts by the Australian Press Council to rate Bolt's articles as offensive on the grounds that they breach rules regarding factual accuracy; the presentation of balanced and fair material; and the requirement that material does not cause substantial offense, distress, or prejudice appear to have little impact. Australia has never had a publicly trusted or effective system of media accountability (Muller 2018).

In her track 'The Matrix', *Élkato* (2019)[8] envisages that strategic media portrayals and media devices are *'part of the tactics'* which are likened to *'assimilation of the mind'* or *'people getting brainwashed'*. Gua camp focus group participants (2019) also suggest that they believe the media portrayal of their community as not integrating or as being criminals is *'no accident'*. As another example of media tactics perpetuating racialising discourses, *Titan*'s track 'Cheques and Balances' (2020)[9] notes the ways in which racialising discourses, through the portrayal of the African gangs narrative (mentioning Apex specifically), are considered to be a selling point. Referring to some politicians and owners of media networks, he states that *'suits and ties make money off us'*. SSA participant Ezra discusses a similar opinion describing corporations making money. He then jokingly suggests that the media is responsible for putting his community on the map where *'everybody knows us now!'* Not everyone sees this as humorous. Cambodian Australian participant Akra describes how these entities *'put all the other communities through it'*. In the case of South Sudanese communities in Australia, he identifies the similarities in these stories to his own former refugee experience. As his family fled Cambodia and as a youth worker, he is aware of the common narratives, stereotypes, and misrepresentations that surround former refugee communities. For SSA communities, however, he also describes the unique ways these narratives play out by highlighting that the young people getting in trouble are a *'small demographic of young people that are kind of stereotyped or victimised by the media'*.

Young SSAs point out their experiences, along their own unique journey in Australia, of extended racial profiling (a form of racialising discourses) and systemic racism that they believe was due to their Blackness (see chapter 4). This makes their experiences in Australia different from other recently migrated communities. Akra goes on to share his frustrations around how the media exacerbates and sensationalises information:

> we spend so much time reversing and making up for fucking bad journalism. You know, fear mongering . . . it's exhausting. But it's a small minority with all this offending stuff . . . and it wrecks it for the large majority.

Rather than the commonly perpetuated term *youth gangs,* which does indicate extensive organised crime, the correct term is *co-offending* and *co-offending networks,* which point to when two or more individuals act collaboratively, sometimes for an extended period (Bright, Whelan, and Morselli 2020). One of the *BCM* crew, Ibrahim, also declares how this kind of reporting using the terminology of 'gangs' '*should be illegal!*' Tina resigned from her role in television after her disgust over how mainstream media networks operate. She started up her own company '*working for the good of humanity*' and '*portraying positive and more nuanced stories*' as a result.

Consideration is then given to the impact of seeing the phrase *Apex gang* in predominantly mainstream newspapers 173 times in one year during the peak period of 2016 (Shepherd, Newton, and Farquharson 2018). If you liken this repetition to marketing practices and similarly consider Apex gang a form of 'branding', when exploring its impact on society and democracy, Jocz and Quelch (2008, 202) suggest that linking marketing tools to 'political science begins to connect individual-level outcomes with societal outcomes'. It also has implications for how young SSAs choose to explore other mixed-multimedia channels to develop alternative media (explored in chapter 6).

Existing research suggests that media representations impact the degree to which migrants experience rights in terms of both of how they are viewed by other members of society and the degree to which they feel empowered to exercise their right to communicate (Marjoribanks, Nolan, and Farquharson 2010). As an example of this, in his interview with *Voice for Change*, *Krown* (2018, 1) explores his realisation of the 'power of media platforms' to 'influence their particular audience's perceptions of other people'. This occurs to the extent that 'people don't really realise what that perception is. All they come to see is things that they see from an external point of view' (Mushroom-Creative 2018, 1). Whilst this was not the first time young SSAs were linked with crime reporting, Liep Gony's murder was a significant event in the perpetuation of racialising discourses. To demonstrate the impact of racialising discourses, it is therefore important to shed light on the media and political discourses around that period based on the findings from participants' perspectives.

TRUTH LEFT IN THE DARK: LIEP GONY'S MURDER

Referring to media representations of his community and youth incarceration rates of young SSAs, *Titan* in his spoken-word poem 'Deng and Katie' says that *'the truth will always be left in the dark'*.[10] He is referring to the ongoing depiction of young SSAs in Australian narratives and how he wants Australians to know the 'truth'. Through narrative spoken-word format, the story of

Deng (a South Sudanese male) and Katie (a Caucasian female) details *Titan's* truth as a young SSA:

*I am not responsible for Deng, like you're not responsible for Katie
But apparently if Deng commits a robbery then his sins Titan must also carry.
However, if Katie goes on a crime spree, slaps an Officer and blows the world up
Then Katie is just crazy.* (Titan 2019)[11]

There was resounding agreement amongst participants that an example of truth 'left in the *dark*' surrounds the murder of Gony in September 2007 (see table 1.1). Whilst abstracts of this finding have been presented in previous chapters, participants in Gua focus groups (2017/2019) determined that it is important to outline the steps surrounding this moral panic of young South Sudanese not integrating in Australia as it relates to the role played by mainstream media in consequential order. In summary, The Australian newspaper initially reported, and then retracted, that a South Sudanese gang had killed Gony. As suggested, it was later found that two Anglo-Australian young people (aged 19 and 21 at the time of the incident) were responsible for Gony's murder (Farouque 2007; Kuai 2009). In the week surrounding Gony's death, Australian media sources portrayed young SSAs as forming gangs and blamed them for violence in the suburbs of Naarm. Reports claimed that this was evidence that Sudanese crime gangs were on the rampage (Barry 2007), leaving residents living in terror (Marshall 2007). The media also misrepresented areas in the southeast of Naarm such as Noble Park by taking photos and making it 'look like a ghetto' (VEOHRC 2008, 27). Media Watch (Barry 2007, 1) and the Australian Communications Media Authority (ACMA) conducted a media investigation, finding the Channels 7, 9 and 10 mainstream media networks in Australia guilty of misreporting on this subject (Fray 2009). Participants felt that by this time, the damage had already been done in terms of damaging Australian society's perceptions of young African diaspora in Australia. The general public would not necessarily be aware of these findings (nor to some extent care).

Despite reform in some areas of Australian journalism since this period, A Current Affair's 'African gangs' (2018) and 'Race War' (2019) programs have been reviewed by ACMA for misleading audiences and inciting violence (Zhou 2019; Carmody and Duke 2019). These portrayals of SSAs were followed by other documentaries attempting to debunk some of the myths (Joined-Up-Films 2018) but essentially still focused on topics of 'African crime' rather than looking at the communities from a strengths-based approach. This monograph alternatively broadcasts South Sudanese communities' counter-narratives to forms of white nationalism and expectations to 'assimilate' into the Australian way of life.

BTSO artivists have always been presenting counter-narratives through Hip Hop. Nyok, Shaker, Amir and Emmanuel claim that *'racialising discourses forced [their] hand to write lyrics addressing media portrayal of [their] community'*. Through presenting Hip Hop-based counter-narratives, they wish to define themselves and not by their skin colour (Malesh-P 2020).[12] CRT identifies that the colour of skin is positioned as the point of contention. The main feature of racism is prioritising Whiteness and white skin over other skin tones. Rather than being defined by this and racialising discourses, Jamal considers *'how to project yourself despite the noise [of Whiteness]'*. One way, as identified in this monograph, is through young SSAs' Hip Hop expression via other arts-based community development alternatives explored below and in chapter 7.

This section has demonstrated that a set of insidious 'media tactics' under the umbrella of 'moral panics' and racialising discourses have been at play when depicting SSAs in harmful and racist narratives. I now turn to research participants' views on the way in which media corporations have been linked to specific political agendas, further limiting young SSAs' freedom to not be further Othered in Australian public discourse.

POLITICAL FOCUS – FEARMONGERING TACTICS AMONGST 'THE SUITS'

As chapter 3 demonstrated through a systems analysis considering CRT, part of the consciousness-raising journey is going through the process of formulating the links between different aspects of the neoliberal system, that is, how the media might be linked to politics. The youth justice or education systems were used as examples. Linking the media to Australia's political focus on their communities, Ibrahim and Amir also described how misinformed opinions are *'born out of ignorance'* and that it *'is political'*. Continuing with the example of the influence of the Murdoch media empire, this essentially means that the conglomerate also has control over how 'news' is depicted. A founded criticism is that it is becoming increasingly right-leaning (Tiffen 2020). Power is therefore maintained through Murdoch and those associated with his ideologies by espousing political agendas on his media platforms (Muller 2018). Linked to a similar political persuasion, of further concern is Kerry Stokes' ownership of the Channel 7 news network (Muller 2018). These further examples illustrate how the *'truth is left in the dark'* (Titan 2019)[13] when piecing together the impact conglomerates and political persuasions stemming from racialising discourses have on Australians and racialised communities.

My master's research (Williams 2015) (outlined in chapter 1) explored the initial impact when South Sudanese communities' ability to integrate was questioned by former immigration minister Kevin Andrews in a negative media campaign targeting the community after the death of Gony (Caldwell 2007) during an election year. South Sudanese Australians have identified that it has been difficult to recover from such a campaign as similar racial profiling of this cultural group has continued (Topsfield 2008). These incidents led to growing nationalism, which continues to exclude by utilising fear-based narratives of the Other (Khan and Pedersen 2010; Marjoribanks, Nolan, and Farquharson 2010). Minister Andrews then reduced the humanitarian intake of Africans to Australia as a result of these beliefs in October 2007 (Cowan 2007). This sparked community outrage as he was accused of being the perpetrator of racial hostility towards Sudanese migrants (Oakes and Cooke 2007; SMH 2007), fitting perfectly with the political interests of those supporting the freeze on African migrants (Barry 2007).

Amir attributed this form of racialising discourse as *'fearmongering tactics'*. These tactics continued when Liberal Home Affairs Minister Peter Dutton and former Liberal Prime Minister Malcolm Turnbull made statements in 2018 about Melbourne not being safe due to African gangs (Lord 2018). Young SSA Thon in a Vice Australia interview (Vice-Australia 2018, 1) suggests that subsequent race-baiting public statements by state Liberal MP Matthew Guy stating he will initiate 'gang busting laws' if he were to be elected are dangerous narratives constructed to 'demonise our community and sets a very scary precedent for other politicians'.

This again had very real implications for young SSAs, where again politicians used the African gang narrative to spread fear in the community before an election. In a group interview with young SSAs after the Channel 7 protest (see below) talking about the topic of politics, media and the police, Flora and Titan expressed their unhappiness with the discourse in the political climate. Flora describes that after Turnbull's national television appearance, young SSAs had to be very aware of their presence 'as a black person in every single space that is dominated by white people' (Vice-Australia 2018). Rather than being perceived as 'different in public' for positive reasons (explored in chapter 3), alternatively as a result, they felt they had to 'make yourself small' (Vice-Australia 2018) so as not to get in the way of white hegemony. *Titan* urges us to consider that the role of politicians in this 'mess' is to look after *all* Australians not just the ones they are protecting through political and race-baited agendas (Vice-Australia 2018).

Demonstrating participants' views on the roles that politicians play in creating moral panics leads to their views on institutional decision-making, often led by federal and state politicians, in the policies they make. These findings are further evidence that *'the system ain't playing'* as depicted by *Krown* (2018b)[14] described in chapter 3.

INSTITUTIONAL FOCUS – FURTHER EVIDENCE THAT THE 'SYSTEM AIN'T PLAYING'

The previous sections have unpacked participants' views on how public discourse and academia conceptualise the nature of the possibility of gangs. Shedding light on African gang narratives perpetuated by racialising discourses, alternative language concedes that 'networks of crime' is the phenomena that had been occurring in pockets of Naarm. This is due to the fact that 'gang behaviour' fulfills the wider definition of organised, systemic, criminal syndicates (Fraser 2013; Dimitriadis 2003; Nayak 2003; R.E. White and Mason 2006; Baker and Wiedersehn 2018). The use of more accurate terminology has not been established in the scenarios depicted. Contentions of young people in public space has also been a focus (NEMBC 2016; B. Smith and Davy 2018; Furlong 2013; Kelly and Kamp 2015; Grossman and Sharples 2010; Kamp and Kelly 2015). Broader data tells a complex story outlining a number of socio-political, xenophobic, and environmental risk factors that increase the likelihood of young SSAs engaging in crime (Shepherd 2021; Baak 2011, 2018, 2019). An extended focus from participants' perspectives of these narratives, which make up racialising discourses, was important to set the scene for what young SSAs are resisting and the counter-narratives they present through forms of Hip Hop expression. This chapter presents further themes of the specific ways young SSAs expressed their political voice by creating specific political and 'conscious' tracks and forms of protest in response. Worth noting is the phrase from artist *Amac's* track (2019)[15] '41 Bars of an African gang member' exploring how the topic of large groups hanging in public spaces was typified by the media as 'African gangs'. He raps:

African gang is no African gang. We have big families when we hang. The numbers that looks like a gang. We've got a few delinquents, we're sorry goddamn. The issue is being politicised.Amac is not necessarily considered a 'political rap' artist. His tracks mostly consist of vibrant Dancehall and Afrobeat beats that unite South Sudanese diaspora and fans across the world. *Amac's* (2019)[16] track is however an expression of his political voice due to the *'noise'* being created by racialising discourses spreading African gangs propaganda all *'over the news'*. Specifically,

The newsroom, the public and the authorities
Judging the many

Based on minorities.
(Amac Don 2019)[17]

Returning to some of his earlier rap roots, *Amac* released this track due to being *'victimised'* and his parents being *'traumatised'*. This resulted in a *'divided voice'* and *'the whole community judged based on a few'*. He does not deny that there are *'a few young-uns who need help'* but calls on society to *'define the problem'* and work together *'finding solutions'* and *'putting them to use'* (Amac Don 2019).[18] The examples below of alternative counter-narratives developed through arts-based community development initiatives demonstrate the importance of self-determination being the core of BIPOC leading this process of finding solutions (Dinerstein 2015).

What this extensive period of media focus on 'African youth crime concern' (Oakes 2012, 1) reinforced is the notion of a white Australian 'we' and a non-white 'Other' (Marjoribanks, Nolan, and Farquharson 2010). Amir noted how it was the start of an *'us versus them narrative narrated by racialising discourses, not started by us'*. This statement also mirrors the way in which the concept of 'race' was constructed by eugenicists and colonisers who prioritised Whiteness at the top of the racial hierarchy instead of recognising humans as equals.

After the extension of racist narratives and the following treatment of SSAs by some Australians, you only needed to mention the word 'Apex' to participants, and it was as if their 'skin boiled'. Research participants such as Felicia posed similar responses to *Daniel Elia's* (2017)[19] or *Krown*'s (2018a, 2018b)[20] tracks where they suggest *'my skin ain't Apex'* by stating that she is *'sick of this topic'*. Essentially, drawing from participants' reactions, young SSAs do not wish to be associated with the term 'Apex' but they are inescapably branded with it as a result of racialising discourses. Young people at the Gua focus groups noted how SSAs are forced to confront and discuss Apex on many occasions (2017, 2019). From a local teacher's perspective, Bella remembered how the media depiction of young SSAs after Gony's death meant that her students *'walked with heaviness as they shouldered this burden'*, particularly as *'eyes were looking at you through a filter that is unsympathetic'*. She recalled discussing this dynamic with her Italian Australian family members who lived in the area, who suddenly described *'Noble Park as changing'*. Through these conversations and in her interview, she clarified that as a 'growth corridor' this region had a rapidly growing population of many ethnic communities at the time.

The overarching theme from participants discussing the Apex gang narrative was *'young people from our community being focussed on as violent and singled out because of our noticeably darker skin'* (Khalid). In his interview with Vice Australia (2018, 1), Thon noted that as a young black male, it was his experience that when the 'media comes down on us hard, the police will act brutally towards us'. Throughout interviews, it was suggested that *'generally young people get a bad rap'* (Veronica). The way this differentiated for young SSAs were that *'responses from the general public'* included South Sudanese communities being *'treated positively on arrival however the African gangs narrative put a negative spotlight on us'* (Abdul). From Jamal's perspective, he felt it has been *'a battle since we arrived'*.

The years 2007–2018 were a significant period in terms of negative media spotlight on the SSA community. Felicia felt that the *'Apex thing caused more segregation'* in society and between her communities. She asserted that South Sudanese communities are *'slowly coming back'* by presenting a more adequate representation of themselves. On the topic of existing in a black body (Channing-Brown 2018), similar sentiments were expressed by multicultural participants Akra, Niki, Bella, Tina and young SSA participants (Felicia, Mumor) alike, namely that if you are a certain kind of migrant (i.e., predominantly non-white), you must *'prepare to get shit on!'* (Niki). South Sudanese participants distinguished that they felt the combination of the longitudinal focus on their community in media and moral panics and treatment due to their Blackness has led to new levels of 'Othering'. This treatment has led to significant consequences (as explored in chapter 3). The most dominant responses to racialising discourses in SSA participants' expression of their political voices are now discussed through involvement in phase two of the Grounded Project.

YOUNG SOUTH SUDANESE AUSTRALIANS RESPONSES TO RACIALISING DISCOURSES THROUGH PARTICIPATING IN AN NEW SOCIAL MOVEMENT

The forms of social action that this section addresses are classified under the concept of NSMs. Young (cited in Bernstein 2005, 64) outlines that NSMs fall within the category of identity politics, formed by the new Left as a world-historical movement subverting politics. As young SSAs also seek to subvert the portrayal of their communities, key messages identified focusing on black liberation point out that young SSAs do not organise to 'obtain recognition of their group's suffering, but rather seek the ability to participate in social life' and 'alter how decisions are made' and 'how worth is evaluated' (Young cited in Bernstein 2005, 64). NSMs in this setting are not conceived as dramatic events but as movements of young people who share cultural orientations and respond to everyday experiences of oppressive structures. Therefore, as Touraine (cited in Escobar 1992, 404) describes, the forms of social mobilisation depicted consist 'of struggles for the process of social change and development'. Rather than deficit Eurocentric discourses of under-represented communities of colour, the participants and artists who are actors in the NSM portrayed were selected due to representing agency (Escobar 2004) through their chosen creative form of Hip Hop.

In this context, Hip Hop as an NSM has always represented the ability to develop and support strong counter-narratives to racialising discourses (Iglesias and Harris 2019). Coupled with a strengths-based approach depicted in Yosso's (2005) *Cultural Wealth Model*, this monograph examines the lived experiences of Communities of Color through CRT as the primary theoretical lens. Through this model, we can see at least six dynamic and overlapping forms of capital depicted by participants. These include the interplay of cultural assets such as the Hip Hop BTSO artivists themselves and resources such as arts-based projects which illuminates a multifaceted view of community cultural wealth (Yosso 2005). *Aspirational capital* refers to the ability to maintain hopes and dreams for the future, even in the face of real and perceived barriers such as systemic racism. *Linguistic capital* includes the intellectual and social skills attained through communication in multiple languages and/or language styles such as through Hip Hop lyrics and storytelling through spoken-word. *Social capital* can be understood as networks of people and community resources formed through participation in an NSM or arts-based project. *Navigational capital* refers to skills in manoeuvreing through social institutions, such as those created by those instigating media and moral panics. Historically, this implies the ability to manoeuvre through institutions that often host arts-based projects or public spaces not always created with communities of colour in mind. *Familial capital* refers to those cultural knowledges nurtured amongst families or kinship connections that carry a sense of community history, memory, and cultural intuition, such as the passing on of Indigenous knowledges through oral storytelling practices. Finally, *resistant capital* refers to those knowledges and skills fostered through oppositional behaviour, such as representing one's political voice that challenges inequality and resists racialising discourses (Yosso 2005). Each of the forms of capital within the kaleidoscope of the Cultural Wealth Model, and their multifaceted dimensions builds on extensive bodies of critical social research that has consistently reframed culture as a resource for communities of colour, rather than as a detriment or deficit (Asante 2003).

I suggest that we do not yet have this social movement 'imagination' in the Australian context to the same level that community-organising (activism) plays in the United States. However, I envisage that through debunking some myths in relation to the African gangs narrative, this monograph contributes to global approaches towards advocacy amongst racialising discourses. It offers a unique perspective on this discourse not yet portrayed in social research in Australia by determining the process of how culture and politics is intertwined in the practices of the 'new actors' (Escobar 1992, 405). The following section, therefore, discusses Hip Hop as an arts-based form of resistance which serves as an example of young SSAs participating in an NSM by developing counter-narratives to racialising discourses.

THE GROUNDED PROJECT (PHASE TWO) – HIP HOP AS AN ARTS-BASED FORM OF RESISTANCE – DEVELOPING A COUNTER-NARRATIVE

Continuing on from the previous chapter discussing the consciousness-raising journey for participants, this section uses the theoretical and evaluation framework of the CCA (Dutta 2015) to review the Footprints YPAR project – the Grounded Project (discussed further in chapter 7). It builds on findings from previous sections in this chapter which details specific narratives perpetuated by racialising discourses, using these narratives as a guide, this section details what counter-narratives young SSAs portray using their political voice through the Grounded Project. Following the Gua camp (phase 1) described in chapter 4, this section focusses on phase 2 which occurred between February and March 2019. SSA spoken-word artist Abe Nouk, featured in figure 5.2, who performed at the very first Grounded in 2009 and at the second Grounded Festival in 2017, describes his journey and frustrations and the need for such projects:

> I know and believe that our youth can make an outstanding image. There are those at every corner of our suburbs who want to pick out our wrongs instead of looking at our bright rights. I am talking about the newspaper articles and their writers. Even if we were all to be deported tomorrow . . . where else would we get this opportunity for so much cultural unification in the world? We need to feel that our unseen work of arts is being appreciated. (Footprints, Grounded Project Acquittal, 2009)

In 2019, the project addressed the impacts of negative media and political portrayals on SSA communities. To counteract these claims, and with considerations of different expressions of political voice in chapters 4–5, Footprints outlined that 'frustrated and disconnected young people are in desperate need of unity within their diverse communities and the wider community' (Footprints, Grounded Project funding application 2019). Despite racialising discourses, through my extended observations as a community cultural development practitioner over a decade, I have repeatedly observed the reality that young SSAs living in CGD's multicultural community (where the project was hosted) are mostly achieving great things.

Figure 5.2 Spoken-word Artist Abe Nouk Performing at the Grounded Festival, 2017.
Source: Footprints.

With the inspiration, support, and opportunities provided by organisations like Footprints, the Grounded Project sought to highlight the positive contributions of young people in the community. The goal of the project, as developed by previous Footprints participants, was to present a counter-narrative to racialising discourses. This goal was taken up by exploring how Hip Hop arts intervention supported further building young SSAs' political voice (Grounded Project fieldwork notes 2019). In the subsequent sections, I discuss research participants and BTSO artivists' overall counter-narratives presented (which are then further taken up in chapter 6). Through a CCA, the youth development initiative provided a platform for subaltern and minoritised actors to demonstrate active agency in expressing their political voice through alternative forms of artivism. In this way, the intended goal of social change is reviewed in the context of emphasis on social justice imperatives in development and social change (Raj-Melkote and Singhal 2021). A specific lens of NSMs is the key focus.

THE GROUNDED YOUTH STAGE – ARTS-BASED FORMS OF RESISTANCE

The Grounded Youth Stage was hosted at Harmony Square Dandenong on Sunday, 17 March 2019 as part of the broader Harmony Festival in partnership with Springvale Neighbourhood House and set in Cultural Diversity Week. Over the course of two hours, approximately 300 people attended. Performers at the Grounded Festival included Gua camp participants and established artists who were predominantly from African diaspora communities across Naarm, with the majority from South Sudanese backgrounds. Through observation of the Grounded Project in its entirety, from the Gua camp to pop-up performances to the public festival, I identified three key themes which conveyed how young SSAs' political voice was enacted through forms of Hip Hop expression. These three key themes are spread across chapters 5–6. These include the depiction of counter-storytelling through the demonstration of 'little publics' (building on chapter 3);3), identity politics on display through public performances, and *Afrocentricity* and *Afropolitanism* – an expression of political voice through representations of Blackness.

This final section of this chapter discusses the first theme in relation to public performances. Figure 5.3 depicts BTSO artivists presenting a counter-narrative resisting deficit discourses portrayed by racialising discourses. Young SSAs demonstrated variations of their political voice in alternative forms of artivism throughout the Grounded Project.

As suggested in chapter 3, urban youth appear to 'stand out' when congregating in large numbers in public. Chapter 4 also depicts how Harmony Square in Dandenong, the site of the Grounded Youth Stage, can also be a contested space due to incidences of antisocial behaviour with groups of young people from different multicultural backgrounds sometimes disrupting public safety in what is often portrayed in the media as 'gang behaviour' (Footprints, Grounded Project Acquittal 2019:2).

One of the narratives that racialising discourses promotes is that it is not safe for a large group of predominantly black youth to be present in public. Multiple sources (R.E. White 2009; Furlong 2013; YACVIC 2017) identify that the foremost reason for potential fear of groups of young people in public spaces is due to media reports that label young people as 'troublemakers'.

Figure 5.3 The Grounded Youth Stage Featured at the Harmony Festival, March 2019, at Harmony Square, Dandenong. *Source*: Footprints.

Alternatively, the Grounded Youth Stage, 2019 is presented in this research as a representation of *little public spheres* (Hickey-Moody 2013a). This is a performance paradigm presenting a counter-narrative to what is portrayed by racialising discourses as urban youth wreaking havoc in society. Hickey-Moody explores how a 'counter-public' can be an oppositional space to recreate a given status quo. *Little publics* can also be spaces of resistance. To constitute a little public, a group of young people need to:

> author a text that calls an audience to attention. . . . For example . . . sing a song that is heard. Little publics articulate the expression of youth voice in the many political tones it can have. I use the term 'little' to refer to young people's diminutiveness as well as to signify the small size of the public formed. (Hickey-Moody 2013b)

My observations of the Grounded Youth Stage were that it was 'sharing discourse in a public space, this deliberate act was about creating art and expressing yourself. This practise, in itself, can be quite political' (Fieldwork notes 2019). This section explores how the Grounded Youth Stage represented a counter-public as an alternative form of artivism. The first thing I noted was that:

> the sad thing is that events like this do not often occur in Harmony Square which are led by young people of diverse cultures themselves. It was almost as if we were reclaiming this space and the African gang narrative and turning it on its heels by representing the BTSO narrative. Although there was not a

large crowd of thousands, it was enough to create a sense of solidarity. It was also the beginning of creating a counter-narrative by being different in public. (Fieldwork notes 2019)

The reason that I noted that this event marked a 'beginning' of creating a counter-narrative was due to the critical consideration of noting whether Footprints intended measurement of social change for this project in creating a counter-narrative to racialising discourses was achieved. This was due to the fact that no demonstrable dint in disrupting racialising discourses in Australia was achieved. Footprints and project partners sent out extensive media releases and creative promotional videos; however, no mainstream media accepted the invitation to attend. Only the local newspaper covered the story, which was consistent with Footprints' experiences over the years (Fieldwork notes 2019). If racialising discourses are predominantly projected by mainstream media, the question remains within the field of social change communication whether the media's non-attendance and failure to capture the project's essence meant that this project therefore did not reach its intended outcome. However, within the framework of CCA, Dutta (2021, 1) alternatively points towards the subversive locations of social change communication through the ways in which 'individual and collective agencies are enacted within and in resistance to structural constraints'. U.S. jazz and soul artist Gil Scott-Heron in 1971 made an important observation when he stated, 'the revolution will not be televised!'[21] Through his spoken-word poetry in the 1970s, Scott-Heron was considered to be a major influence in the development of African American genres of Hip Hop and neo-soul. In understanding how these artivist revolutionaries of the 1970s perceived their role, we gain the clarity that they never conceived of their consciousness-raising as trying to tap into the mainstream. They always remained a visceral voice from the margins critiquing the mainstream and providing alternative forms of community (Pope 2020). The Grounded Project appears to be no different.

The first alternate communicative measures displaying a counter-narrative to racialising discourses were demonstrated on the Grounded Youth Stage when the local mayor, other councillors, council members and passers-by got to see the square filled with young people (particularly of African background) who were in their element (passionate, thriving, displaying their strengths). Some of them even joined in (Fieldwork notes 2019).

As a youth worker and community cultural development practitioner, I have been in many meetings in the CGD where senior stakeholders such as those identified above gather to discuss impending events, like the Grounded Youth Stage, to consider public safety. If perceived antisocial behaviour continues to occur amongst young people where violence is discussed repetitiously, certain views can be formed about young people, whether consciously or unconsciously. Therefore, I noted that,

Figure 5.4 depicts how the audience stayed into the early evening as the event was finishing.

> if the Gua camp was about igniting social change and consciousness-raising, the Grounded Youth Stage was about the opportunity of using Hip Hop to showcase the real story of what young SSAs can achieve in public spaces by displaying a counter-narrative with important people observing such as the Mayor and council members. Here they displayed true unity and connection despite media depiction of [SSA] community in large groups. (Fieldwork notes 2019)

Tina also described how the event was a

> *safe place for kids. I've never seen that many kids of colour in one public community event. . . . This event was a 'testing ground' to consider other broader public spaces. . . . And so I thought it was a more safe place.*

Figure 5.5 depicts a police member appearing to enjoy the festival. I have spoken to many police members who often say they see 'the worst of people'. Today they were seeing 'the best of people' also in large numbers (Fieldwork notes 2019).

In summary, participants identified some of the alternative messages to racialising discourses demonstrated in this project in table 5.1.

These counter-narratives, youth-arts and public pedagogies,

> make citizen states [called] 'little publics' and teach specific ideas about young people to these audiences. Little publics facilitate the articulation of youth voice and are constituted through aesthetic citizenship. They are a means of giving social visibility to the tastes and perspectives of young people. (Hickey-Moody 2013b, 12)

Hickey-Moody 'suggest[s] that we take young people's actions in making little publics seriously; that the materiality of their arts practices constitutes a form of citizenship' (Hickey-Moody 2013b, 19). Furthermore, through identifying how a counter-narrative is presented through alternative forms of artivism, the 'vision of the excluded offers the possibility of correcting certain inequalities [such as access to after-hours activities] and widening the larger social vision [through art], social participation [through youth-led projects], and democratic processes [through collaboration]' (Rosaldo 2006, 125). Similar to this notion, the second counter-narrative that the Grounded Youth Stage demonstrates through this sense of active citizenship is that most young SSAs are flourishing and are not criminals as racialising discourses often suggest.

'My Skin Ain't Apex'   167

Figure 5.4 Footprints Vice-President (Stage Manager) and Co-founder Thank the Audience for Attending the Grounded Youth Stage, 2019. *Source*: Footprints.

Figure 5.5 Audience Members Enjoying the Grounded Youth Stage, Including a Police Officer Standing with the General Public. *Source*: Footprints.

Table 5.1 Alternative Narratives to Racialising Discourses (Fieldwork notes 2019)

Alternative Narratives to Racialising Discourses: 'This project was my first exposure to this community. I was able to make connections'.
'A support network and open community helps'.
'Advocacy to government is needed that involves the inclusion of all voices'.
'Breaking down barriers takes time, people are scared of the unknown'.

THE MAJORITY OF YOUNG SOUTH SUDANESE AUSTRALIANS ARE NOT 'CRIMINALS' AND ARE FLOURISHING

Given the narratives of racialising discourses outlined above, which include young SSAs being perceived as criminals and, as a result to be feared in public, I noted how it was at first 'peculiar to me' that BTSO artivists at the Grounded Youth Stage did not choose to express their political voice overtly in relation to these damaging perspectives of their communities. Initially, I wondered whether the impact of the project and the message communicated in relation to political voice was clear or whether alternative counter-narratives were presented adequately to engage the broader public (Fieldwork notes 2019). After reviewing the goal of social change of the project to present a counter-narrative to racialising discourses, I realised that the purpose of the Grounded Youth Stage was actually 'not specifically to enhance political voice in the overt sense' (Fieldwork notes 2019). As one audience member, Elizabeth, fed back, the message they received was *'people can talk about something they believe in'*. As a result, this 'is infectious to the audience'

(Fieldwork notes 2019). This is despite Hip Hop culture and rap as being perceived to have been associated with negative connotations, equating them with profanity, misogyny, violence and crime (Crooke and Rachael 2017). Despite these types of microaggressions or stereotypes perpetuated about young people involved with Hip Hop culture, this observation of a peaceful event, therefore, reflects some of Hip Hop culture's core tenets or values of social justice, peace, respect, self-worth, community, and having fun. Because of these values, exposure to these types of events and observations in this light, the utilisation of Hip Hop culture can be a therapeutic tool for engagement with young people (Dale, Burnard, and Travis 2024).

This section depicts how the 'interactions of human agency' between young SSAs demonstrate 'communicative processes in bringing about social change and structural transformation' (Dutta 2021, 1). Through practitioner observations (as described earlier), I have repeatedly observed the reality that despite depictions of criminal activity through racialising discourses, many young SSAs are flourishing. To illustrate this observation, young SSA Hip Hop artist Jesko describes how other diverse artists from different generations are *'rising up'* and *'making a statement of our own sound in Australia'*. BTSO artivists in this study also demonstrate how they make statements and make a noise in the context of racialising discourses.

Whilst these are common narratives presented in Australian discourse discussed in this chapter, participants who had explored a consciousness-raising process positioned their responses in terms of *'having a different mindset whereby with the Apex narrative we don't know this narrative'* (Mumor). It was therefore suggested that what was often portrayed by racialising discourses is *'nothing close to the reality'*. BCM crew member Kiir mentions that it is also his preference to bypass negative stereotypes and *'try not to give [them] too much power'*. Instead, as a popular Hip Hop collective, *BCM* prefers to focus on the *'success stories'* of members of their communities.

Alternatively, the *BCM* crew and Mumor, who is a filmmaker gives examples of how you can *'create your own [narrative]'*. Through this approach of self-determination, participants note that *'we have a lot of talent and we don't get the attention we deserve'* (Marley). Khalid and Ibrahim from the *BCM* crew describe how they see that *'positive change can come of [presenting their own narratives]'*. Through this process, you can *'end up creating your own support system from within'* which bypasses racialising discourses. As I discussed in chapter 1, one way this narrative was bypassed was when Australians responded creatively by taking over the #AfricanGangs hashtag to highlight the positive achievements of young SSAs (Faruqi 2018). *Malesh P* in the Voice for Change documentary describes how 'there is an opportunity to flip the narrative where many people are doing great things' (Mushroom-Creative 2017). I suggest that the way 'flipping the narrative' occurred on the Grounded Youth Stage was through utilising Hip Hop culture as a space for an NSM to take shape. As actors in an NSM, young SSAs developed 'counter-knowledge', an 'alternative knowledge system intended to challenge mainstream knowledge producers such as news media and academia' (Gosa 2011, 187). It reveals how Hip Hop 'resembles the "cultic milieu", a space where disparate countercultural ideas propagate and create unlikely political alliances . . . addressing legitimate but complex political grievances in contemporary society' (Gosa 2011, 187).

One way this was demonstrated was through *Krown's*[22] performance featuring On Track[23] students. On Track is a youth program that *Krown* worked on at a school in the southeast of Naarm with Mushroom Group, a music industry organisation. The role of *Krown* in On Track to support students in high school to make collaborative tracks with artists they admire. *Krown* could have performed overtly political tracks such as *Let Us Live* (2018b),[24] which presents a counter-narrative to racialising discourses. However, he focused his performance at the Grounded Youth Stage on how he can support the next generations through music mentoring (Fieldwork notes 2019). Figure 5.6 depicts how *Krown's* aspiration to make a difference through his calling (discussed in chapter 4) is passed down to budding performers. This is taken from the video Mills and Boom created for the project, which portrays students performing their co-written track for the first time. With *Krown* as their mentor, they promote positive energy with the counter-message: *Be M.A.D, be M.A.D, be M.A.D, make a difference* (Krown 2019).[25]

Krown and other young SSAs, whilst juggling multiple identities, are keenly aware of the criminal stereotypes created about their communities. *Krown* has chosen to transcend these narratives. Whilst he is an artist who has voiced his concerns and participated in political struggles, he also uses popular culture to construct a unique identity for himself. *Krown* outlines how young SSAs contribute to Australian society, thus countering the racialising discourse of not integrating (Macaulay and Deppeler 2020; Mhando 2014).

The way that *Krown* and other BTSO artivists resist racialising discourses is through providing 'counter-stories to community and wider public perception and how they play out in lyrics. The motivation is to change the narrative on power imbalance through self-determination' (Fieldwork notes 2019). Two South Sudanese supporters and audience members responded that this occurred at the Grounded Youth Stage because *'there was an opportunity to remember the good (news stories)'*. There was also an opportunity to *'support local artists who are our role models'*. Therefore, the artists selected demonstrated a representation of our *'superheroes'*. Overall, this formed aspects of alternative expression through Hip Hop narratives. Predominantly African diaspora youth demonstrated a CCA by rapping and showcasing their strengths when bringing young people from various cultures together. These

'My Skin Ain't Apex' 171

Figure 5.6 Up-and-coming Melbourne-based Artist Krown Invites to the Stage His Students from Mushroom Group's 'On Track' Program, to Showcase Their Collaborative Song at the Grounded Youth Stage at Harmony Square Hosted by Footprints (Krown 2019). *Source*: Footprints.

are depicted in the following alternative message to racialising discourses: *As multicultural kids, we have one message – give us the benefit of doubt, a fair go*. (Abiel)

The last artist group selected to perform at the Grounded Youth Stage, who shared this message, was the *BCM* crew. They performed their signature track titled 'Gasoline' from their *Realness for Sale* (2020)[26] album. They rap that they are a part of the *'no hate club, in a room full of culture and we show love'*.

Burn City Movement's (BCM)[27] performance at the Grounded Youth Stage incorporated other artists associated with the SSA 'movement' such as *Wantu ThaOne, i.OG, A1 Krashn, 4Fo,* and *Jacki Tut* (see Figures 5.7 and 5.8 below). They can be described as 'the hottest Hip Hop collective coming out of Australia' (Grounded Project media release 2019).

BCM are that 'new wave of young people with killer tracks, oozing outrageous personalities and trendy fashion sense. Their vibes make people want to follow' (Fieldwork notes 2019). Figure 5.8 demonstrates this in their charismatic performance style.

In their group interview, I asked the *BCM* crew how they felt about this depiction. Commenting on their catchy lyrics of *BCM 'why don't you go tell a friend'* repeated in the 'Gasoline track' (2020),[28] I was keen to hear their vision of what they have portrayed as a movement and not just a crew. Whilst they not only did this through their performance and the fashion show they curated at the event, *BCM* also cast their vision broadly through their own depiction of how positive social change can have lasting effects. They manage to achieve this through the development of new subcultures and use of

Figure 5.7 Jacki Tut Performing at the Grounded Youth Stage, 2019. *Source:* Footprints

Figure 5.8 Burn City Movement (BCM) Members Wearing Their Own Fashion Styles. Wantu ThaOne, A1 Krashn and i.OG performing the track 'Ridiculous' by A1 Krashn. Yoannes Tor is filming in the background. *Source*: Footprints and Kimberley Summer.

alternative media. This fulfils an Afrofuturistic vision calling young people to bigger possibilities.

These ideas are likened to what Scott (1985) posits as *everyday resistance* or what Dinerstein (2015) calls the *politics of autonomy,* preferring community-organising and self-determination under the construct of an NSM. There is limited scope to discuss other alternative forms of artivism identified in my research in any more detail. These included young SSAs responding to racialising discourses and the prevailing SSAs presented in other sub-genres of Hip Hop, including trap and drill Hip Hop, which as presented as flavours of overall Hip Hop culture. These ideas are mentioned here to link the ideas promoted in the 2019 Grounded Project fieldwork to broader sustainable dialogue and events that occur post-project. This chapter has specifically discussed an alternative form of artivism that presents counter-narratives to racialising discourses through an arts-based community development project. The final findings in chapter 7 further discusses the other themes identified through the Grounded Youth Stage as forms of resistance to racialising discourses.

ARTIVISM TO RESPOND TO RACIST NARRATIVES

Utilising participants' responses to the impacts of racialising discourses amongst young SSAs and fieldwork data from the Grounded Youth Stage performances, this chapter further unpacks the systems power analysis discussed in chapter 3 and how it relates to mainstream media and politics. In her article published in the *Saturday Paper*, Naarm-based activist and SSA lawyer, Nyadol Nyuon (2018, 1), discusses the racialising discourses by writing about the *politics of fear* evident after the 2018 Victorian elections:

> when the voting is done, and political careers are secured or lost, when the journalists put down their 'pens' and head to their families for bed, and when the publishers are onto the next story, the resultant scars from this episode of moral panic will still be carved into our lives. And they will still be there, weakening the ties that bind us into a shared identity as Victorians. (Nyuon (2018, 1)

This chapter has explored how racialising discourses are pervasive within our daily existence and have the most effect on BIPOC communities. The main assertion in this monograph is that young SSAs utilise alternative forms of expression, such as artivism, to respond to racist narratives. Through the presentation of young SSAs' counter-narratives to racialising discourses, this chapter has demonstrated that the narrative needs to change for real systemic justice to occur and for the possibility of a 'beloved community' (a term highlighted by Martin Luther King) to be explored (James 2013; K.L. Smith and Zepp 1986). Footprints' attempts in the Grounded Project are described to begin this process, at least on a small, local scale. Through exploring cross-media retrieval of news stories depicting Gony's murder and the Apex gang narrative, this chapter demonstrates that upon further analysis the data 'tells a more complex story' (Shepherd 2021, 1).

Empirical depictions of young SSAs' lyrics, interviews and artefacts presented in this chapter suggests that a form of *truth-telling* (Hill-Collins 2013) is an essential component in these young people's acts of resistance against racialising discourses. Exploring participants' views on how media devices and political 'click-bait' are used as tactics of racialising discourses reframes the depiction of African gangs in Australia by presenting alternative counter-narratives in Hip Hop artivism. This chapter has used CRT as a theoretical framework to explore how participants feel that racialising discourses are to 'blame' for how this narrative grew to the extent it did. It is my contention that this perspective has not been thoroughly enough established for this kind of behaviour to never be repeated, despite extensive contributions already made in the way in which media outlets can operate under 'best practice' (Farquharson, Marjoribanks, and Nolan 2018).

This research utilises extensive qualitative knowledge to expand scholarly developments in racialising discourses. At the same time, it formulates new pathways for alternatives that utilise Antiracism discourse. Despite the significant contributions of research and journalistic initiatives discussed in this chapter, which ascertain the impact on the South Sudanese and African diaspora's focus in the media and politics, this research points towards the need for further focus on how young SSAs are exploring their own counter-narratives and displays of agency. This is the context that this research addresses, and it provides unique perspectives on how young SSAs' political voice manifests in important new ways that conventional theories of activism and resistance do not capture. Before venturing further into this discussion, it is important to 'sit with' the impact that moral panics have had on SSA communities and their identity politics, which has been described as limiting their freedoms.

Relating to the topic of Australian media device tactics, one recommendation of the Foundation for Young Australians (FYA) is that Australian media needs to start displaying more positive news stories about young people in general. This recommendation came after FYA's review of news stories about young people during the COVID-19 pandemic (FYA 2020). It is these positive news stories and further counter-narratives that participants developed to resist racialising discourses through expression of a political voice through Hip Hop that I next explore.

NOTES

1. Krown (2018) 'Let us Live', Military Mind: https://www.youtube.com/watch?v=lxjsHiLgFJs.
    See blogpost #15.
2. Amac Don (2019) '41 Bars from an African Gang Member', Future Records: https://soundcloud.com/hbkfam/amac-don-41-bars-of-an-african-gang-member.
    See blogpost #30.
3. See Notes '1'.
4. See chapter 4 for implications on the 'war on Blackness'.
5. See Notes '1'.
6. The Lost Boys of Sudan refers to a group of over 20,000 boys of the Nuer and Dinka ethnic groups who were displaced or orphaned during the second Sudanese civil war and walked for weeks to neighbouring countries in Ethiopia and Kenya (Atem-Deng 2006).
7. See Notes '1'.
8. Élkato (2020) 'The Matrix', YSAS Studios: https://soundcloud.com/user-940608762/lkato-matrix.
    See blogpost #17.
9. Titan (2020), 'Cheques and Balances', GRID Series: https://www.youtube.com/watch?v=oBjfFvsdP6w&feature=emb_logo;
    https://open.spotify.com/album/4mNPnY2Tl2WomjI9FircUe?si=BN6QKnBXQcaUBZrXGFBrGw.
    See blogpost #10.

10. Titan (2019) 'Deng and Katie', performance at *Yah Yah's* on 12 July 2019, Titan Debirioun:
>   See blogpost #31.

>   *I said my story is longer than any news article could describe, or someone can investigate to shed light upon*
>   *So, the truth will always be left in the dark*
>   *I am Sudanese yes, but I am so much more*
>   *I am a human being that is complex to my core yet misunderstood by the place to call home*
>   *Surrounded by community as you're walking along*
>   *I am not responsible for Deng, like you're not responsible for Katie*
>   *But apparently if Deng commits a robbery then his sins Titan must also carry*
>   *However, if Katie goes on a crime spree, slaps an Officer and blows the world up*
>   *Then Katie is just crazy*
>   *I wake up every morning and I see beauty in my community*
>   *The same beauty I conveyed at school*
>   *They looked to me and said 'cool'*
>   *They looked at the t.v. and said 'wait'*
>   *They looked at me and said 'oooooooh'*
>   *By then said 'you n****'s don't belong here mate!'*
>   *I looked at my watch and said 'world change'*
>   *If I came here an hour ago and you came here 30 mins before are we both heading back?*
>   *Silence . . .*
>   *Other times portrayed as blinded*
>   *but if you read between the lines you will see there's more to the story than you and I*
>   *Enough with the suit with truth and lie*
>   *Contradicted by people with suit and tie*
>   *Making the money off me and mine*
>   *Family,*
>   *It's deeper than headlines it's more to my life*
>   *It's telling the story*
>   *Where there is wrong, there is right*
>   *Time to breathe.*

11. See Notes '10'.
12. Malesh P (2020) 'Be Free' (Soli x Mez Mariyé: Malesh P Remix), Malesh P: https://soundcloud.com/malesh/be-free-soli-x-mez-mariye-malesh-p-remix.
>   See blogpost #32.
13. See Notes '10'.
14. See Notes '1'.
15. See Notes '2'.

16. See Notes '2'.
17. See Notes '2'.
18. See Notes '2'.
19. Daniel Elia (2017) 'Lonely' (Remix), ALIA Records: https://www.youtube.com/watch?v=Qb4gzkFKQI0.

See blogpost #5.
20. See Notes '1'.

Krown (2019) 'Hold the Flag', Military Mind: https://www.youtube.com/watch?v=4FsiK_-2pVk.

See blogpost #19.
21. *The Revolution Will Not Be Televised*, track featured in *Features of a Man* album – Gil Scott-Heron https://www.youtube.com/watch?v=QnJFhuOWgXg.
22. https://www.facebook.com/militarykrown/.
23. This item was booked as a collaboration with the Voice for Change project from *Mushroom Group*.
24. See Notes '1'.
25. Krown (2019) '*Be M.A.D.,* 2019', Performance at Footprints Grounded Youth Stage, On Track program by Mushroom Group. Lyrics not available.
26. BCM (2020) 'Gasoline', as part of their *Realness for Sale* EP, Noble Studios: https://tidal.com/browse/album/131189065.

See blogpost #33.
27. https://www.facebook.com/BurnCity.Movement/ https://www.facebook.com/FoFoMUZIC/
28. See Notes '26'.

Chapter 6

Born to Stand Out

'We Want to be Free from Our Chains'

Excerpt from *Malesh P's* track 'Be Free' (2020)[1]

Let me go, I'm demanding my freedom,
Let me go, fuck your sorry's
I don't need them
Let me go, no longer using your eyes to see
Let me go
Let me be FREE.

Artist *Malesh P* utilises Australian Eritrean artist Soli Tesema's remix[2] of U.S. Hip Hop artist J Cole's track 'Be Free' to express his frustrations as a black South Sudanese man dealing with racialising discourses and to further explore the concept of freedom. In the chorus, J Cole (2014) states:

All we want do is take these chains off
All we want do is break the chains of pain

He ends with the refrain

All we want do is be free (x2)[3]

Whilst *Malesh P* identifies as a Hip Hop artist who produces conscious content, he usually steers away from releasing political content. The content of this track, with charged tones and seething anger, is however directly political. It was released soon after the global BLM movement in Australia protested forms of racial injustice such as disproportionate deaths in custody of First Nations peoples and incarceration rates of BIPOC in Australia (Guardian 2020; Henriques-Gomes and Visontay 2020). *Malesh P's* track provides an Australian context to our own localised ramifications as we struggle to address the racism and systemic oppression outlined in chapter 3. These tracks and the statements in Sampa's spoken-word *'we are our own freedom'* (Sampa-the-Great 2020)[4] are analogous to Sen's concept of *freedoms* (Sen 2001[1999]) in laying out the terms of recognition for BIPOC people globally. Whilst BIPOC people experience further intersecting disparities in striving for freedoms, communities of colour nonetheless lay visible claim to their own self-determination, which links to a long history of black liberation activism (Taylor 2016; Kelley 2003; Hart 2020). All three tracks by J Cole, Tesema, and *Malesh P* highlight how a 'post-racial/colonial' society as conceptualised through Critical Race Theories (CRT) does not yet exist (Kendi 2019; Moreton-Robinson 2015; Prentis 2017).

This chapter explores the concept of *freedom* (Sen 2001[1999]) and expressions of political voice expressed in the motto of being 'born to stand out', through alternative forms of resistance. The first section reviews the broader discourse of what it means to be BTSO. This is followed by further detail in the subsequent section about phases two and three of the Grounded Project involving pop-up performances and the Grounded Youth Stage. The accounts of these phases of Footprints YPAR and the arts-development project set the scene outlining the next stages of the consciousness-raising journey as part of participating in a New Social Movement (NSM). Narrative and arts-based inquiry identify the ways BTSO participants envisage their involvement with this project in practical settings as sites of resistance. Participants' views are also captured in BTSO lyrics in tracks and artefacts (choice of public performances) featured in the Grounded Project whilst cross-referencing other Grounded Projects since 2007 for a longitudinal approach.

Additionally, through Bulhan's (1985) stages of *black identity development*, this details how the third stage, *radicalisation,* took place where young SSAs synthesised their identities of both being informed by Eurocentric worldviews but choosing to prioritise their sense of 'Africanness' in their performances throughout the Grounded Project. Likened to Cross' (1971) *black consciousness identity development* theory, young SSAs display their black identity through public performances which meet their personal needs, which in this case was (but not always) Afrocentric.

Chapters 4–6 identify the actions of young SSAs who are *'breaking free'* from *'chains'* (J. Cole 2014; Malesh 2020).[5] BTSO artivists narrate their experiences of life in Australia through the lens of racialising discourses. Namely, the chains include the media and political moral panics fixated on SSAs. As the final findings chapter, this chapter addresses the last research sub-question: *How might building of political voice for young SSAs contribute to enhanced freedom and affirmations of identity?* Through analysis of the exploratory and creative process utilising CHHP (Akom 2009) and the

CCA (2011, 2020), this chapter concludes the presentation of findings of this research, and contributes to the broader dialogue on Australian identity politics. The chapter closes with implications for further understanding racialising discourses. The key themes pertaining to being BTSO were analysed through the lens of a CCA: SSA artivists demonstrate their Blackness and put their African identities on display, as public expressions of identity. Through this process, which involves an interplay with identity politics, this chapter demonstrates their motto of being born to stand out, which they developed essentially as a counter-narrative to existing racialising discourses. Finally, a brief account on young SSAs' preference for other forms of resistance is addressed.

BEING 'BORN TO STAND OUT'

This chapter utilises a CRT lens to show how people from BIPOC backgrounds are frequently disadvantaged through their placement at the bottom of the socially constructed race hierarchy (Williams 2022). This social grouping and colour-coding behaviour can lead to social exclusion and discrimination for BIPOC individuals and communities, whilst others within these communities use these experiences to deliberately carve out their own space (Oxoby 2009; Carver & Scheier cited in Vaughan 2011). Considering these phenomena and the notion of carving out space, the concept and motto of being 'born to stand out' (BTSO), introduced in chapter 1, is another term used in this monograph to conclude the analysis of the CCA and the final stages of the NSM through Hip Hop. It is discussed to demonstrate the nature of young SSAs' resistance to racialising discourses. This section extends notions of identity politics specifically as it pertains to African diaspora identities whilst examining the notion of being BTSO.

Within the concept and motto of BTSO, there is the complexity of wanting to state 'we're all the same' as demonstrated in the understanding of human genomes and common humanity, but also wanting to be distinct and assert differences or forms of self-expression. This involves the possibility of being more self-reliant in identities (Du Bois 2018[1903/1989]). If the notion of achieving aspirations (Appadurai 2004) is the benchmark of achieving racial justice through a BTSO standpoint, the goal is therefore not merely 'equality' but 'equity' and 'justice' or even 'liberation' (Berman and Paradies 2010). In this context, the cultural origins of liberating work for BIPOC communities come through many actions – whether it be through Malcolm X's focus on black liberation through feasible self-determined actions, or the formation of the Black Panther Party, or through Cone's focus on black liberation theology in Turtle Island (USA). The language of decoloniality (Wilder 2015;

Ndlovu-Gatsheni 2015; Sithole 2014) also provides a longstanding political and epistemological movement aimed at the liberation of (ex-)colonised peoples from global coloniality but also from the resulting way of thinking, knowing, and doing (Kendi 2019). Historically, these marginalised, often targeted, but persistent movements 'merged from struggles against the slave trade, imperialism, colonialism, apartheid, neo-colonialism, and underdevelopment as constitutive negative elements of Euro-North American-centric modernity' (Kosley 2020, 1). With these goals of equity, justice, and liberation in mind, Kendi (2019, 18) explains that racial equity is 'when two or more racial groups are standing on a relatively equal footing'. Therefore, rather than any racial group having to 'measure themselves against the benchmark of Whiteness' (Kendi 2019, 29), they position themselves in their own multiple identities with equity not having to conform. Practically, freedom from a duelling consciousness is when:

> the white body no longer presents itself as the [Australian] body; the black body no longer strives to be the [Australian] body, knowing there is no such thing as the [Australian] body, only [Australian bodies] racialised by power. (Kendi 2019, 33–34)

Whilst acknowledging the goal of being BTSO, Channing-Brown (2018, 18) depicts the struggle of 'surviving in a world not "made for me"'. She articulates how it can be 'dangerous for black women to attempt to carve out space for themselves . . . in places that haven't examined the prevailing assumption of white culture' (Channing-Brown 2018, 21). She shares that for BIPOC people:

> the danger of letting Whiteness walk off with our joy, our peace, our sense of dignity and self-love, is ever present. But it doesn't have to be this way. Togetherness across racial lines does not have to mean the uplifting of Whiteness and harming of Blackness. (Channing-Brown 2018, 21)

Within the framework of being BTSO and bringing attention to strength in culture, Pan-Africanism and Afrocentricity are concepts linked to assertions of identities. Additionally, as political doctrines and a movement, their aims focus on self-determination for the universal African community whilst reclaiming African agency as distinguished from Eurocentric ideals (Asante 2003, 2020; Yaw 2018). Alongside post-colonial theorist Ahluwalia (2012) and BTSO artivists, this research asserts the nuances of how African identity has been constituted and reconstituted. It explores African youth agency as many artists have portrayed in their Hip Hop music aligning with or influenced by the following concept of Afrofuturism. One way that Afrocentricity has reclaimed subject place in historical and cultural phenomena is through Afrofuturism. This concept is described here as another way young SSAs and BTSO artivists in this research express themselves through Afrofuturistic notions of creativity and as a form of resistance to racialising discourses. Through a mystical process, they reimagine global Africans' past, present, and future by 'combining traditional culture with futuristic elements' (Yusuf 2018, 1). Using cutting-edge Hip Hop with a BTSO motto, Afrofuturists strive to critique racial, ethnic, and social limitations by empowering and freeing individuals to be themselves and centre their experiences (Womack 2013).

The theme of BTSO focuses on the imperative of knowing who you are and where you come from as being critically important for young SSAs. As an aesthetic sensitivity and whilst refusing victim mentality, *Afropolitanism* is therefore described by Mbembe (2021) as a way of being true to oneself by reflecting one's African origins whilst recognising transnational culture and expanding one's future through one's own authentic forms of self-determination. The Black Power and Consciousness Movements are examples of forms of Afropolitanism where, in the case of black or African Americans, they identified what cultural resistance may look like through their practices. These are noted to show how SSAs may form their own contextual resistance through a Black Consciousness analysis (explored in chapter 4) focusing on social creativity as a cognitive alternative (McKeown, Haji, and Ferguson 2016; Kosley 2020).

Further exploration of CRT and identity politics is required in an Australian context. I build on this body of work by considering the goals that young SSAs pursue through their political voice being recognised. The title *Born to Stand Out* reflects this pursuit whereby SSAs assert their uniqueness through their Blackness, equal citizenship status, and contributions to Australian society. This section has drawn on African diasporic identity politics and forms of resistance. It outlines that in spite of the ideal BTSO narrative of being distinct as human beings with creativity, flair and self-determination, given the more recent debate in Australia about gangs, race and young SSAs being involved in alleged significant crime statistics (Butt 2018; Shepherd and Spivak 2020; Day 2018), it is becoming more important to understand young SSAs' attempts at self-determination. Specifically, how they are developing a counter-narrative through building their own political voice.

BORN TO STAND OUT – SOCIAL INDICATORS

Before proceeding to explore the second and third phases of Footprints' YPAR project, this section details the social indicators of this chapter. These are namely the social, political and historical contexts that necessitated the motto 'born to stand out' (BTSO); second documenting participants' views of how this motto is lived out. Young SSAs' narratives regarding their participation in a New Social Movement-making (NSM) process of everyday and arts-based resistance are discussed. Participants' accounts describe this journey as an individual process for young SSAs, as the findings indicate it is not a homogenous experience. This results in unique accounts of research participants' experiences explored in this research in their search for, or demand for, freedom and their creative demonstrations of how they are BTSO. Rather than being bound by racial hierarchies, this research shows that through young people's 'sameness' as humans but 'uniqueness' when observing multiple identities, they are clearly resolute that they have no desire to fit in. Rather, they clearly prefer to 'stand out' and maintain their non-white identities.

In a verse of *Malesh P's* 'Be Free' track, he further reiterates these sentiments by rapping:

Humanity's a race but white flags don't confirm you're a winner.
You see the pain caused, it's time lost
But I'm determined to flourish and get it going no matter the cost
Fuck no, you didn't plant these seeds
Nah, But rather planted diseases in my skin. (Malesh-P 2020)[6]

Malesh P is adamantly stating that racialising discourses do not define him despite attempts to belittle his Blackness through the concept of race hierarchies. He reinforces the notion that we share a 'common humanity' and that 'there is only one race, the human race' (Kendi 2019, 52, 56). Artist *Daniel Elia* in the *Born to Stand Out* documentary taster clip produced by Footprints and Mills and Boom (2020), explains that 'society here expects a black male or black female to act a certain way. You almost have to make yourself small'.

This is similar to the statement that *Titan* made in his interview with Australian broadcasting channel SBS. Referring to his black skin he states 'it's beautiful skin but people don't see it the same way I do' (SBS 2020, 1). He became conscious of this public perception when he moved to Tarneit, an outer-western suburb of Naarm (Melbourne) in Australia, noting 'when I came here, you immediately realised you were different' (SBS 2020). Flo, in her Vice Australia interview, also described feeling like young SSAs have to 'act small' in Australia so as not to be seen and avoid appearing threatening when travelling on public transport (Vice-Australia 2018). This act of diminishing your black identity is similar to Fanon's (1968) and Channing-Brown's (2018) recognition of the need to wear a white mask over your black face to remain less conspicuous in predominantly white spaces. Picking up on the imagery of having to make yourself small, the negative connotations of 'standing out' and having to diminish yourself for having a dark complexion were captured in three participants' comments. First, *Burn City Movement (BCM)*, an artist collective, were told they 'stand out' when patrons at an inner-city café in Naarm (Johnson 2019). *BCM* advised that one of the takeaways they received from this statement is that they appeared to draw attention to themselves just for their black presence. Second, Emmanuel stated:

> *when you stand out, it's almost like we have this stigma or responsibility as black people because wherever you go, you're representing your community.*

Emmanuel's statement builds on the themes of being different in public described in chapters 4 and 6. He elaborates on this topic by highlighting the pressure of holding one's Blackness in public. Thirdly, participants note that one's black presence may elicit fear in public where their noticeably darker skin leads to them being perceived as a potential threat. Gabriel stated that *'when someone sees you, there's always stuff that jumps through your head. Because you already stand out so much'*.

The 'stuff that goes through your head' might include not wanting to scare people due to narratives of racialising discourses that push a perception that you might be a dangerous criminal because you are a tall, young black male. This links back to statements in chapter 4 in which participants describe experiencing racism and feeling like you 'have to cross the street' to 'keep the peace'.

These statements allude to the notion of 'standing out' for all the wrong reasons and portray a deficit approach to one's black presence in an Australian context. The result of these deficit narratives is that African diaspora young people are left questioning *where do I belong?* (Anthias 2002). Additionally, due to racialising discourses, society has further developed racialised narratives of black bodies in or out of place in the general public (Kwansah-Aidoo and Mapedzahama 2018a). BTSO artivists discuss this in the initial montage in Footprints' *Born to Stand Out* trailer:

> I'm black, I have dark skin, really dark skin . . .
>
> You feel like you're representing your skin colour for everyone who looks just like you . . .
>
> You have to be an extra nice person, extra smart, even if you're not feeling it that day. You have to have a smile on because if you don't, you look scary. (Summer and Footprints 2022b)

This links back to Ayuen K. Bol's poem[7] in chapter 1, in which she states that whilst *'tears [are] flowing'* she was *'convinced to shed [her] skin . . . shrinking even smaller'*. These accounts demonstrate that media and moral panics have limited SSAs' sense of freedom and well-being (Adusei-Asante 2021; Udah 2017). My previous research (Williams 2016) sought to understand how SSAs negotiate life in Australia despite this by addressing the question is it possible to 'fit in' if you obviously stand out? Through YPAR in this earlier project, we discussed whether the goal was to 'fit in' or rather, 'stand out' on your own terms.

When I checked back with participants in this current research, Peter's description was notable; he spoke of expectations for him to *'behave like'* or *'adopt white culture'* in order to *'integrate'* into the Australian way of life. This is an essential theme that Tuan (1998) explores in her book *Forever Foreigners or Honorary Whites*? where she identifies imposed acculturation discourses and how these subtly oppresses non-whites through constant identification as 'different' from the supposed-normality of Whiteness (see chapter 4). This is relevant for participants in this study as they also question the often-imposed goal of becoming honorary whites through integration discourse. For example, Peter shares that he later realised the true sense of integration can mean *'bringing my own culture and integrating that with whatever culture/s exist within Australia and carrying both/many together'*.

Like the multi-coloured giraffe image depicted in photo 3 in chapter 1 to represent the motto of being 'born to stand out', this explanation is a practical example of the broader definition of *transculturalism*. Peter explains that in his context you can identify as South Sudanese, Australian, potentially Pan-African in ideology and also belong to multiple subcultures such as through the Hip Hop community. His vision portrays how transcultural capital and community building are possible (Hebert, Hoerder, and Schmitt 2006; Mansouri, Beaman, and Hussain 2019; Triandafyllidou 2009). It also fits within the formation of Hip Hop, for example, where one founder, Afrika Bambaataa promoted hybrid identities (Whitaker 2021). Peter's explanation also feeds into the notion of being 'born to stand out'. BTSO participants identified their counter-narratives to these forms of racialising discourses as depicted below.

The counter-narrative that participants in this research demonstrate is that rather than being 'the wretched of the earth' as black peoples (Fanon 1968), they are, as *Malesh P* (2020)[8] raps, *'determined to flourish and get it going no matter the cost'*. He is echoing the key research finding that BTSO artivists in this research are determined to boldly claim their identity. The notion of 'flourishing' indicates that humans have the freedom to live the lives they wish to live (Sen 2001[1999]). Through claiming the idea of being 'born to stand out', they can pursue their own defined ways to self-determine. Their claims can be summarised as Titan rhymes about what he wishes Australians to see: Open up your eyes, see the greatest that is black already ... greatness that is us already (SBS 2020, 1).

Whilst *Titan* and other BTSO artists want Australians to celebrate Blackness and their dark melaninated skin (Queen-P 2018),[9] similar to proponents of CRT not placing a hierarchy on skin colour, they do not wish to be defined by their skin colour (Malesh-P 2020; Elia 2017; BCM 2020; SBS 2020).[10] In this chapter, BTSO artists portray black excellence and put black power on display in public performances under this overarching theme as they 'attune to the political dimensions of the cultural' (Escobar 1992, 402). For *Titan*, this includes the ways in which:

> you still know you're different, and at times when it's like 'who am I, why am I hearing stuff?' You know where your house is, you know who your tribe is, you know who your people are. (SBS 2020, 1)

BTSO artivists depicted in this monograph had to develop a knowledge of their identities and hold on to this despite the costs and do so whilst their identity politics are often on display. This was specifically outlined in chapter 4, which describes the consciousness-raising journey upon which participants embarked when engaging in CHHP. Through the ongoing iterations of the Grounded Project depicted in this chapter, BTSO artivists have demonstrated the effectiveness of the arts-based project guided by different theories/perspectives (discussed in chapter 2) aimed at addressing the discrimination experienced by this specific community of young SSAs. Here, they explored their responses to racialising discourses and instead chose to prioritise the exploration of, and proclamation of their strengths through Blackness. This process was discussed as the first step of an NSM during the Gua camp focus groups. This is demonstrated through the way Ibrahim and Marley from the *BCM* crew questioned the notion of responding to people's limited expectations of them, as conditioned through consistent racialising discourse narratives. In their group interview, they discussed that a stereotype of a black man might be that you will not amount to much, or the perception that because you are black you may just end up involved in crime. Ibrahim commented that he prefers to set his own standards: *'when you try to pretty much react to someone else's opinion, you kind of give them power already'*.

He continued to speak more of an alternative approach prioritising not having to prove yourself but rather focusing on self-expression:

> *The best option would be to even just completely neglect them [people who propagate Whiteness] and work on yourself from within. If you feel like you should show them who you are, really make it because all you're trying to show*

is you feeling like you're expressing yourself at the end of the day. . . . And that way, it gives you freedom to do what you feel. Because there's no extra disdain in your heart that connects you to what you're doing. It's really all just purely from you.

This statement of having the 'freedom to do what you feel' largely aligns with Sen's ideas around following your own aspirations (Sen 2001[1999]) and suggests that individuals and communities have to find their own unique paths as they pursue their goal of being BTSO. In their *Voice for Change* interview, which depicts some of the broader discourse SSAs may face of not integrating, young SSA artist *Krown* and Australian rules footballer Majak Dau question 'what is normal society?' as 'people are going to react to it differently'. They highlight that the reality is that 'people might embrace you and some people might not' (Mushroom-Creative 2017, 1). Rather than fitting into categories of preferred Whiteness identity as the social norm in Australia, in his track 'Road to Success', *Malesh P* appears to be reassured in his Blackness and therefore does not mind this narrow path of asserting his unique identity. He declares:

They got me misunderstood. Told you never be successful. Another dreamer. It's all good, I ain't fighting for your love. (Malesh 2015)[11]

Nyuon suggested there is a 'high cost of standing out' (Nyuon 2021, 1). Participants explained that some of these costs can include following your sense of 'calling' as a lonely lifestyle; not everyone will agree with you and sometimes you might experience negative consequences (such as how participants discussed their 'visions from the kitchen' in chapter 4 meaning that not everyone will understand their dreams). Within the context of public identity politics, Salvidar (2006, 158) ponders on Foucault's statement noted in *The Subject and Power,* emphasising that the point is 'not to discover what we are but to refuse [depictions of] what we are'. This phrase may also be referring to personal portrayal and resistance of perceived identities within oneself, Footprints therefore partnered with Mills and Boom and SSA Film Director Ezeldin Deng to create the *Born to Stand Out* documentary (Mills-and-Boom 2020; Footprint-Enterprises-Inc. and Mills-and-Boom 2020) in order to address some of these themes. In the documentary narrative synopsis (2021), Deng and scriptwriter Mariam Koslay depict the untold story of the evolution of Hip Hop in Naarm. They claim that:

the movement, which most do not know about, was led by the sons and daughters of African migrants who came to Australia for a better life. Their children – who matured among the backdrop of conflict and refugee camps – found a uniting force in music, sharing their experiences and futures through song in their new land.

Deng and Kosley describe:

> the two central questions *Born to Stand Out* explores: Is Australia's music industry and Australian society willing to see the undeniable talent and future of these African artists who, for too long, have been sidelined and ignored? And, [can] Australia more broadly redefine the South Sudanese migration story that has, to date, been incorrectly analysed?
>
> At its core, this documentary is proof that regardless of the national music industry and Australian society; these artists, once children of migrants, will forever fight for their music, vision and people. (BTSO Narrative Synopsis 2021)

These artists fight for their vision through the lens of being 'born to stand out'. Photos in table 6.1 are taken from the trailer of a documentary developed out of this research. It identifies how BTSO artivists (also included in this research) are 'born to be seen, born to be heard and born to stand out' (Mills-and-Boom 2020). In the BTSO writer's room hosted by Footprints in August 2020, Deng and Mosley asked selected artists from African diaspora backgrounds: What makes you born to stand out? Their responses were grouped following these themes depicted in figures 6.1 and 6.2; tables 6.1, 6.2 and 6.3:

As these statements suggest, the current generation of SSA young people in Naarm have developed innovative ways to display agency, expression,

Figure 6.1 Lerato Masiyane – Afrobeats and Dancehall Dancer from Burn City Queens and Jungle City Projects (Footprints Project Partner) Is Born to Be Seen. *Source*: Kimberley Summer.

Figure 6.2 Artist Daniel Elia Is 'Born to be Heard'. In the clip he states 'I want to see you guys dance. I want you to leave here with a perspective'. *Source*: Kimberley Summer.

Table 6.1 What Makes You Born to Stand Out? – Themes 'Be Seen'; Perspectives on Being BTSO

Theme	Be Seen
Zii Music -	I don't believe in coincidences. We are in the process of imagining ourselves, no one can be like me. The majority of people are different looking than me in Australia. My worldview is also different.
Queen P -	Being in Australia I naturally stand out due to my noticeably darker skin but mentally I have a different input, a different story and experience.
Daniel E -	I started the race in this creative thing so late but I quickly learned. I had been disadvantaged by not speaking English but I learned a way to articulate and express my emotions through music.

and counter-narratives through Hip Hop. They have essentially created their own lane and carved out space in the face of racialising discourses (Tuan 1998) (see further discussion below). This links back to a long history of civil rights arts-based activism. This was explored in chapter 4, which detailed key themes of their representation of black excellence and power. The ways they continue to represent these themes are further outlined in the following section on the next stages of the Grounded Project, which discusses the third part of the main fieldwork component of this study. I discuss how young people are often at the forefront of expressing their political voice through creating alternative forms of resistance whilst developing subcultures, alternative

Table 6.2 What Makes You Born to Stand Out? – Themes 'Be Heard'; Perspectives on Being BTSO

Theme	Be Heard
Malesh P -	We have a very unique journey we are on, we are resilient but full of resistance. Us as black people are the most resilient on the face of the earth. We therefore stand out.
i.OG from BCM -	Born to stand out to me is what we have in our untold stories and what we have to offer.
	We have different experiences whilst being able to put that in a story and moulding it into a creative aspect. We have the opportunity of planting different thoughts and emotions than how we are portrayed. There are no limitations in how we can deliver it.

media, and as expressed through the notion of being different in public through their uniqueness in identity.

GROUNDED PROJECT CONTINUED – ARTS-BASED FORMS OF RESISTANCE

Considering the overarching theme of 'born to stand out', this section continues to use the theoretical and evaluation framework of the CCA (Dutta 2015) to review Footprints' YPAR project – the Grounded Project. It focuses on stage 2 of the project hosted from February to March, 2019. Drawing on themes in chapter 6, this section continues exploring the community development process and pop-up performances which led up to and include the Grounded Youth Stage previously discussed. Specifically, in the final subsequent sections, the aspects of culture that are reviewed are urban youth cultures and the ways in which SSAs might identify transculturally. This includes how they might identify with their specific South Sudanese cultural origin, their Australian and African identity, but also how they also identify with subcultures such as Hip Hop.

Being Born to Stand Out in Public – Creating Sites for Dialogue

Footprints' critical youth praxis in a transformative youth organising framework is applied to the Grounded Project (described in chapter 2). As chapter 4 outlined, the Grounded Project began with the Gua camp due to the need for 'local sites of dialogue' within the framework of CCA (Dutta 2011) and NSM theory. After participating in consciousness-raising activities at the Gua camp utilising CHHP to discuss the central themes of dialogue important

Figure 6.3 Artist i.OG from BCM Is 'Born to Stand Out' at the Dandenong Market Pop-up Performance as Part of the Grounded Project. He is wearing a 'Sudanese are dope though' t-shirt, an example of involvement in a standpoint project. *Source*: Kimberley Summer.

Table 6.3 What Makes You Born to Stand Out? – Themes 'Born to Stand Out'; Perspectives on Being BTSO

Theme	Born to Stand Out
Lerato from Burn City Queenz and Jungle City Projects -	Other than the physical element (for example, the colour of our skin), even though the way we rap or dance is very different from everybody else. I developed my own unique talent.
Wantu from BCM -	I have a unique perspective in just my story overall. I grew up with my story back home in South Sudan and then here, and then I had the additional road of finding my identity.
	Being able to look like me in the Hip Hop world and celebrate us here is my ultimate goal and achievement.

to young SSAs, camp participants and project partners co-constructed the further phases of the Grounded Project. The subsequent sections describe the moderate theme of how Footprints' YPAR process following the Gua camp engaged participants in creating public sites for dialogue. It is highlighted as a moderate theme as whilst creating public sites for dialogue was moreso a priority of the Grounded Project, it is identified that this was not a major focus of participant voices in the same way. Chapter 2 describes how it was initially conceived that one of the Grounded Project's intention was the opportunity to create overt opportunities to express political voice through Hip Hop expression. Findings point towards how young SSAs participated in the interim phase of engaging in NSM practice by venturing out into public performances following the initial consciousness-raising process described in chapter 4. The first two sections in this chapter gauge participants' views and project observations on how it felt to start presenting their political voice in public after the Gua camp through social media campaigns and pop-up performances. This resulted in the sub-theme of building confidence and building momentum in expressing political voice through engaging the general public. This sub-theme was developed through the first step whereby figure 6.4 depicts being involved in meetings and practises of the spoken-word performances and pop-up dance performances at YSAS Dandenong from February to March 2019. Participation at this stage of the Grounded Project involving further consciousness-raising and team building of participants was in order to be ready to perform at the Grounded Youth Stage in March, 2019.

The second sub-theme evident in considering the capacity to create dialogue through the CCA is by assessing project observations of Footprints' and project participants' social media strategies. The Grounded Youth Stage event discussed below was devised to create social change by creating several social media platforms to promote the overall Grounded Project as part of the broader CCA approach. This theme is not included here due to the analysis

Figure 6.4 Jungle City Project Teaching the Pop-up Performance Dance at the Gua Performance and Leadership Camp in 2019, Followed by Practices at YSAS in March 2019. *Source*: Footprints.

of this theme being better suited through the lens of Dutta's broader *communication for social change* strategy (Dutta 2020). This limitation is discussed in chapter 9, outlining that further strategising is required when considering NSM practice.

Relevant here is a brief discussion on capturing longitudinal YPAR outcomes and identifying the strengths and limitations of this project in relation to Footprints' social change strategy. In summary, these outcomes are documented through the design of structural communication and community partnerships to challenge racist discourses in the Australian context. A limitation of this project, however, is the capacity to create or address structural 'systems' change (Dutta 2015). I now address my observation of the established community partnerships and promotional approaches of the Grounded Project, which assisted the structural communication design of the project as identified in a CCA approach.[12] Participants' thoughts on their experiences of being born to stand out in public through engagement in this phase of the Grounded Project are also captured. The next section therefore discusses how Footprints sought to bypass engaging mainstream media outlets by featuring pop-up performances in public spaces and at schools to engage new fans and audiences. This further ensures an interpersonal approach rather than just relying on 'views' to increase dialogue as part of the CCA approach.

Pop-up Performances and Schools Tour

Following attendance at practices and planning meetings after the Gua camp, pop-up performances at Brunswick street parade, the Southern Migrant Refugee Centre's International Women's Day event, and at Dandenong High School's CDW celebration followed. Footprints identified that organisations with whom they collaborated to develop the Grounded Project over its three iterations since 2009 have been involved in piloting smaller grassroots projects in their local areas. These resulted in a thorough evaluation process pointing to up-scaling ideas to a larger concept, which includes multiple entry points for CCA opportunities. By listening to community voices, specifically those that include locating the cites of resistance, discursive politics and social change communication processes occurred as a result (Dutta 2020).

The key themes detailed in this section discuss how a wider platform is provided for the artists involved to perform and spread their message containing different forms of political voice to a broader audience (Footprints, Grounded Project Acquittal 2017). In my 2019 Grounded Project fieldwork, Footprints arranged for three pop-up performances in the lead-up to the Grounded Youth Stage. I now turn to these performances and discuss their unique contributions to the YPAR project, considering a CCA approach and participants' involvement in an NSM.

Dandenong High School Lunchtime Performance

The public performance aspects of the Grounded Project were an opportunity to present a 'co-constructive' approach where, through collective resistance, the voices of resistance are foregrounded (Dutta 2011, 273). The stages of this project therefore simultaneously offer a critique of hegemony within the narratives of racialising discourses, but also 'foster spaces for democratic participation to enable the alternative stories of development voiced through the participation of people and communities who have been historically erased from discursive spaces' (Dutta 2011, 273).

The first pop-up performance consisted of the Dandenong High School performance where performers *BCM,* Culture Queens (as part of Jungle City Projects), and *Krown* performed at their Harmony Day event during CDW in March 2019. The guest performers were invited by the school and Footprints to host lunchtime performances to celebrate diversity and promote the upcoming Grounded Youth Stage. The Grounded Project artists performing at schools is seen as a sign of outreach to the broader community to offer a taste of the project. Here, the artists came to the school to share their talent with the hope that young people can see themselves in someone performing from culturally diverse backgrounds (Footprints, Grounded Project Acquittal 2019). Once again, this idea aligns with the idea of access to and prioritising culturally diverse mentorship. Considering a CRT analysis of centring Whiteness, Gosa (2011, 191–192) identifies that the:

> key to Hip Hop culture is the de-privileging of expert knowledge gained through participation in white controlled spaces such as schools, and the problematisation of passive acceptance of dominant narratives. The 'truth' and valuable skills, in the world of Hip Hop, can also be attained through lived-experience and 'feeling it'.

This statement can ring true for many young people in Western school systems. In an interview with Jesko, a young artist who had recently graduated from high school in the last couple of years, he highlights the necessity of representation in performance opportunities, *'every time we do shows I get that feeling. We're representing who we are and where we're from. And for all our friends'.*

Figure 6.5 depicts *BCM* featuring Californian U.S. Hip Hop artist A1 Krashn, the Culture Queens dancers (involved in the previous Gua camp), and *Krown* (now a renowned artist in Naarm) who performed a mixture of party songs that acted as 'hype music', exciting the students and tracks with lyrics uniting culturally diverse communities, which linked the BTSO theme to CDW (Summer and Footprints 2022a).

Rather than being defined by the themes of racialising discourses and considering the theme of being BTSO, after also attending Gua camp and performing at a school for the first time, *BCM* thanked Footprints for:

Figure 6.5 Krown, A1 Krashn, Wantu ThaOne and i.OG from Burn City Movement (BCM), and Karabo and Lerato from Culture Queenz Pictured with Footprints Co-founder Sarah Williams at Dandenong High School Harmony Day Event during Cultural Diversity Week, 2019. *Source*: Footprints.

> *showing us what is possible with us, we knew it in ourselves but you have connected us to the bigger picture and what we can do.* (*Wantu ThaOne* from *BCM*) (Fieldwork notes 2019)

i. OG from the *BCM* crew also reflected on this experience, stating that the school performance was:

> *an amazing opportunity to grow and learn more then what we already know of ourselves. This was definitely a life-changing experience that really made me realise what we can do as we collective combine for the greater side of the community despite the negative energy out there . . .* [namely racialising discourses].

Figure 6.6 depicts observation of the spontaneity of pop-up performances and school tours where open-mic time and crowd participation were encouraged.

Participants' accounts demonstrate that they are now building self-confidence when engaging in an NSM. Linking these performances to young SSAs' plans to help others engage in their cause, it appears that young people observing young SSA Hip Hop artists really were '*like sponges*' (Marley from *BCM*). It appears that young students were soaking up the atmosphere and learning tactics for public engagement in a non-confrontational manner. This demonstrates the idea that it is 'okay to be born to stand out as you

Figure 6.6 Burn City Movement (BCM) Performing at Dandenong High School's Harmony Event in CDW, 2019. Culture Queenz Performing at Dandenong High School's Harmony event in CDW, 2019. *Source*: Footprints.

can be creative with showcasing your artistry and identity, mixing it with a social message and reach new audiences' (Fieldwork notes 2019). From these accounts, it is evident that performance and workshop facilitation opportunities inspire individuals to be proactive about their cause within the context of an NSM (Footprints, Grounded Project Acquittal 2019, 17). This was evident in the following pop-up performance at the Southern Migrant Refugee Centre as part of the project.

The Dandenong Market Pop-up Performance

Traditionally, the Grounded Project pop-up performances have been conducted as flash mobs hosted with Jungle City Projects during peak hour outside of the State Library Victoria in the CGD of Naarm one week before the Grounded Festival. Rather than being further exposed to the themes of racialising discourses, the strategy was to promote the upcoming Grounded Festival to a broader audience rather than just the local suburban area. Additionally, it aimed to expose the broader public to the positive things BIPOC young people are doing within their communities in the outer suburbs of Naarm and engage the broader public in NSM practice. In 2017, it was an opportune time to have positive and vibrant young people host this flash mob as it was Moomba weekend at a time when previously the Apex gang narrative had recently erupted (see figure 0.2) and there was a strong police presence around the CBD.

Instead of previous Grounded Project approaches to pop-up performances and flash mobs moreso located in Naarm CBD, in 2019 the Grounded Project consisted of a series of two pop-up performances at the Brunswick Festival Street Parade and the Dandenong Market located in the western and southeastern outer suburbs of Naarm. Whilst it was still the ideal intention to host these public performances in Naarm CBD, the outer-suburb locations were chosen due to the context of the scope of the project, including broader project partners' interaction with the project and funding limitations (Fieldwork notes 2019). The Dandenong Market performance was hosted by the Southern Migrant Resource Centre's CDW tent at the Dandenong Market also in March, 2019. Footprints booked in *BCM* once again as they enjoyed community interaction and the opportunity to engage new audiences. Whilst the audience was not as large as a CBD performance, the benefit of pop-up performances at places like Dandenong Market, where thousands of people come to shop, is that they have a 'lot of impact' due to a 'ready-made audience' (Fieldwork notes 2019). Figure 6.7 shows artist *i.OG* from *BCM* and Footprints' Vice-President wearing the 'South Sudanese are dope [cool] though t-shirts' and a tradesperson enjoying the show. Considering the purpose of engagement with NSMs in each stage of the project, I reflected with artist *i.OG,* who considered that performance is an opportunity to influence future generations as a

> *small glimpse of what is possible . . . I see a shift coming on [from racialising discourses] . . . with the right amount of pressure and access I believe it will happen very soon . . . by force by fire.*

Once again, this appears to continue the theme of building self-assurance and valuing small-scale engagement activities to build dialogue. This then leads to more strategic pop-up performances with larger crowds.

The Brunswick Festival Street Parade Pop-up Performance

Whilst the more central CBD flash mob was not able to occur at the State Library in 2019 as part of the Grounded Project, Footprints project partner Jungle City Projects in Brunswick arranged for any Gua camp participants who wanted to perform to be a part of their Brunswick Festival Street parade

Figure 6.7 Artist i.OG from BCM Performed at the Dandenong Market Wearing a 'Sudanese Are Dope Though' T-shirt, an Example of Involvement in a Standpoint Project.
Source: Kimberley Summer and Footprints.

pop-up performance. Here, they were invited to participate in the choreographed dance routine that they learned at camp (Mills-and-Boom 2019b). The strategy of this stage of the project was young people from southeastern and Western suburbs of Naarm continuing to unite through urban youth culture to create positive social change (Footprints, Grounded Project Acquittal 2019). This overarching theme was identified in presenting a counter-narrative to racialising discourses which have targeted large groups of young SSAs in public as people to be feared. Specifically, this included 'being different in public' demonstrated as multicultural young people representing themselves as 'loud and proud' which coincides with the BTSO narrative (Fieldwork notes 2019) and is depicted in figure 6.8.

When considering a strategic focus of young SSAs being different in public (i.e., being BTSO and demonstrating the freedom of self-expression) and representing their political voice more publicly, I began to wonder, 'what if these types of pop-up performances or flash mobs[13] occurred more often?' Many

Figure 6.8 Burn City Queens Dance Crew as Part of Jungle City Projects Leads the Pop-up Performance of Their Choreographed Dance at the Brunswick Street Parade in March 2019 as Part of the Grounded Project. *Source*: Kimberley Summer and Footprints.

flash mobs I have observed are often filmed and have a broader impact on social media when shared. I wondered, 'what would happen if young SSAs in particular considered being more overt with their political voice in resistance to racialising discourses and potentially 200 of them or so conducted a flash-mob or pop-up performance at the State Library in peak-hour wearing the "South Sudanese are dope though" t-shirts (pictured above)?' (Fieldwork notes 2019). I asked four participants what they thought the impact of this approach might be (considering Footprints previous projects) or if the Grounded Youth Stage was moved to the CBD of Naarm instead of suburbia in the Southeast, what would the impact be? It is beyond the scope of this project to present in detail the varying views of the five participants that I discussed this with. However, to summarise their views, their responses depended on the consideration of a CBD having further exposure to the broader public who might represent a broader cross-section of society, including more Caucasian peoples. But the location of Dandenong was considered to be more suitable for launching their ideals in a safer space (involves more of their own communities in the audience), which could be followed by considering more potentially contentious, white-dominated spaces. There was a consensus that participants questioned the viability of public performances if the social message in resistance to racialising discourses was not more clearly addressed more explicitly. Amina, also from Footprints, felt very strongly about arts-based approaches and how, when she reflects on her own political voice, her

mind does often go to towards the arts. I definitely think art is a form of resistance. Historically, and I guess in present day context.
Yeah, because it's that opportunity to say your voice in your thoughts in a way that can be listened to. Yeah, that doesn't necessarily need an invitation to speak, I suppose. . . .
Marginalised groups should have the loudest voice of all!

Amina's statement sums up the purpose of such pop-up performances where young people do not need to be invited; they can be 'different in public' through their own creativity, expressions of multiple identities, and through different improvisational mechanisms such as pop-up performances rather than formal arts installations. Table 6.4 summarises the key themes identified.

The following section captures how SSA artists in the 2019 Grounded Project did not choose to express themselves with an overtly political voice in resistance to racialising discourses. The way that I captured their message at

Table 6.4 Summary of the Grounded Project Communication Strategies and Pop-up Performances Key Themes

Summary of Grounded Project Communication Strategies and Pop-up Performances Key Themes	Chapter
1. Participation in practices and project meetings after the Gua camp involved building confidence and building momentum in expressing political voice and freedom of self-expression. This was achieved through participants having their voice heard by offering strategic ideas for the project and continuation of networking opportunities.	6
2. Capacity to create local sites of dialogue through social media strategy requires an additional analysis process and further strategising beyond scope in this research.	6
A limitation of the Grounded Project is capacity to create or address structural 'systems' change.	
3. Pop-up public performances represent: • Sites of arts-based resistance – 'being different in public' and 'young people uniting'. • Engages a broader audience, sometimes less targeted. • An opportunity for participants to develop skills in presenting their political voice publicly; build confidence in performing and beginning to participate in the next stages of movement building through engaging members of the public in positive social change.	6

their final Grounded Youth Stage performances represents the project's 'unexpected outcomes': instead of an overtly political message, the strong theme that came across was the way participants chose to represent their *Afrocentricity* and Blackness (still a political paradigm) in more subversive ways. This links to how they express their identity politics in chapter 5. I discuss below how this is a different form of resistance and an alternative type of artivism for young SSAs in developing their own counter-narratives through self-determination at the Grounded Youth Stage, the final stage of the Grounded Project.

The Grounded Youth Stage Continued – Arts-based Forms of Resistance

As suggested in chapter 5, through observation of the Grounded Project in its entirety from the Gua camp to pop-up performances to the public festival, the first key themes conveyed how young SSAs' political voice was displayed through forms of resistance and presenting counter-narratives to racialising discourses – one of the major themes is that the majority of young SSAs are not criminals and are flourishing. This was presented as a form of counter-storytelling through Hip Hop and through the demonstration of 'little publics' (see table 6.5).

This section describes how further themes were identified through observation of the Grounded Youth Stage.

The theme I observed in the previous chapter was how Grounded Project participants shared counter-narratives to racialising discourses after their consciousness-raising journey. With a presentation of diverse identities, this reflects the importance of moving towards *Afrocentric* counter-narratives of race and racism in Australia (Kwansah-Aidoo and Mapedzahama 2018b). The final major themes addressed in subsequent sections surround how, for young SSAs, identity politics are expressed through public performances, *Afrocentricity, and Afropolitanism* – an expression of political voice through Blackness on display.

Table 6.5 Summary of the Grounded Youth Stage Key Themes

Summary of Grounded Youth Stage Key Themes	Chapter
1. Depiction of counter-storytelling through the demonstration of *Little Publics*. Sub-theme:	5
• The majority of young SSAs are not 'criminals' and are flourishing.	
2. Identity politics on display through public performance.	6
3. Afrocentricity and Afropolitanism – An expression of political voice through Blackness. Sub-themes:	6
• Capturing black excellence and Black Power on display through showcasing talents.	

204   Chapter 6

Drawing on findings from chapter 4 to 5, this section discusses how this unintended outcome of featuring Afrocentricity and Blackness to express political voice was established, the key strengths of the Grounded Youth Stage, and any limitations which came up after observing Footprints' YPAR. This leads to the final section on the broader impacts and critical analysis of the project addressing key considerations in relation to creating public sites for dialogue using the CCA. Figure 6.9 demonstrates how the BTSO theme was captured with a picture of camp participants on the front of the festival flyer. Specifically, the main slogan that was communicated in relation to the BTSO theme was that the 'Grounded Project focuses on the commonalities of individuals whilst celebrating and respecting our differences' (Footprints, Grounded Project Acquittal 2019, 1).

With this goal in mind, BTSO artivists demonstrated their agency to assert their uniqueness through their Blackness, equal citizenship status, and contributions to Australian society. These findings are outlined below, where I explore how this project demonstrates the complex interplay of structure and culture through the CCA (2011, 2020, 2021).

Figure 6.9 Grounded Youth Stage Flyer, 2019. *Source*: Malual Deng and Footprints.

Identity Politics on Display through Public Performance

The second strong and nuanced theme carried on from the *Gua* camp and focus group discussions of identity politics was that through public performances, BTSO artivists' identity politics are now on display, representing the BTSO theme. This is seen as how they chose to demonstrate expression of their political voice. Emmanuel shares:

> *When I'm doing things on stage, I'm expressing myself, but sometimes artists are also there to entertain people. That's where Hip Hop comes in as an art form to be able to express myself.*

Three artists articulated this theme; however, *LEZA* most strongly emphasised it through a spoken-word artefact created out of the Gua camp focus groups. *LEZA* declared '*I don't follow society not meant for me. I am living on de facto*' (by herself).[14] She was responding to the themes of racialising discourses and how she did not wish to comply with having to become an honorary white in order to express herself. After picking up spoken-word skills by attending the Gua camp focus groups and camp, *LEZA* then performed her 'White Privilege' poem[15] developed at the Gua camp after experiencing racism on the journey to camp (discussed in chapter 5). She and her group of friends came across as quite loud, rather flamboyant, and opinionated about many topics within identity politics, racialising discourses, and their interactions with the system. Through this journey, it appeared *LEZA* had found her calling as she impacted the crowd with her unapologetic lyrics and was now flourishing – a key component of the BTSO motto.

These types of bold statements and lyrics are likened to Anzaldúa's (cited in Salvídar 2006, 351) Chicana feminist claim that a '"braided tongue" [like a spoken-word performance] is centrally and dramatically at war with colonialism', henceforth she 'will not "tame a wild tongue", or "train it to be quiet", or "make it lie down"'. This fits into the CCA's priority of 'articulating identities' (Dutta 2018, 99). Using the example of *LEZA's* poems, the process of articulating identities is seen to be a strategic response to racialising discourses and participating in an NSM where

> communities with diverse and plural understandings of development come together in communicative spaces forged by subaltern movements to articulate the meaning of community and to construct an identity tied to community life. (Dutta 2018, 99)

This statement describes some of the intangible impacts of the project.

Élkato performed her track 'The Matrix' (Élkato 2019)[16] (discussed in chapter 4) at the Grounded Youth Stage. The significance of this track includes the importance of waking up to how she perceives young people need to be aware of how the system might limit them. By choosing to perform this track and through engaging in CHHP during the Gua focus groups at the camp, *Élkato* offers a form of 'counter-knowledge' to the audience, which can be described as an 'alternative knowledge system intended to entertain whilst challenging white dominated knowledge industries' (Gosa 2011, 191). Therefore, rather than being 'squarely within the realm of political resistance', performing this track as entertainment was a type of 'calculated identity politics' (Gosa 2011, 191). Secondly, Zimbabwean-born spoken-word and Hip Hop artist Simba Mak[17] captured the attention of the crowd, asserting his identity and purpose (Mills-and-Boom 2019a) by declaring,

I'm a peace ambassador, never quick to grab a sword
But equipped to be secure
But my future is fortified
with or without a 9–5pm [job]
Cross my heart and never lie
Hit the beat, take the mic
. . .
So don't get it twisted I'm not a rapper I'm a culture shifter
I'm following my mission to the letter like it's algebra
My brothers and sisters . . .

Figure 6.10 below depicts Simba Mak's and *Élkato's* spoken-word and Hip Hop performances.

I have repeatedly observed many young SSAs actively partaking in the complex activity of forming their identity through self-expression, finding their political voice, and contributing to Australian society despite the racialising discourse narratives of not integrating. Khan (2021) identifies this trajectory as a type of pragmatic belonging, where migrant young people are making claims on the nation. Additionally, it draws on the concept of identity as a 'calling' (Sawyer 2006). Chapter 4 discusses how one might 'awaken' to this calling, which involves a personal consciousness-raising process (also occurring in the context of communal settings in this research). Afterward, one might publicly display snippets of one's identity such as demonstrated through this YPAR project.

In this final findings chapter, it becomes apparent that the way young SSAs are making claims on the nation of Australia is through being BTSO, but not in the ways we might suspect. Through my observation of the final stages of

Figure 6.10 Grounded Youth Stage MC Simba Mak Hosting the Event and Performing Spoken-word, 2019. *Source*: Kimberley Summer and Footprints.

the Grounded Project at the pop-up performances and the Grounded Youth Stage. I anticipated that the consciousness-raising journey would lead to public performances where the participants involved would overtly express their political voice in resistance to racialising discourses. I understood that this project provided a platform with this intention. Whilst they still presented forms of resistance to racialising discourses through this arts-based development project, I observed a more nuanced portrayal of young SSAs' political voice.

The first observation was that all the performers had developed a strong sense of themselves via many avenues, with the project's consciousness-raising journey as a contributor. It was evident they had developed their own internal security as an artist. As chapter 4 demonstrated, the artists involved in this research see Hip Hop as a vehicle to a higher calling of spreading multiple messages about their lives and making an impact in the arts scene in Naarm through this form of storytelling. For some BTSO artivists, this also extends nationally or globally. It was only on certain occasions when public discourse called for it that they felt compelled to express their political voice publicly.

The first theme introduced from observations of the Grounded Youth Stage of identity politics on display came through these observations of culture, practice, and politics in NSMs (Escobar 1992). Here, I consider this an arts-based resistance project under the umbrella of NSMs, where identity politics and a collection of multiple identities or social actors are often at the forefront (Rosaldo 2006, 122). By filtering my observations, and participant and audience responses, this section picks up on the less obvious 'cultural and symbolic aspects' of the project (Escobar 1992, 404). I asked Elizabeth, an audience member who had never really been exposed to Hip Hop or spoken-word, about her first impressions:

Really, I just liked how it made the performers act on stage.
Not act, but how their presence and what they were saying meant something to them and it meant something to the audience.

The next significant theme that was carried on from the *Gua* camp to the Grounded Youth Stage in Footprints' YPAR surrounded how participants displayed Afrocentricity and Afropolitanism. This major theme includes an expression of political voice through Blackness and a CRT analysis (Fieldwork notes 2019). Specifically, this means that the topics discussed at the Gua camp and the lyrics created in response to racialising discourses are now portrayed in strategic public performances.

Afrocentricity and Afropolitanism – An Expression of Political Voice through Blackness

Asante's Pan-Africanist vision suggests that the Afrocentric black diaspora reclaim African agency by considering how Eurocentric ideals dominate their lives (Asante 2020). As many Africans have now become a global diaspora, such as young SSAs in Australia, Mbembe (2020) engages with this decolonising notion by noticing the ways in which the Afropolitan reconstructs black identities. This is through an 'aesthetic sensitivity' and 'political and cultural stance in relation to the nation, to race, and to the issue of difference in general' (Mbembe and Chauvet 2020, 60). This occurs through 'developing a transnational culture' (Mbembe and Chauvet 2020, 60). This is another way of expressing political voice. Whilst I am not aware if participants identify specifically with the terms *Afrocentricity* and *Afropolitanism*,[18] these key themes emerged as a result of the project's CCA, which prioritises centring cultural expression. Centring cultural expression is also discussed as the fourth significant theme which carried on from the Gua camp to the Grounded Festival. This was achieved by the way in which Grounded Project participants represented their Blackness on display, further celebrating the BTSO theme (discussed in chapter 4).

The two sub-themes which were identified under this umbrella theme captured black excellence and power on display through showcasing talents. This was particularly strong amongst female Afrocentric artists. The montage of figure 6.11 below depict Soli Tesema,[19] an Ethiopian artist. Her rhythmic soul and R&B rhythms, presence, and performance epitomised 'the way in which black artists can grace a stage with one soulful voice and microphone with powerhouse vocals and incredible vocal flexibility' (Fieldwork notes 2019). Later, Hip Hop artist *Daniel Elia* and Akimera joined with Tesema on stage for a collaborative performance, which I noted was like 'Hip Hop magic' (Fieldwork notes 2019). It was a moment to remember as all artists are now seasoned performers starting their own trends and music labels, doing bigger shows with larger audiences. Tesema noted that this is '*something Naarm needs more of!*' Like Sampa the Great discussed in previous chapters 4 and 5, this comment reflects Tesema's interactions with the Australian music industry, where they have experienced racism and racialising discourses. However, her statement also demonstrates what is possible when creatives unite for a good cause and continue to resist racialising discourses via arts-based formats.

Another artist who performed at the Grounded Youth Stage and who represented this theme was Achai[20] who is promoted as a black woman who knows and celebrates her black identity (Grounded Project media release 2019). She attended the first Gua camp as a teenager in 2011 and is now an SSA soul, RnB artist whose music has a global reach, particularly with her home country of South Sudan and Uganda. Achai mourns the fact that

> there are a lot of talented SSA and African musicians, however the Australian music industry is still adapting in the sense that there is not a huge fan base for Afro-Australian artists. (Hot-in-Juba 2021, 1)

However, she is hopeful that 'in due time, this will change as more and more artists are on the come-up and will change the music scene' (Hot-in-Juba 2021, 1).

In contrast to the dominating spaces of Whiteness in Australian society and limited representation in the Australian music scene, Lizzy commented on how she was astonished by how many talented black artists there were performing at the Grounded Youth Stage,

Figure 6.11 Achai and Soli Tesema (above) Performing at the Grounded Youth Stage, 2019. *Source*: Footprints.

> *seriously, seeing my sister and the whole event, I guess, like the vibes there was awesome, seeing like all my black people all together, not just black people but everyone in the community all together.*

As it was not just young SSAs booked to perform, I observed how each performer expressed solidarity with each other, 'recognis[ing] one's face in a foreigner' (Mbembe and Chauvet 2020, 60). Whilst considering the complexities evident in black African Australian youths' processes of identification and belonging (Zwangobani 2008), they had perhaps partaken in many similar experiences through their forced-migration journey. These shared experiences therefore create the opportunity for an awareness of the 'interweaving of here, and there' whilst also observing some differences (Mbembe and Chauvet 2020, 59). These varying and similar identifications continue building through the development of a transcultural identity, as well as ways in which they have also interacted with racialising discourses. In this section,

I have identified five artists or groups who performed at the Grounded Youth Stage who represented these ideals in different ways through their gender, geopolitical origins and celebration of strengths.

This leads to the final sub-theme in this section of displays of black excellence and power as forms of cultural innovation. The final way Afrocentric and Afropolitan themes were evident was through 'Hip Hop culture's connection to African musical and social traditions' (Clark 2021, 1). These traditions 'moves beyond borders' (Clark 2021, 1). This was not tokenistic, as I observed it came from the idea of 'identity as calling' (Sawyer 2006). This was a key theme discussed in chapter 4, where Afrocentric artists demonstrated that they are aware of creating an African community conscious of its own myths, origins, and economic, cultural, and philosophical traditions (Asante 2020).

This section portrays that whilst the aim of resisting racialising discourses is difficult to measure and requires further consideration, the positives of this event occurred in unexpected ways. Moreover, by portraying black power and excellence through displays of Blackness rather than overt political discourse discussing racism in a public space and overtly resisting racialising discourses (like the Channel 7 protest), it appears that the event was more about the sense of community that was developing amongst artists and their friends where onlookers were invited in, rather than trying to overtly convince people to change attitudes through art (Fieldwork notes 2019). Santos (2014) argues that attitudes may alternatively change by establishing a space where 'one is unconditionally free and is thus free from the need to prove one's own freedom' (Bautista 2018, 36). Therefore, the angle of the social message through this aspect of an NSM is shifted around. This occurs through participants and artists inviting the broader public into this sense of freedom through an organic process. Lizzy also reinforced this observation, particularly as she had been rather vocal about experiences of racism and racialising discourses:

But like the there's always going to be haters. . . . But, it's all up to you. You don't have to let people's opinion affect you. Like, we don't really care. Like, we're really talking to the black youth, it's up to you if you want to listen. . . . Like, I'm talking to my brother and my sisters, if you want to listen, you're gonna hurt your own feelings. But it's all up to you, stop being ignorant!

This speaks to the BTSO motto of not trying to 'fit in' or convince people not to be racist, but rather for BIPOC individuals and communities to question and not placate racial hierarchies that dictate societal structures in the first place. This has implications for Antiracism policy and practice addressed in chapter 8.

Two artists who embodied black power and excellence through having their own full band and showcasing talents at the Grounded Youth Stage are *Malesh P*[21] and FLEXX.[22] As a duo, their biography for the event described them as having 'sweet sounds and powerful lyrics, you will walk away with your fists in the air' (Grounded Project media release 2019). As suggested above, rather than overtly political Hip Hop, *Malesh P* and FLEXX prefer 'old-school lyrical Hip Hop' from the 1980s and 1990s era, which do have conscious undertones. They have spent many years perfecting their stage presence and sharing their experiences through narrative lyrics which tell a story about their lives and concerns (Fieldwork notes 2019). Also wearing a 'Sudanese are dope though' t-shirt, figure 6.12 depicts their engaging and interactive performance and 'undeniable presence' (Fieldwork notes 2019).

Malesh P and FLEXX performing demonstrates a vision of 'what is possible' as a form of liberatory praxis in Hip Hop in resistance to racialising discourses (Fieldwork notes 2019). Another artist representing this theme is *Akimera*.[23] Her ancestors are of Afro-Caribbean descent and have a history of showcasing their Afrocentric talents in the arts scene. As mentioned, *Akimera* was one of the Grounded Projects mentors. As Afrobeats features a dance component, depicts *Akimera,* a seasoned and evocative performer formerly in the Massive Hip Hop Choir[24] (one of Naarm's premiere Hip Hop collectives), who engaged the audience by getting people to showcase their moves.

The significance of Akimera being involved in the overall Grounded Project and in consideration of the BTSO theme is that she comes across as someone comfortable in her own skin. This is demonstrated by the fact that

Figure 6.12 FLEXX and Malesh P Performing with Their Live Band at the Grounded Youth Stage, 2019. *Source*: Footprints.

Figure 6.13 Akimera Engaging the Audience in Dance Moves at the Grounded Youth Stage, 2019. *Source*: Footprints.

she is a talented performer but also in the cool and calm way she conducts herself when hosting the Gua workshops in spoken-word (Fieldwork notes 2019). Here, Akimera was able to help participants feel comfortable sharing their talents and strengths and build lasting memories by taking a therapeutic approach where belief in self and each other was emphasised. Akimera was also the lead vocalist in the chorus and melodies of the track 'AfriCAN' (2018)[25] (discussed in chapter 5), celebrating the identity of the African diaspora in Australia through the lyrics *'Oh yeah, I am African'*. This track also played at the Grounded Youth Stage.

One of the key messages of 'AfriCAN' (2018) is *'sparking change in the minds of generations'* through a consciousness-raising journey. This ensures that the notions of identity politics, which have a strong truth-telling component, carry through with the overall vision of black excellence and power. One specific aspect is highlighting one's sense of Blackness as an appropriation of style. These lyrics demonstrate some of the sub-themes of using art for resistance to racialising discourses at the Grounded Youth Stage discussed below in a critical review of the project. As a form of imagery that also communicates a message, Lizzy exuberantly stated that her key takeaway from this experience is that '*I love being black*!' This statement highlights that this experience provided a safe space to celebrate and showcase Blackness.

Figure 6.14 Jungle City and Culture Queenz Interactive Dance with Crowd at the Grounded Youth Stage, 2019. *Source*: Kimberley Summer and Footprints.

The final way themes of black excellence and black power were represented is through *Culture Queenz's* performance from Jungle City Studios[26] (figure 6.14) who were a project partner of the Grounded Project. Their collective boasts of 'dancehall, street, and world dance, music, culture and community in the heart of Brunswick' (Grounded Project media release 2019). The five South Sudanese and Zimbabwean dancers represented their Afrocentric style by wearing dashikis, brightly coloured tunics originating from West Africa, and invited the Gua camp participants up to perform the Afrobeats flash-mob dance. They then proceeded to invite the crowd and onlookers to join in by learning new moves. The ability to engage people from all walks of life in this way demonstrates their confidence and exuberance in celebrating the BTSO motto.

Within the BTSO theme of celebrating diversity in identities, this section demonstrates how diverse these identities are, contributing to the exploration of how multiple and diverse civilisations are (Majavu 2015; Ndhlovu 2014). The Grounded Youth Stage challenges mainstream notions about Australian national identity through racialising discourses to encourage a formal recognition of different cultural identities that constitute Australia. As a result, this broadens how we conceptualise diversity. Considering these themes and findings, I critically reflect on the outcomes of the Grounded Project.

CRITICAL REVIEW OF THE GROUNDED PROJECT – CULTURE AS RESISTING AND STORYTELLING

The assumption I have tested throughout this research (specifically through the CCA) was that if young SSAs build their political voice and forms of resistance, sites of social change can be created. Whilst social change was the goal, the reality of the project was that it was rather experimental, as is the nature of YPAR generally. Primarily, the project valued innovation, lived experience, and inclusion of multiple voices through counter-narrative storytelling. Whilst gauging audience impact was not the focus, I asked audience member Elizabeth what she thought the key themes of the project were. Her response:

> *Really, I mean, as much as this is about the South Sudanese community, it's really more to start connection as humans and humanity.*

It was important to hear from an audience member with no prior knowledge of the event. After hearing this response, I reflected in my notes that the higher purpose of the project is achieved but through perhaps a different mechanism than the intended outcome of influencing the general public's perceptions of young SSAs through racialising discourses narratives. (Fieldwork notes 2019)

Following Elizabeth's response and with this reflection in mind, Darder (cited in Bautista 2018, 235) contends that demonstrations of diverse people coming together in dialogue create 'political, "dialectical force that simultaneously unites and respects difference" . . . supports the type of kinship necessary to engage "our shared curiosity, creativity, and imagination, giving meaning to both our resistance and counter-hegemonic practice"'. These qualitative responses demonstrate that for a bystander, the objective was to

listen, respect people with a platform, specifically BIPOC people who do not often have a platform or 'opportunity to hold the mic' uninterrupted. . . . This was achieved through courage, vulnerability and an extensive engagement process. (Fieldwork notes 2019)

Therefore, the Grounded Project demonstrated that through civic engagement, BIPOC urban youth can increase community vitality, challenge injustices, and address social problems (Wray-Lake and Abrams 2020).

Whilst this chapter summarises overall observations, we now move to consider some of the unintended outcomes and limitations of the Grounded Project. Following observation of the whole project, the critical reflection questions in response to these reflections are posited in table 6.6.

This section reviews the impact of the YPAR project with these critical reflections in mind. Considering forms of resistance to racialising discourses

Table 6.6 Afrocentricity and Afropolitanism – An Expression of Political Voice through Blackness

Critical Reflections on the Grounded Youth Stage, March 2019
- Was it more for the performers than the general public – a space to be themselves?
- Did the fact that it all occurred last minute affect the impact? For example, there was no mainstream media pick-up and the final event involved last-minute promotions, which meant large crowds did not attend.
- There were limitations on how the message of being BTSO was communicated. Did the participants and artists understand what the event was all about?
- One participant who attended the Gua camp asked whether these projects should be run by young SSAs themselves? Were there any other similar projects happening around the same time?
- A consideration of the resources involved: A reflection that this was an extensive project with a few phases and had multiple sources of funding, risk-management processes, involved a lot of collaboration with project partners and young SSA communities.

as the main indicator, forms of resistance have been embedded in accounting for this project by detailing the importance of a counter-narrative and a counter-public. An artistic platform provided commentary on political, racial or social injustice (Bonnette 2015, 34) through participating in an NSM. Considering this broad goal, from Footprints' perspective, the strength of the Grounded Project involved:

> offering young people the opportunity to have their voices heard, to build stronger relationships with each other, to discuss issues facing their communities [such as racism] and to come up with strategies to face those challenges. . . .
>
> The project provided an important opportunity for organisers and project partners to better understand the barriers many of the BIPOC young people faced in getting involved in the community. . . . Despite apparent hardships, young people continue to thrive and build resilience with social connections that are there for them. (Footprints, Grounded Project Acquittal 2019:17)

Considering this platform for young SSAs, and CCA more generally, the cultural transformation of racialising discourses needs to involve two approaches. The first approach is: *Culture as storytelling.* To recognise culture as a site of storytelling is to 'open up the processes and practices of development communication to multiple interpretations and re-interpretations, intertwined with the stories people construct of development' (Dutta 2018, 97). This research has demonstrated this approach by providing a rich description and multiple interpretations of the data. Through this process, cultural members which include young SSAs, Footprints members, and project partners participate in both

> the production of cultural stories as well as in the transformation of these stories through their articulation of values that are tied to community life. The metabolic flows and ecological relationships constituting community life are envisioned from other cultural stories, expressing community values in resistance to the dominant development structure. (Dutta 2018, 97)

This research has demonstrated, however, that through the second approach to the CCA and the cultural transformation of racialising discourses, the idea of *Culture as resistance* (2018, 2015) requires further consideration and practical application of self-determination by the communities in question. This involves the

> incorporation of culture into the development structure and into its top-down framework of development interventions is resisted through the participation of

subaltern communities in articulating cultural right as an organising framework for articulating development. (Dutta 2018, 98)

Whilst further improvements could be considered in future YPAR approaches, this chapter has addressed some of these outcomes through considering Hip Hop expression as a form of resistance. In the public performances throughout the Grounded Project, young SSAs demonstrated the power of their presence in public space together and resistance to racialising discourses. Their message exemplifies demonstrating 'we have a voice' and knowledge of self and identity in its many forms is power (Fieldwork notes, 2019). With the goals of CCA described as focusing on culture through storytelling and resistance, I have captured six participants' perceptions of the impacts of the whole project. Themes captured are particularly in relation to their opinions on how discursive spaces of dialogue are created (2018, 2012). Marley from *BCM* shared his thoughts on the general structure and observations of his involvement in the project. Whilst he missed out on the Gua camp and focus groups, he stated that:

> *[this project] definitely would have been a first time for certain people. But then also, just another chance for a lot of people to try to connect with more people who are like minded like themselves . . . and just speak about things like this, and give them a platform.*

Participants such as Kwan from *BCM,* who went on the consciousness-raising journey starting at the Gua camp, relayed his reflections of being involved in the Grounded Project, where he realised:

> *Okay, I do have people like myself, and we can team up to change this. So I guess that's a big thing too, because a lot of the times knowing what we know, I meet a lot of people who supposedly know the same thing, but they've accepted that change can't happen. And that's like a whole different thing that then we need to do. That is also in empowering those who do know, because I guess being the power, being a bystander is bigger than you know. So just seeing that for myself, like being involved with everything, to just knowing like, Okay, if you know better, then you can definitely do better consistently. For me . . . I try to take this step forth.*

Amina, a member of Footprints, echoed many participants' feelings discussed in chapter 5 that expressing your political voice can have ramifications. She therefore felt it was only safe to express her political voice in *'some groups and certain settings'*. She identified how this feeling contributes to the ways in which groups choose to develop forms of resistance through self-determination. Amina reiterated that

> it comes back to ... doing something like that in a safer space in a community setting and then moving towards reaching out to the wider public. So ... doing it in Dandenong would be so effective, and could also ... get more ... like-minded people involved and people who get it to understand it and relate to that. ...
>
> And it only makes us stronger to fight this fight. We're all a part of it, I guess, and the common factor in all of it is that they all resist through art.

Whilst resistance was not an explicit message, I was interested in an audience member, Tina's, take on how she felt forms of resistance might be portrayed. Tina stated that

> I thought it was a positive. I think anytime you have a public showcase of People of Colour, it's important.
>
> I feel like my entire life, it's always been like, everyone's white. And I will like turn around to Pat (my co-worker) and say 'this is such a white room right now'. Because it's becoming less normal for us.
>
> You know, like, the more we get events like Grounded, ... it's important, I think, for more Australians to have that experience ... any public example of that is good.

Tina's statement fits with the CCA's concept of *culture as deconstruction* and *culture as co-construction* (Dutta 2011, 280). Similar to the Grounded Project, which is de-emphasising a Eurocentric focus, culture

> emerges as a marker for returning the gaze at the imperial undertones of neo-liberalism, offering localised forms of participation, recognition, and representation that then become the very bases for offering alternative rationalities of organising. Furthermore, through the networks of solidarity, cultural values from hitherto marginalised spaces are not recognised. (Dutta 2011, 280)

Emmanuel, who has now been a part of several Grounded Projects, comments on the feasibility of the project:

> They are effective. I think art is a tool we can use to change the narrative of a community. Why? Because there is so many sub-sections within art itself because you've got like music or spoken-word or the list goes on. And all that can be used to share people's story, to be able to express their feelings, their own stories and even be able to create stories about themselves with themselves or engage other people within that as well.

Emmanuel also refers to the significance of new performance opportunities created to bring people together to share in dialogue. He similarly noted how, for artists such opportunities are rare. Finally, Akur thinks that performance art and arts-based projects:

> *play a big role in the sense that they allow people to have the opportunity to have a voice and to share their creative knowledge and aspects and works for the people around them and for the community. And even just to be able to express who you are as an artist. You know, it's good to be able to have those platforms from these organisations or communities or, you know, arts-based workplaces and . . . even councils. So . . . it's important . . . because we need that . . . in order for us to give the next lot that responsibility and that platform.*

These experiences, specifically going through the consciousness-raising journey and participating in an NSM, may lead to young SSAs creating their own platforms (Fieldwork notes, 2019).

To summarise this section, discursive spaces as a form of resistance fits in with the central research theme of the ways young SSAs demonstrate new forms of artivism (2018, 2012). BTSO artivists instead want to communicate their feelings of being BTSO through wanting to contribute to society in their own unique ways. Gabriel from Footprints summarises how this occurred through the Grounded Project:

> *was also good because a lot of artists are just expressing themselves in all different sort of art forms. Yeah, that was fine. . . . As an artist, as an arts enthusiast, as a music lover who enjoys Hip Hop . . . it just so great to see all the different communities, different cultures and the music, it was just awesome. And then when you look deep you can also see the messages. Yeah, so that was really good.*

The hope in conducting these experimental projects 'is that the participation of subordinated groups in democratic politics [such as through NSMs] will yield an improvement for the whole society, without reducing everyone to the same identity' (Rosaldo 2006, 124).

SITES OF ARTS-BASED RESISTANCE TO RACIALISING DISCOURSES

This chapter began with young SSAs' accounts of what it means to be BTSO. As identified, diversity and complexity are at the core of the findings outlined in this body of work. Stories about goal setting and ambition provided a foundational narrative arc that was present within many young SSAs' accounts of their experiences living in Australia.

By answering the last sub-question: *How might building of political voice for young SSAs contribute to enhanced freedom and affirmations of identity?* this chapter represents strong research findings that young SSAs were able to build and express their political voice through first resisting the notion that they needed to 'fit in' or to be honorary whites. Instead, further consciousness-raising as part of an NSM enabled participants to pursue their freedom and aspirations (Sen 2001[1999]; Appadurai 2004). The sub-themes developed through participating in pop-up performances in the lead-up to the Grounded Project resulted in BTSO artivists creating sites of arts-based resistance to racialising discourses through being different in public and young people uniting for a social cause. Performance opportunities supported artists in developing skills in presenting their political voice publicly, building confidence in performing, and beginning to participate in the next stages of movement-building by engaging members of the public in positive social change amongst diverse young people.

Building on chapter 5, key themes demonstrated in this chapter also outline the further ways in which young SSAs resist racialising discourses through presenting counter-narratives. This is identified through the more subtle theme that young SSAs' identity politics are on display through public performance opportunities at the Grounded Youth Stage. This is followed by a presentation of the strong theme that young SSAs prefer to express their political voice through Blackness – namely through Afrocentricity and Afropolitanism. The sub-theme captured in this topic demonstrates this finding by capturing Black excellence and power on display through showcasing talents. By doing so, BTSO artivists created public sites of dialogue by performing forms of conscious Hip Hop in public.

As a matter of ethnographic method, capturing the careful selection of artists, involvement of project participants, engagement of the general public and the audience, this chapter has demonstrated that through 'plac[ing] social relations at the heart of the analysis along with the intersubjective world of the participants', the BTSO theme and 'politics of citizenship' was foregrounded (Rosaldo 2006, 120). This was as per research participants' views that they did not prefer to spend too much time considering the narratives of racialising discourses. Instead, they demonstrated their messages through alternative forms of artivism through forms of Hip Hop expression. As a result of participating in this form of NSM, it results in 'the emergence of new citizens with new identities who demand their rights and know that they have the right to demand their rights' (Rosaldo 2006, 120). This emergence of new social actors in a NSM occurs with the backdrop of the social challenges that exist in current globalisation politics. Through enacting critical cultural agency in promoting an alternative to mainstream racialising discourses, these young SSAs built their own freedom to enact the BTSO narrative rather than accepting an expectation of having to be honorary whites (Tuan 1998).

These findings were foregrounded through depictions of how young SSAs are able to build and express their political voice through Hip Hop and pose alternative forms of artivism in response to forms of socio-political disadvantage through arts-based community development projects. By describing individual artists' messages and observations of themes in this chapter, I conclude that the aim of the Grounded Project has been achieved in creating the impetus for activating social change, albeit at a more limited level due to the limitations described. More clarity and strategic focus are needed to explore possibilities for creating further spaces for structural transformation. Chapter 7 summarises the key findings of chapters 4–6 and interacts with these key themes to form a broader discussion surrounding the contributions of this monograph.

NOTES

1. Malesh P (2020) 'Be Free' (Soli x Mez Mariyé: Malesh P Remix), Malesh P: https://soundcloud.com/malesh/be-free-soli-x-mez-mariye-malesh-p-remix.
    See blogpost #32.
2. Soli (2020) *'Be Free'* feat. Mez Mariyé, shotbymez: https://www.youtube.com/watch?v=JQjSLRLniIo.
    See blogpost #34.
3. Cole, J. (2020) 'Be Free', Roc Nation Records: https://www.youtube.com/watch?v=_g02ECRXCtE.
    See blogpost #35.
4. Sampa the Great's (2020) performance of 'Black Power' at her Black Atlantis set at Planet Afropunk, Anastasia Tsobanopoulis: https://www.youtube.com/watch?v=Mx2a9s3mOgU.
    See blogpost #1.
5. See Notes '3' and '1'.
6. See Notes '1'.
7. See Chapter 1, Notes '1'.
8. See Notes '1'.
9. Queen P (2018) 'Hummingbird', featured on *Bring Black Back* EP, Queen P: https://open.spotify.com/track/76GoDC8lvnA4bzJgRxv42A?si=3VvbFuLJRmiq4zY29EL7TQ.
    See blogpost #28.
10. See Notes '1'.
    Daniel Elia (2017) 'Lonely' (Remix), ALIA Records: https://www.youtube.com/watch?v=Qb4gzkFKQI0.
    See blogpost #5.

Burn City Movement (BCM) (2020) 'Trials n' Tribulations (TNT)' featured in Burn City Movement's Realness for Sale EP, Noble Studios: https://tidal.com/browse/album/131189065.

See blogpost #4.

11. Malesh P (2015) 'Road to Success', featured on the *Dreamer. Believer* EP, Malesh P: https://music.apple.com/ca/album/dreamer-believer/1029172750.

See blogpost #36.

12. The summary of these strengths and limitations are condensed due to the scope of this thesis but will be published elsewhere, as they represent important, more nuanced findings of this research in relation to arts-based community development projects.

13. The difference between a *pop-up performance* and a *flash-mob* is due to how they are conducted. A flash mob is a group of people who seamlessly arrive at a venue separately unbeknown to the general public, and traditionally start performing or doing street theatre in unison and draw in a crowd of interested onlookers to create a 'buzz'. A pop-up performance may be something more planned, where an artist is booked to perform at a public event. They may have the sound system and infrastructure set up in advance whereas in a flash mob the artists might be carrying the sound system with them and turn on the music unexpectedly.

14. LEZA (2019), spoken-word poetry on the topic of exploring identity at Gua camp, 2019:

See blogpost #37.

I don't know why it took me so long to write down a poem
To catch a second in the life
It's hard to type so I use my pen
It's easy using my first camera because it was only the click of a button
Why is it so hard to think?
Mind blank
Why is it so hard to go out and capture a second?
Lonely
That's right, I need my inspiration
Tired of feeling that desperation
Digging my thoughts deep I need that medication
Wait, ego is that you?
Why are you knocking on my door so late?
Please, I need a break!
Knock knock, who's there?
Motivation
Finally got me to that station
My biggest creation
The duration of my greatest formation slowly unsaturates and pours out into isolation
Empty, slowly deflating like a balloon
I'm quick to dip, flip and slip and but all I hear is get a fucking grip
Equipped, but I'm still spiritually connected to that slave ship

> *I'm drowning, I need my ancestors to guide me while I am currently playing battlefield*
> *My mind thinks if only I can turn back time I would use all my ghosts to start over*
> *Would you take the red pill or the blue pill?*
> *If only we got asked that question right?*
> *Like a daffodil the yellow fills up my every hollow*
> *And the mellow tunes make me feel less shallow*
> *I wear my Afro high and reminisce upon the times my soul sits next to my Pharoahs*
> *Call me Agro Fiasco! Ha ha*
> *I don't follow a society not meant for me*
> *I'm living on de facto . . .*

15. See Chapter 4, Notes '45'.
16. Élkato (2020) 'The Matrix', YSAS Studios: https://soundcloud.com/user-940608762/lkato-matrix.
    See blogpost #17.
17. https://www.facebook.com/itssimbamak.
18. Two participants identified with a Pan-African identity.
19. https://www.facebook.com/pg/itsSoli/about/?ref=page_internal; https://www.youtube.com/watch?v=MxDJkJcV_uQ
20. https://www.facebook.com/AchaiD7/.
21. https://www.facebook.com/OfficialMalesh/.
22. https://www.facebook.com/YoannesTOR/.
23. https://www.facebook.com/akimera/.
24. https://soundcloud.com/massive-hip-hop-choir#:~:text=Melbourne,harmonies%20and%20body%20percussion%20MASSIVE%20%E2%80%A6 .
25. 'Afri– CAN' (2019) produced by *Malesh P* - GUA Project - AfriCAN.mp3
    See blogpost #2.
    Created by workshop facilitator Malesh P at Gua Performance and Leadership Camp hosted by Footprints in January 2019.
    See chapter 3, Notes '4' for full lyrics of the track.
26. https://www.facebook.com/Junglecityprojects/.

Chapter 7

Discussion

Alternative Forms of Artivism for Young South Sudanese Australians through Hip Hop

This monograph has detailed how young SSAs are dealing with the pervasive problem of racialising discourses that promote the idea that SSAs are failing to integrate into Australian society and are instead forming criminal gangs. Alternatively, young SSAs counter that 'we do not know that narrative' and have identified how their story has been 'incorrectly analysed' (BTSO Director synopsis 2020, 1). The broader scope of this research investigated different expressions of their political voice through protest, dissent, and arts-based community development projects focusing on the topic of how 'being born to stand out' manifests. This monograph has explored young SSAs' efforts towards self-determination manifested through alternative forms of artivism, as most clearly demonstrated through the sub-genres of conscious and political message Hip Hop expression (Oware 2018; Bonnette 2015).

Due to the recent global uprising concerning matters of racial injustice and the fight for black lives, it was important to capture an ethnographic account of this time in the history of the South Sudanese communities' resettlement in Australia between 2007 and 2021 from a truth-telling perspective (Hill-Collins 2013). Depicting young SSAs' own accounts of this timeline involved an extensive community engagement process. The participants in this PhD research, presented in monograph format, worked with me to co-construct the timeline of key events, which is captured in figure 0.1. This timeline began with the murder of young SSA Liep Gony in 2007 and explored a counter-narrative to the prevalent African gangs narrative in subsequent years. Detailing the impact of these narratives in chapter 6 demonstrated some of the ways in which Australians perceive 'Blackness'.

Whilst truth is an elusive term in postmodern times (Clammer 2021), hearing young SSAs' own accounts of the impacts of racialising discourses through song lyrics, interviews, and abstracts of mixed multimedia is devastating. The findings have demonstrated that the suicide of young SSAs and experiences of systemic racism are still prevalent in the Australian context. Whilst acknowledging societal and structural limitations, the extent of this impact and what young SSAs are doing to move towards their own freedoms and aspirations has not yet been captured to any great extent in pre-existing research. By also documenting young SSAs' personal and communal counter-narratives through multi-modal research data, this research contributes to extending the research terrain and forges new paradigms of activist research through ethnographic writing on the topics of urban youth politics and resistance. This addresses Escobar's (1992, 421) concern that any such representations urge us to 'account for the many voices within social movements and their discursive positioning (including the ethnographer) and the complex epistemological and political negotiations at stake'.

SUMMARY OF FINDINGS AND STRUCTURE OF THIS CHAPTER

The main contention of this monograph is that young SSAs express new forms of artivism by expressing their political voice through the medium of Hip Hop. This is a form of participation in an NSM. The findings chapters 4–6 demonstrate this by outlining some of the messages of their political voice in resistance to racialising discourses and actions they have taken so far. This emerging area of study mapping strengths-based approaches requires further investigation led by young SSA communities/scholars themselves or in collaboration with existing scholars who identify as allies, as will be addressed in chapter 9.

Summarising the key findings, the sub-questions presented in chapters 3–6 were used to structure the background and findings chapters, and to capture several new findings that contribute to both youth and community development studies in pursuit of my overarching research question: *What is the role of Hip Hop for young South Sudanese Australians in building their political voice to resist racialising discourses?*

The first background chapter, chapter 3, outlined the stories that young people shared about their experiences with urban youth culture and systemic racism. This necessitated the need to build political voice. To unpack the overarching research question, the first sub-question explored in chapter 3 was: *How do young South Sudanese Australians build agency and develop their political voice?* Whilst all participants agreed that young SSAs have a voice, there were various opinions presented about whether young SSAs had a political voice and what constituted limitations to the expression of that political voice. Participants noted that this was due to the insidious nature of racialising discourses as experienced through various forms of racism.

Participants explained that they developed their voice (freedom of expression) and then their political voice through various avenues. This may have been through either a mentor believing in them or modelling themselves off limited role models from their communities. Engaging in Hip Hop was seen as a pivotal moment that provided a forum for voicing concerns about what they see occurring within the community or an outlet for self-expression on other topics. Chapter 3 demonstrated that Hip Hop is the primary modality for the young SSAs featured in this research to express their political voice. They noted that they chose Hip Hop because racialising discourses was so pervasive in their lives that they felt an outlet was necessary.

Chapter 3 was followed by three findings chapters detailing the consciousness-raising journey in order to build political voice and an expression of alternative forms of artivism through an arts-based development project – the Grounded Project. In consideration of the continuous role Hip Hop plays for young SSAs in building their political voice, the findings in chapters 4–6 elaborated on how this modality of self-expression and resistance functions as a genre of music, but also an identity-based New Social Movement (NSM) chosen by their communities. Young SSAs' accounts of political voice expression throughout this research demonstrates the enduring presence of agency and, in some cases hopeful narratives.

However, the impact of racialising discourses on SSA young people led many to feel frustration and uncertainty about their future. This research argues that the ways young people reflect on and narrate their experiences have a significant influence on their internal and external manifestation of selfhood and the expression of their multiple emerging identities. As a key feature of identity-based NSMs, Hip Hop remains a vehicle for oppressed communities to express political voice and identity politics on their own terms. Having a global impetus, but also building on local forms of expression, ensures that a variety of experiences are heard in the messages that young SSAs wish to portray.

Therefore, the second sub-question addressing these themes: *What role does Hip Hop specifically play in building political voice?* was primarily addressed in chapter 4. This chapter discussed the importance of the consciousness-raising journey young SSAs might embark upon when engaging in CHHP and before determining how their expressions of political voice might become public. Whilst young SSAs did not necessarily view political voice in the conventional sense of engaging in mainstream modes of politics, in chapter 5 a small number of artists saw expressing their identities through Hip Hop as a higher calling that enabled them to get their messages of conscious or political Hip Hop across to the broader public and their own communities. The messages of these artists through alternative forms of storytelling, primarily depicted in this monograph as BTSO artivists are summarised in the following sections.

The third sub-question: *What role does political voice play for young SSAs in resisting racialising discourses?* is covered in chapter 5 through varying views depending on young SSAs' individual socio-political dispositions. This study finds that some young SSAs have gone through a consciousness-raising journey to become 'woke' (aware) of the power imbalances in society created by the social construct of race as detailed in Critical Race Theories (CRT). They, therefore, express themselves through conscious forms of Hip Hop to resist racialising discourses. Whilst further findings suggest that others prefer to respond to society in their own fashion through forms of dissent such as trap, grime, and drill Hip Hop, one thing that unites young SSAs is their expressions of political voice through various sub-genres of Hip Hop. Chapter 5 depicts how artivists used their Hip Hop personas to engage the general public in the Grounded Project public performances to provide a counter-narrative to racialising discourse tropes.

The final sub-question: *How might this contribute to enhanced freedom and affirmations of identity?* is addressed in chapter 6. This chapter describes the preference of young SSAs to self-determine how their political voice is represented through an alternative expression of being 'born to stand out' (BTSO). This aligns with a CCA. Finally, chapter 6 portrays how alternative forms of resistance narratives can be displayed through arts-based youth community development projects. Young SSAs, therefore, present their own flavour and mixed-modal expertise to consistently present the BTSO theme.

By focusing on BTSO as their main motto, SSAs choose to prioritise strength in Blackness and transcultural identities through an Afrodiasporic vision for the future. This is as opposed to spending all their time trying to debunk the narratives of racialising discourses. This is not a homogeneous vision, with findings beyond the scope of this monograph outlining various opinions and highlighting the emergence of new subcultures, creation of alternative forms of media and business outlets, and the rise of Hip Hop artists and other leaders in various industries gaining influence. By highlighting strength in culture as a hyphy-discourse (another demonstration of political voice) (Pope 2020), the preference for Afrocentric and even sometimes Afrofuturistic formats became evident. They specifically depict the African diaspora's vision for a future they are bringing about through forms of alternative artivism.

Through the YPAR approach and critical analysis of the BTSO theme, participants asserted that whilst they are in the process of 'becoming' (Bloch 1970, 1986), they wish to articulate their own shifting and hybrid identities. Furthermore, they wish to reclaim much of what was lost in their diaspora transition and redefine a future for themselves. Whilst this is the case, I have demonstrated the opportunity to examine the communicative processes, strategies, and tactics through which social interventions are constituted in response to the challenge. I have documented the ways in which those in power create conditions for the many (e.g., media outlets and some politicians) and provide a theoretical base for discussing the ways in which these positions of power are resisted through pursuing freedoms (Sen 2001[1999]).

This monograph has described how, due to their sense of 'identity as calling' (Sawyer 2006), BTSO portray conscious lyrics about social norms and therefore deliver social messages as a result. Whilst others prefer to influence their communities in less overt ways through the formation of emerging subcultures. Younger generations of Hip Hop artists are also using hybrid approaches that blend all genres of Hip Hop with messages about the things that affect their lives. In their orientation towards Afrocentricity and deep knowledge, and experience in constructing Hip Hop that connects with young SSAs, they aim to reach new youth audiences in less conventional ways than mainstream youth development practices.

This chapter is comprised of four sections distilling the findings from chapters 4 to 7 and explaining the significance of the PhD research findings, namely, that SSA have chosen alternate routes to express their political voice through the sub-genres of political and conscious Hip Hop. The use of this alternative method, in conjunction with other methods beyond the scope of this monograph, redefines our understanding of political voice and the pursuit of justice, equity, and freedom. As suggested, the broader focus of the research was on the way young SSAs have chosen to pursue these things through protest, dissent, and everyday resistance. This monograph and therefore this discussion chapter only focuses on arts-based community development approaches utilising Hip Hop as an alternative form of artivism.

The following sections unpack the key concepts raised throughout the findings, which surround consciousness-raising and resistance, racial justice and equity, and the theme BTSO. Any additional gaps in social research literature that suggest areas for future study are discussed in the conclusion chapter 8.

CONSCIOUSNESS-RAISING AND RESISTANCE

Rather than focusing on deficit approaches in response to dominant racialising discourses, such as societal narratives around what young SSAs are doing 'wrong' in relation to the 'integration' discourse, the ethnographic focus in the findings chapters highlights the importance of a consciousness-raising journey for building counter-narratives through forms of Hip Hop expression that focus on their 'bright rights' (what they are doing well) (Abe Nouk,

Fieldwork Notes). The discussion in this section extends Akom's CHHP (2009) which incorporates CRT theories (D.G. Solórzano and Yosso 2002) of counter-storytelling (Delgado and Stefancic 2000). This is demonstrated through the monograph's exploration of key findings through PhD research about the ways young people narrate a consciousness-raising journey at the Gua Performance and Leadership Camp (chapter 5), which led to forms of resistance at the Grounded Youth Stage and other public performances incorporated into Footprints Grounded Project (chapters 5–6).

The tenets of CHHP and its application in exploring CRT will be used here to structure my discussion of five key findings relating to consciousness-raising and resistance (D.G. Solórzano and Bernal 2001, 312–315). As outlined in chapter 3, CHHP utilises the following elements: (1) The centrality of race and racism and their intersectionality with other forms of oppression; (2) challenging traditional paradigms, texts, and theories used to explain the experiences of BIPOC; (3) the centrality of experiential knowledge of BIPOC; (4) commitment to social justice; and (5) a transdisciplinary approach (Solórzano and Delgado Bernal cited in Akom 2009). They are not discussed in Akom's original order as I have presented each tenet as it pertains to the themes of centrality of race and the BTSO narratives participants portrayed. Tenets two, four and five are therefore discussed in this section, whilst tenets one and three are discussed in the subsequent sections.

THE COMMITMENT TO SOCIAL JUSTICE AND A TRANSDISCIPLINARY APPROACH

The analysis conducted throughout this research identifies stories of young SSAs who became 'woke' (Mirzaei 2019) or 'conscious' of geopolitical events of recent years and the roles various social actors play in an NSM. This was the first stage of participants' journeys when participating in an identity-based NSM utilising Hip Hop. This section explores how they conceptualise this journey within the opportunity that Hip Hop presents for broader listeners to engage with the same consciousness-raising journey. By surveying the ways in which young SSAs embark on a consciousness-raising journey to develop their political voice, the findings that young SSAs' demonstrations of little publics through 'black public spaces' that evolve into 'counter-spaces' becomes pertinent (addressed in chapter 5). Through their 'role as a place of comfort and nurturance and as a place of building communities of resistance' (D.G. Solórzano and Yosso 2002, 336), this study demonstrates how elements of Hip Hop culture can effectively use everyday narratives to transform individual, subaltern positions into sources of community power (Pope 2020).

This follows Dutta's (2011, 2020) CCA which uses consciousness-raising to increase public awareness about issues of racial social justice as conceptualised through CRT. These sources of power were demonstrated by research participants' engagement with consciousness-raising at the Gua camp (discussed in chapter 4). In alignment with the proximate origins of NSMs, for example beginning with the feminist movement and their processes of change, which often involve consciousness-raising, the processes specifically included intimate sessions where participants shared stories from their lives about the hurts and wounds they suffered. Through discussions in a 'safe' or 'intimate' setting hosted by young BIPOC facilitators and their artistic peers, these discussions are likened to the broader Black Consciousness Movement, a significant era when a mass consciousness-raising process occurred in the 1950s and 1960s.

This was a movement for 'black solidarity, black cultural pride, and black economic and political self-determination' which had 'enraptured the entire black world' (Kendi 2019, 16). In its current iterations, conscious Hip Hop artists like USA artist common promote the idea that 'black is beautiful' (Asante 2008, 79), which offers a counter-narrative to racialising discourses and dispels 'inferiority' theorised in CRT. The discussions detailed in the Gua camp (discussed in chapter 5) also involved a process of understanding connection to culture and place, noting young people's yearnings to connect to their homelands in South Sudan. To discuss this yearning, Asante (2008, 75) also draws on the imagery of *Sankofa*, symbolised by a mighty and mythic bird that soars forward while looking backward. This Afrocentric Akan (West African) concept means 'go back to your roots in order to move forward'.

For Gua participants, essentially this meant 'if we want to move forward, it is essential that we understand where we came from' (Asante 2008, 75). Understanding this element of consciousness-raising was identified as a key aspect of building political voice for young SSAs and an essential part of beginning to participate in an NSM and anti-deficit discourse.

The other element of this journey of consciousness-raising involves what fellow artivist and academic Kelley (2003, 191) describes as a 'revolution of the mind', a conception for black liberation. This asset and strengths-based approach involves refusing to take on victim status and instead engaging creative capacity to begin fighting for change. This has implications in determining what the struggle for human freedom looks like in relation to racial social justice, whereby BIPOC are conceptualised at the bottom of the 'race' hierarchy. This monograph continues to challenge these racist social structures by discussing how young SSAs pursue liberation from racialising discourses by somewhat bypassing it altogether through the theme of BTSO. In poetic format, surrealist writer and blues scholar Garon articulates the process towards human freedom. Garon suggests that if a restructuring of the mind occurs, this can lead to:

> new modes of poetic action, new networks of analogy, new possibilities of expression. All help formulate the nature of the supersession of reality, the transformation of everyday life as it encumbers us today, the unfolding and eventual triumph of the marvellous. (Garon cited in Kelley 2003, 192)

It is my contention in this research that this iterative and creative process of 'bridging the gap between dream and action' (Kelley 2003, 193) has occurred through YPAR hosted by Footprints and through young SSAs building their political voice. This occurs through the process that BTSO artivists articulate through Hip Hop to create the 'marvellous' (Kelley 2003, 193). By responding to the African gangs narratives (a key feature of racialising and deficit discourses), 2018 in Naarm was a particularly strong year in which young SSAs flourished in their artivism. They were working towards building 'new movements, new possibilities, new conceptions of liberation' (Kelley 2003, 192). This approach to movement-building essentially leads to the broadening of one's mind to strive towards Black Consciousness. Like Biko (the founder of South Africa's Black Consciousness Movement), rather than conceiving of blacks as debilitated people, Black Consciousness was an 'inward process of understanding identity'. Biko wanted to 'channel the anger and frustrations of black people into something they could all fight for' (Kosley 2020, 1).

Through the Gua camp focus group and workshop process, participants realised that their individual issues were, in fact, collective. Rather than being 'depressed', they discovered they were both 'oppressed and angry' – hence moving from a personal to a political consciousness of their issues, that is, where the 'personal is political' (Rosaldo 2006, 119). Realising this is a key feature of beginning to participate in an NSM as it relates to the consciousness-raising journey. This was, however, just one step in the Black Consciousness process; the next step was the conscious realisation that young Hip Hop artists can be 'voices of revolutions' (Asante 2008, 82), resulting in the key concept that 'when we have a true sense of who we are, we are unstoppable' (Asante 2008, 175). This leads to the next phase of being involved in an NSM through Hip Hop artivism.

The final stage of the consciousness-raising journey that BTSO artivists went on is their choice of Hip Hop culture, which intertwines with NSMs and seeking social change. This was not only chosen for the 'spiritual dimension' (Asante 2008, 256) and personal healing element, but in this context was chosen by young SSAs to articulate and spread their messages of the racial disparities they were experiencing, as well as their counter-narratives (addressed in the next tenet of CHHP). The significance of this choice, as Kelley (2003) and Asante (2008) identify, is that through the use of poetic expression, as an identity-based NSM, Hip Hop builds upon real affinities with Afrodiasporic vernacular culture and connects with the deeply African roots of Hip Hop.

One example of how Afrodiasporic vernacular culture is linked to African roots is by clarifying the origins of how the word 'Hip Hop' came about. By doing so, Afrocentric scholar Asante (2008, 250) takes us on a consciousness-raising exercise. He explains that *Hip* comes from the Wolof language, spoken by the Wolof people in Senegal, Gambia, and Mauritiana. He suggests that 'in Wolof, there's a term *"hipi"* which means "to open one's eyes and see". So *"hipi"* is a term of enlightenment' (Asante 2008, 250) in order to understand the social conditions. Further linking to the Black Consciousness framework, Asante emphasises not only the revolution of the mind but the importance of the action component – that is, he suggests that *Hop* is the English word meaning 'to spring to action' (Asante 2008, 255). Understanding the etymology of Hip Hop provides insight into the actions and messages of Afrocentric young SSAs who use the format of conscious Hip Hop, in particular, seeking first to enlighten us about their experiences with creative and accessible messages. This is often with the intention that we too might become 'conscious' and spring into action in response to their experiences of systemic racism.

Krown's track 'Trials n' Tribulations (TnT)' (Krown 2018b)[1] and through his presence in his own recording label Military Mind, is one example where this approach is applied. In 'TnT' he describes using *'the mic as a weapon'*. Asante's (2008) powerful interpretation of the etymology of Hip Hop links these terms together to suggest that Hip Hop culture is a weapon of the mind and a call to action. An important differentiation is made here to suggest that one approach alone, such as the writing of a Hip Hop track, does not accelerate social change through an NSM. Kelley (2003, 193) stresses the importance of considering multiple angles and actions within the broader NSM approaches, suggesting, for example that unlocking potential to effect change through creative devices emerges through the following dynamics considering:

> love and poetry and the imagination as powerful social and revolutionary forces, not replacements for organised protest, for marches and sit-ins, for strikes and slowdowns, for matches and spray paint. Surrealism recognises that any revolution must begin with thought, with how we imagine a *New World* [emphasis added], with how we reconstruct our social and individual relationships, with unleashing our desire and building a new future on the basis of love and creativity rather than rationality.

Linking chapter 4 into this discussion around urban youth culture, Kelley (2003, 193) also argues for the 'recognition of the ghetto as a site of creativity, a call for solidarity with oppressed classes'. The uniqueness of this research and this approach to consciousness-raising is however that rather than an emphasis on service delivery to create social change, by participating in an NSM, BTSO artivists create 'tracks designed to invigorate or call to action, to prepare people for struggle, to elevate their consciousness' (Kelley 2003, 255). This has implications discussed in the conclusion around the design of development projects, and it challenges traditional paradigms for conducting social research into NSMs, which I now address.

Challenging Traditional Paradigms, Texts, and Theories Used to Explain the Experiences of Young BIPOC

By challenging traditional paradigms through prioritising young BIPOC experiences, this tenet seeks to answer previously unaddressed research questions in social research, such as the way in which young SSAs demonstrate the capacity for agency. Through this exploration, they demonstrate playing a dynamic and powerful role in narrating and creating counter-stories of resistance. One example given of these was the politically fuelled tracks by artist *Krown* (2018a) 'Let Us Live'[2] or *Amac's* (2019) '41 Bars of an African Gang member'[3] discussed in chapter 6. The study participants' stories of black excellence and power, for example through *Queen P*'s *Bring Black Back* EP[4] (discussed in chapter 4) confirms earlier scholarship that considers the 'triumphant tradition of black arts as a means to elevate, uplift and inspire collective change' (Asante 2008, 6).

By utilising Indigenous storytelling approaches that considered young SSAs' experiences, these findings were thus highly relational, with young people identifying specific structural features of their experience as either promoting or hampering their ability to flourish. Participants significantly highlighted that this also occurs whilst also additionally considering their dual identities as South Sudanese nationals and experiencing an interplay with the notion of 'identity politics playing tricks' (Williams 2022) when considering ongoing identity formation in Australia. This is evidenced in BTSO artivists alternatively narrating counter-knowledges in resistance to racialising discourses, thus demonstrating the multiple ways they are enacting agency in their lives in Australia.

Delgado (2000) suggests that oppressed groups have known instinctively that stories are an essential tool for their survival and liberation. Through the process of reflecting on CRT and forms of resistance, counter-storytelling is a technique of telling the story of those experiences that are not often told (i.e., minoritised voices). It is also a tool for analysing and challenging the stories of those in power and whose story is a natural part of the dominant discourse – the majoritarian story (D.G. Solórzano and Yosso 2002; D.G. Solórzano and Bernal 2001). The imagery of one presenting a counter-story to dominant narratives of racialising discourses is powerful. In this research, this is demonstrated through BTSO artivists having access to a microphone to express their political voice either in public or through the Hip Hop track recording process. In the broader context of Hip Hop and linking to NSMs, Clay's (2006, 105) citing of U.S. conscious rapper Nas' lyrics 'all I need is one mic to spread my voice to the whole world' demonstrates this significance. Clay discusses contemporary youth activism in the context of mobilising young people for social change in the post-civil rights era.

The trajectory of their consciousness-raising journeys was generated by individuals seeking out conscious Hip Hop artists they admire. Through conscious lyrics iterating prominent social messages, participants were educated around potential political content through CHHP. Collective consciousness-raising journeys occurred throughout the Grounded Project, with the bulk of relevant data on this process captured during the Gua camp – the first stage of the project detailed in chapter 5. The outcomes of this process were represented when an artist on stage at a community event articulated, for example, a celebration of the strengths within their community. These experiences thus serve as 'political communication', which includes the collection of lyrics, project artefacts, and observation of local scenes, representatives, and movements (Pope 2020). This is further discussed in the next subsection.

After observing the full project and when considering the process of participating in an NSM, I noted that the Gua focus groups in the first stage of the overall Grounded Project enabled participants to discuss and develop their understanding of identity politics. This occurred in intimate spaces in small groups, which provided them with the opportunity to determine when and how to go public with their identity and political voice (Fieldwork notes 2019). Commenting on the interactions with people she observed during the performances, Elizabeth, an audience member at the Grounded Youth Stage (discussed in chapters 6–7), identified that this process was noticeable. She stated:

> *it's probably quite nice to have a space like that initially to get people combined but then if you perhaps go to larger spaces the group's already got those interactions. I mean, they already connected to each other, so then they would have more confidence as they have other people coming in a really magical environment.*

I have established that alternative forms of resistance are present; however, further discussion and research are required to understand the implications, lessons and sustainability or trajectory of this resistance as expressed through arts-based community development projects or forms of dissent and protest.

Some of these implications will be briefly discussed as an impetus for future research in the conclusion. It is imperative, however, to understand the nature of processes by which young SSAs build their political voice after the initial and ongoing consciousness-raising journey, to which I now turn.

YOUNG SOUTH SUDANESE AUSTRALIAN HIP HOP ARTISTS POLITICAL VOICE

In chapters 4–5, alongside Majavu (2018), I argued that deficit narratives as depicted through racialising discourses directed towards SSAs have had long-lasting impacts on how society perceives them. The discourses about non-integration and criminality are racialising discourses and forms of *necropolitics* - death-dealing regimes operationalised by proponents of Whiteness which are forms of violence young SSAs are navigating and can lead to 'deathworlds' (implications discussed in chapter 3) (Mbembe and Corcoran 2019). This section addresses the key learnings that have emerged from an analysis of the various ways young SSAs build their political voice through Hip Hop in response to these damaging narratives, discussing them particularly in relation to CHHP practice (described in chapter 2). The practice of CHHP has the benefit of eliciting young people's unique voices through going on a consciousness-raising journey towards liberation (Akom 2009).

Despite an acknowledgement that urban young people are often caught within 'urban strife' and are 'sometimes limited by things outside of their control' (Pope 2020, vii), the findings challenge the perception that young SSAs do not have a political voice and remain somewhat apathetic to issues surrounding their communities, such as the perception that they are criminals without reform. Furthermore, as pointed out by Majavu (2018) and Gatwiri et al. (2020, 2022), these findings do not support scholarship which primarily focusses on incidences of criminality and deficit approaches that deplete the sense of agency young SSAs demonstrate.

Indeed, my overall PhD research showcased in this monograph instead portrayed the myriad ways young SSAs see and represent themselves as being BTSO through alternative forms of artivism. Within each BTSO artivist's story and song lyrics, and through the artefacts collected, they present themselves as running their own race in the Australian context. This includes building on examples of hard work and connection despite the media and political portrayal of their communities. As such, they provided examples of how their attitudes and actions contribute to disrupting notions of racialising discourses by bypassing them, alternatively preferring to author their own narratives along the lines of their BTSO motto.

Hip Hop as an NSM provides a framework that enables alternate narratives and should be understood through a number of modalities defined as sub-genres of the art form. U.S. rapper Mos Def describes how

> people treat Hip Hop like an isolated phenomenon. They don't treat is as a continuum, a history or legacy. And it really is. And like all mediums or movements, it came out of a need. (Asante 2008, 75)

Chapters 3 and 5 identify that the claims of disenfranchised young people evident in this research is that the *'system ain't playing'* (Krown 2018a)[5] and that systemic racism still exists extensively within Australian society. Whilst rap artists in the 1990s had to deal with record labels and music management, young artists in the current generation do not necessarily have to go through the traditional record label management structure, circumventing this by using social media platforms such as YouTube. If there is something young people 'want to respond to in real time, they can do so via this new technology' (Bonnette 2015, 146). Rather than always having to 'dumb down' content to sell music, this technology assists in diversifying the genre and allowing more politically relevant rap (or Hip Hop) to be created that depicts issues young people are interested in and that impacts their communities within local or national politics (Bonnette 2015; Oware 2018).

Whilst conscious or political forms of Hip Hop expression are the focus here, Asante (2008, xii) urges young people to consider the words of post-colonialist Fanon, who states that 'each generation must out of relative obscurity, discover its mission, fulfill it or betray it'. This statement is relevant for young SSAs as they direct their sense of agency through various sub-genres of Hip Hop. Asante (2008, 7) introduces a new term, 'post Hip Hop' which describes a period of time – *'right now* – of great transition' or a 'generational tipping-point' for a new generation in 'search of a deeper, more encompassing understanding of themselves in a context outside of the corporate Hip Hop monopoly'. Linking this back to the idea that Hip Hop is an NSM and a strong representation of urban youth culture, he argues that he does not think Hip Hop is dead. But, with this in mind, he suggests that

> the post Hip Hop generation [current generation who have taken the genre far from its original form] must be brave enough to fully engage in exploration, challenge and discovery, acts that will ultimately result in a revelation of contemporary truths that will help define us, and in turn, the world. (Asante 2008, 12)

Some would argue that pushing cultural boundaries has always been the way that Hip Hop has evolved through an NSM perspective. Observation of the

BTSO artivists in this research showed that these artists are in a good position to take heed of these remarks and will continue to reformulate our preconceived ideas about how they are portrayed by racialising discourses and who they should become. Like Simba Mak's spoken-word poem at the Grounded Youth Stage in chapter 7, they will remain the *'culture shifters'* and we will be seeing more of them in the Australian music industry landscape and through their own projects. Asante (2008) leaves us with a philosophical quandary by highlighting the social issues that artists have failed to address. Asante (2008, 7) warns that:

> history teaches us that both action and inaction lead us to dramatic shifts. If the post Hip Hop generation chooses to act, what values, whose ideas, will inform that action? If they choose not to act, not to 'wake up' as it were, whose values and ideas will be imposed upon them?

However, in terms of issues surrounding their own communities, this research demonstrates that young SSAs are not failing to act. The three aspects of ethnographic focus in findings chapters 4–6 demonstrate expression of political voice through a form of consciousness-raising and involvement in arts-based community development projects through a CCA. Chapter 4 describes Bonnette's (2015) political rap model to identify specifically political Hip Hop songs which consider more overt forms of protest and political voice.

In chapter 5, I drew on three tracks by *Krown*, *Titan* and *Amac Don* which addressed the racist Apex gang narrative that portrays young SSAs as criminals without reform. These artists provide a counter-narrative about their community by describing how young SSAs are *'not as bad as they think we are'* (Krown 2018a).[6] Whilst racialising discourses perpetuated by Whiteness have not really changed, the impacts of this are briefly taken up in the next section and in chapter 8, describing how the transformation of the social construct of Whiteness and racialising discourses was not really an outcome that could be achieved through this approach alone.

The findings suggest, however, that these overtly political tracks and actions are often written as a last resort as young SSAs prefer to present other music which represents their lifestyles and vibrant personalities. Like the Black Arts Movement and the long history of message or protest music in the traditions of NSMs, young SSAs demonstrate that they are not afraid to assert their voice, discuss discontent, and mobilise the broader community to address injustices concerning race relations (Bonnette 2015; Pope 2020). This is a long-held view of Kenyan scholar Ngũgĩ in his book *Penpoints, Gunpoints, and Dreams* where he explores the relationship between art and political power in society and:

calls for the alliance of art and people power, freedom and dignity against the encroachments of modern states. Art . . . needs to be active, engaged, insistent on being what it has always been, the embodiment of dreams for a truly human world. (Ngũgĩ 1998, 1)

Using the pen as a tool, the role of the artivist is to make us not only see and understand the world of humanity and nature but also to see and understand it in a certain way (Ngũgĩ 1983).

There was, however, a debate amongst research participants about the purpose of Hip Hop expression as an art form and its involvement in NSM practice. Whilst some participants resisted the term 'political voice', as they initially had no intention of being involved in the political realm, after further discussion they came to understand the nature of this term, confirming misconceptions about political voice and Hip Hop. Whilst not all may agree with this statement, Asante (2008, 206) suggests that 'all arts and artists – ALL – are political, even if their politics are disguised as indifference'. He purports that the notions of neutrality or indifference aid oppression, whereas an artivist has the opportunity to bring value back to human life (Asante 2008, 206). Whilst this statement does not necessarily take into account the many reasons why a person may make art, including therapeutic purposes, Asante does ask an important question: 'How can we make arts for arts-sake in a world that is crying out for artists to save it?' (Asante 2008, 207).

Oware (2018, 17) takes a more nuanced approach, asserting that 'ultimately context matters', which suggests that need for a 'multi-layered approach for understanding emcees' [Hip Hop artists] lyrics'. This involves understanding that Hip Hop artists are 'provocateurs who pushed the envelope by articulating playful, boastful, or unconventional rhymes. They posture and present over-the-top personas more than anything else' (Oware 2018, 17). This has implications for the interpretation of the data presented in this monograph, which I address in chapter 8. Oware (2018, 17) suggests that 'throughout it all, affirming or disempowering, political or apolitical, rap artists continue to make their voices heard'.

Therefore, attention to youth political voice is not just about listening to young people's voices but centres the notion of *democratic practice* when engaging young people in participatory processes such as being involved in NSMs. It is important to understand that the term *youth participation* can be used loosely when offered as a cliché in government rhetoric, failing to recognise significant obstacles for young people's participation or sending a mixed message as to whose voices have been heard and to what extent (Bessant 2004). When implementing such initiatives (such as those described in chapters 5–6), the task is not simply giving youth voice; it is making sure that voice will be heard by focusing the goals and then building the necessary bridges to local organisations and policy makers. (Campbell and Erbstein 2012, 72)

Key indicators for successful culturally competent initiatives consider 'what specific contributions will youth engagement provide?' and a transparent selection process to identify which youth might benefit most. This is due to different youth populations having different experiences in the same community (Campbell and Erbstein 2012, 73). This discussion on the purpose of political voice, therefore, leads to the next section on how young SSAs use their political voice for the purposes of sharing specific socio-political messages around racial justice issues in the Australian context.

RACIAL JUSTICE AND EQUITY

Messages around racial justice and equity for young SSAs are the key theme that this research addresses in young SSAs' expression of their political voice. This expression is achieved through sub-genres of Hip Hop, but primarily conscious Hip Hop. Drawing on the intersections of justice-oriented YPAR and CRT, this research explores the possibilities embedded in the theoretical, ethicalethical, and methodological overlaps between the two (Akom 2009, 2011; Torre 2009). Post-colonial theorist Anzaldúa's *Borderlands/La Frontera, The New Mestiza* (Anzaldúa and Moraga 1983; Salvídar 2007; Torre 2009) use the term *nos-otras* translated as [us/we] – whereby research is designed to seek knowledge at the nexus of everyday lived experience and intricate social systems. She asks questions that allow individuals to hold multiple or even opposing identities; to provoke analyses that requires historical re-memory and to destabilise naturalised power hierarchies. She prioritises research that calls for socially engaged questions that demand to be answered collectively through research and action. This is therefore why the first tenet of CHHP further explored in this section touches on the implications of this message and on what calls for action young SSAs are seeking.

The Centrality of Race and Racism and Their Intersectionality with Other Forms of Oppression

The tenet of CHHP describing the centrality of race, racism, and recognising intersectionality was explored through the way in which young SSAs articulated the interplay of 'systems'. Chapter 4 describes how Critical Race Theories (CRT) are a derivative of critical theory which uses Marxian analysis to challenge power structures (Ritzer 2005; Habermas 2007[1987]). This is noted through the lyric, *'the system ain't playing'* (Krown 2018a)[7]. As depicted in chapter 4, experiences of this system through the lens of racialising discourses can be death-dealing (Mbembe and Corcoran 2019).

By looking specifically at the media and moral panics that occurred in Naarm between 2007 and 2021 and the resulting impact of racialising discourses on SSAs, this research has demonstrated a more complete picture and understanding of the intersection of 'race, social movements, and urban politics' (Pope 2020, 4). BTSO artivists' roles depicted in this research are therefore ultimately 'leveraged as a basis for social justice campaigns towards de facto equality' (Pope 2020, 3) through participation in NSMs. Finally, through public performances and by presenting a counter-narrative resisting deficit racialising discourses, young SSAs demonstrate variations of their political voice in alternative forms of artivism as part of the Grounded Project (chapters 5–6).

The dominant racialising discourse narratives surrounding depictions of young SSA were debunked by counter-narratives presented through Hip Hop expression. The question of whether racial justice and equity can be achieved is considered, necessitating discussion of limits that can be reasonably set and achieved. The following section addresses some of these concerns.

Towards Freedoms and Aspirations for Young South Sudanese Australians

Asante (2008, 254) asserts that the question remains, in relation to Hip Hop as an NSM: 'Do you really think your music can liberate black people?' In the case of this research, can building young SSAs' political voice really support them to resist racialising discourses? In answer to this question, and like the cultural origins of this form of liberating work for BIPOC communities described in chapter 4, young SSAs' artivism in this research was not about 'saving' black people. Instead, it was about black people 'liberating' themselves from oppressive structures and racialising discourses through the first step of consciousness-raising. This led to the possibility that others might join in this liberation when presenting their key messages and freedom of self-expression in public (Kendi 2019, 16; Hart 2020).

One might suggest that the efforts of young SSAs described in this research may have only put a dint in altering racist views of young SSAs as depicted through racialising discourses. Different views are also presented regarding whether this is in fact the goal. This notion is further discussed below around young SSAs' intentionality when considering the purpose of their expression of political voice. When considering the expression of political voice as a form of artivism linked to NSMs, Asante (2008, 254) clarifies his purpose – that through Hip Hop, just as music is a part of every freedom struggle or social movement, his answer to his question of purpose is that: 'not by myself . . . but in the context of a movement, my music can be the soundtrack'.

In terms of a philosophical and practical discussion on what the goals of young SSAs' forms of artivism/Hip Hop expression are in this research, the theme of moving towards liberation is further picked up. Similar to other identity-based NSMs that may not consider emancipation as a priority, poet Toure, who is linked to aspects of Black Power in the 1960s, emphasises that this 'movement' was more about

> self-transformation, changing the way we think, live, love, and handle pain. While the music frequently negatively mirrored the larger culture, it nonetheless helped generate community pride, challenged racial self-hatred, and built self-respect. It created a world of pleasure, not just to escape the everyday brutalities of capitalism, patriarchy, and white supremacy, but to build community, establish fellowship, play and laugh, and plant seeds for a different way of living, a different way of hearing. (Kelley 2003, 11–12)

This explanation of the purpose of young people's artivism/expression broadens our initial ideation of a struggle towards freedom and achieving aspirations (Sen 2001[1999]). This articulation of NSM goals certainly reflects the findings of the Grounded Project, which were presented in chapter 6. Through detailing the project's unintended outcomes, it was identified that instead of an overtly political message through forms of Hip Hop expression, the theme that came across was the way young SSAs chose to represent their Afrocentricity and Blackness in their Hip Hop and African identity personas (still a political paradigm) in more subversive ways. As suggested in chapter 6, working towards liberation does not necessarily lead to full emancipation. This is due to the extent to which systemic racism is embedded in our society. For example, after audience member Elizabeth's initial impression, she felt that an arts-based community development project expressing political voice

> *progresses the journey of the South Sudanese Australians to be more wholly respected in the community.*
>
> *[Rather than focusing on a smaller minority perpetuating racialising discourses], you know, the majority of community now, I think acknowledges them as more as a respected part of the community.*

Whilst this outcome may be a by-product of artivist interventions and the expression of political voice through Hip Hop, the findings suggest that the overwhelming majority of young SSAs who participated in this research rejected the notion that they needed to appease forms of racialising discourses by looking to be accepted or by just seeking equality alone. This type of outcome mentioned by Elizabeth broadly aligns with Australian integration policies over the years (Hage 1998, 2014). As discussed, this focus on *colourism* tones may still expect young SSAs to become like 'honorary whites' (Tuan 1998, 21). Before he was assassinated, Dr King reflected, 'I sit here deeply concerned that we're here leading people on an integration trip that has us integrating into a burning house' (Asante 2008, 258). While probably not the intention, this outcome of 'being respected' could align with integration outcomes expecting young SSAs to become 'more like us' rather than being dignified in their own forms of self-expression.

As suggested, my previous research (Williams 2015, 2016) questioned whether integration or social inclusion is in fact the goal. The final section on the theme of BTSO discusses some of the nuances of this proposed alternative messaging and perhaps a more suitable goal in terms of young SSAs' aspirations of being 'born to stand out' rather than becoming 'honorary whites'. Chapter 9 explores areas of future policy improvement in these areas with the suggestion of interculturalism being a more ideal focus (Mansouri and Modood 2021).

In the Australian context, youth studies sociologist Anita Harris' (2013) research on multicultural young people's identities is crucial in understanding the crux of this monograph, particularly how young people articulate problems of race, power, and negotiating identity formation. Within their culturally diverse urban environments, young people from different backgrounds now routinely encounter one another in their everyday lives, negotiating and contesting ways of living together and sharing civic space. Whilst this might be the case 'on the ground' in society, Harris (2021) joins other CRT scholars in demonstrating that due to the absence of reckoning with race in Australian youth studies and in private and public spheres, this has produced an imaginary of young people that centres Whiteness within youth experiences. An alternative vision is honouring the multiplicity of different intercultural experiences as this research also demonstrates.

Through a race-critical analysis, I also contend that concepts which foreground colonialism, racialised migration schemes, multicultural policies, and everyday racism have yet to be applied in any substantial way in analysing the experiences of racialised youth in Australia (Idriss, Butler, and Harris 2021). This work is crucial whilst considering how 'race as a complex, global, structural phenomenon comes to bear on the development of young people's identity making, life choices and lived experiences' (Idriss 2021, 1). The research presented in this monograph has demonstrated that it is an important time to hear the voices of young SSAs and contextual views on these matters alongside the current global fight for black lives and freedom struggles. The Australian context cannot be divorced from this. Through decoding young Hip Hop artists' lyrics in chapter 6, which analysed the ways young SSAs resist racialising discourses through conscious Hip Hop, it became apparent that if Australian society continues to emphasise racialising discourses, we will continue to see different forms of dissent which may include forms of civil unrest.

Through lyrical forms, these views are represented in artists' viewpoints. For example, U.S. artist Dead Prez raps and echoes calls for freedom: 'I'm like a black Steve Biko, raised in the ghetto by the people. . . . I'm an African, Let's Be Free' (Asante 2008, 87). These claims are also echoed in the famous activist chant at public rallies/protests, 'no justice, no peace' in which young SSAs joined First Nations communities in Australia as part of the global BLM marches in 2020 (Henriques-Gomes and Visontay 2020; Asante 2008). In fact, Dead Prez warns:

> If I had to deliver a message to the youth, I'd say to keep your eyes open and your fist clenched. I'd say they can try to kill the messenger but they can't kill the message, they can try to jail the revolutionary but not the revolution. (Asante 2008, 168)

Chapters 5–6 allude to the ramifications of young SSAs expressing their political voice more publicly and incessantly. Their public forms of resistance to racialising discourses are due to the fact that there is a growing sense of urgency in these matters. BIPOC across the globe are extremely frustrated about getting *tone-policed* (a tactic that dismisses ideas particularly when people appear to be angry or frustrated) and have expressed that enough is enough as they wish to stop politely asking for real change and instead demand freedom. Channing-Brown (2018, 210) explains her perspective when having discussions with people about their realisations of the impact of racism:

> So I don't accept confessions like these anymore. Nowadays, when someone confesses about their racist uncle or that time they said the N word, I'm determined to offer a challenge toward transformation. For most confessions, this is as simple as asking, 'So what are you going to do differently?'

Here, Channing-Brown implies that she is not responsible for the transformation of 'Whiteness' by explaining that the repositioning of her question

> lifts the weight off my shoulders and forces the person to move forward, resisting the easy comfort of having spoken the confession. The person could, of course, dissolve or enter excuses, but at that point the weight of that decision belongs to them, not to me. (Channing-Brown 2018, 110)

In addition, participants discuss various views on whether they feel there is a sense of hope that the transformation of racialising discourses is occurring or can occur with enough discipline whilst having the intention of also 'dismantling Whiteness'. This all remains a pertinent question. Further discussion is required as to the implications of participants' expressions of their political voice and messages highlighted. For example, the topics of countering racism, decolonial and *Antiracism* practice, and the implications of this research, including dialogue around policy and programme implementation are explored in chapter 9. Discussion of whether there is any potential for 'race-neutrality', or a 'post-racial society' likewise remains pertinent. This is mostly due to the current extensive and systemic racism that recent migrant young people experience in society and its debilitating effects. Whilst the possibility of a post-racial society remains an existential question, the theme of 'born to stand out' (BTSO) served as an iterative language for young SSAs striving towards freedom from race-based characterisations of their communities.

BORN TO STAND OUT

The final section of this chapter extends McAdams' (1993, 1996, 2001, 2006) theories of *applied narrative inquiry* through a discussion of this monograph's key findings about the ways young people narrate their sense of agency and freedom of self-expression in the face of racialising discourses. The findings uniquely capture urban youth of colour's civic engagement. Their vitality and assets are on display as they challenge injustices and address a specific social problem (Wray-Lake and Abrams 2020). The findings below outline that BTSO artivists were able to demonstrate a CCA through local sites of artivism and voices of collective resistance (Dutta 2012, 2020). Resisting the depiction of SSA communities as passive, Grounded participants narrate their 'stories of active meaning making and participation in processes of change directed at altering social structures' (Dutta 2011, 270). Within this section, the original concept of the BTSO theme is proposed, in which young people's capacity for agency is explored as playing a dynamic and powerful role in how they narrate and create forms of resilience and continued resistance through participating in an NSM. Research participants' stories of narrating how they are BTSO upholds scholarship that considers both the personal and social contexts of resilience and resistance. This leads to a discussion on the third tenet of CHHP, which prioritises the centrality of BIPOCs' experiential knowledge.

The Centrality of Experiential Knowledge of Young BIPOC

This research has demonstrated that despite deficit narratives portrayed about them, young SSAs are the experts in determining lives they value. The examination of the theme BTSO offers a new scope, framework, and method through the CCA (discussed in chapter 7) when considering future analysis of urban locales. Through examples given in this research of how young SSAs participate in an NSM, this approach has demonstrated the 'political development of local underground power, protest media, and representatives; the tools and technologies used in the production of local messages' (Pope 2020, 4).

Through focusing on the BTSO narrative, a key finding of this research focusses on an exploration of how BTSO artivists are carving out space in the face of racialising discourses; they essentially 'create their own lane' rather than focusing on racialising discourses. Specifically, young SSA Hip Hop artists create their own lane by drawing on the musical roots of rap music. BTSO artivists such as *Krown, Titan, Queen P, Malesh P, Daniel Elia, Élkato* and *Amac Don* emerge as 'black folk heroes' who have risen out of crisis utilising Hip Hop culture to reclaim identities (chapter 5). They create their own messages, subcultures and forms of political voice. Through the newly created power bases prioritising participant self-expression, the discourses created were messages about being seen, being heard, and being born to stand out (chapter 6). The banks of artefacts which include everyday accounts are therefore understood as the 'foundation of a parallel political community' (Pope 2020, 4). This fulfills the research aim of presenting alternative forms of resistance and counter-storytelling narratives as displayed through arts-based youth community development projects and forms of artivism.

Rather than spending all their time trying to debunk the narratives of racialising discourses, the other way young SSAs are carving out space and creating their own lane through the exploration of the BTSO theme is by prioritising strength in Blackness and transcultural identities. This is through an Afrodiasporic vision for their future in an Australian context. The ways that they determine their own pathways through articulating their own black identity development was outlined in chapter 4–6 which details how young SSAs have had to develop the vocabulary to talk back to racialising discourses by borrowing the revolutionary black American language of Antiracism but are also detailing a journey of their black identity development. For instance, research participants' narratives echo Bulhan's (1985) three stages of *black identity development*. The first and second stages of *capitulation* and *revitalisation* is demonstrated in chapters 5 and 6 where young SSAs go through a consciousness-raising journey when participating in an NSM. Upon arrival in Australia and going through adolescent development, they are confronted with the first stage, capitulation, which involves the expectation of increased assimilation into the white dominant culture, while simultaneously rejecting one's own black heritage. Once individuals and communities become more conscious about their black heritage, the second stage, revitalisation, takes place when young SSAs, as BIPOC rejected the ubiquitous Eurocentric culture for their African heritage. Chapter 6 details how the third stage, *radicalisation*, took place where young SSAs synthesised their identities of both being informed by Eurocentric worldviews but choosing to prioritise their sense of 'Africanness' in their performances throughout the Grounded Project. Bulman's (1985) analytical perspective is cross-referenced with Cross' (1971) *black consciousness development* theory, which, on the other hand, has five stages. In the first *pre-encounter stage*, in chapters 1 and 4, young SSAs identify their sense of excitement and gratitude for coming to Australia, due to not being exposed upon early arrival to notions of Blackness and Whiteness, it is demonstrated that they appear to hold attitudes towards race that range from low salience to race neutrality. Whereas, the second *encounter* stage detailed in chapters 1, 3 and 5 is characterised by a dramatic event, such as being assaulted by white racists or watching a televised report of a racial incident (e.g., Liep Gony's 2007 murder), which shatter the black person's understanding of race and Blackness. The third *immersion* stage is characterised by efforts to develop a black identity that is anchored in Black Consciousness detailed in chapter 4. In this stage, black people often attend political or cultural meetings, the person goes to black music sessions and attends seminars and art shows that focus on Blackness; everything of value to this person becomes about being black. In this research, participants do that via Hip Hop. The fourth *internalisation* stage marks the point of racial dissonance resolution detailed in chapter 4, and as a result, the person feels calmer and more at ease with their black identity. In the fifth *commitment* stage, young SSAs display their black identity through public performances which meets their personal needs, which in this was (but not always) Afrocentric.

In summation of these analytical perspectives, a key narrative explored in this monograph is the acknowledgement of the power within Blackness (e.g., through black hype lyrics (Pope 2020) discussed in chapter 4). This set participants on a trajectory of asserting the multiple ways they see themselves as being BTSO. This notion was expressed in *Malesh P's* lyric *'I ain't fighting for your love'* (Malesh-P 2015).[8] By highlighting strength in culture, the preference for Afrocentric and even sometimes Afrofuturistic formats became evident (discussed in chapters 4 and 6). When research participants claim to be 'born to stand out', they deeply understand that the free-floating anxieties about Blackness in twenty-first-century Australia has roots in a multi-layered narrative that has a long lineage in Australian political culture.

The power of this process and journey demonstrated through the research findings is that instead of deficit and defeat with a focus on criminality, an alternate strengths-based narrative presented by young black artists creates worlds in which people who experience oppression are in power positions (Pope 2020). For example, a person holding the microphone to share young BIPOC voices as a viable alternative to the centering of Whiteness narratives through mainstream Australian media. Culture-building practices continue the traditions of black folklore; of passing on songs, dance, arts, and speech throughout the generations and during times of oppression and exploitation (Pope 2020; Kelley 2003). I now turn to summarising the key messages from this chapter and research.

SUMMARY OF DISCUSSION

Through their common approach of essentially bypassing forms of racialising discourses, other more prevalent ways young SSAs demonstrate their political voice expression is through the portrayal of identity politics in Hip Hop lyrics. Therefore, through the expression of their political voice, they re-create or re-orient the narrative typified about them. For example, *Queen P's* EP *Bring Black Back*[9] and the 'AfriCAN' track[10] produced at Gua camp brought to attention the topics of black excellence and power (chapter 5). Drawing this together with fieldwork conducted with Footprints through the Grounded Project (chapters 4–6), the secondary aspect of young SSAs expressing their political voice through conscious forms of Hip Hop was through being able to perform identity politics in public. Once again, audience member Elizabeth articulates this sentiment on the impact she experienced when seeing a young SSA perform for the first time:

> *Having your first time on stage or being able to get up in front of a group of people will definitely have more impact. They may even be more confident to get up in front of groups in the future, be it to sing or to expose themselves to people [to showcase] what wonderful people they are, but not to hide away as much.*
>
> *Whether that be on a physical side but I just think visibility lead to more visibility. Hopefully some more famous singers!*

I note that it was important that Elizabeth used the word '*visibility*'. As I discussed when considering the BTSO theme in chapter 6, young SSAs are often labelled as standing out for all the wrong reasons. In this context and from this conversation, the Grounded Youth Stage was an alternative, positive visibility with the BTSO theme in terms of standing out like that, standing tall, or standing up straight with dignity. She wished to clarify her thoughts from the conversation,

I think, whenever I've seen South Sudanese people, they all stand tall. I mean, they've all got wonderful posture.
So they are tall but what I mean, it's more like their eyes are more on the ground than where they are going, they've learned not to look at other people around them.
And maybe because of bad experiences around them or the smears they got or what they're seeing in the news [through integration discourses]. And they just perceive that is best for them, just to go about their business, and just engage with each other, but not with a wider group.
So it wasn't like at the event, no one came and specifically spoke to me, there was no object there to make other others welcome. It was just a by-product of the event that, you know, I can start talking to people, it just felt like a very warm, welcoming environment and nothing false about it.

Therefore, in relation to the Grounded Youth Stage's overall relationship with the 'born to stand out' motto, standing out is more about doing so *in public*. The main square in CGD, as a demonstration of *little publics* (Hickey-Moody 2013, 2016), was one such example (described in chapters 3 and 5) recognising urban youth agency. Elizabeth's description of her experience observing the South Sudanese community before this event, where she described their eyes being lowered (often due to not wanting to stand out in public), juxtaposes her description of her experience at this event. Alternatively, through engagement in an arts-based community development process hosted by Footprints, she describes her observations of their ability to '*stand tall with confidence*'. Here, the notion of standing taller relates to well-being and visibility. She noted that the point is to demonstrate confidence and articulate yourself, which occurs after the process of consciousness-raising. After this process, a young person might be able to stand taller and rise above the public's perception of them as conceived through racialising discourses.

Elizabeth's perception of the overall message of the Grounded Youth Stage necessitates further consideration. Did she hear the messages through the Hip Hop tracks? She described this as the 'vibe' she received, noting she had not been exposed to Hip Hop really before this event. However, it appears the general messages of the artists singing funky Hip Hop tracks was that they wished to portray a sense of fun and a form of black excellence. BTSO artivists' expressions throughout the Grounded Project indicate that the unintended impact was more about the participants' self-expression rather than influencing the general public to reconsider racist and harmful narratives. A more detailed exploration of the impacts of these performances on audiences was beyond the scope of this study, although it does merit further attention.

Nevertheless, the impact on performers fits in with revolutionary Sankara's (1989) renaming of the country Upper Volta to Burkina Faso. The meaning of this new name translates as *to stand upright*. This renaming fits within the overall BTSO theme that participants of this research are not trying to appease or make white society like them. Rather, they are standing upright in their own self-determination and identity expression. As Lizzie put it *'people can come along for the journey if they want to'*. This leads to final considerations in terms of the exploration of the implications of the specific forms of resistance approaches to racialising discourses young SSAs demonstrate. Contributions and limitations of this monograph, as well as suggestions for future research, are explored in the conclusion chapter 8.

NOTES

1. Krown (2018) 'Trials n' Tribulations', Military Mind: https://www.youtube.com/watch?v=dZHsb0D0pZE.

See blogpost #22.

2. Krown (2018) 'Let us Live', Military Mind: https://www.youtube.com/watch?v=lxjsHiLgFJs.

See blogpost #15.

3. Amac Don (2019) '41 Bars from an African Gang Member', Future Records: https://soundcloud.com/hbkfam/amac-don-41-bars-of-an-african-gang-member.

See blogpost #30.

4. Queen P (2018) *Bring Black Back* EP, Queen P: https://open.spotify.com/album/1nuXWCzyYpyDjmgQgrPx3v.

5. See Notes '2'.

6. See Notes '2'.

7. See Notes '2'.

8. Malesh P (2015) *Dreamer*. Believer EP, Malesh P: https://music.apple.com/ca/album/dreamer-believer/1029172750.

See blogpost #38.

9. Queen P (2018) *Bring Black Back* EP, Queen P: https://open.spotify.com/album/1nuXWCzyYpyDjmgQgrPx3v.

10. 'Afri– CAN' (2019) produced by *Malesh P* - GUA Project - AfriCAN.mp3

See blogpost #2.

Created by workshop facilitator Malesh P at Gua Performance and Leadership Camp hosted by Footprints in January 2019.

See Chapter 3, Notes '4' for full lyrics of the track.

Chapter 8

Creating Sites for Social Change

Implications and Conclusion

Examination of 35 young SSAs' stories and artefacts in this monograph, triangulated against over a decade's worth of programme documentation from Footprints' YPAR programmes, has contributed to new understandings of young SSAs' experiences as they navigate racialising discourses. This research documents and analyses the impacts of how young SSAs present counter-narratives through Hip Hop expression in the face of racialising discourses, particularly in response to over a decade of media and moral panics targeted towards South Sudanese communities. Using the motto, 'born to stand out' (BTSO), this research depicts how they conceive of themselves. My analysis of the stories of people living within oppressive circumstances illuminates ways their sense of freedom has been limited. In far too many cases, this has resulted in a rise of SSA youth suicide.

The PhD research design explored in this monograph used an innovative narrative and arts-based methodology to capture young SSAs' alternative forms of artivism through protest, dissent, everyday resistance, and arts-based community development formats. Using these data sources to form an ethnographic account, this monograph provides a unique strengths-based insight into the lives of young SSAs, as evidenced in the Footprints' YPAR – the Grounded Project. This approach challenges previous deficit-based approaches that focused on young South Sudanese potential for criminality. Rather than trying to 'fit in' as explored in my earlier research (Williams 2015, 2016) or acquiescing to expectations of assimilation, findings clearly show that young SSAs prefer to 'stand out'. BTSO artivists are carving out space in the face of racialising discourses and essentially create their own alternative subcultures.

Each young person who participated in this study shared a unique story as they participated in artivist events or constructed Hip Hop lyrics. Through a consciousness-raising journey, Hip Hop is the chosen modality for how BTSO artivists in this cohort of young SSAs express their political voice. Conducting narrative interviews with all the artists felt as if I was sitting with U.S. rapper Tupac as we yarned about their philosophical views on the birth of Hip Hop and how it relates to them. This challenges the perception that young SSAs remain apathetic to issues surrounding their communities (Gatwiri and Moran 2022). Rather, Hip Hop artist *Daniel Elia* stated in chapter 4 that 'Hip Hop artists are like super-heroes'. He feels like he is figuratively wearing a cape when performing. *Queen P*'s catchy lyrics are 'like an earworm' (they remain). *Malesh P* is an artist that many young people look up to in his community both on and off the stage. *Krown* and *Titan* set the trajectory for what mass forms of political voice can look like in public, demonstrating 'what is possible' when we unite. *Élkato* has a message for the black youth if they choose to listen. *BCM* form alternative subcultures and forms of community; their infectious energy is welcoming and inclusive.

This chapter is future-focused and touches on participants' visions. It discusses approaches towards the transformation of racialising discourses. This research is timely and has implications for Antiracism policy and praxis through its contribution of new knowledge detailing the experiences of young SSAs through the BTSO theme. The PhD research's innovative theoretical framework blended Australian and international critical race theorists, NSM theory and YPAR methodology, thus ensuring an empirical portrayal of how the social construct of race continually perpetuates discontent and resistance.

Through advancing interdisciplinary approaches, this study has also identified how young SSAs developed, enacted and maintained their political voice and agency through a consciousness-raising journey. Through their participation in an identity-based NSM, they illustrate examples of everyday resistance. The metanarrative of my research explored how political voice manifests in important new ways that conventional theories of activism and resistance may not capture. The key contributions and considerations of my research are outlined in the following section.

KNOWLEDGE SURROUNDING WHITENESS STUDIES AND APPLICATION OF CRITICAL RACE THEORY

This monograph provided the opportunity to better understand the motivations, experiences, and perspectives of young SSAs as they resist racialising discourses. Moreover, through the metanarrative of how political voice manifests, I have identified ways young SSAs narrated agency and resilience within challenging experiences by presenting alternative counter-narratives to racialising discourses. The key contributions have emerged in three discrete areas: (1) the privileging of young people's stories about their experiences of racialising discourses; (2) a record of participants' lived experience of systemic racism in an urban Australian context; and (3) the impact of how integration policies conceive of young BIPOC in Australia as 'not fitting in' whilst detailing their alternate sense of self and their attitude about their future in Australia. These themes are now briefly addressed.

In the process of a collective CRT analysis, it became evident that participants held varying and nuanced views on how Whiteness or Blackness exists. Due to scope, participants' opinions on whether they feel that the social construct of Whiteness and racialising discourses can be dismantled could not be included in this research. Further investigation into the theoretical and epistemological approaches one might take when deciphering these offerings is required. Participants posed alternatives to racialising discourses (see Antiracism discussion below) and suggested that change is slow if it happens at all. When considering the process of social change through a culture-centred lens, cultural theorist Wynter (2015) provides insight by re-orienting what concepts of change might look like. Wynter syntheses insights on how race, location, and time together inform what it means to be human and the interconnectedness of creative and theoretical resistances. Chapters 4–6 demonstrate how we might reconceptualise social change within these concepts by focusing on human interconnectedness and slow-relational movements promoting advocacy towards systemic change. This approach is alternative to a focus on deficit approaches which are 'issues' and not individual and communal 'strengths-based'.

Linking with a critique of how humans were placed in a hierarchy prioritising Whiteness, theories of resistance and human interconnectedness highlight what is possible instead of deconstructing humanness as solely bitter and twisted and without reform. This section, therefore, demonstrates a key contribution of this research that surrounds its description of 'processes of articulation that start out of submerged networks of meanings, proceed through cultural innovation in the domain of everyday life, and may result in visible and sizable forms of collective action for the control of historicity' (Escobar 1992, 420). Another contribution to knowledge and a topic of further consideration is the impact of racialising discourses on young SSAs' experiences of living in Australia.

The Impact of Racialising Discourses on Young South Sudanese Australians' Experiences of Living in Australia

The presentation of artefacts, artist lyrics and extended narrative interviews with young SSAs, alongside an analysis of the systemic challenges they experience in the face of racialising discourses, supports the establishment of new knowledge about the lived experience of young SSAs. The focus of this research around the BTSO motto additionally notes how young SSAs articulate the freedom to live the lives they wish to choose in order to flourish. To reach this discussion, after hearing about how they self-identify (explored in chapter 4), participants were asked if they could imagine an Australia beyond racialising discourses. This led participants into the central theme of this research, where they considered what it means to 'stand out' rather than trying to fit in or be honorary whites. Touching on this theme of black dignity instead of black pain, Antiracist educator Channing-Brown (2018, 80) states:

> we must remind ourselves and one another that we are fearfully and wonderfully made, arming ourselves against the ultimate message of Whiteness – that we are inferior. We must stare at ourselves in the mirror and repeat that we, too, a fully capable, immensely talented, and uniquely gifted. We're not tokens. We are valuable in the fullness of our humanity. We are not perfect, but we are here, able to contribute something special, beautiful, lasting.

This research is therefore unique as 'social relations' are placed at the heart of the analysis along with the 'intersubjective world of the participants' (Rosaldo 2006, 120). Unlike earlier generations who may not have articulated their voices to the same extent (Oluo 2018), it showcases how 'the politics of citizenship derives from the emergence of new citizens with new identities who demand their rights and know that they have the right to demand their rights' (Rosaldo 2006, 120).

Primarily, the stories that young people have shared provide new and valuable insights into how young SSAs would like to be portrayed and their role in the decision-making process to facilitate participation and belonging within the Australian community. The terms of 'belonging', however, need to be negotiated. These sentiments of contributing in their own unique ways are captured by participant Jikany's statement noting common humanity and discussing Australian multiculturalism: '*At the end of the day we're all the same*'. Whilst some caution is noted regarding policies of multiculturalism, there appeared to be genuine optimism and a sense of encouragement for a way forward described by further participants considering the BTSO theme (see table 8.1 below). Notions towards multiculturalism and a way forward could be further explored in future studies.

Considering these statements, Rosaldo (2006, 123) clarifies that a 'vision of social good' or 'utopian hope that identity politics can offer' is not one of a world inhabited by young BIPOC and nobody else. Instead, Rosaldo (2006, 123) sees contributions in this area as 'general recognition that we all are positioned subjects and we all speak from distinct points of view shaped by identities that have to be socially recognised'. One must therefore take into

Table 8.1 Participants Contribution Statements towards Australian Multiculturalism

Participants Contribution Statements towards Australian 'Multiculturalism':
'There is shame attached to not being able to have this – "wasting opportunity"'
'Make the most of your life – "find purpose"'
'Be careful what we're leaving for the next generation – "I want my kids to feel comfortable here"'
'Other communities have done well over time, they tend to support each other'
'I am a positive person and many of my people are doing positive things'
'We are trying to transition, contribute'
'It takes work. Not so much negativity'; 'Bickering is useless, a waste of time and energy'

account, 'distinct points of view. In this case, one must think of the point of view of marginalised, excluded, and subordinated groups' (Rosaldo 2006, 123). This has implications for further research on multiculturalism discourse. Castells (cited in Harding 2006, 258) notes that he is especially interested in multiculturalism as a potential source of 'transformative subjects'. Castells (cited in Harding 2006, 258) specifically refers to the 'multiplicity of potentially progressive resisting identities and the cognitive diversity of their standpoints that multiculturalism promises to provide for social justice transformations'.

Through these accounts, the additional existential question remains: can you fight for liberation or freedom if you think you are not going to win? This is in line with *Malesh P*'s track where he suggests that proponents of racialising discourses:

Tied a noose around my head when I attempt to fight back
Crying for equality but you don't work like that, hmmm
You want me oppressed, you want me a mess
You want me in debt begging for cheques
Liberation for us should only exist in vain
You want my ankles forever shackled in these chains.

(Malesh-P 2020)[1]

His lyrics imply that if racism will always be present and we are not living in a post-racial society (Channing-Brown 2018) how do we redefine what kind of society we intend to build? Kelley (2003, 14) describes how the Black Freedom movement and notions of Pan-Africanism/Afrocentricity/Afropolitanism explain freedom as the 'goal our people were trying to achieve; *free* was a verb, an act, a wish, a militant demand'. Through notions of black nationalist dreams, and recalling a history of freedom struggles, this cultural movement inspired young artists to 'talk openly of revolution and dream of a new society, sometimes creating cultural works that enable communities to envision what's possible with collective action, personal self-transformation, and will' (Kelley 2003, 7). This research is therefore a 'taster' of articulation of some of those dreams for young SSAs through forms of creativity.

Considering forms of creativity through an artivist approach to social change, Hip Hop provides a framework of an 'international revolutionary movement concerned with the emancipation of thought' and involves the 'exaltation of freedom, revolt, imagination and love' (Kelley 2003, 7). Through a more subversive approach than perhaps public protest, such resistance-oriented thought and action are intended not only to 'discredit and destroy the forces of repression, but also to emancipate desire and supply it with new poetic weapons' (Kelley 2003, 7). With this approach in mind, there is the possibility of moving towards 'develop[ing] . . . potentialities fully and freely' (Kelley 2003, 7). It is through the context of hope for change that we explore what forms of cultural resistance may look like in the following section.

Locating Youth Agency: Young South Sudanese Australians' Alternative Forms of Artivism through the Born To Stand Out Motto and Participation in New Social Movements

This monograph has explored the proposition that through the alternate stance of being 'born to stand out' young SSAs are engaged in a complex negotiation between forces that act upon them (racialising discourses) and their ability to enact agency within these circumstances. In doing so, this research has contributed to interdisciplinary scholarship through a presentation and analysis of young SSAs' stories that preserve the diversity and complexity of their experiences. Furthermore, the collection and presentation of these stories and artefacts challenge the strategy of Whiteness proponents perpetuating racialising discourses who attempt to keep stories of young SSAs' success from the public (discussed in chapter 5). This monograph privileges young SSAs' stories and their alternative forms of artivism and involvement in NSMs. These findings disrupt the dominant cultural narrative and societal discourse about young BIPOC living in Australia. Moreover, they are humanised through sharing their words and cultural artefacts.

Chapter 2 established that there is a tendency to focus on deficit narratives and somewhat traumatic events of African gangs' saga. Additionally, findings chapters demonstrated the systemic, social and oftentimes daily challenges of living and adapting in potentially hostile host societies. Considering the demonstration of youth agency, this research is well positioned to alternatively narrate an articulation or

> account of the processes of identity formation that are historically specific, to this time and place, without being completely determined by social structures. And we need an account of subjects – collective identities – that are capable of transforming society and history. (Harding 2006, 255)

These deficit approaches have been challenged within the current study. Stories of young people's experiences have been analysed to explore the emergence of agency within their conception of alternative forms of artivism through political voice expression and involvement in NSMs.

Through foregrounding CRT and NSM theory with a specific grounding in Hip Hop pedagogy, alongside Hill-Collins (2006, 2013), this monograph has demonstrated that race-talk and the exchange of non-expert knowledge are essential for challenging racial stratification. Specifically, in the absence of more explicit conversations about racism and privilege, this provided an opportunity to demonstrate that forms of Hip Hop expression for young SSAs have become a proxy for public discussions about race, particularly in the Australian context. Through a consciousness-raising journey, the exploration of identity politics through participants' artefacts and expressed views on these topics provides discursive resources and space for individuals and communities to deconstruct popular understandings of social identity. By doing so, they create new narratives about inequality and alternative realities. In this setting, CHHP provides a meaningful space in which cultural understandings about racial identity and inequality can circulate (Dimitriadis 2001).

Young SSAs' stories tell us that though they navigate compounding, somewhat toxic social environments during their resettlement and consequent generations of settlement as 'forever refugees' who are allegedly 'not integrating', they are able to narrate their world as meaningful and share stories of agency and resilience despite racialising discourses. A key finding of this research is that by linking forms of Hip Hop expression with an NSM, young SSAs have narrated their own versions of 'pro-democratic, identity-based, new social movements' (Harding 2006, 246). This is achieved through building an *'identity for resistance'* which leads to the 'formation of *communes* or *communities*' which 'may be the most important type of identity-building in our society' (Harding 2006, 246). This is due to the way themes of identity for resistance comprises

> forms of collective resistance against otherwise unbearable oppression, usually on the basis of identities that were, apparently, clearly defined by history, geography, or biology, making it easier to essentialise the boundaries of resistance. (Harding 2006, 246)

Poignantly, the concept and motto of BTSO and theoretical tools like *little publics* and *public pedagogy* in an Australian context give a distinctive lens on the framing of the monograph overall in CRT. Specifically, one of the unique contributions of knowledge that this text defines is how Australian-based black Afrodiasporic youth cultures and youth movement literatures, which include Hip Hop, lead to a distinctive socio-political positioning contrasting the often privileging of U.S. perspectives. Whilst this section has addressed the strengths of this research, the next section discusses the validity of the research and explores some limitations and considerations for how NSMs evolve in the Australian context.

VALIDITY AND LIMITATIONS

Whilst findings in this research do not extrapolate to the whole population in Australia, participants represented a broad cross-section of gender and tribal-diverse young SSA artists across Naarm who settled in Australia as former refugees. A limitation is that this small sample of participants does not represent demographic diversity across Australia. Whilst the scope was narrowly focused, relying on interviews with young SSAs from relatively socio-economically disadvantaged urban areas in Naarm, the PhD research design incorporated opportunities for increasing depth of understanding through ethnographic methods of observation, interview, and analysis of artefacts. In addition to observing Footprints' project work, observation at the youth organisation YSAS broadened the incorporation of a diversity of young people with varying experiences, and thereby helped to triangulate my findings.

Considering validity, the value of narrative inquiry is concerned with how past experiences impact current attitudes and behaviours; thus, this was an appropriate and effective method for exploring their emerging resistance to racialising discourses. Through incorporating elements of Indigenous research methods, such as relational inquiry, one strength of this research is that participants all knew each other in the grassroots arts community in Naarm. A feature of this research was that it allowed for a nuanced and in-depth exploration of a discrete group of young SSAs. Further research is recommended to better understand the experiences and demonstrations of young SSAs' agency more broadly.

A Narrative Process

Conversations with young SSAs were not linear. Therefore, the presentation of this monograph's findings jumps between personal experiences, storytelling, a person's perception of historical context, a disagreement on context, a clarification that that is your *'truth'* whereas *'I saw it from this perspective'* to form an ethnographic account. Through this iterative process, a few key themes emerged. The power of this research is, as Oware (2018, 3) claims, in that the most 'compelling and ground-breaking work on Hip Hop comes from ethnographies'.

Furthermore, those working with youth and their evolving identities frequently lament that they do not stay with the community long enough to see the changes implemented by communities (D. Harris 2017, 164). Conversely, due to its longitudinal nature, the research claims presented here are reliable in that they provide sustainable, grounded outcomes due to the length of time I have been walking alongside SSA communities. Escobar (1992) and Bevington and Dixon (2005) suggest that researchers embedded amongst social movement actors are better positioned to capture the immediate mood, tone, emergent direction and impact that is often missed by external observers. This has led to 'important theoretical reorientations and the emergence of new topics' (Escobar 1992, 404).

In addition, the research participants articulated their appreciation for the representation of data through the consultative process, which reinforced their interest in research outcomes (see chapter 2). This research would only be replicable if other researchers had the same longitudinal access to these communities using similar methods. Considering the use of aspects of Indigenous methods – that is a

> researching with' process – together with a CCA approach, the strength of this research has involved emphasis on 'co-creating theoretically grounded spaces of change by working dialogically with subaltern communities through participatory communication strategies. (Dutta 2021, 1)

One of the perceived limitations of creative and community research is the level of subjectiveness displayed in analysis (Fine et al. 2021). Harding (cited in 2006, 247–248), however, suggests that mainstream research disciplines and social institutions 'do not hesitate to insist that they know precisely what are, and how to serve, the knowledge needs of everyone, including those represented by such new social movements'. He goes on to suggest, however, that *standpoint projects* [discussed below] involving the unique positionality of co-researchers and fellow artivists challenge traditional social research ideals by maximising rationality, objectivity, and prevailing conceptual frameworks and methods by instead prioritising iterations of what it means to be involved in an immersive process amongst NSMs. Harding (cited in 2006, 247–248) ascertains that unique positioning provides the opportunity to offer unique points of view and more practical outcomes.

Therefore, the observation of NSMs is inherently a 'dialectical and intersubjective process' (Alcoff et al. 2006, 122). Through the stories and counter-narratives of young SSAs, researchers can add to the understanding of resistance as a site of possibility and of human agency (D.G. Solórzano and Yosso 2002, 337). It is therefore suggested by Alcoff et al. (2006) that perhaps the point of research in this context can best be developed through a personal narrative rather than through a theoretical statement. Andreotti (2011, 381) also suggests that any social research will only offer 'a partial and limited perspective on an issue: the complexity cannot be captured by any one theory'. Andreotti's (2011) approach emphasises that walking (and pushing) the edges of a theory's limits is part of our ethical responsibility as researchers. Freire (2014[1968]) in *Pedagogy of Hope* counsels that bringing out the truth will always be an experiment.

I argue, however, that this monograph offers both theoretical and inferential praxis-led generalisation. Through the qualitative application of social theories such as CRT and NSMs, this research has identified how the actions of young SSAs 'have something to tell us about the underlying social processes and structures that form part of the context of, and the explanation for, individual behaviours or beliefs' (Denzin and Lincoln 2017, 279). Additionally, empirical evidence exists to support inferential generalisation by demonstrating thorough knowledge and providing a rich description of the data and socio-political contexts as presented by myself as a pracademic (discussed in chapter 3). Through an ethnographic format, this traces a map of the 'range of views, experiences, outcomes or other phenomena under study and the factors and circumstances that shape and influence them, that can be inferred to the researched population' (Denzin and Lincoln 2017, 268).

Oware (2018, 17), however, points to the futility of critical 'rap' analysis by suggesting that 'sometimes art defies interpretation'. Whilst this may be the case, he does believe such a critique seems possible by suggesting that 'artists' words can speak to real conditions and imagine realities' and often involve a sense of 'bravado' or 'breaking the rules of decorum' which is 'integral to rap music' (Oware 2018, 17). The strength of this artistic inquiry (Leavy 2015) is that through music, it may 'reflect everyday concerns and desires that allow for a more sophisticated understanding of gender, race, sexuality and the meaning making of social consciousness' (Oware 2018, 17).

Though this PhD research had been undertaken following recommendations for good practice and after cultural consultation with SSA communities, whilst there are pros and cons, it is a limitation that data elicitation and analysis has been conducted by an insider-outsider (a white researcher but engaged longitudinally in the communities discussed). Aligning with the values of decolonising methodologies (Tuhiwai-Smith 2021; Fine et al. 2021), future research would benefit by being led by researchers from within the cultural background of the participant group or through using a peer-interviewer or critical Action Research model (Akom 2011; Fine 2021).

Participants, however, suggested that the reason they were happy to be involved in this research was due to the strengths-based approach and the opportunity to explore alternatives from their own perspectives, which they had not previously been involved in previous consultations and social research. With future research in these areas, the application of CRT and NSM theory could be developed with a focus on refining the accommodation of newly found variations in behaviours or reviewing circumstances in a fluid collection over time (Denzin and Lincoln 2017). Other suggestions for future research are now considered.

FUTURE RESEARCH: IMPLICATIONS FOR EFFECTIVENESS OF APPROACHES

Four areas for future research have been identified. The first area involves recommendations for future research design involving young SSAs and their articulation of what social change could look like. One example given is the development of new subcultures. The second recommendation involves framing these aspirational goals within the context of Antiracism. Thirdly, transformative organising and critical YPAR approaches detail one way that a further systemic analysis could be included in order to consider targeted social change as directed by young SSAs. Finally, through consideration of engaging the broader public in communicative processes articulating social change, the concepts of prefigurative politics and communication for social change are briefly explored. This section details these recommendations and some of the factors to consider.

The first example for future consideration is the implied limitations of young SSAs' messaging in articulating what type of change they would like to see in response to challenging racialising discourses. This is not a criticism of the young people involved who were responding rapidly to racist behaviours. As argued in chapter 7, alternative forms of artivism did not include extensive 'organising' in the broader tradition of historical Antiracist work and NSM practice. Nevertheless, whilst this research is experimental in nature through YPAR, the need for a clearly articulated vision of freedom became evident as a foundation for further artivism. This is an important finding for future initiatives established by young SSAs. If participants continue to link to global movements for black emancipation and equality, they can learn and engage with each other on movement tactics. For example, the Black Panthers created a ten-point program that set an agenda to address their prioritised needs of black oppressed people. Specifically, their first agenda item is the most pertinent to this study: 'We want freedom. We want power to determine the destiny of our black and oppressed communities' (Asante 2008, 60).

Whilst to some, the Black Panther's demands may seem like basic requirements for humanity to flourish, that is, basic food, shelter, education and self-determination, their goal was in fact 'the total liberation of all black people' (Asante 2008, 127). This research demonstrated that at the very least, young SSAs 'want to remain unencumbered, free of police brutality, racial profiling, and the hardships held on by the strong arm of the state' (Oware 2018, 190).

The second recommendation for future research is contextualising young SSAs' goals for social change through the lens of Antiracism. Findings have suggested that future consideration needs to be given to how this all-pervasive phenomenon of racialising discourses needs to be dismantled for racial social justice to occur and for young SSAs to work towards achieving their freedom/aspirations. In order to achieve these aspirational goals, the tradition of Antiracist organising amongst NSM practice involves organising to 'attack injustice at its root' through confronting the 'ladder of power' (Asante 2008, 169). In this manner, Antiracist educator Kendi (2019, 215) suggests that the

> most effective demonstrations (like the most effective educational efforts) provide methods for people to give their Antiracist power, to give their human and financial resources, channelling attendees and their funds into organisations and protests and power seizing campaigns.

Working towards freedoms/aspirations within the context of Antiracism fits into a larger framework regarding Dr King's dream of a *beloved community* (Smith and Zepp 1986; James 2013), which ponders whether the goal is racial reconciliation or racial transformation, challenging the social construct of race. The rhetorical and practical question of 'what will you do differently?' is where this conclusion chapter and the (YPAR) ethnographic process described in this research invites us to enter into this transformational process to consider a radical context. Malek described how trying to have conversations about racial justice with people who are not prepared is said to '*cause more tension/separation*' where it can get '*emotional very quickly on both sides*' as often both parties often want to '*feel like we're right*'.

Spoken-word artist Abe Nouk shares that he knows what this kind of '*love feels like*' as '*love is the extensiveness of a handshake between friends not foes*' (Australian-Poetry-Slam 2014)[2] and therefore deems it possible. Kendi (2019), however, warns on calls for unity without recognising the fundamental disadvantages that some communities experience. This research also points to these important factors through utilising a systems analysis within a CRT framework (see below final implications for Antiracism approaches). There is therefore a need to understand and begin to articulate through *standpoint theory* processes (see below) of transformative organising (Bautista 2018), which is a decolonising social movement framework.

The third recommendation for future research involves the incorporation of *transformative organising* approaches which 'encourage both organisers and youth to shift their thinking in order to participate together in forms of individual and collective healing that can mobilise social transformation' (Bautista 2018, 13). This leads to the potential for notions of 'transformational resistance' (D.G. Solórzano and Bernal 2001) where the transformation of the social construct of Whiteness and racialising discourses may take place. This can only be fulfilled through *standpoints for pro-democratic transformation* whereby resistant (collective) identities moving beyond mere resistance must first understand that the kinds of knowledge that their oppressors produce are socially situated through' distinctive kinds of knowledge' (Rosaldo 2006, 258). Following this, they must identify the

> particular concepts and practices through which their distinctive forms of oppression are enacted and maintained. And, fourth, they must engage in political struggles to change those concepts and practices, struggles that will produce collective 'subjects' of knowledge and history. (Rosaldo 2006, 258)

With movement tactics in mind, BTSO participants described that they had their own plans for continuing sustained actions which had not yet fully come to fruition. This was due to the impact of the COVID-19 pandemic and the mental load present when embarking on making a dint in systemic change. Lizzie also asked the important question after the Grounded Project, '*what's next?*' – pointing towards the need for a more sustainable approach. Participants also described how young SSAs are tired after their extensive efforts. In order to claim your rights for freedom/aspirations, this is a very long road with many casualties whilst experiencing the ongoing effects of racism. Whilst '*trying to transition*' however over the years, young SSAs '*felt victimised*' and so this means '*we can't sit and be comfortable*' (BCM crew group interview).

Whilst this research has demonstrated new knowledge about counter-narratives and alternative forms of artivism, one of the limitations that NSMs explores is the need for coordinated efforts if movements are to have momentum. Whilst it does not appear that young SSAs will continue sustained efforts of utilising this form of arts-based development projects at this point in time (after COVID-19), they express interest in the ways in which they continue to define themselves in everyday resistance and identity politics. Chapter 7 and this chapter have depicted how they are able to develop this capacity through Hip Hop. There are now more arts events than ever run by young people. Chapter 5 depicted how some prefer black-only safe space whilst chapters 6–7 depicted how some do not mind collaborating with allies to come up with alternatives.

Additionally, new kinds of subcultures will continue to develop, particularly amongst urban youth culture and the Hip Hop world. This is an exciting space that requires further consideration. Although these experiences might be painful, young people describe how they are building resilience in following their dreams. Revisiting the notion of *'visions from the kitchen'* described in chapter 4, *BCM* (2020b)[3] describe how they have that *'realness for sale'* and their dream is *'getting booked'* where on the weekend they see themselves shining when performing and being *'in the big league'*.

Escobar (1992, 407) suggests that the reality is that NSMs emerge 'only in limited areas, for limited phases, and by means of moments of mobilisation which are the other, complementary phase of the submerged networks'. What nourishes collective action is the 'daily production of alternative frameworks of meaning, on which the networks themselves are founded and live from day to day' (Escobar 1992, 407). The question that comes into play here is whether focusing on the goal of reform of racialising discourses or revolution is the best tactic (Luxemberg 1973). Through a critical exploration of the approaches to mobilisation for the expression of political voice, this question urges the actor (in this case artivists) to consider how much time is required or where they may be best placed to spend their efforts.

Whilst this research has a strong research design, future research could benefit from the critical YPAR approach, which adds a *critical* element to the YPAR approach. This approach considers further a *power analysis* where very differently positioned people bring distinct levels of power, lines of analysis, experience, and forms of expertise, and together craft research design always centering the perspectives of those most impacted by injustice and draws extensively from the praxis, engaging interdisciplinary scholarship and activist work (Fine et al. 2021).

When considering a goal to retain freedoms, here it is necessary to explore the concept of prefigurative politics (Dinerstein 2015) as a topic for future research – what it means to bring about hope in oppressive circumstances. Young SSAs' social movement goals could further be explored as part of this. As suggested, this does not necessarily mean abstract goals of unity as some would position (Lentin 2018; Channing-Brown 2018). Further research would therefore involve more specific articulation of *communication for social change* through CCA approaches (Dutta 2011). This would involve further investigation of the transformation of racialising discourses. This suggested approach changes the imperative from young SSAs to do something about their social cause to those who benefit from Whiteness interrogating their own identity politics. These further investigations would contribute to key discussions about contemporary politics of belonging (Yuval-Davis 2007). The benefits of conducting such research would be to 'present an ongoing and emerging framework of organising that outlines a politics of social change' (Dutta 2011, 276).

Doing Things Differently Going Forward: Policy, Research and Practice

Through a CRT and NSM analysis, the core question remains, what can one do to really create social change in this context if it is perceived that racism will always appear to be in our midst? Hage (2016) also recalls Antiracism indicating that as a social movement, he suggests that through this urgent task, accumulative gain has been made throughout history and always requires a critical re-examination of how it can be modified and made more efficient. As the research design included ethnographic methodology (Kelly 2022), the core focus was elevating young SSA participant voices. Research participants had several recommendations they wished practitioners to consider, not included in this study, particularly in relation to arts-based community development and standpoint projects.

As there was not scope for this PhD research represented in this monograph to utilise auto-ethnographic methodologies (Cann and DeMeulenaere 2012), the researcher's personal positionality and discussion about their specific role in this research as co-founder of Footprints as an arts-based community development in cultural-policy ecology remains limited. For the purpose of cultural policy contributions (Clammer 2015; Stephenson Jr, Tate, and Goldbard 2015), there is further scope to analyse the power, potential biases and decision-making in the Grounded Project and the role of the white researcher utilising Indigenous methodologies in this. As it stands, one limitation of this research is that it is unclear whether political voice emerged organically in the practice of individuals and groups and/or was fostered through the organisation/project's direct interventions and explicit focus on conscientisation – an important distinction. It is, however, clear that delivery of projects involving self-determination and defined collaboration involves providing an opportunity for dialogic spaces which are quintessential to the politics of social change. Additionally, they need to be contextually situated in relationship with the structures at local, national and global sites (Dutta 2011, 2020). These findings are particularly poignant due to the fact that the Australian government has released a 5-year National cultural policy to revive the arts in Australia whilst ensuring there is a 'place for every story, and a story for every place' (Australian Government 2023, 1).

Young SSAs' actions in this research stemmed from the idea that black people are not in 'powerless defence'. Like other social movements such as the Black Panthers, whilst fairly short-lived due to systemic state-sanctioned targeting of the chapters, this movement left a legacy where 'black minds were awakened to the ongoing reality of racism' (Kendi 2019, 139). Many of the successes of these movements are attributed to contributing to alternative policymaking, which can be developed once an adequate analysis and assessment of an issue is achieved. This can only be achieved if the first step of an NSM is conducted through a consciousness-raising process with the oppressed (Kendi 2019, 139).

In terms of examining the results depicted in this monograph alongside youth and community development literature, this process highlights disjuncture between dominant expectations facing young SSAs and their aspirational community development values. Rather than choosing to resist racialising discourses at a public youth event by performing overt political Hip Hop tracks, BTSO artivists preferred to subvert the event by portraying Afrocentric notions of themselves. This finding leads to epistemological considerations in identity projects, thereby providing additional resources for racial justice movements. In this format, identity-based groups participating in NSMs provide 'distinctive kinds of knowledge that are claimed to become available through the strategies of the identity-based groups' (Rosaldo 2006, 249).

Whilst this has not been a main feature of this monograph as it requires an additional, more detailed conceptual approach, it is important to note briefly that Hip Hop audiences may, too, go through the consciousness-raising process. Through seeing young SSAs perform, or through listening to the content of their tracks, or being amongst a group of young black artists in a performance space, findings from Footprints' YPAR and some limited interview data suggested there was potential for the transformation of attitudes towards young SSAs. This indicates the potential for the transformation of the social construct of Whiteness and racialising discourses requiring a more strategic focus. This experience may lead towards a more general open-mindedness towards culturally diverse communities over time; however, this needs to be further substantiated.

Addressing the 'buzz' that was felt at projects like the Grounded Project, which involved intercultural dialogue (with multiple cultures present), little is yet known of the potential gains that transculturalism (young people identifying with multiple or hybrid cultural identities across continents) offers migrant youth. Further exploration of this concept would involve exploring what attributes and capacities young people accumulate from balancing, concurrently, the demands of their cultural identities and wider social belongings (Mansouri and Modood 2021).

Similar to the PhD research featured, other scholars conclude that there is an urgent need to examine the multifaceted everyday experiences of migrant youth to better understand not just the broader processes of social integration, but also the utility of *transcultural capital* for them, their communities, and their wider societies (Wyn, Cuervo, and Cook 2019). This may lead to a broader focus on interculturalism rather than multiculturalism whilst recognising the limitations of any approach within an ongoing colonial context (Mansouri and Modood 2021).

With this future focus and with consideration of the motto 'born to stand out' (BTSO), a precedent for the development of political voice iterates that Australia has the potential to make changes over time. There is hope through this context. BIPOC communities such as SSAs can begin to account for the 'entangled relations of power between the global division of . . . racial and ethnic hierarchy, identity formation, and Eurocentric epistemologies' (Salvídar 2006, 340). Through a consciousness-raising process and acknowledging the coloniality of power, BIPOC communities have the opportunity to restructure the 'process of identity, experience, and knowledge production articulating geo-strategic locations and subaltern (minor) inscriptions' (Salvídar 2006, 340).

In many cases, the notion of black power or aspects of the BTSO motto, which involve the refusal to be caged in society's expectation of you can cause quite a bit of controversy. The reality is that through the headway achieved through NSMs, Lentin (2020, 16) also identifies that the ramifications are a 'constant production of outrage about the apparent excesses of 'identity politics'. This is 'having a negative effect on the possibilities for Antiracist solidarity grounded in a race-critical politics' (Lentin 2020, 16). Whilst acknowledging that contemporary Antiracism appears unable to make sense of the function of race in racism, she therefore calls for longitudinal studies of Australian-based Antiracism initiatives (Lentin 2016). Whilst the Grounded Project was not specifically a targeted Antiracism project, it has some stark likeness to some Antiracism goals. These goals are expressed by Lentin (2018, 1) who identifies 'what Antiracism is not' by suggesting that the

> enduring power of Whiteness and Eurocentrism obscures the focus by presenting fluffy ideas of intercultural communication or a discourse of 'unity in diversity' which silences difference. . . . It does however involve multiple discourses and movement practices that can be called Antiracism.

This has implications for an evolving Australia where 'we can create dialogue' and 'write our own description of what it means to be Australian' where we are 'figuring it out together' (SBS 2020, 1). If this approach is possible, *Titan*, in an interview with an Australian broadcast, feels 'there is definitely hope'. He is not interested in the old Australia where you can 'get rid' of people through assimilation and white policy (SBS 2020, 1).

Through focusing on the political practice of collective social actors, today's social movements are seen as 'playing a central role in producing the world in which we live, its social structures and practices, its meanings and cultural orientations, its possibilities for change' (Escobar 1992, 395–396). The initial measurement of social change outcome intended in this research utilises a YPAR process through an arts-based community development project and explores the ways in which young SSAs are challenging deficit representations through racialising discourses utilising this methodology. For young SSAs, this is an ideal time to formulate resistance towards racialising discourses, not just through their migration experience or through the lens of their visibility and experiences of racism but also through asserting their own positive contributions. Here, it is not just about tolerance or feelings of social inclusion, but an opportunity to express their identity in Australia. As a result, they may impact white Australian perceptions towards this community and other BIPOC.

CONCLUDING STATEMENT

Upon arrival in Australia, young SSAs recalled their hopes that this would be a land of opportunity. Instead, due to racist narratives, many are forced to repeatedly consider their Blackness (Mushroom-Creative 2017). This was not something they necessarily had to consider when living in countries where being black was the norm. These discussions point towards broader experiences of racism and anti-Blackness sentiments in Australia (Majavu 2020; Gatwiri and Anderson 2020). Activist and lawyer Nyadol Nyuon believes Australia is currently in the process of deciding what it can become (Nyuon 2021). This history of race politics in Australia provides a pertinent foundation for the empirical research discussed in this monograph, grounding consideration of racialising discourses in radical contexts to fundamentally reconstruct our thinking and build a better Australia. The term born to stand out therefore offers a further contribution to knowledge about urban youth identities.

Facing complex challenges (Mansouri 2009a, 2009b; VIC-Health et al. 2017), multicultural young people already frequently and routinely interact across diversity (A. Harris 2013). This research has demonstrated the importance of not stereotyping young people from various cultural or sub-cultural backgrounds, as insisted by racialising discourses. Whilst acknowledging this necessity, perceptions of limited choice emerge for young BIPOC experiences when determining their own directions in life. This is due to portrayals of African diaspora identities through deficit approaches and narratives in Australia (Majavu 2015; Gatwiri and Anderson 2020). These focus on what they are doing 'wrong' instead of focusing on what they are doing 'right'.

By presenting counter-narratives to racialising discourses, this research has reinforced that members of diasporas have sharable knowledge about their social world that has valuable implications. As shown in the #African-gangs response discussed in chapter 1 and subsequent findings discussing young SSAs' expression of their political voice through alternative forms of artivism, young SSAs do have collective responses to their depiction in the media (Nunn 2010). This research has demonstrated that they wish to define themselves through the lens of identity politics, documenting what young SSAs are doing to shed new light on how they enact their agency through building their political voice. This has implications for policymakers, the public sector, youth, justice and education practitioners who are seeking innovative ideas to engage young people in determining their own outcomes rather than shaping a homogenous 'one-size-fits-all' or 'top-down' approach.

Through negotiating transcultural lives as part of NSMs, young people can build social capital (Hebert, Hoerder, and Schmitt 2006; Oxoby 2009; Wray-Lake and Abrams 2020). From BCM's (2020a, 1) perspective, this kind of momentum can create 'a movement that makes sense' whilst not seeking anyone's approval. This research has demonstrated the start of that momentum through participation in NSMs. There will always be young people who have a higher calling and will continue to call people to account and raise consciousness through Hip Hop (Sawyer 2006). Through their witness, we are left with the consideration: 'what shall we build on the ashes of a nightmare?' (Kelley 2003, 196). Through marches, performance and narratives circulated through social media, through the images, participatory articulations, and community-based mobilising efforts presented in Footprints' YPAR, the representations of voices documented in this research amplify forms of 'resistance from the global margins' which contribute to the 'global politics of resistance' and 'social transformations and transformations in structures of oppression and exploitation' (Dutta 2011, 275).

The BTSO artists depicted in this monograph and young people throughout history have shown us that artists can be revolutionary actors. One of the main contributions of this research is, therefore, the quest to understand what future 'revolutionary dreams' can 'erupt out of political engagement' as it has been demonstrated that 'collective social movements are incubators of new knowledge' (Kelley 2003, 8). Therefore, the findings are unique in the ways in which they capture urban youth of colour's civic engagement, where their community vitality and assets are on display as they challenge injustices and address a specific social problem (Wray-Lake and Abrams 2020). Through their Hip Hop personas and narratives, ultimately, young SSAs in this research have demonstrated that they are 'born to stand out'.

NOTES

1. Malesh P (2020) 'Be Free' (Soli x Mez Mariyé: Malesh P Remix), Malesh P: https://soundcloud.com/malesh/be-free-soli-x-mez-mariye-malesh-p-remix.

    See blogpost #32.

2. Abe Nouk (2014) 'Love Looks Like', Abraham Nouk: https://www.youtube.com/watch?v=Jtb_FjtJd5U.

    See blogpost #39.

3. Burn-City-Movement (2020). Realness for sale. In *Realness for Sale*. Tidal: Noble Studios. https://tidal.com/browse/album/131189065.

    See blogpost #40.

A Note on Terminology

African diaspora: I also acknowledge the complexity of the term 'diaspora' due to the fact that my participants may be first or second-generation migrants or forced migrants. However, participants who identify as SSA are first-generation and all came to Australia either on a #200 or #202 visa (former refugee or humanitarian Visa) and therefore fit the 'African diaspora' category. Therefore, in consideration of the socio-political complexity of the term African diaspora, use of this term in this text for young SSAs refers to the conceptual homeland of South Sudan and the interplay between their arrival as forced migrants in Australia being classified as perpetual refugees failing to integrate (Brubaker 2005; Ang 2014).

Antiracism: Recognised as a New Social Movement (NSM). One who is supporting an Antiracism policy through their actions or expressing an Antiracist idea (Kendi 2019).

Black and white: Skin colour is not capitalised throughout the text to differentiate between *Blackness and Whiteness*, which are capitalised as they refer to forms of constructed identities. Whilst the concept of race is a social construct, Blackness is often referred to in a cultural or socio-political environment either referring to claiming or being proud of 'ones black [racialised] identity/ies' or acknowledging the systemic inequities that have formed as a result of being labelled at the 'bottom' of a racial hierarchy as a result of being classified with black skin pigmentation or attributes. The concept of Whiteness is a dominant paradigm that humans are socialised into whereby Whiteness is perceived to be at the 'top' of the racialised hierarchy depicting white racialised identities, customs, culture, and beliefs, attributes as operating as the 'normal' or 'ideal' standard by which all other groups are compared. Where I am describing social movements such as *Black Lives Matter (BLM)*, *Black Power* or *Black Consciousness,* capitals are used in these instances. Advancing the civil rights movement in the United States, global BLM movement/s recognise and seek to dismantle structural inequities experienced by black peoples. To be a part of the Black Consciousness movement is to highlight the strengths of being a part of a positive unifying identity and be aware of the awakening of one's self-worth as black peoples. As a revolutionary movement, Black Power emphasises racial pride, economic empowerment and self-determination through cultural and political gains of black peoples worldwide.

*Blak***:** It refers to First Nations identities in the lands we now call Australia who may identify as bla(c)k and with Bla(c)kness.

Cultural Codes and Critical Creative Agency: If one identifies as black or with Blackness, or as Indigenous or as Person of Colour (BIPOC), these are terms recognised to be 'cultural codes'. Whilst contested, such terms support these people groups to communicate amongst themselves and use recognised symbols and systems of meaning that are relevant to members of a particular culture (or subculture). 'Critical creative agency' involves becoming aware of these codes in relation to systems which either advantage or disadvantage some community groups and using creative methods to highlight, resist, dismantle, reclaim or develop counter-narratives through individuals or through communities' self-determination. Agency in this context refers to the power to choose what cultural codes represent oneself or one's sub-culture or community.

First Nations terminology: In the first mention of the country in this text, I shall use the First Nations name. For example, 'the lands we now call Australia' (Australia), Turtle Island (now known as the United States of America (U.S.)), Aotearoa (New Zealand). The map of my research locale also recognises First Nations names representing the Kulin Nations (traditional owners of the parts of the state we now call 'Victoria').

Hip Hop: Recognised as the name of a sub-culture and a New Social Movement (NSM); therefore, requiring capitals (proper noun) and no hyphen as indicated elsewhere.[1]

N****: While Hip Hop artists and urban youth culture recast 'nigga' as an endearing term, 'ni***rs' remained a derisive term outside and inside black mouths (Kendi 2019, 137). This is due to the term having racist links to references to black slaves. It is not recommended for anyone who does not identify as bla(c)k to use the term 'nigga', therefore I have chosen to represent participants' use of the word by writing 'n****' after consultation with them about their preferences.

South Sudanese Australian (SSA): It is recognised that young people from South Sudanese Australian communities may identify with this term or other terms (Williams 2022). I have chosen one acronym 'SSA' for consistency as I use this term frequently. I have chosen to say communities (plural) due to there being multiple tribes and inter-ethnic considerations.

NOTE

1. As advised in consultation with Dr Tasha Iglesias, Board Member of the *Hip Hop Association of Advancement and Education* (HHAAE) and *Hood Scholar*, NYC in 2021, who advocated for this approach to the *APA* and *Merriam Webster Dictionary*: https://www.hhaae.org/?fbclid=IwAR2qj9D23lTmmuYq8fmPpIa2104un-8FsRo91ElODqKV-Xe0mvYjtYXzhmg.

Glossary of Terms and Key Events

Apex gang:Allegations of young SSAs' involvement with the 'Apex gang' surfaced following a public brawl during the March 2016 Moomba Festival in Naarm (Melbourne) (Wahlquist 2018). From the period of 2016–2018, the Apex gang was known for a series of 'car-jackings, burglaries and home-invasions. Later described as network offenders and a non-entity, their violence sparked a moral panic (Farnsworth 2017; Joined-Up-Films 2018).

Moomba Riots:The etymology of the word Moomba was said to be an 'Aboriginal word' meaning 'coming together to have fun', (Dee 2015). Featuring fair-like activities, sporting competitions, and a big street parade on the Labour day public holiday, Moomba is the festival of the city of Naarm (Melbourne). The Moomba 'riot' of 2016 was Victoria's most significant episode of public disorder since the G20 protests of 2006. The rioters, who were allegedly of South Sudanese descent (but found to be a group of different ethnicities), attempted to pick fights with festival-goers in Federation Square (a public landmark/gathering place) on the Saturday night. Initially, factions of Victoria police and the media claimed a gang based in Naarm (Melbourne's) southern suburbs, called Apex, was responsible for the riot. Most visibly, these claims and the incident sparked a wave of heavily racialised media narratives about 'African gangs' that gained further momentum in the lead-up to the 2018 Victorian state elections (Benier et al. 2018; Maher et al. 2020).

Multiculturalism, Interculturalism and Transculturalism:*Multicultural* refers to a society that contains several cultural or ethnic groups. *Intercultural* describes communities in which there is a deep understanding and respect for all cultures. Referring to different forms of diversity and conceptual complexities resulting in policymaking (Guilherme and Dietz 2015), critique of *multicultural policy* involves questioning the notions of integration and assimilation that proponents imply. There are other proposed options. Critiques of *Interculturalism* are that it is often discussed as a type of utopia when, in practice, at best, it talks of dialogue without taking conflicts into account. *Transculturality* is a concept that captures some of the living traits of cultural change as highly diverse contemporary societies become globalised. In this context, observing that people's identities can be made up of more than one cultural or ethnic influence, *transculturalism* offers a conceptual landscape for considering cultures as relational webs and flows of significance in active interaction with one another (Mansouri and Modood 2021). This research therefore considers a transcultural approach to belonging and engagement amongst forced-migrant youth, whereby transcultural capital claiming a new channel of respect (or rejection) of the Other might be possible (Triandafyllidou 2009; Mansouri, Beaman, and Hussain 2019).

Murder of Liep Gony in 2007:South Sudanese communities in Australia ability to integrate was questioned by former immigration minister Kevin Andrews in a negative media campaign targeting the community (Collins 2007) after the murder of young South Sudanese Australian Liep Gony in Noble Park, (Naarm) Melbourne in 2007. It was initially alleged that a Sudanese gang had killed him, but found to be a racially motivated attack by two Caucasian males. A spate of incidents involving African Australian young people (and others) resulted in some groups of mainstream media and politicians claiming the city was in the grip of a gang crisis (NewMatilda 2010; Bonica 2018). SSAs have identified that it has been difficult to recover from such a campaign as similar racial profiling of this cultural group has continued (Topsfield 2008).

Standpoint Theory and Projects:Standpoint theory is traditionally understood to be the combination of intersubjective discourses proposing that authority is rooted in individuals' personal knowledge and perspectives and the power that such authority exerts (Ritzer 2005). An example of applied standpoint theory in this monograph comes in the form of a *standpoint project* involving arts-based methodology stemming from a social position on racism and involving *transformative youth organising* (Ritzer 2005; Bautista 2018). An example of transformative youth organising as part of a standpoint project depicted in this PhD thesis is photo 21, where young South Sudanese Australian (SSA) artist *i.OG* wears a 'Sudanese are dope [cool] though' t-shirt with a caption 'Immigrants make Australia great!' Footprints, the organisation that this research focuses on, created these t-shirts in response to the Apex gang moral panic for people to wear in public and at pop-up performances. Instead of being fearful of seeing a young SSA in public after widespread discussion about riots and gangs, wearing this t-shirt is a form of artivism (activism using a creative format) depicting a counter-message.

References

AAP. 2011. "Racist pole murder: 20-year term upheld." *The Age*, August 23, 2011, National. Accessed December 12, 2012. https://www.theage.com.au/national/victoria/racist-pole-murder-20-year-term-upheld-20110823-1j7tj.html.

ABC, Australian-Broadcasting-Corporation. 2007. "Protesters angry over govt immigration policies." *ABC News*, October 11, 2007. Accessed July 22, 2020. https://mobile.abc.net.au/news/2007-10-11/protesters-angry-over-govt-immigration-policies/695374?pfm=sm.

ABS, Australian-Bureau-of-Statistics. 2016a. "2016 Census." Accessed June 19, 2018. https://www.abs.gov.au/websitedbs/censushome.nsf/home/2016.

———. 2016b. "ANC1P/ANC2P/ANCP Ancestry 1st response/Ancestry 2nd response/Ancestry multi-response." 2016 Census Classifications. Accessed June 1, 2018. https://www.abs.gov.au/ausstats/abs@.nsf/Lookup/2901.0Chapter602016.

Abur, W. 2018. "Systemic vilification and racism are affecting on the South Sudanese community in Australia." *International Journal of Scientific Research* 7 (11): 47–52. https://www.worldwidejournals.com/international-journal-of-scientific-research-(IJSR)/article/systemic-vilification-and-racism-are-affecting-on-the-south-sudanese-community-in-australia/MTczMTM=/.

———. 2019. *A new life with opportunities and challenges: The settlement experiences of South Sudanese-Australians*. Osborne Park, WA: Africa World Books.

Abur, W., and C. Mphande. 2020. "Mental health and wellbeing of South Sudanese-Australians." *Journal of Asian and African Studies* 55 (3): 412–428. https://doi.org/10.1177/0021909619880294.

Adichie, C.N. 2021. *Chimamanda Ngozi Adichie*. New York: Columbia University Press.

Adusei-Asante, K. 2021. "'Where are you really from?' The harsh realities of Afro-Aussie life are brought to stage in Black Brass." *The Conversation*, March 11, 2021. Accessed May 10, 2021. https://theconversation.com/where-are-you-really-from-the-harsh-realities-of-afro-aussie-life-are-brought-to-stage-in-black-brass-156110.

Ahluwalia, D.P.S. 2012. *Politics and post-colonial theory: African inflections.* Online. London: Routledge.

AHRC, Australian Human Rights Commission. 2010. *In our own words: African Australians: A review of human rights and social inclusion issues.* Sydney, NSW: Australian Human Rights Commission.

Akom, A.A. 2009. "Critical Hip Hop pedagogy as a form of liberatory praxis." *Equity & Excellence in Education* 42 (1): 52–66. https://doi.org/10.1080/10665680802612519.

———. 2011. "Black emancipatory action research: Integrating a theory of structural racialisation into ethnographic and participatory action research methods." *Ethnography & Education* 6 (1): 113–131. https://doi.org/10.1080/17457823.2011.553083.

Al-Jazeera. 2022. "South Sudan: President Kiir, VP Machar agree to resume talks." *Al Jazeera*, April 4, 2022, News. https://www.aljazeera.com/news/2022/4/4/south-sudan-president-kiir-vp-machar-agree-to-resume-talks.

Alcoff, L., M. Hames-Garca, S. Mohanty, M. Hames-García, Paula M.L. Moya, and M. Hames-García. 2006. *Identity politics reconsidered.* First edition. ed. Bibliographies. The future of minority studies. New York: Palgrave Macmillan.

Allan, D., and V. Duckworth. 2018. "Voices of disaffection: disengaged and disruptive youths or agents of change and self-empowerment?" *British Journal of Special Education* 45 (1): 43–60. https://doi.org/10.1111/1467-8578.12201.

Alvesson, M., and K. Sköldberg. 2018. *Reflexive methodology: New vistas for qualitative research.* Third edition. ed. Bibliographies. London; Thousand Oaks: SAGE Publications.

Amac-Don. 2019. *41 bars of an African gang member.* Melbourne: Future Records.

Anderson, E., and C. West. 2011. *Against the wall: Poor, young, black, and male.* Vol. 9780812206951. The city in the twenty-first century. Philadelphia: University of Pennsylvania Press, Inc.

Anderson, W.P. 2005. *The cultivation of whiteness: Science, health and racial destiny in Australia.* New edition. ed. Bibliographies. ACLS Fellows' publications. Melbourne: Melbourne University Press.

Andreotti, V.O. 2011. "(Towards) decoloniality and diversality in global citizenship education." *Globalisation, Societies and Education* 9 (3–4): 381–397. https://doi.org/10.1080/14767724.2011.605323.

Andrews, K. 2020. "'Urban' sounds: It's time to stop using this hackneyed term for black music." *The Guardian*, August 14, 2018. https://www.theguardian.com/music/shortcuts/2018/aug/14/urban-time-stop-hackneyed-term-black-music.

Ang, I. 2014. "Beyond Chinese groupism: Chinese Australians between assimilation, multiculturalism and diaspora." *Ethnic and Racial Studies* 37 (7): 1184–1196. https://doi.org/10.1080/01419870.2014.859287.

Anthias, F. 2002. "Where do I belong?" *Ethnicities* 2 (4): 491–514. http://journals.sagepub.com/doi/abs/10.1177/14687968020020040301.

Anzaldúa, G., and C. Moraga. 1983. *This bridge called my back: Writings by radical women of color.* Second edition, [that is first edition reprint] ed. Bibliographies. Latham and New York: Kitchen Table: Women of Color Press.

References

Appadurai, A. 2004. "The capacity to aspire: Culture and the terms of recognition." In *Culture and public action*, edited by V. Rao and M. Walton, 59–84. Redwood City, CA: Stanford University Press.

Asante, M.K. 2003. *Afrocentricity: The theory of social change*. New and Revised edition. Chicago, IL: African American Images.

———. 2008. *It's bigger than Hip Hop: The rise of the post-Hip Hop generation*. New York: St. Martin's Press.

———. 2020. *An Afrocentric Pan Africanist vision. Afrocentric essays*. Online. Critical Africana Studies. Lanham, MD: Lexington Books.

Atem-Deng, S. 2006. "My long journey from suffering to life." *Reclaiming Children & Youth* 15 (2): 71–72. https://www.proquest.com/openview/26bd5372dfd4e1c1c8b71a7352bfcb5e/1?cbl=33810&pq-origsite=gscholar.

———. 2016. "South Sudanese youth acculturation and intergenerational challenges." Paper presented at the 39th African Studies Association of Australasia and the Pacific (AFSAAP). https://afsaap.org.au/assets/19-Santino-Atem-Deng.pdf.

Australian-Council-Arts. 2020. *Towards equity: A research overview of diversity in Australia's arts and cultural sector*. Australian Council for the Arts (Sydney). http://diversityarts.org.au/app/uploads/Towards-Equity-Report.pdf.

Australian-Government. 2016. *Country information summary - South Sudan*. Department Home Affairs (Website). https://www.homeaffairs.gov.au/mca/files/2016-cis-south-sudan.pdf.

———, 2023. "National cultural policy—Revive: A place for every story, a story for every place." February 9, 2023. https://www.arts.gov.au/publications/national-cultural-policy-revive-place-every-story-story-every-place.

Australian-Poetry-Slam. 2014. "Abe Nouk - 'love looks like' - Australian poetry slam 2013." https://www.youtube.com/watch?v=Jtb_FjtJd5U.

Ayala, A. 2017. "Youth giving voice in research ethics." *Narrative Inquiry in Bioethics* 7 (1): E1–E4. https://doi.org/10.1353/nib.2017.0023.

Baak, M. 2011. "Murder, community talk and belonging: An exploration of Sudanese community responses to murder in Australia." *African Identities* 9 (4): 417–434. https://doi.org/10.1080/14725843.2011.614415.

———. 2018. "Sudanese heritage youth in Australia are frequently maligned by fear-mongering and racism." *The Conversation*, January 11, 2018, Politics and Society. Accessed May 24, 2021. https://theconversation.com/sudanese-heritage-youth-in-australia-are-frequently-maligned-by-fear-mongering-and-racism-89763.

———. 2019. "Racism and Othering for South Sudanese heritage students in Australian schools: is inclusion possible?" *International Journal of Inclusive Education* 23 (2): 125–141. https://doi.org/10.1080/13603116.2018.1426052.

Baker, A., C. Sonn, and K. Meyer. 2020. "Voices of displacement: A methodology of sound portraits exploring identity and belonging." *Qualitative Research* 20 (6): 892–909. https://doi.org/10.1177/1468794120909765.

Baker, N., and S. Wiedersehn. 2018. "Are Australia's African communities really experiencing a 'gang' crisis?" *SBS News*, July 24, 2018, Immigration. Accessed July 14, 2017. https://www.sbs.com.au/news/what-s-behind-the-african-gangs-fallout.

Barber, T.E., R. Anderson, M. Dery, and S.R. Thomas. 2018. "25 years of Afrofuturism and black speculative thought: Roundtable with Tiffany E. Barber, Reynaldo Anderson, Mark Dery, and Sheree Renée Thomas." *TOPIA: Canadian Journal of Cultural Studies* 39: 136–144. https://muse.jhu.edu/article/706962/pdf.

Barlow, J.N. 2018. "Restoring optimal black mental health and reversing intergenerational trauma in an era of Black lives matter." *Biography* 41 (4): 895–908. https://muse.jhu.edu/article/719282.

Barry, P. 2007. "Ganging up." In *Media watch.* ABC, July 2007. Accessed July 27, 2008. http://www.abc.net.au/mediawatch/transcripts/s2054150.htm.

Bautista, E.E. 2018. "Transformative youth organising: A decolonising social movement framework." Doctor of Education Dissertation, Loyola Law School, Loyola Marymount University, p. 522. https://digitalcommons.lmu.edu/etd/522.

BBC. 2017. "The Anzac post, outrage and a debate about race." *BBC News*, August 10, 2017, Australia. Accessed June 2, 2021. https://www.bbc.com/news/world-australia-40712832.

BCM, Burn-City-Movement. 2020a. "Burn city movement." https://www.facebook.com/bcmthemovement.

———. 2020b. "Realness for sale." In *Realness for sale*. Tidal: Noble Studios, Melbourne.

———. 2020c. "Scary hours feat. A1 Krashn." In *Realness for sale*. Tidal: Noble Studios, Melbourne.

———. 2020d. "TnT (Trials n' Tribulations)." In *Realness for sale*. Tidal: Noble Studios, Melbourne.

Beat-Magazine. 2017. "How the next generation of creators are using their voice for change." *Beat Magazine*, March 2017. Accessed July 18, 2020. https://beat.com.au/how-the-next-generation-of-creators-are-using-their-voice-for-change/.

Bell-Villada, G.H., N. Sichel, F. Eidse, and E. Neil Orr. 2011. *Writing out of limbo: International childhoods, global nomads and third culture kids.* Newcastle: Cambridge Scholars.

Benier, K., R. Wickes, and C. Moran. 2020. "'African gangs' in Australia: Perceptions of race and crime in urban neighbourhoods." *Australia and New Zealand Journal of Criminology* 55 (2): 220–238. https://doi.org/10.1177/0004865820965647.

Benier, K.J. , J.B. Blaustein, D. Johns, and S.L. Maher. 2018. *'Don't drag us into this': Growing Up South Sudanese in Victoria after the 2016 Moomba 'riot'.* Centre for Multicultural Youth and Monash Migration and Inclusion Centre (MMIC) at Monash University and the School of Social and Political Sciences at the University of Melbourne. (CMY website). October 31, 2018. https://www.cmy.net.au/resource/dont-drag-me-into-this-growing-up-south-sudanese-in-victoria-after-the-2016-moomba-riot/.

Berman, G., and Y. Paradies. 2010. "Racism, disadvantage and multiculturalism: Towards effective anti-racist praxis." *Ethnic and Racial Studies* 33 (2): 214–232. https://doi.org/10.1080/01419870802302272.

Bernstein, M. 2005. "Identity politics." *Annual Review of Sociology* 31: 47–74. https://www.jstor.org/stable/29737711.

Bessant, J. 2004. "Mixed messages: Youth participation and democratic practice." *Australian Journal of Political Science* 39 (2): 387–404. https://doi.org/10.1080/1036114042000238573.

Bevington, D., and C. Dixon. 2005. "Movement-relevant theory: Rethinking social movement scholarship and activism." *Social Movement Studies* 4 (3): 185–208. https://doi.org/10.1080/14742830500329838.

Bhattacharya, K. 2017. *Fundamentals of qualitative research: A practical guide.* Bibliographies. New York: Routledge.

BICOC-Project, The. 2020. "A Black indigenous people of colour movement." Accessed February 14, 2020. https://www.thebipocproject.org/.

Black, S. 2014. "'Street music', urban ethnography and ghettoised communities." *International Journal of Urban and Regional Research* 38 (2): 700–705. https://onlinelibrary.wiley.com/doi/abs/10.1111/1468-2427.12098.

Bleiker, R., D. Campbell, E. Hutchison, and X. Nicholson. 2013. "The visual dehumanisation of refugees." *Australian Journal of Political Science* 48 (4): 398–416. https://doi.org/10.1080/10361146.2013.840769.

BLM. 2021. "Black lives matter." Accessed June 18. https://blacklivesmatter.com/.

Bloch, E. 1970. *A philosophy of the future. Non-fiction. An Azimuth book.* Freiburg: Herder and Herder.

———. 1986. *The principle of hope.* First American edition. ed. Online. Studies in contemporary German social thought. Cambridge, MA: MIT Press.

Bonica, D. 2018. "Liep Gony memorial: Mother urges politicians to change language around youth crime." *ABC News*, September 26, 2018, 2018. Accessed May 22, 2020. https://www.abc.net.au/news/2018-09-26/liep-gony-memorial-shines-spotlight-on-racism/10306476.

Bonnette, L.M. 2015. *Pulse of the people: Political rap music and black politics.* ed. Bibliographies. American governance: Politics, policy, and public law. Philadelphia, PA: University of Pennsylvania Press.

Boulet, J. 2018. "Researching is relating time and space: From methodological straightjackets 'against method', to 'nothing about us without us'." In *Positioning research shifting paradigms, interdisciplinarity and indigeneity*, edited by M. Kumar and S. Pattanayak, 106–141. New Delhi: SAGE Publishing.

Boulet, J., and L. Hawkins. 2021. *Practical and political approaches to recontextualizing social work.* Social Science. Melbourne: IGI Global.

Bourke, L. 2009. "Reflections on doing participatory research in health: Participation, method and power." *International Journal of Social Research Methodology* 12 (5): 457–474. https://doi.org/10.1080/13645570802373676.

Bowden, E. . 2018. "Melbourne's Sudanese community reclaims 'African gangs' slight in powerful campaign." *The Age*, January 11, 2018. Accessed March 24, 2018. https://www.theage.com.au/national/victoria/african-gangs-slight-reclaimed-in-powerful-campaign-for-sudanese-community-20180110-h0g2ao.html.

Braun, V., and V. Clarke. 2012. *Thematic analysis.* Washington, DC: American Psychological Association.

Briese, J., and K. Menzel. 2020. *No more 'Blacks in the Back'. Adding more than a 'splash' of black into social work education and practice by drawing on the works* of Aileen Moreton-Robinson and others who contribute to Indigenous standpoint theory. Book Chapter. New York and London: Routledge.

Bright, D., C. Whelan, and C. Morselli. 2020. *Understanding the structure and composition of co-offending networks in Australia*. Australian Institute of Criminology, Australian Government, June 2020. https://www.aic.gov.au/publications/tandi/tandi597.

Brown, B. 2010. *The gifts of imperfection: Let go of who you think you're supposed to be and embrace who you are*. Bibliographies. Center City, MN: Hazelden.

Brubaker, R. 2005. "The 'diaspora' diaspora." *Ethnic and Racial Studies* 28 (1): 1–19. https://doi.org/10.1080/0141987042000289997.

Bruner, J. 1991. "The narrative construction of reality." *Critical Inquiry* 18 (1): 1–21. https://doi.org/10.1086/448619.

Buechler, S.M. 1995. "New social movement theories." *The Sociological Quarterly* 36 (3): 441–464. http://www.jstor.org/stable/4120774.

Bulhan, H.A. 1985. *Frantz Fanon and the psychology of oppression*. New York and London: Plenum Press.

Burke, K.J., S. Greene, and M.K. McKenna. 2017. "Youth voice, civic engagement and failure in participatory action research." *Urban Review: Issues and Ideas in Public Education* 49 (4): 585–601. https://link.springer.com/article/10.1007/s11256-017-0410-4.

Butt, C. 2018. "Are Sudanese people over-represented in Victoria's crime statistics?" *The Age*, September 5, 2018, National News. Accessed 22nd December, 2020. https://www.theage.com.au/melbourne-news/are-sudanese-people-over-represented-in-victoria-s-crime-statistics-20180904-p501qx.html.

Caldwell, A. 2007. "Australia closes door to African refugees." October 3, 2007. Accessed December 13, 2012. https://www.abc.net.au/worldtoday/content/2007/s2049830.htm.

Campbell, D., and N. Erbstein. 2012. "Engaging youth in community change: Three key implementation principles." *Community Development* 43 (1): 63–79. https://doi.org/10.1080/15575330.2011.645042.

Cañas, T. 2013. "Self-actualisation through conscientisation." *Journal of Pedagogy, Pluralism, and Practice* 5 (1): 77–100. https://doi.org/https://digitalcommons.lesley.edu/jppp/vol5/iss1/1.

Cann, C.N., and E.J. DeMeulenaere. 2012. "Critical co-constructed autoethnography." *Cultural Studies ↔ Critical Methodologies* 12 (2): 146–158. https://doi.org/10.1177/1532708611435214.

Carmichael, S., and C.V. Hamilton. 1969. *Black power: The politics of liberation in America*. ed. Bibliographies. Pelican book. London: Penguin.

Carmody, B., and J. Duke. 2019. "Seven Network slapped on the wrist over 'African gangs' coverage." *The Sydney Morning Herald*, March 21, 2019, News and Current Affairs. Accessed May 26, 2021. https://www.smh.com.au/entertainment/tv-and-radio/seven-network-slapped-on-the-wrist-over-african-gangs-coverage-20190321-p5169g.html.

Carroll, T.W. 2017. "Intersectionality and identity politics: cross-identity coalitions for progressive social change." *Signs* 42 (3): 600–607. https://www.journals.uchicago.edu/doi/pdf/10.1086/689625.

Cassell Jr, W. 2020. "How Rupert Murdoch became a media tycoon: Strategic acquisitions propel Murdoch's wealth and empire." *Investopedia*. Accessed May 20. https://www.investopedia.com/articles/investing/083115/how-rupert-murdoch-became-media-tycoon.asp.

Castells, M. 2009. *The power of identity*. Second edition, with a new preface. ed. Bibliographies. The information age: Economy, society, and culture: Vol. 2. NJ: Wiley-Blackwell.

CGD. 2016. "Greater dandenong: A summary." Accessed June 19. https://www.greaterdandenong.vic.gov.au/_flysystem/filerepo/A6819537.

———. 2018. "Statistical data for Victorian communities - City of greater dandenong." Accessed July 11. www.greaterdandenong.com/document/.../statistical-data-for-victorian-communities.

Chang, J. 2005. *Can't stop, won't stop: A history of the Hip Hop generation*. [First Picador edition] ed. History of the Hip Hop generation. New York: Picador.

Channing-Brown, A. 2018. *I'm still here: Black dignity in a world made for Whiteness*. First edition. ed. Non-fiction. Colorado Springs, CO: Convergent Books.

Checkoway, B.N., and L.M. Gutierrez. 2006. "Youth participation and community change." *Journal of Community Practice* 14 (1–2): 1–9. https://doi.org/10.1300/J125v14n01_01.

Chilisa, B. 2020. *Indigenous research methodologies*. Bibliographies. Second edition. Thousand Oaks, CA: SAGE Publications.

Clammer, J. 2012. *Culture, development and social theory: Towards an integrated social development*. Bibliographies. London: Zed Books.

———. 2015. *Art, culture and international development: Humanising social transformation*. ed. Bibliographies. Rethinking development. New York and London: Routledge.

———. 2021. "Can art embody truth? Ethics, aesthetics and Gandhi." *Social Change* 51 (1): 92–103. https://journals.sagepub.com/doi/full/10.1177/0049085721996859.

Clark, M.K. 2021. "Hip Hop and Pan-Africanism: From Blitz the Ambassador to Beyoncé." *The Conversation*, January 29, 2021, Arts and Culture. Accessed September 19, 2021. https://theconversation.com/hip-hop-and-pan-africanism-from-blitz-the-ambassador-to-beyonce-151680.

Clay, A. 2006. "'All I need is one mic': Mobilising youth for social change in the post-civil rights era." *Social Justice* 33 (2): 105–121. http://www.jstor.org/stable/29768373.

Cleland, J. 2016. "Tkay Maidza, Remi, Sampa and the changing face of Australian Hip Hop." *The Sydney Morning Herald*, October 26, 2016, Culture Music. Accessed August 14, 2020. https://www.smh.com.au/entertainment/music/tkay-maidza-remi-sampa-and-the-changing-face-of-australian-hiphop-20161024-gs9f1e.html.

Cockett, R. 2016. *Sudan: The failure and division of an African state*. Second edition. ed. Online. New Haven, CT: Yale University Press.

Cohen, S. 1987. *Folk devils & moral panics: The creation of the mods and rockers*. New edition. ed. Non-fiction. Oxford, England: Basil Blackwell.

Colbert, S.D. 2017. *Black movements: Performance and cultural politics*. New Brunswick, NJ: Rutgers University Press.

Cole, J. 2014a. "Be free." In *2014 Forrest hills drive*. You Tube: Roc Nation Records.

———. 2014b. "No role modelz." In *2014 Forest hills drive*. You Tube: Roc Nation/Columbia.

Cole, M. 2016. *Racism: A critical analysis*. London: Pluto Press.

Colic-Peisker, V. 2005. "'At least you're the right colour': Identity and social inclusion of Bosnian refugees in Australia." *Journal of Ethnic & Migration Studies* 31 (4): 615–638. https://www.tandfonline.com/doi/abs/10.1080/13691830500109720.

Colic-Peisker, V., and F. Tilbury. 2008. "Being black in Australia: A case study of intergroup relations." *Race and Class* 49 (4): 38–56. https://journals.sagepub.com/doi/abs/10.1177/0306396808089286.

Collins, S.J. 2007. "Murder 'Shame on entire community.'" *The Age*. Accessed December 15, 2012. http://www.theage.com.au/articles/2007/10/10/1191695968357.html.

Connelly, M.F., and J.D. Clandinin. 1990. "Stories of experience and narrative inquiry." *Educational Researcher* 19 (5): 2–14. http://www.jstor.org/stable/1176100.

Cooper, N. 2021. "How serious is the threat of white supremacy in Australia?" *The Sydney Herald*, August 20, 2021. Accessed August 31, 2022. https://www.smh.com.au/please-explain/how-serious-is-the-threat-of-white-supremacy-in-australia-20210820-p58ki8.html.

Cowan, J. 2007. "Andrews stands by remarks on African refugees." *PM*, October 11, 2007. Accessed December 12, 2012. https://www.abc.net.au/pm/content/2007/s2057250.htm.

Cranswick, T., and S. Wicks. 2021. "Nyadol Nyuon — the girl who gave refugees a voice." In *Fierce girls*. https://www.abc.net.au/radio/programs/fierce-girls/nyadol-nyuon-the-girl-who-gave-refugees-a-voice/13270048.

Crenshaw, K., N. Gotanda, G. Peller, and C. Inglis. 1996. *Critical race theory: The key writings that formed the movement*. New York: The New Press.

Crooke, A., and T. Rachael. 2017. "The healing power of Hip Hop." *The Conversation*, July 27, 2017, Arts and Culture. Accessed July 22, 2024. https://theconversation.com/the-healing-power-of-hip-hop-81556#:~:text=But%20while%20many%20people%20struggle,%2C%20community%2C%20and%20having%20fun.

Cross, W.E. 1971. *The negro to black conversion experience*. Brooklyn, NYC: The East.

Dale, P., P. Burnard, and R. Travis. 2024. *Music for Inclusion and Healing in Schools and Beyond: Hip Hop, Techno, Grime, and More*. Oxford: Oxford University Press.

Dandy, J., and R. Pe-Pua. 2015. "The refugee experience of social cohesion in Australia: Exploring the roles of racism, intercultural contact, and the media." *Journal of Immigrant & Refugee Studies* 13 (4): 339–357. https://doi.org/10.1080/15562948.2014.974794.

Daughter's-of-Jerusalem. 2017. "South Sudanese 'daughters of jerusalem' providing support to community." *SBS World News*, October 18. https://www.facebook.com/Daughters123/; https://www.sbs.com.au/news/south-sudanese-daughters-of-jerusalem-providing-support-to-community; https://www.sbs.com.au/language/english/audio/south-sudanese-the-daughters-of-jerusalem.

Davis, A. 2016. "Angela Davis on abolishing prisons, Indigenous incarceration and the US election." In *ABC RN Drive*, interview by Karvelas, P. Online: ABC Radio National. Accessed March 30, 2021. https://www.abc.net.au/radionational/programs/drive/angela-davis-on-mass-incarceration-black-lives-matter-and-the/7950414.

Day, L. 2018. "What statistics can and can't tell us about Melbourne's African crime issue." *ABC News*, January 23, 2018. Accessed April 13, 2018. http://www.abc.net.au/news/2018-01-17/what-statistics-tell-us-about-melbournes-african-crime-issue/9336604.

De Block, L., and D. Buckingham. 2007. *Global children, global media: Migration, media and childhood*. New York: Palgrave Macmillan.

Debirioun, T. 2019. *Ghetto tears*. Soundcloud: Titan Debirioun.

———. 2020. *Cheques and balances*. You Tube: Grid Series.

Dee, P. 2015. "Moomba." In *Social life and customs, such is life* (blog), *State library of Victoria*, June 19. https://blogs.slv.vic.gov.au/such-was-life/moomba/.

Dei, G.J.S. 2018. "'Black like me': Reframing blackness for decolonial politics." *Educational Studies* 54 (2): 117–142. https://doi.org/10.1080/00131946.2018.1427586.

Delgado, R., and J. Stefancic. 2000. *Critical race theory : The cutting edge* Book. Philadelphia: Temple University Press.

Denzin, N.K., and Y.S. Lincoln. 2017. *The SAGE handbook of qualitative research*. Fifth edition. ed. Bibliographies. London: SAGE.

Dimitriadis, G. 1996. "Hip Hop: From live performance to mediated narrative." *Popular Music* 15 (2): 179–194. https://doi.org/10.1017/S0261143000008102.

———. 2000. "'Making history go' at a local community center: Popular media and the construction of historical knowledge among African American youth." *Theory & Research in Social Education* 28 (1): 40–64. https://www.tandfonline.com/doi/abs/10.1080/00933104.2000.10505896.

———. 2001. "'In the clique': Popular culture, constructions of place, and the everyday lives of urban youth." *Anthropology & Education Quarterly* 32 (1): 29–51. https://doi.org/10.1525/aeq.2001.32.1.29.

———. 2003. *Friendships, cliques, and gangs: Young black men coming of age in urban America*. New York: Teachers Publishers Press.

———. 2007a. "Chapter five: Looking toward the past and the future." In *Studying Urban Youth Culture*, edited by G. Dimitriadis, 129–156. New York: Peter Lang Primer.

———. 2007b. "Chapter four: Studying urban youth culture." In *Studying Urban Youth Culture*, edited by G. Dimitriadis, 109–128. New York: Peter Lang Primer.

———. 2007c. "Chapter two: Traditions of studying urban youth culture." In *Studying Urban Youth Culture*, edited by G. Dimitriadis, 25–80. New York: Peter Lang Primer.

———. 2015. "Framing Hip Hop: New methodologies for new times." *Urban Education* 50 (1): 31–51. https://journals.sagepub.com/doi/10.1177/0042085914563185.

———. 2016. "Reading qualitative inquiry through critical pedagogy." *International Review of Qualitative Research* 9 (2): 140–146. https://www.jstor.org/stable/26372189.

Dinerstein, A.C. 2015. *The politics of autonomy in Latin America: The art of organising hope.* New York: Palgrave Macmillan.

Diversity-Arts-Australia. 2018. *Voice, agency and integrity: A report on 'beyond tick boxes': A symposium on cultural diversity in the creative sector.* Parramatta, NSW: Diversity Arts Australia, October. http://diversityarts.org.au/app/uploads/Beyond-Tick-Boxes-Report_FINAL1.pdf.

———. 2019. *Shifting the balance: Cultural diverstiy in leadership within the Australian arts, screen and creative sectors.* Parramatta, NSW: Diversity Arts Australia, August. http://diversityarts.org.au/app/uploads/Shifting-the-Balance-DARTS-small.pdf.

Du Bois, W.E.B., and Shawn Leigh Alexander. 2018[1903]. *The souls of black folk: Essays and sketches.* Bibliographies. Amherst, MA: UMass Amherst Libraries.

Dutta, M. 2011. *Communicating social change: Structure, culture, and agency.* London: Taylor and Francis.

———. 2012. *Voices of resistance: Communication and social change.* West Lafayette, IN: Purdue University Press.

———. 2015a. *Communicating health: A culture-centered approach.* Online. New York: Polity Press.

———. 2015b. "Decolonising communication for social change: A culture-centered approach." *Communication Theory (1050–3293)* 25 (2): 123–143. https://doi.org/10.1111/comt.12067.

———. 2018. "Culturally centering social change communication: Subaltern critiques of, resistance to, and re-imagination of development." *Journal of Multicultural Discourses* 13 (2): 87–104. https://www.tandfonline.com/doi/abs/10.1080/17447143.2018.1446440.

———. 2020. *Communication, culture and social change: Meaning, co-option and resistance.* Cham, Switzerland: Springer International Publishing AG.

———. 2021. "What is CCA?." Last modified October 9. Accessed October 1. http://culturecenteredapproach.com/index.php/what-is-cca.

Dwyer, M. 2018. "Bad times behind them: Refugee rap heads festival." *The Sydney Morning Herald*, September 13, 2018, National. https://www.smh.com.au/national/bad-times-behind-them-refugee-rap-heads-festival-20080912-4fj7.html.

Eddie, R. 2018. "Channel Seven protest over African gang 'fear mongering' on Sunday Night program." *The New Daily*, July 12, 2018, Victorian News. Accessed May 26, 2021. https://thenewdaily.com.au/news/state/vic/2018/07/12/channel-7-african-gang-sunday-night-protest/.

Eddie, R., and Y. Zhuang. 2019. "Teen girls stabbed as dozens of women brawl near Fountain Gate." *The Age*, May 15, 2019, Crime. Accessed May 20, 2019. https://www.theage.com.au/national/victoria/teen-girls-stabbed-as-dozens-of-women-brawl-near-fountain-gate-20190515-p51ner.html.

Eitle, T.M., and D.J. Eitle. 2002. "Race, cultural capital, and the educational effects of participation in sports." *Sociology of Education* 75 (2): 123–146. https://doi.org/10.2307/3090288.

Elia, D. 2016. *Daniel Elia - Visions from my kitchen (Feat. Wantu ThaOne) [Explicit]*. You Tube: ALIA Records.

———. 2017a. *Daniel Elia - Shook (Official Video)*. Edited by C.K. Michael and Jordan Montgomery. You Tube: ALIA Records.

———. 2017b. *Lonely*. You Tube: ALIA Records.

———. 2018. *I know it very well*. You Tube: ALIA Records.

———. 2019a. "Daniel Elia - WAKE." In *Thamaniya*, edited by Mills & Boom. You Tube: ALIA Records.

———. 2019b. *Fear (Feat. Elysia Gomez & Tenda Mcfly)*. You Tube: ALIA Records.

Elias, A., F. Mansouri, and Y. Paradies. 2021. *Racism in Australia today*. First edition. ed. Bibliographies. Singapore: Palgrave Macmillan, Springer Nature.

Élkato. 2019. *Matrix*. Soundcloud: YSAS Studio.

Elston, R. 2019. "Melbourne's South Sudanese youth say they're sick of losing their friends to suicide." *SBS News*, June 7, 2019, Australia. Accessed June 20, 2020. https://www.sbs.com.au/news/melbourne-s-south-sudanese-youth-say-they-re-sick-of-losing-their-friends-to-suicide.

Entman, R.M. 2007. "Framing bias: Media in the distribution of power." *Journal of Communication* 57 (1): 163–173. https://doi.org/10.1111/j.1460-2466.2006.00336.x.

Escobar, A. 1992. "Culture, practice and politics: Anthropology and the study of social movements." *Critique of Anthropology* 12 (4): 395–432. https://doi.org/10.1177/0308275X9201200402.

———. 2004. "Beyond the Third World: Imperial globality, global coloniality and anti-globalisation social movements." *Third World Quarterly* 25 (1): 207–230. https://doi.org/10.1080/0143659042000185417.

Esenadus-Squad. 2012. "Esenadus Squad 2012 Ft Bangs & A-Mac. [Music Video]." Malesh P Official. https://www.youtube.com/watch?v=MU7WymNd7x4.

Everest, K. 2019. "Push from Australian State Government and Victorian youth activists against racism." Online: The Organisation for World Peace. Accessed August 30, 2020. https://theowp.org/reports/push-from-australian-state-government-and-victorian-youth-activists-against-racism/.

Exley, B., S. Whatman, and P. Singh. 2018. "Postcolonial, decolonial research dilemmas: Fieldwork in Australian Indigenous contexts." *Qualitative Research* 18 (5): 526–537. https://doi.org/10.1177/1468794118778611.

Eyerman, R., and A. Jamison. 1998. *Music and social movements: Mobilising traditions in the twentieth century*. Cambridge Cultural Social Studies. Cambridge and London: Cambridge University Press.

Fanon, F. 1968. *Black skin, white masks / Frantz Fanon*. Translated by Charls Lam Markmann. Book. New York: Grove Press.

Farnsworth, S. 2017. "Apex crime gang declared a 'non-entity' by Victoria Police." *ABC News*, April 12, 2017. Accessed June 24, 2021. https://www.abc.net.au/news/2017-04-12/victoria-police-declare-apex-crime-gang-non-entity/8440312.

Farouque, F., A. Petrie, and D. Miletic. 2007. "Minister cuts African refugee intake." *The Age*, October 2, 2007. Accessed December 12, 2012. https://www.theage.com.au/national/minister-cuts-african-refugee-intake-20071002-ge5yb1.html.

Farquharson, K., T. Marjoribanks, and D. Nolan. 2018. *Australian media and the politics of belonging*. Online. Melbourne: Anthem Press.

Faruqi, O. 2018a. "African-Australians are using the #AfricanGangs hashtag To fight racist fearmongering." *Junkee*, January 10. 2018, Politics. Accessed May 24, 2021. https://junkee.com/african-gangs-hashtag/141854.

———. 2018b. "Victoria's top cop has ripped into Peter Dutton's comments over 'African gangs'..." *Junkee*, January 10, 2018. Accessed March 24, 2018. http://junkee.com/police-commissioner-african-gangs/141999.

Fenderson, J. 2019. *Building the Black arts movement: Hoyt Fuller and the cultural politics of the 1960s*. ed. Bibliographies. The new black studies series. Urbana, IL: University of Illinois Press.

Ferguson, R. 2018. "Melbourne's Sudanese gangs are real, says Turnbull." *The Australian*, July 18, 2018. Accessed July 29, 2018. https://www.theaustralian.com.au/national-affairs/state-politics/melbournes-sudanese-gangs-are-real-says-turnbull/news-story/422db0dded3541a6b25cda4e9220cfb0.

Fine, M., M.E. Torre, A.G. Oswald, and S. Avory. 2021. "Critical participatory action research: Methods and praxis for intersectional knowledge production." *Journal of Counseling Psychology* 68 (3): 344–356. https://doi.org/10.1037/cou0000445.

Footprints. 2019a. "Grounded project workshops." https://www.youtube.com/watch?v=9wL6A2Tee1o.

———. 2019b. "Gua performance and leadership camp photo's." https://www.facebook.com/media/set/?vanity=footprintsfam&set=a.2733105790095019.

———. 2020. "Footprint enterprises Inc." *Facebook*. https://www.facebook.com/footprintsfam/.

Footprint-Enterprises-Inc., and Mills-and-Boom. 2020. "Born to stand out -a documentary." Naarm: City of Melbourne; Film Victoria; City of Greater Dandenong; Documentary Australia. Accessed May 30, 2022. https://www.facebook.com/borntostandoutproject; https://documentaryaustralia.com.au/project/born-to-stand-out/.

Fraser, A. 2013. "Street habitus: Gangs, territorialism and social change in Glasgow." *Journal of Youth Studies* 16 (8): 970–985. https://doi.org/10.1080/13676261.2013.793791.

Fray, P. 2009. "ACMA names and shames networks for Sudanese coverage." *Crikey*, December 1, 2009, TV & Radio. Accessed December 12, 2012. https://www.crikey.com.au/2009/12/01/acma-names-and-shames-networks-for-sudanese-coverage/.

Freire, P. 1972. *Cultural action for freedom*. Government documents. Penguin education. London: Penguin.

Freire, P., R.R. Barr, and A..M.A. Freire. 2014[1968]. *Pedagogy of hope: Reliving pedagogy of the oppressed*. Bloomsbury Revelations edition. ed. Bibliographies. Bloomsbury revelations. London: Bloomsbury.

Freire, P., D.P. Macedo, M.B. Ramos, and I. Shor. 2018[1968]. *Pedagogy of the oppressed*. Fiftieth anniversary edition. ed. Bibliographies. London: Bloomsbury Academic.

Furlong, A. 2013. *Youth studies: An introduction*. Bibliographies. New York and London: Routledge.

Future-of-the-Rap. 2012. The future of the rap - Amac tha Don feat. Abe and Chingiling. In *Future of rap*. Soundcloud: A-mac Don, Melbourne.

FYA, Foundation-Young-Australians. 2020. *Missing: Young people in Australian news media: Examining the representation of young people by Australian news media in the first six months of COVID-19*. Foundation for Young Australians (FYA) (Online). https://www.fya.org.au/young-people-in-aus-news-media/.

Gartner, M.F. 2024. "Weaving the space between: Navigating identities and institutions as a third-sector pracademic." *Development in Practice (Foerthcoming special issue)*: 1–6. https://doi.org/10.1080/09614524.2024.2353721.

Gatt, K. 2011. "Sudanese refugees in Victoria: An analysis of their treatment by the Australian Government." *International Journal of Comparative and Applied Criminal Justice* 35 (3): 207–219. https://doi.org/10.1080/01924036.2011.591904.

Gatwiri, K., and L. Anderson. 2020. "Boundaries of belonging: Theorising black African migrant experiences in Australia." *International Journal of Environmental Research and Public Health* 18 (1): 38–50. https://doi.org/10.3390/ijerph18010038.

———. 2021. "The Senate has voted to reject critical race theory from the national curriculum. What is it, and why does it matter?" *The Conversation*, June 22, 2021. Accessed June 10, 2021. https://theconversation.com/the-senate-has-voted-to-reject-critical-race-theory-from-the-national-curriculum-what-is-it-and-why-does-it-matter-163102.

———. 2022. *Afrodiasporic identities in Australia: Articulations of Blackness and Africanness*. Singapore: Springer Singapore.

Gatwiri, K., and C. Moran. 2022. "Reclaiming racial dignity: An ethnographic study of how African youth in Australia use social media to visibilise anti-black racism." *Australian Journal of Social Issues* 58 (2): 360–380. https://onlinelibrary.wiley.com/doi/abs/10.1002/ajs4.224.

Gatwiri, K., and M. Townsend-Cross. 2022. "'Block, unfollow, delete': The impacts of the #BlackLivesMatter movement on interracial relationships in Australia." *British Journal of Social Work* 52 (6): 3721–3739. https://doi.org/10.1093/bjsw/bcac008.

Genetic-Circus-Productions. 2016. "Wurundjeri Baggarrook ceremony." https://www.geneticcircusproductions.com/wurundjeri-baggarrook.html.

Gentry, B. 2018. "Political identity: Meaning, measures, and evidence." In *Why Youth Vote: Identity, Inspirational Leaders and Independence*, edited by B. Gentry, 19–48. Cham: Springer International Publishing.

Gildart, K., A. Gough-Yates, S. Lincoln, B. Osgerby, and M. Worley. 2017. *Youth culture and social change: Making a difference by making a noise*. ed. Bibliographies. Palgrave studies in the history of subcultures and popular music. London: Palgrave Macmillan.

Gillborn, D., and G. Ladson-Billings. 2019. "Critical race theory." In *SAGE research methods foundations*, edited by Paul Atkinson. London: SAGE Publications, Ltd.

Giugni, M. 2009. "Political opportunities: From tilly to tilly." *Swiss Political Science Review* 15 (2): 361–367. https://doi.org/10.1002/j.1662-6370.2009.tb00136.x.

Goessling, K.P., D.E. Wright, A.C. Wager, and M. Dewhurst. 2021. *Engaging youth in critical arts pedagogies and creative research for social justice: Opportunities and challenges of arts-based work and research with young people. Routledge research in arts education*. Milton: Taylor and Francis.

Gooding, F.W., M. Brandel, C. Jountti, A. Shadwick, and B. Williams-Bailey. 2016. "Think global, act local: How underground Hip Hop gets down down under." *AlterNative: An International Journal of Indigenous Peoples* 12 (5): 466–479. https://doi.org/10.20507/AlterNative.2016.12.5.3.

Gosa, T.L. 2011. "Counterknowledge, racial paranoia, and the cultic milieu: Decoding Hip Hop conspiracy theory." *Poetics* 39 (3): 187–204. https://doi.org/https://doi.org/10.1016/J.POETIC.2011.03.003.

Graeber, D. 2009. *Direct Action: An ethnography*. Oakland, CA: AK Press.

Green, M. 2015. "Victoria Police officially prohibits racial profiling." *The Age*, September 23, 2015. Accessed May 24, 2021. https://www.theage.com.au/national/victoria/victoria-police-officially-prohibits-racial-profiling-20150923-gjt6bt.html.

Greene, S., K.J. Burke, and M.K. McKenna. 2016. *Youth voices, public spaces, and civic engagement*. ed. Bibliographies. Routledge research in education: 159. New York and London: Routledge.

Griffiths, M., P. Sawikar, and K. Muir. 2009. "Culturally appropriate mentoring for Horn of African young people." *Youth Studies Australia* 28 (2): 32–40. https://research-repository.griffith.edu.au/handle/10072/40242.

Grossman, M., and J. Sharples. May 2010. *Don't go there, young people's perspectives on community safety and policing*. Victoria University https://www.vu.edu.au/sites/default/files/mcd/pdfs/dont-go-there-study-may-2010.pdf.

Guardian. 2020. "Australia protests: Thousands take part in Black Lives Matter and pro-refugee events amid Covid-19 warnings." *The Guardian*, June 13, 2020. Black Lives Matter movement. Accessed May 24, 2021. https://www.theguardian.com/world/2020/jun/13/australia-protests-thousands-take-part-in-black-lives-matter-and-pro-refugee-events-amid-health-warnings.

Guilherme, M., and G. Dietz. 2015. "Difference in diversity: Multiple perspectives on multicultural, intercultural, and transcultural conceptual complexities." *Journal of Multicultural Discourses* 10 (1): 1–21. https://doi.org/10.1080/17447143.2015.1015539.

Habermas, J. 1987. *Knowledge and human interests*. ed. Bibliographies. Social theory. Cambridge, MA: Polity Press.

———. 2007[1987]. *The philosophical discourse of modernity: Twelve lectures*. ed. Bibliographies. Studies in contemporary German social thought. Cambridge, MA: Polity Press.

Hage, G. 1998. *White nation: Fantasies of white supremacy in a multicultural society*. Bibliographies. *Radical writing*. London: Pluto Press.

———. 2014. "Continuity and change in Australian racism." *Journal of Intercultural Studies* 35 (3): 232–237. https://doi.org/10.1080/07256868.2014.899948.

———. 2016. "Recalling antiracism." *Ethnic and Racial Studies* 39 (1): 123–133. https://doi.org/10.1080/01419870.2016.1096412.

Harding, S. 2006. "Transformation vs. resistance. Identity projects: Epistomological resources for social justice movements." In *Identity politics reconsidered*, edited by L. Alcoff, M. Hames-Garca, S. Mohanty, Michael Hames-García, Paula M.L. Moya, and Michael Hames-García, 246–263. New York: Palgrave Macmillan.

Harmon, S. 2020. "Archie Roach and Sampa the Great electrify as Tame Impala win big." *The Guardian* (Aria Awards), November 26, 2020. Accessed November 2, 2020. https://www.theguardian.com/music/2020/nov/25/aria-awards-2020-archie-roach-and-sampa-the-great-electrify-as-tame-impala-win-big.

Harris, A. 2013. *Young people and everyday multiculturalism*. ed. Bibliographies. Critical youth studies: 13. Oxfordshire: Routledge.

Harris, D. 2017. *Creativity, religion and youth cultures*. Edited by Yvette Taylor and Sally Hines. *Routledge Advances in Critical Diversities*. New York and London: Routledge.

Hart, D. 2020. *Who will be a witness? Igniting activism for God's justice, love and deliverance*. Harrisburg, Virginia: Herald Press.

Heath, T. 2018. "Moving beyond multicultural counselling: Narrative therapy, anti-colonialism, cultural democracy and Hip Hop." *International Journal of Narrative Therapy & Community Work* (3): 50–55. https://doi.org/10.3316/informit.022141674671328.

Hebert, Y., D. Hoerder, and I. Schmitt. 2006. *Negotiating transcultural lives: Belongings and social capital among youth in comparative perspective*. Book. Toronto: University of Toronto Press.

Henriques-Gomes, L., and E. Visontay. 2020. "Australian Black Lives Matter protests: Tens of thousands demand end to Indigenous deaths in custody." *The Guardian*, June 7, 2020. Accessed August 8, 2020. https://www.theguardian.com/australia-news/2020/jun/06/australian-black-lives-matter-protests-tens-of-thousands-demand-end-to-indigenous-deaths-in-custody.

Henry-Waring, M.S. 2008. *Multiculturalism and visible migrants and refugees: Exploring the yawning gap between rhetoric and policy in Australia*. Melbourne: University of Melbourne,1 January.

Hickey-Moody, A. 2013a. "Little public spheres." *Performance Paradigm* 9 (1): 4–15. http://www.performanceparadigm.net/wp-content/uploads/2013/08/hickey-moody-anna-little-public-spheres.pdf.

———. 2013b. *Youth, arts and education: Reassembling subjectivity through affect*. ed. Bibliographies. Routledge advances in sociology: 85. New York and London: Routledge.

———. 2016. "Youth agency and adult influence: A critical revision of little publics." *Review of Education, Pedagogy & Cultural Studies* 38 (1): 58–72. https://www.tandfonline.com/doi/abs/10.1080/10714413.2016.1119643.

Highmore, Ben. 2016. *Culture*. First edition. ed. Bibliographies. Key ideas in media and cultural studies. London: Routledge, Taylor & Francis Group.

Hill-Collins, P. 2002. *Black feminist thought: Knowledge, consciousness, and the politics of empowerment*. Second edition. ed. Online. Perspectives on Gender Ser.: v. No. 2. New York and London: Routledge.

———. 2006. *From Black power to Hip Hop: Racism, nationalism, and feminism*. ed. Bibliographies. Politics, history, and social change. Philadelphia: Temple University Press.

———. 2013. "Truth-telling and intellectual activism." *Contexts* 12 (1): 36–41. https://doi.org/10.1177/1536504213476244.

Hohle, R. 2018. *Racism in the neoliberal era: A meta history of elite white power*. ed. Bibliographies. New critical viewpoints on society series. New York and London: Routledge.

Holbraad, M., S. Green, A. Jimenez, V. Das, N. Bird-David, E. Kohn, G. Hage, L. Bear, H. Knox, and B. Kapferer. 2018. "What is analysis? Between theory, ethnography, and method." *Social Analysis* 62 (1): 1–30. https://doi.org/10.3167/sa.2018.620103.

Hopkins, T. 2017. *Monitoring racial profiling: Introducing a scheme to prevent unlawful stops and searches by Victoria Police*. Police Stop Data Working Group, September 5. http://www.policeaccountability.org.au/racial-profiling/shrouded-in-secrecy-racial-profiling-by-victoria-police/.

Hot-in-Juba. 2021. "South Sudanese Australia-based female singer Achai talks music, new music video." Accessed October 19. https://hotinjuba.com/south-sudanese-australia-based-female-singer-achai-talks-music-new-music-video/.

Howley, K. 2008. "Through an activist lens: Social movement theory and practice." *Social Movement Studies* 7 (1): 97–100. https://doi.org/10.1080/14742830801969399.

Hugo, G. December 2009. *Migration between Africa and Australia: A demographic perspective*. Australian Human Rights Commission AHRC (Website). https://humanrights.gov.au/our-work/african-australians-project-migration-between-africa-and-australia-demographic-perspective.

Hunter, F., and B. Preiss. 2018. "Victorians scared to go to restaurants at night because of street gang violence: Peter Dutton." *The Sydney Morning Herald*, January 3, 2018. Accessed March 24, 2018. https://www.smh.com.au/politics/federal/victorians-scared-to-go-to-restaurants-at-night-because-of-street-gang-violence-peter-dutton-20180103-h0cvu4.html.

Hunter, M. 2005. *Race, gender, and the politics of skin tone*. New York: Routledge.

Idriss, S. 2017. *Young migrant identities: Creativity and masculinity*. Online. Youth, young adulthood and society. London: Taylor and Francis.

———. 2021. "Researching race in Australian youth studies." *Journal of Youth Studies*. https://doi.org/10.1080/13676261.2020.1869193.

Idriss, S., R. Butler, and A. Harris. 2021. "Interrogating race, unsettling whiteness: Concepts of transitions, enterprise and mobilities in Australian youth studies." *Journal of Youth Studies* 25 (9): 1–17. https://doi.org/10.1080/13676261.2021.1948516.

IESRI, Ipsos Eureka Social Research Institute. 2011. "Ipsos McKay report: SBS immigration nation." http://www.sbs.com.au/aboutus/corporate/view/id/556/h/SBS-Ipsos-Immigration-Nation-Research-Full-Report.

Iglesias, T., and T. Harris. 2019. "'I Speak Hip Hop': An informative interview about generation Hip Hop and the universal Hip Hop museum." *Journal of Hip Hop Studies* 6 (2): Article 12. https://scholarscompass.vcu.edu/jhhs/vol6/iss2/12.

International-Crisis-Group. 2021. *Toward a viable future for South Sudan*. International Crisis Group, February 10. Accessed July 22, 2022. https://www.crisisgroup.org/africa/horn-africa/south-sudan/300-toward-viable-future-south-sudan.

James, Joy. 2013a. *Seeking the beloved community: A feminist race reader*. ed. Bibliographies. SUNY series, philosophy and race. Alberta, NY: State University of New York Press.

———. 2013b. *Seeking the beloved community: A feminist race reader*. Bibliographies. *SUNY series, philosophy and race*. Alberta: State University of New York Press.

Jasper, J.M. 2010. "Social movement theory today: Toward a theory of action?" 4 (11): 965–976. https://onlinelibrary.wiley.com/doi/abs/10.1111/j.1751-9020.2010.00329.x.

Jenkins, T.S. 2011. "A beautiful mind: Black male intellectual identity and Hip Hop culture." *Journal of Black Studies* 42 (8): 1231–1251. http://www.jstor.org/stable/41304582.

Jineffer, A. 2022. "UN warns of 'return to violence' if parties fail to implement peace." *Eye Radio*, February 11, 2022. Accessed May 30, 2023. https://www.eyeradio.org/un-warns-of-return-to-violence-if-parties-fail-to-implement-peace/.

Jocz, K.E., and J.A. Quelch. 2008. "An exploration of marketing's impacts on society: A perspective linked to democracy." *Journal of Public Policy & Marketing* 27 (2): 202–206. https://www.hbs.edu/ris/Publication%20Files/Exploration%20of%20Marketing's%20Impact%20on%20Society,%20Quelch,%20Jocz,%202008_c30aca32-351a-49bd-8c45-801f9cac6f98.pdf.

Johansen, J.D., and S. Varvin. 2020. "Negotiating identity at the intersection of family legacy and present time life conditions: A qualitative exploration of central issues connected to identity and belonging in the lives of children of refugees." *Journal of Adolescence* 80: 1–9. https://doi.org/10.1016/j.adolescence.2020.01.016.

Johnson, M. 2019. "In Melbourne, Debunking the African gang 'crisis' over coffee." *Sprudge*, January 31, 2019. Accessed December 22, 2020: https://sprudge.com/in-melbourne-debunking-the-african-gang-crisis-over-coffee-135963.html.

Joined-Up-Films. 2018. *Apex Gang - Behind the headlines*. SBS On Demand.

Junub-Television. 2016. "Malesh P. ft. Tébir - Why are we?" *Facebook Music Video*, December 12. https://www.facebook.com/watch/?v=1828025160800691.

Juris, J. 2007. "Practicing militant ethnography with the movement for global resistance in Barcelona." In *Constituent imagination: Militant investigations, collective theorisation*, edited by S. Shukaitis and D. Graeber, 164–176. Chico, CA: AK Press.

Kabir, N. 2006. "Representation of Islam and Muslims in the Australian media, 2001-2005." *Journal of Muslim Minority Affairs* 26 (3): 313–328. https://doi.org/10.1080/13602000601141281.

Kamp, A., and P. Kelly. 2015. *A critical youth studies for the 21st century*. ed. Bibliographies. Youth in a globalising world: Volume 2. Netherlands: Brill.

Kelley, R.D.G. 2003. *Freedom dreams: The black radical imagination*. London: Penguin Random House.

Kelly, L.M. 2022. "Focused ethnography for research on community development non-profit organisations." *Forum Qualitative Sozialforschung Forum: Qualitative Social Research* 23 (2): 1–22. https://doi.org/10.17169/fqs-22.2.3811.

Kelly, L.M., and A. Rogers. 2022. *Internal evaluation in non-profit organisations: practitioner perspectives on theory, research, and practice*. ed. Bibliographies. Routledge studies in the management of voluntary and non-profit organizations. New York and London: Routledge.

Kelly, P., and A. Kamp. 2015. *A critical youth studies for the 21st century*. Leiden: Brill.

Kende, J., O. Sarrasin, A. Manatschal, K. Phalet, and E.G.T. Green. 2022. "Policies and prejudice: Integration policies moderate the link between immigrant presence and anti-immigrant prejudice." *Journal of Personality and Social Psychology* 123 (2): 337–352. https://doi.org/10.1037/pspi0000376.

Kendi, I.X. 2019. *How to be an Antiracist*. Bibliographies. London: One World.

Kenny, S., and P. Connors. 2017. *Developing communities for the future*. Fifth edition. ed. Bibliographies. Southbank: Cengage Learning.

Keyes, C. 2019. Afrika Bambaataa Interview. Marlborough: Adam Matthew Digital.

Khan, R. 2021. "Pragmatic belonging: Migrant young people making claims on the nation." *Journal of Intercultural Studies* 42 (3): 1–16. https://doi.org/10.1080/07256868.2021.1884054.

Khan, S., and A. Pedersen. 2010. "Black African immigrants to Australia: Prejudice and the function of attitudes." *Journal of Pacific Rim Psychology* 4 (2): 116–129. https://doi.org/10.1375/prp.4.2.116.

Knowles, R. 2021. "Coalition supports Pauline Hanson motion to ban critical race theory teachings." *National Indigenous Times*, June 23, 2021. Education News. Accessed July 10, 2021. https://nit.com.au/coalition-supports-pauline-hanson-motion-to-ban-critical-race-theory-teachings/.

Kosley, M. 2020. "Steve Biko: A man of responsibility and action." *Amplify Africa*, September 13, 2020. https://www.amplifyafrica.org/post/steve-biko-a-man-of-responsibility-and-action#:~:text=On%20September%2012%2C%201977%2C%20intellectual,cell%20of%20Pretoria%20Central%20Prison.

Krown. 2018a. *Hold the flag*. You Tube: Military Mind.

———. 2018b. "Let Us live." In *Hold the flag*. You Tube: Military Mind.

———. 2018c. *Trials n' Tribulations*. You Tube: Military Mind.

———. 2019. "Be M.A.D." In *Be M.A.D performance at Footprints Grounded Youth stage*, edited by Mills and Boom. Facebook: On Track program by Mushroom Group.

Kuai, M.N.A. 2009. "Australia to probe into discrimination against Africans." *The New Sudan Vision*, March 16, 2009. Accessed December 13, 2012. https://www.newsudanvision.com/718-2/.

Kubler-Ross, E., and D. Kessler. 2014. *On grief and grieving: Finding the meaning of grief through the five stages of loss*. New York: Simon & Schuster Ltd.

Kwansah-Aidoo, K., and V. Mapedzahama. 2018a. "Black bodies in/out of place?: Afrocentric perspectives and/on racialised belonging in Australia." *Australasian Review of African Studies* 39 (2): 95–121. https://search.informit.org/doi/10.3316/informit.971944437311288.

———. 2018b. "Towards Afrocentric counter-narratives of race and racism in Australia." *Australasian Review of African Studies* 39 (2): 6–18. https://afsaap.org.au/assets/39_2_6-18.pdf.

Land, C. 2015. *Decolonising solidarity: Dilemmas and directions for supporters of Indigenous struggles*. Bibliographies. London: Zed Books.

Land, R.R., and D.O. Stovall. 2009. "Hip Hop and social justice education: A brief introduction." *Equity & Excellence in Education* 42 (1): 1–5. https://doi.org/10.1080/10665680802631238.

Lane, M., S. Rees, J. Ife, and J. Boulet. 2013. *People, power, participation: Living community development*. Non-fiction. Melbourne: Borderlands Cooperative.

Leavy, P. 2015. *Method meets art: Arts-based research practice*. Second edition. ed. Bibliographies. New York: The Guilford Press.

Lee, M., T. Martin, J. Ravulo, and R. Simandjuntak. 2022. "[Dr]illing in the name of: The criminalisation of Sydney drill group ONEFOUR." *Current Issues in Criminal Justice* 34 (4): 339–359. https://doi.org/10.1080/10345329.2022.2100131.

Lentin, A. 2015. "What does race do?" *Ethnic and Racial Studies* 38 (8): 1401–1406. https://doi.org/10.1080/01419870.2015.1016064.

———. 2016. "Racism in public or public racism: Doing anti-racism in 'post-racial' times." *Ethnic and Racial Studies* 39 (1): 33–48. https://doi.org/10.1080/01419870.2016.1096409.

———. 2018. "Fault on both sides? Racism, anti-Racism and the persistence of white supremacy." *ABC*, February 27, 2018. Accessed July 10, 2021. https://www.abc.net.au/religion/fault-on-both-sides-racism-anti-racism-and-the-persistence-of-wh/10094946.

———. 2020. *Why race still matters*. Bibliographies. New York: Polity Press.

———. 2022. "No room for neutrality." *Ethnic and Racial Studies* 45 (3): 485–493. https://doi.org/10.1080/01419870.2021.1994149.

Lentin, A., and G. Titley. 2011. *The crises of multiculturalism: Racism in a neoliberal age*. Bibliographies. London: Zed Books.

Levin, M. 2012. "Academic integrity in action research." *Action Research* 10 (2): 133–149. https://doi.org/10.1177/1476750312445034.

Levy, I.P. 2020. "'Real recognise real': Hip Hop spoken word therapy and humanistic practice." *Journal of Humanistic Counseling* 59 (1): 38–53. https://doi.org/10.1002/johc.12128.

Lord, K. 2018. "Sudanese gangs a 'real concern' in Melbourne, Prime Minister Malcolm Turnbull says." *ABC News*, July 17, 2018. Accessed May 24, 2021. https://www.abc.net.au/news/2018-07-17/sudanese-gangs-real-concern-in-melbourne-malcolm-turnbull-says/10002556.

Luxemberg, R. 1973. *Reform or revolution*. Education for Socialists: Revolutionary classics edition. Atlanta, GA: Pathfinder.

Macaulay, L. 2020. "Australian Sudanese and South Sudanese youths' perspectives on the youth/parent relationship and its influence on the transition to adulthood." *SAGE Journals: Young* 29 (2): 137–156. https://doi.org/10.1177/1103308820937540.

Macaulay, L., and J. Deppeler. 2020. "Perspectives on negative media representations of Sudanese and South Sudanese youths in Australia." *Journal of Intercultural Studies* 41 (2): 213–230. https://doi.org/10.1080/07256868.2020.1724908.

Macmillan, K. 1995. "Giving voice: the participant takes issue." *Feminism & Psychology* 5 (4): 547–552. https://doi.org/10.1177/0959353595054017.

Mahana-Culture. 2022. "Mahana culture: Awakening cultural dignity." Accessed March 6. https://mahanaculture.com/.

Maher, S., S. Atem-Deng, and N. Kindersley. 2018. "South Sudanese Australians: constantly negotiating belonging and identity." *Sudan Studies* 58: 53–64. https://research.monash.edu/en/publications/south-sudanese-australians-constantly-negotiating-belonging-and-i.

Maher, S., J. Blaustein, K. Benier, J. Chitambo, and D. Johns. 2020. "Mothering after Moomba: Labelling, secondary stigma and maternal efficacy in the post-settlement context." *Theoretical Criminology* 26(2): 304–325. https://doi.org/10.1177/1362480620981639.

Majavu, M. 2015. "Becoming an African diaspora in Australia: Language culture, identity." *Ethnic & Racial Studies* 38 (13): 2452–2454. https://www.tandfonline.com/doi/abs/10.1080/01419870.2015.1011181.

———. 2018. "The Whiteness regimes of multiculturalism: The African male experience in Australia." *Journal of Asian and African Studies* 53 (2): 187–200. https://journals.sagepub.com/doi/10.1177/0021909616677372.

———. 2020. "The 'African gangs' narrative: associating Blackness with criminality and other anti-Black racist tropes in Australia." *African & Black Diaspora* 13 (1): 27–39. https://www.tandfonline.com/doi/abs/10.1080/17528631.2018.1541958?journalCode=rabd20.

Majors, R., and J. M. Billson. 1992. *Cool pose: The dilemmas of black manhood in America*. Chicago: Touchstone Books.

Malesh, P. 2015. *Dreamer. Believer.* Apple Music: Malesh P.

———. 2020. *Be Free - Soli x Mez Mariyé: Malesh P Remix'*. Apple Music: Malesh P.

Mansouri, F. 2009a. *The impact of racism upon the health and wellbeing of young Australians*. Melbourne: Foundation for Young Australians.

———. 2009b. *Youth identity and migration: Culture, values and social connectedness*. Book. Urbana, IL: Common Ground.

Mansouri, F., L.G. Beaman, and S. Hussain. 2019. "A transcultural approach to belonging and engagement among migrant youth." Accessed December 23, 2019. https://www.transculturalyouth.com/.

Mansouri, F., and T. Modood. 2021. "The complementarity of multiculturalism and interculturalism: Theory backed by Australian evidence." *Ethnic and Racial Studies* 44 (16): 1–20. https://doi.org/10.1080/01419870.2020.1713391.

Marjoribanks, T., D. Nolan, and K. Farquharson. 2010. "Media representations of Sudanese people in Australia: An initial analysis." Media, Democracy, Change,

Australian, New Zealand Communication Association, Conference, Canberra, Australia.

Marlowe, J.M., D. Harris, and T. Lyons. 2013. *South Sudanese diaspora in Australia and New Zealand: Reconciling the past with the present*. Book. Newcastle upon Tyne: Cambridge Scholars Publishing.

Marshall, W. 2007. "Australian government resorts to anti-African witch hunt." Accessed May 22, 2021. https://www.wsws.org/en/articles/2007/10/suda-o12.html.

Martin, G. 2015. "Stop the boats! Moral panic in Australia over asylum seekers." *Continuum* 29 (3): 304–322. https://doi.org/10.1080/10304312.2014.986060.

Mason, W. 2018. "'Swagger': Urban youth culture, consumption and social positioning." *Sociology* 52 (6): 1117–1133. https://doi.org/10.1177/0038038517698638.

Matereke, K. 2009. "'Embracing the Aussie identity': Theoretical reflections on challenges and prospects for African-Australian youths." *Australasian Review of African Studies* 30 (1): 129–143. https://search.informit.org/doi/10.3316/informit.767932997992824.

Mauthner, N.S., and A. Doucet. 2003. "Reflexive accounts and accounts of reflexivity in qualitative data analysis." *Sociology* 37 (3): 413–431. https://journals.sagepub.com/doi/10.1177/00380385030373002.

MAV, Multicultural-Arts-Victoria. 2019. "Off the grid." [Project]. Hoppers Crossing Youth Resource Centre. MAV. Accessed April 17. https://www.mav.org.au/event/off-the-grid/2019-11-12/.

Mbembe, A. 2021. *Out of the dark night: Essays on decolonization*. Bibliographies. New York: Columbia University Press.

Mbembe, A., and L. Chauvet. 2020. "Afropolitanism." *Nka: Journal of Contemporary African Art* 46 (1): 56–61. https://doi.org/10.18574/nyu/9781479829682.003.0007.

Mbembe, A., and S. Corcoran. 2019. *Necropolitics*. ed. Bibliographies. Theory in forms. Durham, NC: Duke University Press.

Mbembe, A., and L. Dubois. 2017. *Critique of black reason*. ed. Bibliographies. John Hope Franklin Center Book. Durham, NC: Duke University Press.

McGill, E. 2018. *Response to dark ghettos: Injustice, dissent, and reform*. OhioPhilosophy Documentation Center.

McKenzie, N., and J. Tozer. 2021. "Inside racism HQ: How home-grown neo-Nazis are plotting a white revolution." *The Age*, August 16, 2021, Nazis next door. Accessed August 31, 2021. https://www.theage.com.au/national/inside-racism-hq-how-home-grown-neo-nazis-are-plotting-a-white-revolution-20210812-p58i3x.html.

McKeown, S., R. Haji, and N. Ferguson. 2016. *Understanding peace and conflict through social identity theory: Contemporary global perspectives*. Online. Peace psychology book series. New York: Springer International Publishing.

McNiff, S. 2013. *Art as research: Opportunities and challenges*. Bristol: Intellect.

McPhee, S., and N. Chrysanthos. 2021. "Police Minister calls for teacher to be sacked over BLM posters." *The Sydney Morning Herald*, Apri 21, 2021, Education. Accessed June 10, 2021. https://www.smh.com.au/national/nsw/police

-minister-calls-for-teacher-to-be-sacked-over-blm-posters-20210421-p57kz7
.html.
Mhando, L. 2014. *African youth in contemporary literature and popular culture: Identity quest.* ed. Bibliographies. Routledge African studies: 13. New York and London: Routledge.
Micoleta, J. 2012. "Generation Z teens stereotyped as 'lazy and unaware'." *Huffington Post*, June 3, 2012, Teen. Accessed March 1, 2021. https://www.huffpost.com/entry/apathetic-teens-generatio_n_1323577.
Miller, T., and G. Yúdice. 2002. *Cultural policy.* ed. Bibliographies. Core cultural theorists. London: Sage Publications Ltd..
Mills-and-Boom. 2019a. "Footprints trailer." https://www.youtube.com/watch?v=wcqrRwHvciM; https://vimeo.com/329018892; .
———. 2019b. "The grounded festival." https://fb.watch/8hwyQhL48u/.
———. 2019c. "Grounded youth stage promo video – Footprints." https://vimeo.com/322752500?fbclid=IwAR0841_m4TY0gJB1b5xIDxE8mn0aloOMiYFM_6KEa2mVbUTd-bwfPGr4ArQ.
———. 2020a. *Born to stand out.* Melbourne: Footprint Enterprises Inc.
———. 2020b. "The Matrix music video - Élkato" Mills and Boom." https://vimeo.com/459622010.
Milner, K., and N. Khawaja. 2010. "Sudanese refugees in Australia the impact of acculturation stress." *Journal of Pacific Rim Psychology* 4 (1): 19–29. https://journals.sagepub.com/doi/pdf/10.1375/prp.4.1.19.
Milstein, C. 2015. *Taking sides: Revolutionary solidarity and the poverty of liberalism.* Chico, CA: AK Press.
———. 2017. *Rebellious mourning: The collective work of grief.* Book. Chico, CA: AK Press.
Minestrelli, C. 2017. *Australian Indigenous Hip Hop: The politics of culture, identity, and spirituality.* ed. Bibliographies. Routledge studies in Hip Hop and religion. New York and London: Routledge.
Mirzaei, A. 2019. "Where 'woke' came from and why marketers should think twice before jumping on the social activism bandwagon." *The Conversation*, September 9, 2019, Arts & Culture. Accessed December 9, 2020. https://theconversation.com/where-woke-came-from-and-why-marketers-should-think-twice-before-jumping-on-the-social-activism-bandwagon-122713.
Montero, M. 2009. "Community action and research as citizenship construction." *American Journal of Community Psychology* 43 (1–2): 149–161. https://doi.org/10.1007/s10464-008-9224-6.
Moran, C., and K. Gatwiri. 2022. "#BlackLivesMatter: Exploring the digital practises of African Australian youth on social media." *Media, Culture & Society* 44 (7): 1330–1353. https://doi.org/10.1177/01634437221089246.
Moran, C., and B. Robards. 2020. "Researching connected African youth in Australia through social media ethnography and scroll-back interviews." *African Journalism Studies* 41 (4): 83–102. https://www.tandfonline.com/doi/full/10.1080/23743670.2020.1817765.

Moran, L. 2016. "Constructions of race: Symbolic ethnic capital and the performance of youth identity in multicultural Australia." *Ethnic and Racial Studies* 39 (4): 708–726. https://doi.org/10.1080/01419870.2015.1080375.

Moreton-Robinson, A. 2000. *Talkin' up to the white woman: Aboriginal women and feminism*. ed. Bibliographies. UQP Black Australian writers. Brisbane: University of Queensland Press.

———. 2004a. "Whiteness, epistemology and Indigenous representation." In *Whitening race: Essays in social and cultural criticism*, edited by A. Moreton-Robinson, 75–88. Canberra: Aboriginal Studies Press.

———. 2004b. *Whitening race: Essays in social and cultural criticism*. ed. Bibliographies. EBL ebooks online. Alice Springs: Aboriginal Studies Press.

———. 2015. *The white possessive: Property, power, and Indigenous sovereignty*. ed. Bibliographies. Indigenous Americas. Minnesota, MI: University of Minnesota Press.

Morgan, M., and D. Bennett. 2011. "Hip Hop and the global imprint of a black cultural form." *Daedalus* 140 (2): 176–196. https://doi.org/https://doi.org/10.1162/DAED_A_00086.

Morgan, R. 2018. "Melbournians have taken to social media to bite back at Australian Home Affairs Minister Peter Dutton." *SBS News*, January 4, 2018. Accessed March 24. https://www.sbs.com.au/news/melbournebitesback-dutton-mocked-after-african-youth-crime-comments.

Moussa, T., and T. Tony. 2017. *Fight for freedom: Black resistance and identity*. Book. Accra, Ghana: Sub-Saharan Publishers.

Moyo, N. 2019. "Titan's story." In *Close up: Stories of young African Australians*. Victorian Equal Opportunity Human Rights Commission. https://www.youtube.com/watch?v=-CUFVp_8kOg.

Mpofu, W., and M.E. Steyn. 2021. *Decolonising the human: Reflections from Africa on difference and oppression*. Bibliographies. Johannesburg, SA: Wits University Press.

Muller, D. 2018. "Media power: Why the full story of Murdoch, Stokes and the Liberal leadership spill needs to be told." *The Conversation*, September 18, 2018, Politics and Society. Accessed May 20, 2021. https://theconversation.com/media-power-why-the-full-story-of-murdoch-stokes-and-the-liberal-leadership-spill-needs-to-be-told-103522.

———. 2020. "Whether a ratings chase or ideological war, News Corp's coronavirus coverage is dangerous." *The Conversation*, July 22, 2020, Politics and Society. Accessed May 20, 2021. https://theconversation.com/whether-a-ratings-chase-or-ideological-war-news-corps-coronavirus-coverage-is-dangerous-143003.

Mushroom-Creative. 2017. "Voice for change: Episode 8 - Youth for change." In *Voice for change*. Voice for Change. https://www.youtube.com/watch?v=iEU-4jdirz14&feature=emb_logo.

———. 2018a. "Voice for change - Momo and P-Unique." In *Voice for change*. https://voiceforchange.net.au/series/momo-p-unique/.

———. 2018b. "Voice for change series - Krown." In *Voice for change*. https://voiceforchange.net.au/series/krown/; https://www.youtube.com/channel/UCfZ7O1vOhk0O59RvAutus5w.

Nayak, A. 2003. "'Through children's eyes': Childhood, place and the fear of crime." *Geoforum* 34 (3): 303–315. https://doi.org/10.1016/S0016-7185(03)00003-4.

Nazroo, J., J. Jackson, S. Karlsen, and M. Torres. 2007. "The black diaspora and health inequalities in the US and England: Does where you go and how you get there make a difference?" *Sociology of Health and Illness* 29 (6): 811–830. https://onlinelibrary.wiley.com/doi/abs/10.1111/j.1467-9566.2007.01043.x.

Ndhlovu, F. 2014. *Becoming an African diaspora in Australia: Language, culture, identity*. ed. Bibliographies. Melbourne: Palgrave Macmillan.

Ndlovu-Gatsheni, S.J. 2015. *Decoloniality as the future of Africa*. Hoboken, NJ: Wiley-Blackwell.

NEMBC, National-Ethnic-Multicultural-Broadcasters-Council. 2016. "NEMBC National Conference 2016." NEMBC National Conference 2016, Sydney, Australia, November 26–27.

New-Matilda. 2010. "Learning from Liep Gony's Murder." *New-Matilda*, March 23, 2010, Civil Society. Accessed December 12, 2012. https://newmatilda.com/2010/03/23/learning-liep-gonys-murder/.

Nguyen, J., and G. M. Ferguson. 2019. "A global cypher: The role of Hip Hop in cultural identity construction and navigation for Southeast Asian American youth." In *Globalisation as a context for youth development: New directions for child and adolescent development*, edited by J. McKenzie, 99–115. Hoboken, NJ: Wiley Periodicals Inc.

Nichols, N., and J. Ruglis. 2021. "Institutional ethnography and youth participatory action research: A praxis approach." In *The Palgrave Handbook of Institutional Ethnography*, edited by S. Vaughan and P.C. Luken, 527–550. Cham: Palgrave Macmillan.

Nolan, D., K. Farquharson, V. Politoff, and T. Majoribanks. 2011. "Mediated multiculturalism: Newspaper representations of Sudanese migrants in Australia." *Journal of Multicultural Studies* 32 (6): 655–671. https://www.tandfonline.com/doi/abs/10.1080/07256868.2011.618109.

Ntibagirirwa, S. 2018. "Ubuntu as a metaphysical concept." *Journal of Value Inquiry* 52 (1): 113–133. https://doi.org/10.1007/s10790-017-9605-x.

Nunn, C. 2010. "Spaces to speak: Challenging representations of Sudanese Australians." *Journal of Intercultural Studies* 31 (2): 183–198. https://www.tandfonline.com/doi/abs/10.1080/07256861003606366?journalCode=cjis20.

Nur, A., K. Farquharson, and A. Haw. 2021. "'Foreign thugs' and the new menace. Racialised constructions of 'gangs' in Australian news media discourse." Sociological insights for the new normal conference, TASA Conference, November 23–26. https://www.tasa.org.au/content.aspx?page_id=22&club_id=671860&module_id=378582.

Nyuon, N. 2018a. "Nyadol Nyuon: How racism diminishes humanity." *Saturday Paper*, July 14, 2018, Opinion. Accessed August 14, 2020. https://www.thesaturdaypaper.com.au/opinion/topic/2018/07/14/how-racism-diminishes-humanity/15314904006554#hrd.

———. 2018b. "Nyadol Nyuon: The Victorian election and the politics of fear." *Saturday Paper*, November 24, 2018, Opinion. Accessed August 24, 2020. https://

www.thesaturdaypaper.com.au/opinion/topic/2018/11/24/the-victorian-election-and-the-politics-fear/15429780007185.
———. 2021a. "Australia on the brink of deciding what it can become." *The Guardian*, March 16, 2021. Accessed March 30, 2021. https://www.smh.com.au/national/australia-on-the-brink-of-deciding-what-it-can-become-20210316-p57b0u.html.
———. 2021b. "'Go back to your s---hole country': The high cost of standing out, speaking up." *The Sydney Morning Herald*, March 26, 2021, Lifestyle: Life & relationships, Racism. Accessed March 28, 2021. https://www.smh.com.au/lifestyle/life-and-relationships/go-back-to-your-s-hole-country-the-high-cost-of-standing-out-speaking-up-20210325-p57e75.html.
O'Brien, A. 2017. "Black lives matter founders meet Australia's Indigenous community." *SBS*, November 7, 2017. Accessed April 30, 2021. https://www.sbs.com.au/news/black-lives-matter-founders-meet-australia-s-indigenous-community.
Oakes, D. 2012. "African youth crime concern." *The Age*, August 20, 2012. Accessed May 24, 2021. https://www.theage.com.au/national/victoria/african-youth-crime-concern-20120819-24glt.html.
Oakes, D., and D. Cooke. 2007. "Community's anger spills over." *The Age*, October 11, 2007. Accessed December 12, 2012. http://www.theage.com.au/news/national/communitys-anger-spills-over/2007/10/10/1191695993790.html?page=fullpage.
OHCHR, United Nations Human Rights Office of the High Commissioner. 2022. *Australia: People of African descent living under siege of racism, say UN experts*. United Nations Human Rights Office of the High Commissioner OHCHR (Website). Australia, December 21. Accessed July 6, 2023. https://www.ohchr.org/en/press-releases/2022/12/australia-people-african-descent-living-under-siege-racism-say-un-experts.
Okun, T. 2014. *Emperor has no clothes: Teaching about race and racism to people who don't want to know*. Online. Educational leadership for social justice. Charlotte, NC: Information Age Publishing.
Oluo, I. 2018. *So you want to talk about race*. First edition. ed. Bibliographies. New York: Seal Press.
Oware, M. 2018. *I got something to say: Gender, race, and social consciousness in rap music*. Book. New York: Palgrave Macmillan.
Oxoby, R. 2009. "Understanding social inclusion, social cohesion, and social capital." *International Journal of Social Economics* 36 (12): 1133–1152. https://doi.org/10.1108/03068290910996963.
Parter, C., D. Murray, J. Mohamed, B. Rambaldini, T. Calma, S. Wilson, D. Hartz, J. Gwynn, and J. Skinner. 2021. "Talking about the 'r' word: A right to a health system that is free of racism." *Public Health Research & Practice* 31 (1): 1–5. https://www.phrp.com.au/issues/march-2021-volume-31-issue-1/talking-about-the-r-word-a-right-to-a-health-system-that-is-free-of-racism/.
Payne, A. 2021. "How Hip Hop influences identity development." Last modified March 21. Accessed April 9. https://blogs.missouristate.edu/bearbulletin/2021/03/30/how-hip-hop-influences-identity-development/.
Peng, Y., X. Huang, and Y. Zhao. 2017. "An overview of cross-media retrieval: Concepts, methodologies, benchmarks, and challenges." *IEEE Transactions on*

Circuits and Systems for Video Technology 28 (9): 2372–2385. https://ieeexplore.ieee.org/document/7930456.

Penninx, R., and B. Garcés-Mascareñas. 2016. "The Concept of integration as an analytical tool and as a policy concept." In *Integration processes and policies in Europe: Contexts, levels and actors*, edited by B. Garcés-Mascareñas and R Penninx, 11–29. Cham: Springer International Publishing.

Pittaway, T., and J.A.R. Dantas. 2021. "African youth gangs: The marginalisation of South Sudanese young people in Melbourne, Australia." *Journal of Immigrant & Refugee Studies* 22 (1): 178–194. https://doi.org/10.1080/15562948.2021.2017534.

Poe, J. 2015. "Cornel West: Australia is on the path to US-style fascism." *The Guardian*, June 9, 2015, Politics Books. Accessed March 30, 2021. https://www.theguardian.com/books/2015/jun/09/cornel-west-australia-is-on-the-path-to-us-style-fascism.

Pope, L. 2020. *Rap and politics: A case study of Panther, gangster, and hyphy discourses in Oakland, CA (1965–2010)*. New York: Palgrave Macmillan.

Porfilio, B.J. 2015. "Reimagining solidarity: Hip Hop as revolutionary pedagogy." *Cultural Logic: Marxist Theory & Practice,* 46–66. https://www.academia.edu/8255310/Reimagining_Solidarity_Hip_Hop_as_Revolutionary_Pedagogy.

Potter, R.A. 2012. "'Are you afraid of the mix of black and white?' Hip Hop and the spectacular politics of race." In *Music and identity politics,* edited by I. D. Biddle. New York and London: Routledge.

Precel, N. 2019. "'Mayhem' as brawl erupts at soccer match in city's south-east." *The Age*, August 4, 2019, National - Victoria Police. Accessed December 22, 2020. https://www.theage.com.au/national/victoria/brawl-erupts-at-soccer-match-in-city-s-south-east-20190804-p52dsb.html.

Prentis, B. 2017. "The time for treaty is now." *Arena Magazine* (146): 19.

Priest, N., J. Guo, K. Doery, R. Perry, K. Thurber, and R. Jones. 2021. *Racism, racial discrimination and child and youth health: A rapid evidence synthesis*. VIC Health; Australian National University; Murdoch Children's Research Institute, May 27. https://apo.org.au/node/313551?mc_cid=a341e06236&mc_eid=cd73e20969.

Queen, P. 2018a. "Black panther." In *Bring Black back*. Spotify, Melbourne: Queen P.

———. 2018b. "Hummingbird." In *Bring Black back*. Spotify, Melbourne: Queen P.

———. 2018c. "Queen P - Effort (Music Video)." In *Bring Black back*. https://www.youtube.com/watch?v=-DMKuwgL6ng.

———. 2018d. "Queen with colour [Official Music Video]." In *Bring Black back*. https://www.youtube.com/watch?v=VvairPC3tJM.

Quinn, E. 2003. "Performing identity/performing culture: Hip Hop as text, pedagogy, and lived practice." *Popular Music* 22 (2): 247–258.

Quinn, K. 2020. "Are all white people racist? Why critical race theory has us rattled." *The Sydney Morning Herald*, November 7, 2020. Culture Wars. Accessed January 29, 2021. https://www.smh.com.au/culture/books/are-all-white-people-racist-why-critical-race-theory-has-us-rattled-20201105-p56bwv.html.

Raj-Melkote, S., and A. Singhal, eds. 2021. *Handbook of communication and development*. Edited by Elgar Handbooks in Development, Sociology, social policy and education 2021. Elgar Online: Edward Elgar Publishing.

Rambaree, K., and I. Knez. 2016. "Effects of ethnicity and gender on youth health." *Cogent Social Sciences* 2 (1): 1186136. https://doi.org/10.1080/23311886.2016.1186136.

RCOA, Refugee-Council-of-Australia. 2018. "Key facts on the conflict in South Sudan." Last modified December 23, 2018. Accessed December 22. https://www.refugeecouncil.org.au/south-sudan/#:~:text=Around%2024%2C000%20South%20Sudanese%20people,the%20nation%20declared%20its%20independence.

Reeves, S., A. Kuper, and B.D. Hodges. 2008. "Qualitative research methodologies: Ethnography." *BMJ* 337: a1020. https://doi.org/10.1136/bmj.a1020.

Reeves, S., J. Peller, J. Goldman, and S. Kitto. 2013. "Ethnography in qualitative educational research: AMEE Guide No. 80." *Medical Teacher* 35 (8): e1365–e1379. https://doi.org/10.3109/0142159X.2013.804977.

Reiland, R. 2013. *The Hip Hop movement: From R&B and the civil rights movement to rap and the Hip Hop generation*. Book. Lanham, MD: Lexington Books.

Richmond, M., and A. Charnley. 2022. *Fractured: Race, class, gender and the hatred of identity politics*. London: Pluto Press.

Ritzer, G. 2005. *Encyclopedia of social theory*. Book. Thousand Oaks, CA: Sage Publications.

Rogers, A., and L. Kelly. 2024. *A Toolkit for Effective Everyday Activism*. First edition. London: Routledge.

Romm, N.R.A. 2015. "Reviewing the transformative paradigm: A critical systemic and relational (Indigenous) lens." *Systemic Practice and Action Research* 28 (5): 411–427. https://doi.org/10.1007/s11213-015-9344-5.

Rosaldo, R. 2006. "Identity politics: An ethnography by a participant." In *Identity politics reconsidered*, edited by L. Alcoff, M. Hames-Garca, S. Mohanty, M. Hames-García, Paula M. L. Moya and M. Hames-García, 118–125. New York: Palgrave Macmillan.

Rose, T. 1994. *Black noise: Rap music and black culture in contemporary America*. Music/culture. Hanover, NH: University Press of New England.

Rosenblatt, P.C., and B.R. Wallace. 2005. "Narratives of grieving African Americans about racism in the lives of deceased family members." *Death Studies* 29 (3): 217–235. https://doi.org/10.1080/07481180590916353.

Run, P. 2013. "Unnecessary encounters: South Sudanese refugees' experiences of racial profiling in Melbourne." *Social Alternatives* 32 (3): 20–25. https://search.informit.org/doi/abs/10.3316/ielapa.773643522189678.

Ryan, B. 2018. "Melbourne's African leaders call for calm as Peter Dutton's gangs comment provokes backlash." *ABC News*, January 5, 2018. Accessed March 24, 2018. http://www.abc.net.au/news/2018-01-04/african-communities-meet-to-respond-to-gang-crime-debate/9303228.

Said, E.W. 1994. *Culture and imperialism*. London: Vintage.

———. 2003[1968]. *Orientalism*. [New preface edition] ed. Bibliographies. Westminster: Penguin.

Salvídar, J. 2006. "Border thinking, minoritised studies, and realist interpellations: The coloniality of power from Gloria Anzaldúa to Arundhati Roy." In *Identity politics reconsidered*, edited by L. Alcoff, M. Hames-Garca, S. Mohanty, M. Hames-García, Paula M. L. Moya and M. Hames-García, 152–170. New York: Palgrave Macmillan.

———. 2007. "Unsettling race, coloniality, and caste: Anzaldu'a's borderlands/ La frontera, Martinez's parrot in the oven, and Roy's the god of small things." *Cultural Studies* 21 (2/3): 339–367. https://www.tandfonline.com/doi/abs/10.1080 /09502380601162563.

Sampa-the-Great. 2020a. "ARIA awards." Facebook, November 26. https://www.facebook.com/sampathegreat/photos/pcb.3771695662861089/3771616632868992.

———. 2020b. "Sampa the great - Black Atlantis - Planet Afropunk performance." You Tube. https://www.youtube.com/watch?v=Mx2a9s3mOgU.

———. 2020c. "Sampa the great: Final form | 2020 ARIA Awards #Livestream" (Performance). https://youtu.be/Y4buIYNL01U.

Samuels, A.J. 2018. "The AfroReggae cultural group: A rebirth of hope within Rio De Janeiro's Favelas." Accessed October 1. https://theculturetrip.com/south -america/brazil/articles/the-afroreggae-cultural-group-a-rebirth-of-hope-within-rio -s-favelas/.

Sankara, T. 1989. *Thomas Sankara speaks: The Burkina Faso Revolution, 1983–87*. New York: Pathfinder Press.

Sawyer, P. 2006. "Identity as calling: Martin Luther King on War." In *Identity politics reconsidered. The future of minority studies*, edited by L.M. Alcoff, M. Hames-García, S.P. Mohanty and P.M.L. Moya. New York: Palgrave Macmillan.

SBS. 2020. "The Australian musician fighting racist narratives about African migrants." *My Australia*, January 21, 2020. Accessed April 16, 2020. https://www .sbs.com.au/news/the-australian-musician-fighting-racist-narratives-about-african -migrants.

Scheurich, J.J. 1993. "Toward a white discourse on white racism." *Educational Researcher* 22 (8): 5–10. https://doi.org/10.2307/1176814. http://www.jstor.org/ stable/1176814.

Schweitzer, R., S. Perkoulidis, S. Krome, C. Ludlow, and M. Ryan. 2005. "Attitudes towards refugees: The dark side of prejudice in Australia." *Australian Journal of Psychology* 57 (3): 170–179. https://doi.org/10.1080/00049530500125199.

Scott, J.C. 1985. *Weapons of the weak: Everyday forms of peasant resistance*. London: Yale University Press.

Sen, A. 2001[1999]. *Development as freedom*. Bibliographies. Oxford: Oxford University Press.

Shepherd, S. 2021. "Too many young African-Australians are in jail. Some blame police, but the data tells a more complex story." *ABC News*, March 25, 2021. Accessed March 30, 2021. https://www.abc.net.au/news/2021-03-25/racial -profiling-concerns-african-australian-youth-imprisonment/13252594#:~:text=So %20what%20is%20behind%20the,by%20some%20members%20that%20group. &text=Crimes%20against%20the%20person%20include,often%20involve %20less%20police%20discretion.

Shepherd, S., D. Newton, and K. Farquharson. 2018. "Pathways to offending for young Sudanese Australians." *Australian and New Zealand Journal of Criminology* 51 (4): 481–501. https://journals.sagepub.com/doi/abs/10.1177/0004865817749262.

Shepherd, S., and B.L. Spivak. 2020. "Estimating the extent and nature of offending by Sudanese-born individuals in Victoria." *Australian & New Zealand Journal of Criminology* 53 (3): 352–368. https://doi.org/10.1177/0004865820929066.

Shoneye, T. 2018. "As a Black woman, I hate the term 'person of colour.'" *The Independant*, April 22, 2018. Accessed June 24, 2018. https://www.independent.co.uk/voices/black-women-people-of-colour-racism-beyonce-coachella-black-lives-matter-a8316561.html.

Sithole, T. 2014. "Achille Mbembe: Subject, subjection, and subjectivity." PhD, African Politics, University of South Africa. http://hdl.handle.net/10500/14323.

Smethurst, J.E. 2005. *The Black Arts Movement: literary nationalism in the 1960s and 1970s*. ed. Bibliographies. The John Hope Franklin series in African American history and culture. Chapel Hill: University of North Carolina Press.

SMH, Sydney-Morning-Herald. 2007. "Andrews unbowed, Sudanese tensions brew." *SMH*, October 11, 2007, National. Accessed December 13, 2012. https://www.smh.com.au/national/andrews-unbowed-sudanese-tensions-brew-20071011-gdrbhk.html.

Smith, B. 2011. "From the frontline 1: 'Boys, you wanna give me some action?' Interventions into policing of racialised communities in Melbourne." *Somatechnics* 1 (1): 48–58. https://doi.org/10.3366/soma.2011.0005.

Smith, B., and G. Davy. 2018. "Over-policing of young people: Making youth programs safer." *Police Accountability Project*. Accessed July 14. https://www.policeaccountability.org.au/racial-profiling/over-policing-of-young-people/.

Smith, E.M., R. González, and C. Frigolett. 2021. "Understanding change in social-movement participation: The roles of social norms and group efficacy." *Political Psychology* 42 (6): 1037–1051. https://onlinelibrary.wiley.com/doi/abs/10.1111/pops.12733.

Smith, K.L., and I.G. Zepp. 1986. *Search for the beloved community: The thinking of Martin Luther King, Jr.* ed. Bibliographies. Lanham, MD: University Press of America.

Smith, R. 2018. "Protest planned for Channel 7 headquarters over 'racist' Sunday Night story." *News.com.au*, July 13, 2018. https://www.news.com.au/entertainment/tv/current-affairs/protest-planned-for-channel-7-headquarters-over-racist-sunday-night-story/news-story/401030282572d1a6f2319f5f16b9d35e.

Solórzano, D.G., and D.D. Bernal. 2001. "Examining transformational resistance through a critical race and latcrit theory framework: Chicana and chicano students in an urban context." *Urban Education* 36 (3): 308–342. https://doi.org/10.1177/0042085901363002.

Solórzano, D.G., and T.J. Yosso. 2002. "Critical race methodology: Counter-storytelling as an analytical framework for education research." *Qualitative Inquiry* 8 (1): 23–44. https://doi.org/10.1177/107780040200800103.

Sonn, C., and A. Baker. 2016. "Creating inclusive knowledges: Exploring the transformative potential of arts and cultural practice." *International Journal of*

Inclusive Education 20 (3): 215–228. https://www.tandfonline.com/doi/full/10.1080/13603116.2015.1047663.

Spivak, G.C. 1999. *A critique of postcolonial reason: Toward a history of the vanishing present.* ed. Bibliographies. Cambridge, MA: Harvard University Press.

Stefancic, J. 2014. *Critical race theory.* Chichester: John Wiley & Sons, Ltd.

Stephenson Jr, M.O., S.A. Tate, and A. Goldbard. 2015. *Arts and community change: Exploring cultural development policies, practices, and dilemmas.* ed. Bibliographies. The community development research and practice series. London: Routledge.

Stratton, J. 2020. *Multiculturalism, whiteness and otherness in Australia.* Book. Cham: Palgrave Macmillan.

Subcultures-Network. 2014. *Subcultures, popular music and social change.* Edited by Subcultures Network. Bibliographies. Newcastle upon Tyne: Cambridge Scholars Publishing.

Sudo-Boiz. 2010. "Memory's lane." In *Strive for the stars.* ReverbNation, Melbourne: Sudo Boiz.

Sullivan, J.M. 2018. *Dimensions of blackness: Racial identity and political beliefs.* Edited by J. Winburn and W.E. Cross. ed. Bibliographies. SUNY series in African American studies. Albany, NY: State University of New York Press.

Summer, K., and Footprints. 2022a. "Born to stand out documentary." https://www.youtube.com/watch?v=T7hhRWdvTVA.

———. 2022b. "Born to stand out trailer." https://www.youtube.com/watch?v=pv3zCHm56gc.

Sutherland, N. 2013. "Book review: Social movements and activist ethnography." *Organization* 20 (4): 627–635. https://doi.org/10.1177/1350508412450219.

TACSA, The-Australian-Centre-for-Social-Innovation. 2020. "Improving mental health with South Sudanese Australian communities." Activating Social Health. Last modified November. Accessed August 27. https://tacsi.org.au/work/ssa-mental-health/.

TASA, The-Australian-Sociological-Association. 2021. *TASA MEM Conversations series - Decolonising methodologies: BIWOC perspective.* You Tube: The Australian Sociological Association. Accessed July 21, 2022. https://www.youtube.com/watch?v=J4HiTA5s_74.

Taylor, K.Y. 2016. *From #BlackLivesMatter to black liberation.* ed. Bibliographies. Chicago: Haymarket Books.

The-Drum-Theatre. 2020. "B.C.M. showcased in drum theatre home delivery." In *Drum theatre home delivery.* The Drum Theatre. https://www.youtube.com/watch?v=CvvBj83TgpU.

Thiong'o, Ngũgĩ wa. 1972. *Homecoming: Essays on African and Caribbean literature, culture and politics.* ed. Bibliographies. Studies in African literature. London: Heinemann.

———. 1981. *Writers in politics: Essays.* ed. Bibliographies. Studies in African literature. London: Heinemann Educational Books.

———. 1983. *Barrel of a pen: Resistance to repression in neo-colonial Kenya.* Nonfiction. London: New Beacon Books.

———. 1986. *Decolonising the mind: The politics of language in African literature.* ed. Bibliographies. Studies in African literature. Oxford: J. Currey.

———. 1993. *Moving the centre: The struggle for cultural freedoms.* Non-fiction. Studies in African literature New series. Oxford: J. Currey.

———. 1998. *Penpoints, gunpoints, and dreams: Toward a critical theory of the arts and the state in Africa.* Online. Oxford: Clarendon Press.

Tiffen, R. 2020. "James Murdoch's resignation is the result of News Corp's increasing shift to the right – not just on climate." *The Guardian*, August 2, 2020, Politics and Society. Accessed May 20, 2021. https://theconversation.com/james-murdochs-resignation-is-the-result-of-news-corps-increasing-shift-to-the-right-not-just-on-climate-143799.

Tillmann-Healy, L.M. 2003. "Friendship as method." *Qualitative Inquiry* 9 (5): 729–749. https://doi.org/10.1177/1077800403254894.

Topsfield, J. . 2008. "Sudanese youth feel sharp end of racism." *The Age*, 2008. Accessed December 15, 2012. http://www.theage.com.au/national/sudanese-youth-feel-sharp-end-of-racism-20081217-6zxi.html.

Torre, M.E. 2009. "Participatory action research and critical race theory: Fueling spaces for nos-otras to research." *The Urban Review* 41 (1): 106–120. https://doi.org/10.1007/s11256-008-0097-7.

Touraine, A. 1998. "Social transformations of the twentieth century." *International Social Science Journal* 50 (156): 165–171. https://onlinelibrary.wiley.com/doi/abs/10.1111/1468-2451.00120.

Trapp, E. 2005. "The push and pull of Hip Hop: A social movement analysis." *American Behavioral Scientist* 48 (11): 1482–1495. https://doi.org/10.1177/0002764205277427.

Triandafyllidou, A. 2009. "Sub-Saharan African immigrant activists in Europe: Transcultural capital and transcultural community building." *Ethnic & Racial Studies* 32 (1): 93–116. https://doi.org/10.1080/01419870802196021.

Truman, C., B. Humphries, and D.M. Mertens. 2000. *Research and inequality.* Non-fiction. London: UCL Press.

Tuan, M. 1998. *Forever foreigners or honorary whites? The Asian ethnic experience today.* New Brunswick: Rutgers University Press.

Tuhiwai-Smith, L. 2021. *Decolonising methodologies: Research and Indigenous peoples.* Book. Vol. Third edition. London: Zed Books.

Udah, H. 2017. "'Not by default accepted': The African experience of Othering and being Othered in Australia." *Journal of Asian and African Studies* 53 (3): 384–400. https://doi.org/10.1177/0021909616686624.

Vaughan, G. M., and M.A. Hogg. 2011. *Social psychology.* Sixth edition. Frenchs Forest: Pearson Australia.

VEOHRC, Victorian-Equal-Opportunity Human-Rights-Commission. 2008. *Rights of passage: The experiences of Australian-Sudanese young people*, December. Printmode Melbourne. https://apo.org.au/node/3038.

VIC-Health. 2005. *Social inclusion as a determinant of mental health and wellbeing.* Mental Health and Wellbeing Unit. Carlton: Vichealth.

———. 2008. *Ethnic and race based discrimination as a determinant of mental health and wellbeing*. Carlton: VicHealth.

———. 2009. *Evaluation of the community arts development scheme: Improving health and wellbeing through social connection and the arts*. Victorian Health Promotion Foundation (VIC Health). Carlton: VicHealth.

VIC-Health, Data61, CSIRO, and MYAN. 2017. *Bright futures: Spotlight on the wellbeing of young people from refugee and migrant backgrounds*. Carlton: VicHealth.

Vice-Australia. 2018. "South-Sudanese Australians talk police, politics and the media." *Vice Australia*, August 9, 2018. Accessed March 21, 2020. https://www.facebook.com/watch/?v=879825515549385; https://www.vice.com/en/article/ywkq4w/south-sudanese-australians-talk-police-politics-and-the-media?utm_source=vicefblocalau&fbclid=IwAR1Ypygp-wOeIgg52LZrWIw2eB8yRpV9lgqpeU29RhZQ2LUeGNV4GzSda50.

Victorian-Government. 2018. *Victorian African communities action plan: Building inclusive communities, improving outcomes and creating sustainable opportunities for Victorians with African heritage; Working together now and over the long term*. Online: State of Victoria (Department of Premier and Cabinet). https://www.vic.gov.au/sites/default/files/2020-11/Victorian-African-Communities-Action-Plan.pdf.

Vincent, D.N., and C Nader. 2013. *The boy who wouldn't die*. Non-fiction. Melbourne: Fairfax.

Vrajilal, A. 2020. "ARIA Awards: Sampa The Great delivers epic takedown of racism in the music industry." *Huffington Post*, November 26, 2020. https://www.huffingtonpost.com.au/entry/aria-awards-2020-sampa-the-great_au_5fbe1db2c5b66bb88c62a2da.

Wadsworth, Yoland. 2016. *Do it yourself social research*. Third edition. ed. Bibliographies. London: Routledge.

Wahlquist, C. 2018. "Is Melbourne in the grip of African gangs? The facts behind the lurid headlines." *The Guardian*, January 3, 2018. Accessed April 13, 2018. https://www.theguardian.com/australia-news/2018/jan/03/is-melbourne-in-the-grip-of-african-gangs-the-facts-behind-the-lurid-headlines.

Ware, V., and K. Dunphy. 2019. "Methodological practices in research on arts-based programs in international development: A systematic review." *The European Journal of Development Research* 31 (3): 480–503. https://doi.org/10.1057/s41287-018-0164-1.

———. 2020. "How do arts programmes contribute in International Development? A systematic review of outcomes and associated processes." *Progress in Development Studies* 20 (2): 140–162. https://doi.org/10.1177/1464993420908682.

Waters, J. 2011. "Documents appear to show race profiling by police." May 4, 2011. Accessed April 13, 2018. http://www.abc.net.au/news/2011-05-04/documents-appear-to-show-race-profiling-by-police/2703010?site=melbourne.

Weng, E., and F. Mansouri. 2021. "'Swamped by Muslims' and facing an 'African gang' problem: Racialised and religious media representations in Australia." *Continuum* 35 (3): 468–486. https://doi.org/10.1080/10304312.2021.1888881.

Whitaker, R. 2021. "Reflections on Afrika Bambaataa's universal Zulu Nation: Horizons, Hip Hop, and hybridity." *Journal of Contemporary Religion* 36 (1): 19–36. https://doi.org/10.1080/13537903.2020.1864105.

White, R., ed. 2009. *Concepts and methods of youth work. Doing youth work in Australia vol. 1.* Hobart: Australian Clearinghouse for Youth Studies.

White, R., and R. Mason. 2006. "Youth gangs and youth violence: Charting the key dimensions." *Australian & New Zealand Journal of Criminology* 39 (1): 54–70. https://doi.org/10.1375/acri.39.1.54.

White, R.D. 1999. *Ethnic youth gangs in Australia: Do they exist?* Bibliographies. Carlton: Australian Multicultural Foundation.

Wilder, G. 2015. *Freedom time: Negritude, decolonisation, and the future of the world.* Bibliographies. Durham, NC: Duke University Press.

Williams, S. 2015. "'Representing inclusive communities:' What does social inclusion mean in Australia when you obviously stand out?" Masters of Social Change and Sustainability Youth Participatory Action Research - traditional thesis, Anthropology and Social Change, Oases Graduate School.

———. 2016. "'Representing Inclusive Communities:' What does social inclusion mean in Australia when you obviously stand out?" Proceedings of the 38th AFSAAP Conference: 21st Century Tensions and Transformation in Africa, Deakin University, February https://afsaap.org.au/assets/sarah_williams_AFSAAP2015.pdf.

———. 2020. "'Decolonising the mind provocation' - Community Development Roundtable." *Deakin University Community Development Roundtable*, July 24. https://sarahwilliamsnyagoa.wordpress.com/2020/07/31/decolonising-the-mind-provocation-community-development-roundtable/.

———. 2021. "Resistance and uprising." *Journal of Asian Women's Resource Centre for Culture and Theology* 40: 48. https://awrc4ct.org/.

———. 2022a. "Australian identity politics playing tricks for young South Sudanese Australians." *Journal of Intercultural Studies* 43 (5): 657–674. https://doi.org/10.1080/07256868.2022.2063821.

———. 2022b. "'Born to stand out:' The role of Hip Hop for young South Sudanese Australains in building their political voice to resist Australian Whiteness discourse." Doctor of Philosophy Conventional Thesis, International and Community Development, Deakin University.

Wilson, S. 2008. *Research is ceremony: Indigenous research methods.* ed. Bibliographies. Blackpoint: Fernwood Pub.

Windle, J. 2008. "The racialisation of African youth in Australia." *Social Identities* 14 (5): 553–566. https://doi.org/10.1080/13504630802343382.

Womack, Y. 2013. *Afrofuturism: The world of black sci-fi and fantasy culture.* First edition. ed. Bibliographies. Chicago, IL: Chicago Review Press.

Wray-Lake, L., and L.S. Abrams. 2020. "Pathways to civic engagement among urban youth of color." *Monographs of the Society for Research in Child Development* 85 (2): 7–154. https://doi.org/10.1016/j.childyouth.2014.03.012.

Wyn, J., H. Cuervo, and J. Cook. 2019. *Expanding theoretical boundaries from youth transitions to belonging and new materiality.* Chapter. Blackburn: Taylor and Francis.

Wyn, J., and D. Woodman. 2006. "Generation, youth and social change in Australia." *Journal of Youth Studies* 9 (5): 495–514. https://www.tandfonline.com/doi/abs/10.1080/13676260600805713.

YACVIC. "Youth offending – know the facts." March 28, 2017. https://www.yacvic.org.au/advocacy/youth-offending-know-the-facts/.

Yaw, A-G. 2018. "Afrocentricity: An important feature of the Pan African tradition." Politics and Society. This is Africa. Last modified October 2, 2018. Accessed March 10. https://thisisafrica.me/politics-and-society/afrocentricity-an-important-feature-of-the-pan-african-tradition/.

Yo, J. 2006. *Encyclopedia of multicultural psychology.* ed. Bibliographies. London; Thousand Oaks: SAGE Publications.

Yosso, T.J. 2005. "Whose culture has capital? A critical race theory discussion of community cultural wealth." *Race, Ethnicity and Education* 8 (1): 69–91. https://doi.org/10.1080/1361332052000341006.

Young, J. 1971. *The drugtakers: The social meaning of drug use.* Non-fiction. Sociology and the modern world. London: MacGibbon and Kee.

———. 2009. "Moral panic: Its origins in resistance, resentment and the translation of fantasy into reality." *British Journal of Criminology* 49 (1): 4–16. https://www.jstor.org/stable/23639652.

Yusuf, K. 2018. "On Black Panther, representation and Afrofuturism." [Blog]. *La Grande Afrique.* Accessed February 8, 2021. https://lagrandeafrique.com/on-black-panther-representation-and-afrofuturism/#:~:text=While%20Black%20Panther%20didn't,who%20kept%20the%20movement%20alive.

Yuval-Davis, N. 2007. "Intersectionality, citizenship and contemporary politics of belonging." *Critical Review of International Social and Political Philosophy* 10 (4): 561–574. https://www.tandfonline.com/doi/abs/10.1080/13698230701660220.

Zhou, N. 2019. "A current affair accused of inciting violence in Melbourne 'race war' story." *The Conversation*, January 4, 2019, Australian Media. Accessed May 26, 2021. https://www.theguardian.com/media/2019/jan/04/a-current-affair-accused-of-inciting-violence-in-melbourne-race-war-story.

Zihabamwe, N. 2022. "WGEPAD Australia end of mission statement." African Australian Advocacy Centre. Last modified December 20. Accessed June 1. https://www.africanaustralianadvocacy.org.au/wgepad-australia-end-of-mission-statement/.

Zwangobani, K. 2008. "From diaspora to Multiculture: In search of a youthful Pan-African identity." *Australasian Review of African Studies* 29 (1/2): 51–65. https://search.informit.org/doi/10.3316/INFORMIT.370063163182141.

Index

A1 Krashn, artist, 172–73, 196–97
African Australians/African identity, xi, 12, 28, 123, 182, 193, 242
African diaspora [in Australia], 6–10, 28, 33, 36, 45, 60, 62, 68, 72, 76, 85, 93, 107, 109, 118, 121–22, 125, 131, 145, 154, 163, 170, 181, 185, 189, 213, 228, 268, 271
African Mic Controllers (AMCs), artists, 72
Afrocentric, 100, 118, 180, 211, 228, 231, 247, 266; Afrocentric black diaspora/Afrocentric young South Sudanese Australians, 208, 233; Afrocentric identities/Afrocentric identity politics, 54, 126, 133; Afrocentricity, 203–4, 208, 216, 221, 229, 242; Afrocentric perspective/s/Afrocentric counter-narratives/Afrocentric scholar, 27, 203, 233; Afrocentric style/Afrocentric dance style, 15, 215; Afrocentric talents/Afrocentric artists, 209, 212; Afrocentric tracks, 130
Afrodiasporic, 228, 233; Afrodiasporic experiences [in Australia]/urban contemporary music and visuals, 93; Afrodiasporic influences, 100; Afrodiasporic struggles, 60; Afrodiasporic vision, 246; Afrodiasporic youth cultures, 258
Afrofuturism/black futures, 93, 107, 135, 182–83; Afrofuturistic/Afrofuturistic themes/Afrofuturistic vision, 131, 136, 173, 183, 228, 233, 247, 266; Afrofuturists, 183
Afropolitan/Afropolitanism, 163, 183, 203, 208, 216, 221; Afropolitan themes, 54, 211
Akimera, spoken-word artist, workshop facilitator, 45, 209, 212–13
Amac Don, 130, 141, 158, 238, 246
antiracism/as a social movement, xv, 27, 35, 100, 246, 253, 261–62, 265, 267, 271; antiracism approaches/Antiracism initiatives/Antiracism project/s, 60, 262, 267; antiracism goals, 267; antiracism policy, 25, 211, 252, 271; antiracism practice, 245; antiracism scholarship/Antiracism educator/Antiracism discourse, 14, 55, 108, 123, 174, 254, 262; antiracist perspective, 36
antiracist/Antiracist work/Antiracist organising/Antiracist power, 64, 135, 261–62; antiracist idea, Antiracist ethic/Antiracist perspective/s, xi, 27, 271; antiracist inquiry/Antiracist

research/Antiracist ethnographer, 34–35; antiracist solidarity/Antiracist practice, 135, 267
artivism, 5, 7, 23, 49, 51, 60, 72, 76, 85, 94–98, 102, 110, 144–45, 163–64, 166, 173–74, 203, 220–22, 225–29, 232, 236, 241–42, 245–46, 251, 256–57, 261, 263, 269; artivist/s, Born to Stand Out (BTSO), artivist, artivist identity/ies, 24–25, 35, 37–38, 40–41, 44, 47, 61, 67, 71–73, 76, 77, 79, 81, 85, 94–95, 97–98, 108, 120, 122–24, 126–33, 136, 144–45, 155, 160, 162–63, 165, 168–70, 180–83, 185–87, 189, 204–5, 207, 220, 221, 228, 231–32, 234–36, 238–39, 241–42, 245–46, 249, 251–52, 256, 259, 264, 266, 269
arts-based development project/s, 7, 10, 45, 50, 97, 107, 207, 227, 263
arts-based or artistic inquiry/counter-narrative arts-based inquiry/creative inquiry/critical arts-based inquiry, 22, 24, 48–49, 94, 144, 180, 260
aspirations/capacity to aspire/in relation to freedom, 22, 51, 94–95, 106–7, 181, 188, 221, 226, 241–43, 262–63
Australian society, 4–9, 12–13, 16, 18, 21, 23, 32, 50, 54–55, 59–60, 62, 106–7, 113, 122, 146, 148, 154, 170, 183, 189, 204, 206, 209, 225, 237, 244

belonging/contemporary politics of belonging, 8–9, 12, 16–17, 19, 32, 67, 76, 112, 206, 210, 254, 264, 266
beloved community, xv, 174, 210, 262
BIPOC/Black, Indigenous, People of Colour/BIPOC communities/BIPOC experiences in Australia/BIPOC across the globe, xv, 6–7, 14–15, 19, 34, 36, 44, 46, 51, 56–57, 59, 65, 71, 75, 81–82, 95–96, 98, 105, 107–9, 111, 113–14, 126, 129, 143, 158, 174, 179–82, 198, 210–11, 216–17, 230–31, 234, 241, 244–48, 253–54, 256, 265–68, 272
black/black skin colour/black person, people and communities [in Australia]/black lives/black bodies in or out of place/black experience, xi, 8, 11, 15, 28, 32, 38, 40, 51, 53, 55, 58, 60, 62, 64–67, 69, 70, 75, 77, 82–83, 101, 108, 113–14, 122–23, 125–28, 130–31, 133, 146, 150, 156, 158–59, 184–87, 191, 210, 214, 225, 231–32, 241–44, 247, 262, 265, 268, 271–72; black African/s/ black African immigration/ black African Australians/black American/s/black South Sudanese Australians/black African diaspora, xi, xiii, 3, 8, 12–13, 28, 51, 56, 59–60, 64, 70, 93, 99–101, 119, 122, 127, 133, 179, 183, 208, 210, 246–47; black agency, xi; black arts/Black Arts Movement/black artists, 98, 101, 128, 133, 209–10, 234, 238, 247–48, 266; black business, 130; black culture/black cultural expression/black aesthetic, 66, 99–100, 122, 125, 127, 133; black dignity/black royalty/black is beautiful/black joy, 69, 124, 130, 132–33, 231, 254; black equality/black emancipation/black self-emancipation, xi, 261; black excellence, 62, 130–31, 134, 187, 190, 203, 209, 211, 213, 215, 221, 234, 248–49; black female/black women, 123, 130, 182, 184, 209; black heroes [black Robin Hood]/ black folk heroes/black folklore, 73, 246, 248; black history/ies, 125–27, 135; black identities/black identity development theory/black identity politics/black immigrant identities/ black African-diaspora identities/ black racialised identities, xi, 15, 28, 46, 94, 100, 111, 113, 122, 126,

Index

150, 184, 209, 246–47, 271; black leadership/black leaders, 127–29, 133; black liberation/Black Freedom Movement/struggle/black liberation activism/black liberation theology, xiii, 99, 103, 121, 159, 180–81, 231, 241, 255; black male masculinity/black male/s/black man, 100, 184–85, 187; black music/black 'hype' lyrics/black Afrocentric tracks, 67, 119, 130, 247; black Nationalist/black Nationalist dreams/black political and economic self-determination, 93, 101, 131–32, 231, 255; black oppressed people/s, communities/black slaves/black subjugation/black-white continuum [the system], 55, 57, 261, 272; black pain/black and brown deaths, 56, 254; black politics/black issues/black economic and political self-determination, 101, 118, 126, 231; black public spaces/black-only safe space/black counter-spaces/public/black neighbourhood/black presence, 85, 118, 185, 230, 263; black studies in Australia, 28; black youth/black diaspora youth/black diasporic youth cultures, 110, 113, 125, 128, 163, 211, 252, 258
black consciousness/Black Consciousness Movement/black consciousness framework/black consciousness development theory/black minds, 51, 94, 99, 107, 109, 112, 118–19, 122, 126–27, 131, 133, 135, 150, 180, 183, 230–33, 247, 265, 271–72; black cultural pride/bring black back/black heritage/black cultural form, 68–69, 112–14, 122, 130, 231, 234, 247–48; black solidarity, 231; black visionaries, 53; black world, 231
Black Lives Matter (BLM)/BLM movement, 6, 15, 271

blackness/black identity/ies/black racialised identities/black consciousness identity development/theory, xi, 17, 28, 49, 94, 100–111, 119, 121, 124–25, 132, 150, 180, 184, 208–9, 214, 246–47, 271–72
Black Panther/s/Black Panther Party, 130–31, 181, 261–62, 265
black power/black power movement, 53, 101–2, 121–22, 126, 130–31, 133, 135, 183, 187, 190, 211–12, 215, 234, 242, 248, 267, 271–72
Blak/bla(c)k, 15, 100, 128, 272
Bol, Ayuen, visual artist, 19, 108, 186
born to stand out (BTSO)/BTSO theme, 1, 7, 13–14, 17, 20, 22, 25, 48, 51, 73, 108–9, 131, 133–34, 179, 183, 186, 190–93, 195, 197, 225, 228, 243, 245–47, 256, 268–69; BTSO artivist/s/BTSO artivism, 9, 25, 37–41, 189–92, 256; BTSO documentary, 184–85, 188–89; BTSO motto (definition), xiii, 9, 18, 29, 50, 54, 93, 134, 180–81, 184, 186, 249, 251, 256, 267
Burn City Movement (BCM), artist group, 38, 41, 62, 65, 72, 75, 117, 173, 185, 197–98

Channel 7 television network/Channel 7 protest, 7, 13, 66, 102, 143, 155–56, 211
citizens/citizenship/citizenship status/citizenship system, 4, 83, 166, 204, 221, 254; equal citizens/equal citizenship status, 3, 10, 183; new citizens, 221, 254
Cole, J, artist, 71, 179–80
colour/skin colour/people of colour (POC) or communities of colour, 6, 9, 12, 19, 56–59, 61–63, 65, 99–100, 108, 121, 123, 125, 130, 146, 155, 160, 166, 180–81, 185, 187, 191, 219, 243, 271; colourism/colour

blindness, 123, 146, 243; queen with colour, 130
communication for social change, 50, 194, 261, 264
community development/arts-based CD, 14–15, 17, 22–23, 30–31, 37, 46, 60, 67, 96–97, 155, 158, 173, 191, 222, 225–26, 228–29, 235, 238, 242, 246, 249, 251, 265–66, 268; asset-based CD, 43
consciousness/critical consciousness/conscientisation/consciousness-raising/consciousness-raising journey, xvi, 9, 24–25, 27, 29–30, 35, 43–46, 49, 51, 69, 71, 76, 80, 84–85, 93–94, 96, 98, 102–4, 109–12, 118–28, 130–31, 133–36, 143, 145, 150, 155, 161, 165–66, 169, 180, 182, 187, 193, 203, 206–7, 213, 218, 220–21, 227–36, 238, 241, 246, 249, 252, 257, 260, 265–67, 269
counter-narrative/s/counter knowledge/s/counter-message, 4, 8, 23–25, 29, 52, 75–76, 84, 96–97, 104, 109, 124–25, 127, 130, 141–42, 144, 150, 154–55, 157–58, 160–62, 164–66, 168, 170, 173–75, 181, 183, 186, 190, 200, 203, 206, 215, 217, 221, 225–26, 228–29, 231–32, 234, 238, 241, 251–52, 259, 263, 269, 272; counter-hegemony/counter-hegemonic practice/counter-hegemonic space, 111, 116, 118, 216; counter-narrative arts-based inquiry, 49; counter-public/counter-spaces, 164–65, 217, 230; counter-story/telling, 43–44, 48, 81, 130–31, 145, 163, 203, 215, 230, 234–35, 246
creative agency/critical creative agency, 20, 22, 95, 147, 272
crime/s/crime statistics/crime reporting/criminals/violent crime, 4, 6–7, 11, 13, 66, 99, 147, 151, 153–54, 157–58, 169, 183, 187; criminal behaviour/criminality/criminality

discourse/s, 8, 10, 16, 19, 55, 76, 109, 144, 146–47, 236, 248, 251
critical arts-based inquiry, 48–49
critical race theory (CRT)/CRT theorists, 23–24, 27–28, 30, 49–51, 54–61, 63, 66, 81–82, 94, 110, 121–23, 144–49, 151, 155, 160, 174, 180–81, 183, 187, 196, 208, 228, 230–31, 234, 238, 240–41, 243, 252–53, 257–58, 260–62, 265
culture, xiii, 4, 19, 29, 30, 36, 50, 69, 84, 93, 96–97, 99, 101, 103, 105–6, 108, 111, 115, 118, 120–22, 124, 126–27, 131–34, 148, 172, 186, 191, 204, 206, 208, 217, 219, 242, 271–72; arts-culture/Hip Hop as a culture/youth music culture and fashion/music for the culture, 38, 67–68, 70–72, 95, 97–99, 102, 112, 160–61, 169–70, 173, 193, 215, 230, 232–33, 246; black culture/Blackness and culture/African American culture/Afrodiasporic vernacular culture/culture-building practice through black folklore, 66, 94, 99–100, 113, 125, 127, 130, 233, 238, 248; cancel culture, 106; cultural codes, 19–20, 109, 135, 272; culturally diverse/cultural identity/ies/tribal culture, 23, 106; cultural policy ecology, 265; culture shifters, 206, 238; dominant culture/mainstream culture/Eurocentric or 'white' culture, 95, 105, 112–13, 146, 182, 186, 219, 247; ethnic culture/s/ethnic communities/inter-ethnic tensions/disparities, 1–2, 5, 8, 12, 37, 56, 74, 106, 158, 183, 267, 272; place-based culture/Melbourne culture, 76, 231; political culture, Australian, 247; popular culture, 17, 28, 53, 98, 100, 106, 135, 170; pride in culture/beauty in culture or celebration of culture or strength in culture, 8, 93, 133, 135, 170, 182,

228, 247; subculture/s/alternative subcultures, xvi, 13, 52, 69, 102, 108, 112, 136, 172, 186, 190, 193, 228–29, 246, 251–52, 261, 264, 272; third culture context/mixed cultural identity/ies/transnational culture, 24, 114, 183, 208; traditional culture, 183; youth culture/urban youth culture, 19, 23, 45, 54, 66–68, 70, 72, 74, 85, 99–100, 109, 119, 143, 200, 226, 233, 237, 264, 272

culture-centred approach (CCA), 24, 27, 29–30, 49–50, 85, 93, 95–96, 105–7, 109, 121, 126, 161–62, 165, 170, 181, 191, 193, 195, 204, 206, 208, 215–18, 228, 231, 238, 245–46, 259, 264; culture as deconstruction and culture as co-construction, 219; culture as resistance, 217; culture as storytelling, 217–18

decolonise/decolonisation, xvi, 208; coloniality of power/colonial world system/global coloniality/neo-colonial history/settler-colonial past/context/societies, 2–4, 15, 57–60, 182, 267; decolonising/decolonising conversations, decolonising praxis/decolonising methodologies/decolonising social movement framework, 14, 31, 34, 36, 43, 260, 262; neo-colonial context/influences, Kenya, 120, 127; post-colonial scholarship/post-colonial world, 28, 59

deficit/deficit-based/deficit approaches/models, 52, 96, 130, 160, 185, 194, 229, 236, 248, 251, 253, 257, 268; anti-deficit discourse/resisting deficit [racialising] discourse/s, 85, 163, 231, 241; deficit narratives/deficit [racialising discourse] discourses/deficit Eurocentric discourses, 22, 34, 46, 160, 163, 232, 236, 246, 256; deficit stories, representations, 5, 268

Deng, Achai, artist, 209–10
Deng, Ezeldin, film-maker/Izzy Films, 74, 131, 188
development interventions/social interventions/artivist or arts-based interventions, 29, 49–50, 99, 106, 217, 229, 242, 265
discrimination/racial discrimination/structural discrimination, 3, 10, 12, 15, 42, 61–62, 70–71, 102, 127, 132, 181, 187
dissent/ing, 10, 41, 52, 95, 98, 101, 225, 228–29, 235, 244, 251

Elia, Daniel, artist, 40–41, 65, 67, 72, 128–30, 158, 184, 190, 209, 246, 252
Élkato, artist, 38, 41, 82–84, 123, 125, 152, 206, 246, 252
emancipate/emancipatory/emancipation, 33, 96, 242, 256, 261; emancipatory praxis, 33, 44; self-emancipation, xi
empirical applications/approaches/empirical conditions/empirical depictions/portrayals/empirical work/empirical data/empirical evidence/empirical research, xi, 23, 42, 103, 115, 174, 252, 260, 268
epistemological approaches/epistemological considerations/epistemological terrain/epistemological stances/negotiations/epistemological movement, 23, 49, 60, 182, 226, 253, 266
ethnography/ethnographic data/ethnographic inquiry/ethnographic methods, xi, 14, 17, 24, 29, 31, 42, 47–49, 52, 106, 110, 144–45, 149, 221, 225–26, 229, 238, 251, 258, 260, 262, 265
Eurocentric/Eurocentrism/Eurocentric discourses/focus/Eurocentric worldviews/ideals, 113, 160, 180, 182, 208, 219, 247; Eurocentric epistemologies/hegemonic dominance/hegemonic agendas/

stories/discourse/Western hegemonic approaches/depictions, 2, 76, 85, 104, 118, 125, 127, 267

first nations peoples/First Nations communities/First Nations history/First Nations identities/First Nations struggles/First Nations terminologies, xiii, 4, 7, 15, 57, 60, 68, 179, 244, 272
fitting in, 8–9, 17, 148, 253
flash mob/s/pop-up performances, 30, 199, 203, 223; Dandenong high school pop-up performance, 196; Dandenong Market pop-up performance, 192, 198, 200; Brunswick Street Parade, 199–203; Grounded festival pop-up dance (Afrobeats)/Grounded festival pop-up performances, 199, 203, 207, 215, 221; State library flash-mob/Tébir pop-up performance, xiv, 201
FLEXX, artist, 112, 212
Footprint Enterprises Inc/Footprints, xi, xiv, xv, xvi, 9, 15–18, 20, 24, 29–37, 42–43, 45–47, 49, 65, 72–73, 79, 93, 95, 110–12, 114–18, 120, 128, 134, 144, 161–65, 167–68, 171, 173–74, 180, 183–85, 188–89, 191, 193–202, 204, 207–8, 210, 212–14, 217–18, 220, 230, 232, 248–49, 251, 258, 265–66, 269
freedom/s, 13, 17, 22, 24, 51, 53–54, 67, 69, 78, 84–85, 96, 98, 103, 105, 107, 111, 120, 130, 134, 136, 151, 155, 179–80, 182, 184, 186, 188, 200, 202, 221–22, 227–29, 231–32, 239, 241–45, 251, 254–56, 261–64; achieving/attaining/pursuing/towards freedoms and aspirations, 51, 226, 229, 241, 262, 264, 267; barriers to freedoms/limited freedoms, 29, 150, 175; we want to be free from chains/we are our own freedom, 93, 130, 179–80, 255
Future of Rap, artist group, 38, 130

gang/s/sta/gang behaviour/gang culture/gang violence/anti-gang legislation/'gang-busting' laws/ethnic youth gangs, 5–7, 10–11, 13–14, 16, 61, 63, 71, 95, 99, 101, 107, 113, 146–48, 151, 153–54, 156–57, 163, 183, 225; African gang/s/African gang member, 6–7, 11, 13, 52, 65–66, 75, 102, 141–42, 144, 149–57, 159–60, 164, 174, 225, 232, 234, 256; Apex gang/Apex gang saga/Apex gang moral panic, 4, 6, 11, 24, 63, 65, 70, 130, 142, 144, 149–51, 153, 158, 174, 199, 238
global uprising, xiii, 225
Gony, Liep, young South Sudanese Australian who was murdered, 6–7, 13, 24, 32, 43, 61, 66, 70, 144–45, 147, 149–50, 153–54, 225, 247
Great, Sampa the, artist, 53–54, 68, 93, 109, 123, 180, 209
Grounded project, 24, 29–30, 35–37, 41–47, 49–52, 93, 97–98, 110–11, 114–16, 120, 122, 128, 134, 142, 144, 159, 161–63, 165, 172–74, 180, 187, 190–93, 195–96, 198–204, 207, 209, 212, 215–22, 227–30, 235, 241–42, 247–49, 251, 263, 265–67; Grounded festival, 47, 161–63, 198, 209; Gua performance and leadership camp/Gua focus group, 24, 29, 45–46, 49, 62–63, 65, 71, 74–75, 93–94, 110–12, 114–23, 126, 128, 132–34, 152, 154, 158, 161, 163, 166, 187, 193–96, 199, 202–3, 205–6, 208–9, 213, 215–16, 218, 230–32, 235, 248

hip hop/Hip Hop expression, identity politics, xi, 15, 17, 23, 32, 51, 53–55, 61, 67–71, 74, 76, 78–79, 83, 94, 98–99, 105–7, 109, 112–13, 118–20, 122, 124, 127, 132, 135, 142, 146–47, 155, 157, 163, 170, 205, 220, 221, 225, 227, 239, 241–42, 251, 259, 263; conscious or political Hip

Index

Hop/rap/genre of Hip Hop, xiii, 1, 7, 16, 22–24, 29, 44, 50–51, 54–55, 61–62, 69, 71–72, 74, 76–77, 79–80, 82–84, 94, 97, 99, 101–2, 104–5, 111–12, 120, 122, 125, 127, 131, 133–34, 142–44, 150, 155, 157, 162, 179, 182–83, 190, 193, 212, 222, 225–31, 233, 235–42, 244, 248, 251–52, 256, 266, 269; critical hip hop pedagogy (CHHP), 27, 29–30, 42–46, 49, 94, 96, 102–3, 106, 110–11, 121, 126, 134, 180, 187, 193, 206, 227, 230, 232, 235–36, 240, 245, 257; drill Hip Hop/genre of Hip Hop, 71, 99, 112–13, 173, 228, 237, 240; gangsta or gangster rap/genre of Hip Hop, 71, 79, 101, 112–13, 228, 237, 240; Hip Hop artivists/Hip Hop superheroes/Hip Hop as a New Social Movement (NSM)/Hip Hop as an arts-based form of resistance, xiii, 7, 14, 17, 23, 27, 29–30, 36–41, 45–46, 51–54, 68, 70–75, 77, 81, 85, 93–94, 96–99, 102, 120–21, 124, 127, 130, 133, 136, 143–45, 149, 155, 160–62, 170, 172, 174, 181, 190–91, 196, 206–7, 209, 212, 218, 221, 227–30, 232–33, 235, 237–38, 241–42, 246, 251–52, 256–58, 269, 272; Hip Hop as a culture, 51, 67–72, 95, 97–100, 125, 169–70, 173, 186, 193, 196, 211, 220, 229–30, 232–33, 246–47, 258, 264; historical origins in the US and African influences/origins in Naarm, Melbourne, 47, 69–71, 73, 82, 98–100, 112–13, 165, 186, 188, 211, 233; intersectional nature, 100–101; lyrics and tracks/alternative forms of storytelling, counternarratives, 32, 44, 46–49, 54, 68–69, 77, 80–81, 84–85, 94, 97, 101, 103–4, 112–13, 124, 127, 130, 142, 155, 160, 203, 212, 229, 233, 239, 244, 249, 251, 266; participating in a New Social Movement through Hip Hop, definition, 98; performer/Hip Hop emcees/Hip Hop audiences, 72, 76, 104–5, 114, 166, 197, 203, 208, 228–30, 249, 266, 269; producer, recording process, 67, 72, 235; tenets, 32, 72, 102, 127, 169

identity/ies/construct of identity/identity groups/(negotiating) identity formation/racial or ethnic identity/social identity, 2, 9, 14, 16–17, 19, 29, 42, 54–55, 68, 74, 94, 96, 102, 105–10, 114, 118–19, 122, 126–27, 132–35, 174, 191, 205–6, 218, 220, 232, 234, 243, 257, 266–67; Australian National identity, 14, 57, 215, 268; (forced) migrant identity, 52, 100; hybrid identities/intercultural identity/ies/transcultural identity/ies, 8, 13, 22, 93, 99, 186, 210, 228; identity-based New Social Movement/identity project/s, 27, 30, 93, 121, 129, 227, 233, 242, 252, 257, 266; identity as calling, 94, 127–29, 133, 206, 211, 229; identity expressions through art/identity politics on display through public performance, 109, 111, 130, 198, 205, 242; identity politics, Australian/identity crisis or identity issues/'identity politics playing tricks'/mistaken identity/racialisation of identities, 8, 14–15, 19, 22–24, 29, 35, 43, 51, 54–56, 64, 66, 83, 93–95, 97–98, 100, 103, 105–10, 121–24, 126–27, 130–35, 143, 146, 148, 159, 163, 175, 181–83, 187–88, 203, 205–6, 208, 213, 221, 227, 234–35, 248, 254, 257, 263–64, 267, 269; reclaiming identity/ies/affirming identity/ies/resistance to build identity/forging identity/identity transformation/power of your identity/unique identity or strength in identity/claim

your identity/celebration of identity/
identity for resistance/identity
transformation/*r*epresenting identity/
ies, 17, 19, 22, 27, 30, 51, 68–69,
96, 101, 106, 109–10, 124–25, 127,
132, 135, 170, 180, 186, 188, 191,
206, 213, 218, 221, 228, 232, 250,
257, 272
inclusion, 12, 32, 168, 215; social
exclusion, 9, 12, 181; social
inclusion, 8–9, 14, 243, 268
indigenous methods/blak Indigenous
rights/Indigenous (and relational)
inquiry/Indigenous knowledges/
Indigenous lens of relationality/
Indigenous methodology/Indigenous
people's social movements/
Indigenous post-colonial scholarship,
Indigenous standpoint theory/
Indigenous storytelling/multiple
ways of Indigenous knowing/story
custodian, 28, 31–32, 34–35, 41, 48,
59–60, 108, 128, 160, 234, 258–59,
265
inequity/*s*ystemic inequity, 81–82, 85,
98
injustice/s/challenge injustices/injustice
in Australia/social injustice/systemic
injustices, 52, 77, 98, 101, 105, 110,
127, 142, 216–17, 238, 245, 262,
264, 269
integrate/integration/integration policies,
5, 7, 9–11, 25, 28, 37, 43, 55, 62,
85, 107, 118–19, 144, 146–48, 156,
186, 225, 229, 236, 243, 249, 253,
266, 271
intercultural/interculturalism/
intercultural communication/
intercultural projects, 12, 23, 93,
128, 243, 266–67
i.OG, artist, 62, 65, 73, 124, 126, 131,
172–73, 191–92, 197, 199–200

Jal, Emmanuel, artist, 40–41

Kosley, Mariam, journalist, 182–83,
189, 232
Krown, artist, 39, 41, 73, 81–83, 102,
124–25, 127, 129, 141–44, 148, 151,
153, 157, 170–71, 188, 196–97,
233–34, 237–38, 241, 246, 252

LEZA, artist, 117, 132, 205
liberation/liberation of the mind/
liberation theology/liberating work,
xiii, 36, 93, 99, 102, 105, 111,
120–21, 125–26, 159, 180–82,
231–32, 234, 236, 241–42, 255, 262;
liberatory (and emancipatory) praxis,
29, 44, 102–3, 111, 118, 123, 212;
liberatory politics, xi
little publics/public spheres, 74, 76, 85,
144, 163–64, 166, 203, 230, 249,
257; public pedagogy/ies, 74, 102,
105, 144, 166, 257
lived experience/s, xi, xv, 25, 28, 51, 72,
81, 96, 110, 126, 132, 160, 196, 215,
240, 243, 253–54

Mak, Simba, artist, 206–7, 238
Malesh P, artist, 39, 41, 45, 73, 112–
13, 124, 129–31, 155, 169, 179–80,
184, 186–88, 191, 212, 246–47,
252, 255
media, 7–8, 12, 33, 48, 66, 75, 78, 101,
104, 106, 144–45, 147, 149–55, 170,
246, 248, 269; alternative media/
positive media, 107, 143, 153, 165,
173, 175, 190–91, 228; mainstream
media, 5–6, 8, 11–12, 19, 32, 81, 83,
107, 142, 148–55, 165, 174–75, 195,
216, 229; media and moral panics,
8, 10, 13, 19, 36, 51, 55–56, 60,
62, 74, 109, 144–49, 151, 159–60,
180, 186, 241, 251; racialised media
narratives, 5–7, 10–12, 14, 16, 24,
32, 43, 68, 70, 76, 130–31, 143–44,
147, 149–51, 154, 156–59, 161, 163,
166, 174–75, 236; social media, 45,

47–48, 64, 73–75, 78, 93, 132, 144, 193, 201–2, 237, 269
mental health/youth suicide, 33, 65–66, 119, 147, 150, 226, 251; health disparities, 12, 62
Minoritized/minoritised identity/ies/ voices, border thinking, 2, 34, 44, 99, 107, 163, 234; minority groups/ communities/subaltern/ethnic minority groups/minority rap fans, 8, 12, 32, 44, 68, 80, 104, 111, 152, 242
Moomba/Moomba riots, 6, 11, 13, 62, 151, 199
multicultural/multiculturalism/ multicultural policy/ies/multicultural society, 3, 5–6, 9, 21, 28, 38, 58–59, 71, 111, 114, 159, 161, 163, 172, 200, 243, 268

Naarm, Melbourne, Victoria, place, xiv, 3–4, 118, 154, 157, 163, 170, 174, 184–85, 188–89, 196, 198–201, 207, 209, 212, 232, 241, 258
Nai, Erjok (Eeh), xiii, xvi, 33–34
narrative inquiry, 30, 48–49, 135, 245, 258
necropolitics, 3, 5, 54, 56, 60, 83, 122, 144, 236
new social movement/s(NSMs)/New Social Movement theory, 23–24, 27–30, 49–52, 68, 71, 93–98, 102, 106–7, 110, 112, 116–17, 120–21, 123–24, 128–29, 134–36, 143–44, 147, 159–61, 163, 170, 173, 180–81, 184, 187, 193–95, 197–99, 205, 208, 211, 217, 220–21, 226–27, 230–35, 237–39, 241–42, 245–46, 252, 256–59, 261–67, 269, 271–72
Nouk, Abraham (Abe), spoken-word artist, 161–62, 229, 262

other/non-white other/othering, 4, 8, 15, 19, 22, 51, 58, 146, 156, 158, 159

Pan African/Pan Africanism/Pan African identity, 107, 126, 182, 186, 208, 224, 255
participation/democratic participation/ participation in a project/participation in a New Social Movement/social participation/youth participation, 12, 22, 31, 52, 95–96, 98, 134, 144, 160, 166, 184, 193, 196, 202, 217, 219–20, 226, 239, 241, 245, 252, 254, 256, 269; barriers or limits to, 96, 98; place-based participation/ crowd participation/white-controlled spaces participation, 196–97
policy and practice/cultural policy and practice, 25, 35, 211
political/lly/political actors/agency/ activism/careers/self-determination/ political agenda/s/(click)bait/rhetoric/ political climate/context/dimensions/ politically conscious/ness/roots/ politically driven/fueled/politically divergent/political alliances/interests/ persuasions/political climate/ doctrines/economy/political issues/ grievances/struggles/political education/message/statements/ tones/political negotiations/political commentary/ discourse/ narratives/ perspectives/political moral panics/ devices/political power/political resistance/social movements/political supremacy, 1–2, 5–6, 8–10, 14, 16–17, 19, 23–24, 28–32, 38, 40, 43–44, 47–51, 54–55, 58, 60–61, 76–77, 79–83, 85, 95, 97–98, 101–12, 119–21, 123, 130, 135, 142–46, 148–53, 155–57, 161, 164, 170, 174, 179–80, 182, 184, 187, 203, 206, 208, 211, 216–17, 226, 231–32, 234–40, 242, 246–47, 260, 263, 269, 272; identity/ies, 2, 97, 102, 105; praxis (practice), xii, 84–85, 97, 267; sociopolitical/sociopolitical analysis/

sociopolitical considerations/
context/s/circumstance/undertones/
sociopolitical constructs/origins/
sociopolitical communities/
sociopolitical disadvantage/
sociopolitical structural forces/
systems, 13–14, 23–24, 31, 34, 44,
55–56, 62–63, 65, 71, 83, 102–3,
112–14, 125, 144, 150, 157, 222,
228, 240, 258, 271; voice/s, xi, xiii,
1, 7, 13, 16, 20, 23–25, 27–30, 44,
47, 50–52, 54–55, 57, 60–62, 67–69,
72, 74, 76–80, 83–84, 94–99, 103,
106–7, 110–12, 115, 118–21, 124,
128, 133–34, 142–45, 147, 157,
159–63, 168, 175, 180, 183, 190,
193, 195, 200–208, 212, 218, 221,
225–32, 235–36, 238–42, 244–46,
248, 252, 257, 264–67, 269
post-colonial/post-colonial theorist, 28,
59, 147, 182, 240
praxis/critical praxis/praxiological, xii,
xv, 33, 36, 42–44, 49, 97, 102–3,
107, 111, 123, 125, 193, 212, 252,
260, 264
prejudice, 3, 8–10, 56–57, 70, 124, 152
Projects, Jungle City/Jungle City
Studios/Lerato Masiyane/
Karabo/Burn City Queens/Culture
Queens, xv, 42, 45, 57, 62, 65, 70,
124, 152, 189, 191, 194, 196–99,
201, 208, 214–15
protest/s/ers/protest music, 6–7, 10, 13,
66, 97–98, 101–2, 124, 143, 156–57,
211, 225, 229, 233, 235, 238, 244,
246, 251, 256, 262

Queen P, artist, 39, 41, 62, 66, 109, 130,
133, 187, 190, 246

race/race-based agendas/baiting/
gaslighting/issue/war/race-critical
analysis/neutrality/race literacy
(constructed) race characterisations/
hierarchy/markers/race politics/race
relations/talk in Australia, 15, 19,
23, 28, 44, 51, 54–61, 66, 74, 81,
94–96, 101, 108, 110, 112, 121–23,
132, 144–46, 150–51, 154, 156, 158,
181, 183–84, 190, 203, 208, 228,
230–31, 236, 238, 240, 243, 245,
247, 252–53, 257, 260, 262, 267–68,
271; racial equity/racist inequities,
57, 182, 240–41; racial inequity, 58,
81–82, 85, 98; racial justice/racial
injustice/s/racial justice movements,
xiii, 28–29, 32, 36, 42, 56, 101–2,
119, 181, 229, 240–41, 262, 266;
racial politics, 59; racial profiling, 6,
10–11, 64, 152, 156, 262
racialising discourses/racialising
narratives/racist propaganda, xi, xiii,
1, 5, 7–8, 10, 13–17, 19, 23–25,
27–30, 37, 46, 48–52, 54, 57, 60–62,
65, 70, 74, 76, 81–82, 84–85, 94–97,
100, 106, 109–10, 112–13, 117,
119, 122, 124–27, 130–32, 142–44,
153, 155, 157–66, 168–70, 172–75,
179–81, 183–87, 190, 196–203, 205,
207–11, 214–18, 220–22, 225–29,
231, 234–36, 238, 241–46, 248–58,
261–62, 264, 266, 268–69, 272
racism (experiences of) racism in
Australia/racist/racist attitudes/
behaviour/ beliefs/ propaganda/
tropes, 3–5, 9–10, 12, 14–16,
22–23, 27, 30, 34, 42–44, 51–52,
54–66, 82, 85–87, 98, 100–101,
113, 119, 124, 130–31, 136, 142,
144–47, 155, 180, 185, 203, 205,
209, 211, 217, 227, 230, 238,
240–41, 244, 249, 255, 257, 261,
263, 265–68; biological racism,
63; black c*** n**** [derogatory
and racist terms in this context],
62–63; colour-coded or imperial
racism, 16, 58, 61, 63, 121, 123;
counterring racism/challenge racist
discourses, 195, 245; cultural
racism, 135; everyday racism, 57,

60, 63, 146, 243; institutional, structural or systemic racism/institutional racism/racist social structures 'the system ain't playin', 15, 25, 42, 53–56, 58, 60–61, 64–66, 68, 84, 111, 115, 133–34, 149, 152, 160, 226, 231, 233, 237, 242, 245, 253; internalised (or intrapersonal) racism, 60–63; interpersonal racism, 60–63, 65–66; post-racial or racist society/post-racist future, 59; racist discourses/narratives, 56, 70, 74, 122, 143, 148, 155, 158, 173–74, 268; racist hate crime, 147; racist ideas/racist ideologies/racist hate, 55–57, 62; racist infra-humanisation, 148; racist policies/racist project, 57–58, 60, 146

refugee/former refugee experience/refugee camps/refugee or humanitarian visa/refugee young people, 2, 6, 10, 12, 19–22, 31, 36, 46, 152, 188, 195, 198, 271; Acculturation/acculturative stressors, 5, 13, 186; genocide, 1; recent arrivals/black immigration to Australia, 2–3, 12, 28, 60, 245; resettlement/settlement history/resettlement zone, 2–3, 5, 12, 16, 20–21, 31, 51, 61, 225, 257

resilience, 10, 22, 51, 84, 114, 135, 217, 245, 252, 257, 264

resistance/building or steps of resistance (such as Black Consciousness as a tool for resistance or consciousness-raising as a tool to create awareness, build)/resistance and social change/resistance to racialising discourse, structural forms of racism or 'the system', xv, 14, 16, 24–25, 27–28, 30, 37, 44, 50–51, 69, 84, 95, 105, 107, 110–11, 120–21, 123, 165, 181, 183, 191, 201, 215–16, 218, 229, 250, 252–53, 258, 263, 268–69; culture as resistance/Blackness as resistance/forms of resistance through the culture-centred approach, 97, 105–6, 124, 134–35, 165, 183, 217–18, 256; everyday resistance, 24, 97, 173, 229, 251–52, 263; forms of/creative or theoretical resistances/protest, dissent, multimedia or arts-based development projects/alternative forms of resistance/black business as resistance/black joy as a form of resistance/drivers of resistance projects/Hip Hop, counter-storytelling, political voice as resistance/identities or self-expression as a form of resistance/modes of youth resistance/transformational resistance, 10, 14, 23, 25, 27, 29, 33, 47–50, 52, 69, 84, 94–96, 99, 102, 107, 112, 118, 120, 124, 130, 161, 163, 173–75, 180–81, 184, 188, 190–91, 202–3, 207–8, 214, 218, 220–21, 226–28, 230, 234–35, 246, 251–53, 256–57, 259–60, 263; public displays of, collection of resistance stories/communities of resistance/little publics as a form of resistance/sites of resistance/performance of resistance politics, 8, 13–14, 23, 28, 48, 85, 102, 104–5, 133, 164, 180, 195–96, 202–3, 206–7, 212, 216–19, 230, 244–45, 257, 263

self-determination/resistance through self-determination, 16, 19, 23, 54, 84, 95–96, 103, 112, 127, 134, 158, 169–70, 173, 180, 182–83, 203, 217–18, 225, 231, 250, 265, 272

skin colour, 6, 12, 19, 56, 63, 100, 123, 130, 146, 155, 185, 187, 271; melanated skin, 63, 132, 187

social change, xiii, xiv, 1, 7–8, 14, 17, 23–24, 27, 29–30, 36, 44–45, 50, 95–98, 104–7, 111, 121, 129, 143, 160, 163, 165–66, 168–69, 172, 193–95, 200, 202, 215, 221–22, 232–35, 251, 253, 256, 261–62, 264–65, 268

social cohesion, 12, 147
South Sudan/North Sudan, 1–3, 5, 15, 19, 21, 32, 36, 38–40, 73, 80, 100, 112, 125, 191, 209, 231, 271
South Sudanese Australian/s (SSAs), xi, xiv, 1–25, 27–38, 42–52, 54–57, 59–71, 73–74, 76–78, 81–85, 93–103, 106–14, 116–20, 124–35, 142–59, 161–63, 166, 168–75, 180–83, 186–89, 191, 193, 197, 200–203, 206–10, 215–17, 220–34, 236–38, 240–48, 250–66, 268–69, 271–72
spoken-word poetry, xi, xv, 15, 39, 45, 47, 53, 62, 65, 110, 114, 118–19, 122, 128, 132, 142, 153, 160–62, 165, 180, 193, 205–7, 213, 219, 238, 262
standpoint project/s, 14, 16, 22–23, 29, 81, 98, 192, 200, 259, 265
standpoint theory, 59–60, 262
stereotype/s, 3, 10, 14, 16, 62, 65, 67, 100–101, 109, 126, 130, 132, 147, 152, 169–70, 187
strengths/communal strengths/cultural strengths or strength through Blackness/strengths-based/capabilities, asset-based approaches, 10, 22, 43, 45, 62, 95, 107, 111, 124–25, 127, 131–34, 154, 160, 165, 170, 187, 195, 204, 211, 213, 226, 231, 235, 248, 251, 253, 258, 261, 272
Summer, Kimberley, photographer, videographer, film-producer, 21, 83, 189–90, 192, 200–201, 207, 214

Tebir, artist, xiv, 72–73
Tesema, Soli, artist, 179–80, 209–10
Titan, artist/Titan Debirioun, 38, 41, 62–66, 68, 70–72, 78, 102, 143–44, 152–56, 184, 187, 238, 246, 252, 267
transcultural/transculturalism/transculturality/transcultural capital/transcultural identity/ies, 13, 22, 186, 210, 228, 246, 266, 269

transformative youth organising, 16, 22, 43, 98, 118, 193
tribe/s [from South Sudan]/tribal/tribal ancestry/tribal culture/tribal language/tribal politics, 1–3, 10, 45, 99, 106, 112, 128, 187, 258, 272; Bari (Equatorial), 3; Dinka, 1–3, 38, 128, 175; Nuer, 1–3, 45, 175
truth-telling, 59, 84, 130, 145, 174, 213, 225

unfreedoms, 8, 107
uprising, xiii, xv, xvi, 225
urban youth/urban youth agency/urban youth culture/s/urban youth identity/ies/urban youth politics/young people, 10, 16, 19, 23, 28, 54, 67–68, 82, 84–85, 95–96, 99–100, 106, 113, 119, 121, 131, 143, 163–64, 191, 200, 216, 226, 233, 237, 245, 249, 264, 268–69, 272

Vincent, David, cultural leader, xiv, 6, 147
visions from the kitchen [ideas or strategic visions formed in one's own context], 54, 72, 129–30, 132, 188, 264

Wantu ThaOne, artist, 117, 120, 172–73, 191, 197
war/conflict/war-torn, 1–3, 5, 10, 40, 59, 71, 80, 111, 133, 154, 205; war on Blackness, 54, 60, 175
white/white demographic/white dominant culture or white-centric society or white-dominated industries/white identities/white people/s, communities/white elitism, hegemony, privilege or supremacy/white Australian or Nationalism/white skin colour/white (controlled or dominated) spaces/society/Caucasian, 3–4, 6, 9, 12, 15, 19, 32, 35, 37, 51, 55–59, 63, 65–66,

70, 75, 82, 100–101, 108, 112, 127, 134, 145–48, 150, 154–56, 158–59, 182, 184–86, 196, 201, 205–6, 219, 242, 247, 250, 265, 268, 271; honorary whites, 186, 205, 221–22, 243, 254; white Australia immigration policy, 3–4, 57, 267; white mask, 147, 184
whiteness/Australian Whiteness/ hegemonic Whiteness, 3, 5, 7, 9, 28, 50–52, 56–60, 66, 70, 82, 112, 133, 144–49, 151, 155, 158, 182, 186–88, 196, 209, 236, 238, 243–45, 247–48, 252–54, 256, 263–64, 266–67, 271
'woke'/wokeness, 24, 82–83, 103, 105, 119–20, 228, 230

youth justice/youth justice precinct/ youth justice system, 7, 41, 72–73, 81–82
youth participatory action research (YPAR), 9, 17, 42–43, 120, 144, 161, 180, 183, 186, 191, 193, 195, 204, 206, 208, 215–16, 218, 228, 232, 240, 251–52, 261–62, 264, 266, 268–69
youth work/er/s/youth work practice, 31, 35, 64, 73, 79, 85, 152, 165; development/youth development initiative/youth development practices, 162, 229
YSAS, Dandenong, xv, 41, 45–46, 64, 136, 142, 175, 193–94, 258

About the Author

Dr. Sarah J. Williams has worked as an intercultural community development practitioner and youth worker for almost two decades. Her PhD research methodology involved action research investigating creative sites for social change regarding racial social justice issues. Her interest in arts-based development and standpoint projects is driven by the question of how "being born to stand out" manifests. Sarah was co-founder of Footprint Enterprises Inc. a grassroots organisation which focuses on creating spaces to bring about social change through the creative arts. Sarah has previously served on a number of boards, peak multicultural committees and currently works as a lecturer, researcher and program manager in youth work and youth studies at RMIT University in Naarm (Melbourne), Australia.